Klaus Krogmann

Reconstruction of Software Component Architectures and Behaviour Models using Static and Dynamic Analysis

The Karlsruhe Series on Software Design and Quality

Volume 4

Chair Software Design and Quality
Faculty of Computer Science
Karlsruhe Institute of Technology

and

Software Engineering Division
Research Center for Information Technology (FZI), Karlsruhe

Editor: Prof. Dr. Ralf Reussner

Reconstruction of Software Component Architectures and Behaviour Models using Static and Dynamic Analysis

by
Klaus Krogmann

Dissertation, Karlsruher Institut für Technologie
Fakultät für Informatik,
Tag der mündlichen Prüfung: 02.11.2010
Referenten: Prof. Dr. Ralf Reussner, Prof. Dr.-Ing. Gregor Snelting

Impressum

Karlsruher Institut für Technologie (KIT)
KIT Scientific Publishing
Straße am Forum 2
D-76131 Karlsruhe
www.ksp.kit.edu

KIT – Universität des Landes Baden-Württemberg und nationales
Forschungszentrum in der Helmholtz-Gemeinschaft

KIT Scientific Publishing 2012
Print on Demand

ISSN 1867-0067
ISBN 978-3-86644-804-9

Abstract

Model-Based Performance Prediction (MBPP, [BDIS04a]) is a software engineering discipline which systematically deals with the evaluation of software performance. MBPP's central idea is to predict the performance of a software system based on performance models. MBPP can be applied at design-time to avoid bottlenecks when designing a software architecture but also for existing software systems. For existing software systems, one is interested in scalability analysis and resource sizing without actually buying expensive hardware and setting up the execution environment for each possible execution scenario. Additionally, when extending an existing software system by a new component, software performance models allow to estimate the impact of the extension and help avoiding the introduction of bottlenecks. Consider the example of a legacy accounting application: When extending such an application by a new reporting component, it should be estimated how the overall performance (e.g. response time) of the system is affected.

Applying MBPP requires the presence of up-to-date software performance models. To reason on software architectures, these models must capture the architecture itself as well as the behaviour of each architecture component. Unfortunately, current reverse engineering techniques often aim at the static software architecture and understanding of software systems [CZvD+09]. No approach reverse engineers software performance models at an architectural level which are required to enable software performance engineering. Thus, currently performance models must be created manually when aiming at the support of design decisions for software architectures.

The contribution of this thesis is a new integrated reverse engineering approach for the reconstruction of parameterised software component architectures and software component behaviour models which can serve as software performance models due to the execution semantics of the target model. This approach allows reverse engineering behaviour models for each component's service from code using static, dynamic, and statistical analysis techniques. For performance prediction, the Palladio Component Model Approach [BKR09] is used.

The new reverse engineering approach reconstructs static architecture information (components, interfaces, and connectors) as well as a performance behaviour model capturing control and data flow for each provided service of a component. The reverse engineered models are semantically rich so they can serve for performance simulation approaches without requiring manual complements. Since these models are highly parameterised (avoiding constants) they not only help understanding the *current* state of a software system, the reverse engineered models help planning and changing a software system in an efficient way at the model level. The reverse engineered models support a large variety of *design decisions* at the model level with respect to their performance impact: architectural refactorings, exchanging components, extensions of legacy software systems (e.g. introducing new components), performance optimisations (e.g. introducing caches or distribution), sizing of the hardware environment (e.g. required hardware to support 100 concurrent users for an existing application), and scalability analysis (up to how much load will an application scale until bottlenecks become crucial).

For reverse engineering of software component architectures, the so-called "So-MoX" approach has been developed. It employs various source code metrics and combines them in a flexible way into detection strategies for architectural elements. At the same time, the detection strategies respect interdependencies among metrics. A graph-based hierarchical clustering approach then creates components and composite components including their interfaces and connectors. Behaviour models are reverse engineered by an approach ("Beagle") combining static and dynamic source code analysis. The system under investigation is therefore executed by a test driver and monitored. Using the monitoring results as guide, a genetic programming approach combines results from static, dynamic, and statistical analysis to create the behaviour model which out-performs the results of each single analysis approach. To back up any reverse engineering results, trace models allow to identify the origins of each result model element.

Unlike existing approaches, the reverse engineered models make no assumptions on either of the following so-called *contexts* of a software system or component:

- Usage context. Neither the number of concurrent users nor their interaction with the software system or parameters are assumed to be fixed.

- Assembly context. Neither the caller nor the callee of a component can generally be known to a component. Accordingly, no fixed connection to other components is assumed for a component.

- Allocation context. For a component it cannot be known at design time, in which hardware and software environment it will be executed. For example, which version of a virtual machine, middleware, or processor serve for execution is not fixed. This is also reflected in the reverse engineered models.

Additionally, existing approaches either focus on reverse engineering the architecture of a software system following a relaxed definition of a software component which contradicts use within simulation approaches (e.g. [SAG$^+$06, YGS$^+$04, RLvV06]) with focus on understanding of software systems [CZvD$^+$09] or deal with reverse engineering of not fully parameterised behaviour models (e.g. [HMWR99, IWF07,

CW00, ZWL08, WHSB01]). No approach converges architecture and behaviour model reverse engineering. Consequently, none of the above design decisions is supported.

The approach presented in this thesis has been successfully validated in a total of 11 industrial case studies and reference applications, including among others Co-CoME, Palladio FileShare, SPECjvm2008, and SPECjbb2005 [CKK08, KKR10]. Models were reverse engineered with an overall precision of 78% and a recall of 89% when compared to reference architecture. Performance predictions based on the reverse engineered models deviated 12% in average and 30% in the worst case from measurements of the systems.

Zusammenfassung

Die modellbasierte Performance-Vorhersage (MBPP, [BDIS04a]) ist eine Software-Ingenieursdisziplin, die sich mit der systematischen Evaluation von Software-Leistungsfähigkeit beschäftigt. Die zentrale Idee von MBPP ist die Vorhersage der zu erwartenden Performance eines Software-Systems auf der Basis von Performance-Modellen. MBPP kann bereits zur Entwurfszeit eingesetzt werden, um Flaschenhälse beim Entwurf einer Software-Architektur zu verhindern oder um Flaschenhälse bestehender Software-Systeme auszuräumen. Im Falle existierender Software-Systeme möchte man Skalierbarkeitsanalysen durchführen und Resourcendimensionierungsfragestellungen beantworten ohne die zur Ausführung für jedes Szenario benötigte teure Hardware tatsächlich kaufen oder die Ausführungsumgebung aufsetzen zu müssen. Software-Performance-Modelle erlauben es daneben zu untersuchen, wie sich die Erweiterung eines Software-Systems um eine neue Komponente auf die Gesamtarchitektur auswirkt, ob dabei eventuell Flaschenhälse eingeführt werden oder sich potentielle Flaschenhälse negativ auf die Performance auswirken würden. Soll beispielsweise eine bestehende Buchhaltungsanwendung um eine neue Berichtskomponente erweitert werden, sollte zunächst untersucht werden, wie sich die neue Komponente auf die Gesamt-Performance (bspw. Antwortzeitverhalten) auswirkt.

Um MBPP-Techniken anzuwenden, ist es notwendig, dass aktuelle Software-Performance-Modelle vorliegen. Um Entwurfsentscheidungen auf der Ebene von Software-Architekturen abwägen zu können, müssen Software-Performance-Modelle die Architektur selbst sowie das Verhalten einer jeden Komponente der Architektur erfassen. Derzeit verfügbare Reverse-Engineering-Techniken, die Modelle aus Programmcode erzeugen können, konzentrieren sich auf die statische Software-Architektur und die Unterstützung von Architekturverständnis von Software-Systemen [CZvD+09]. Es gibt keinen Reverse-Engineering-Ansatz, der Software-Performance-Modelle auf der Architekturebene erzeugt, bei dem es die rekonstruierten Modelle erlauben Software-Performance-Engineering-Ansätze auf diesen Modellen anzuwenden. Daher werden Software-Performance-Modelle derzeit manuell erstellt, wenn es um Entwurfsentscheidungen für Software-Architekturen geht.

Der Beitrag dieser Arbeit ist ein neuartiger integrierter Reverse-Engineering-Ansatz für die Rekonstruktion von parametrisierten komponentenbasierten Software-Architekturen und Verhaltensmodellen für Software-Komponenten. Das Zielmodell besitzt Ausführungssemantik, um für Software-Performance-Vorhersagen dienen zu können. Der entwickelte Ansatz erlaubt das Reverse-Engineering der Dienste von Komponenten aus Programmcode auf der Grundlage von statischer, dynamischer und statistischer Analysetechniken. Zur Performance-Vorhersage setzt der Ansatz auf das Palladio Komponentenmodell [BKR09].

Der neu entwickelte Reverse-Engineering-Ansatz rekonstruiert statische Architekturinformationen (Komponenten, Schnittstellen und Konnektoren) sowie ein Performance-Modell des Verhaltens von Komponenten, das den Kontroll- und Datenfluss eines jeden angebotenen Komponentendienstes enthält. Die rekonstruierten Modelle sind semantisch derart reichhaltig, dass sie für Performance-Simulationsansätze dienen, ohne, dass manuelle Ergänzungen notwendig sind. Da die rekonstruierten Modelle hochgradig parametrisiert sind (und dabei Konstanten im Modell vermeiden), können Sie nicht nur beim Verstehen des *aktuellen* Zustands eines Software-Systems dienen, sondern auch bei der Planung und Änderungen eines Software-Systems helfen. Die Analyse kann dank der Parametrisierung der Modelle auf der Modellebene erfolgen. Die rekonstruierten Modelle unterstützen eine Vielzahl von *Entwurfsentscheidungen* auf der Modellebene in Bezug auf ihre Performance-Auswirkung: Architekturrefaktorisierung, Austausch von Komponenten, Erweiterung von Altsystemen (bspw. Einführung neuer Komponenten), Performance-Optimierung (bspw. Einführung von Puffern oder Verteilung), Bemessung von Ausführungsumgebungen (bspw. benötigte Hardware um 100 parallele Nutzer bei einer bestehenden Applikation zu unterstützen) und Skalierbarkeitsanalyse (bspw. wie viel Last kann eine Anwendung maximal verarbeiten bevor Performance-Flaschenhälse kritisch werden).

Zur Rekonstruktion von komponentenbasierten Software-Architekturen wurde der sogenannte SoMoX-Ansatz entwickelt. Er verwendet eine Vielzahl von Quellcodemetriken und kombiniert diese in einer flexiblen Weise zu Erkennungsstrategien für Software-Architekturelemente. Die Erkennungsstrategien berücksichtigen dabei auch Abhängigkeiten zwischen Metriken. Ein graph-basierter hierarchischer Ansatz zur Analyse von Bündeln dient dabei der Erstellung von Komponenten und zusammengesetzten Komponenten inklusive ihrer Schnittstellen und Konnektoren. Verhaltensmodelle von Komponentendiensten werden vom sogenannten Beagle-Ansatz rekonstruiert, der statische und dynamische Quellcodeanalyse kombiniert. Die untersuchten Systeme werden dabei von einem Testtreiber ausgeführt und beobachtet. Mit den beobachteten Ergebnissen als Referenz kombiniert dann ein Ansatz zur genetischen Programmierung aus statischer, dynamischer und statistischer Analyse ein Verhaltensmodell, das die Qualität eines jeden einzelnen Ansatzes übertrifft. Zur Vervollständigung der Reverse-Engineering-Ergebnisse wird ein Modell zur Ablaufverfolgung (Tracing) erstellt, das die Rückverfolgung aller rekonstruierten Architekturelemente auf ihren Ursprung im Programmcode ermöglicht.

Im Gegensatz zu bestehenden Ansätzen, machen die rekonstruierten Modelle des entwickelten Reverse-Engineering-Ansatzes keine Annahmen über einen der folgenden sogenannten *Kontexte* eines Software-Systems oder einer Komponente:

- Benutzungskontext. Weder die Anzahl der gleichzeitigen Benutzer noch ihre Art der Interaktion mit dem Software-System oder die verwendeten Aufrufparameter werden als fest angenommen.

- Verbindungskontext. Weder der Aufrufer noch die Aufgerufenen können einer Komponente im Allgemeinen bekannt sein. Daher werden keine festen Verbindungen zwischen Komponenten angenommen.

- Allokationskontext. Für eine Komponente kann zur Entwurfszeit nicht bekannt sein, auf welcher Hardware- oder in welcher Software-Umgebung diese ausgeführt werden wird. Zum Beispiel ist für eine Komponente unbekannt, welche Version einer virtuellen Maschine, Middleware oder welcher Prozessor sie zur Ausführung bringt. Diese Unabhängigkeit wird ebenfalls in den rekonstruierten Modellen widergespiegelt.

Es ist festzuhalten, dass bestehende Ansätze häufig das Reverse-Engineering von Architekten fokussieren, die einer schwachen Komponentendefinition folgen und damit einer Nutzung in Simulationsansätzen (für Software-Performance) zuwider laufen (bspw. [SAG⁺06, YGS⁺04, RLvV06]). Solche Modelle eignen sich vor allem zum Verstehen von Software-Systemen [CZvD⁺09]. In anderen Fällen sind die rekonstruierten Modelle unvollständig parametrisierte Verhaltensmodelle (bspw. [HMWR99, IWF07, CW00, ZWL08, WHSB01]). Kein Ansatz führt das Reverse-Engineering von Architektur- und Verhaltensmodellen zusammen. Daher werden die zuvor genannten Entwurfsentscheidungen auf der Architekturebene nicht oder nur bruchstückhaft unterstützt.

Der in dieser Arbeit vorgestellte Reverse-Engineering-Ansatz wurde erfolgreich in insgesamt elf industriellen Fallstudien und Referenzapplikationen, inklusive CoCoME, Palladio FileShare, SPECjvm2008 und SPECjbb255 validiert [CKK08, KKR10]. Im Vergleich mit der Referenzarchitektur dieser Systeme hatten die rekonstruierten Modelle insgesamt eine Präzision (precision) von 78% und einen Rückruf (recall) von 89%. Die auf den rekonstruierten Modellen basierenden Performance-Vorhersagen wichen nur um durchschnittlich 12% – im schlechtesten Fall um 30% von Messungen dieser Systeme ab.

Acknowledgements

A dissertation is not possible without the support of numerous people which contribute in discussions, reviews, help in implementations, or other kinds of collaborations. I will try to keep the acknowledgements brief and try to not forget someone.

First of all, I would like to thank my wife Taalke Krogmann, my family Johanna, Eduard, and Martin Krogmann and Heidi, Götz-Ulrich, Ole, and Ulfert Reuss for their enduring support throughout the last years.

Ralf Reussner is a great adivisor, mentor, group leader, and personality. It is always a pleasure to work with him. He enabled me to write this thesis. Furthermore, I would like to thank my supervisor Gregor Snelting for his fruitful comments, constructive feedback, and valuable discussions. Michael Kuperberg, Thomas Goldschmidt, and Martin Krogmann supported me during proof reading and provided very valueable feedback on my research.

The whole Software Design and Quality group, its associated members, students, and student researchers made the time of writing my dissertation enjoyable and exiting research in an excellent atmosphere. Thank you: Andreas Rentschler, Anne Koziolek, Benjamin Klatt, Christof Momm, Christoph Rathfelder, Dennis Westermann, Elena Kienhöfer, Elke Sauer, Erik Burger, Fabian Brosig, Fouad ben Nasr Omri, Franz Brosch, Giovanni Falcone, Grischa Liebel, Heiko Koziolek, Heinz Hermann, Henning Groenda, Iulia Chirila, Jens Happe, Jörg Henß, Johannes Stammel, Landry Chouambe, Lucia Kapová, Martin Küster, Matthias Huber, Michael Hauck, Mircea Trifu, Nikolaus Huber, Pierre Parrend, Qais Noorshams, Samuel Kounev, Steffen Becker, Steffen Kruse, Tatiana Rhode, Thomas Fischer, Thomas Knapp, Tom Beyer, Vanessa Martin Rodriguez, Viktoria Firus, and Zoya Durdik.

This thesis is further based on support and discussions in the fields of reverse engineering, performance, component technology, symbolic execution, and validation by the following people: Andrea Ciancone, Christian Hammer, Clemens Szyperski, Frank Eichinger, František Plášil, Ivica Crnkovic, Jürgen Ebert, Jan Harder, Jan Kofroň, Jochen Quante, Lubomír Bulej, Lukáš Marek, Mattias Ulbrich, Michael Ernst, Petr Hnětynka, Petr Tůma, Raffaela Mirandola, Rainer Koschke, Roland Klug, Wilhelm Hasselbring, and Wolfgang Weck.

Thank you all! Thanks to all I forgot to thank to.

Contents

Contents

Contents

1. Introduction

The ability to design a system and predict its properties before actually implementing it is one of the core properties of any engineering discipline. Design rules, basic principles, theoretical background, and prediction approaches help engineering disciplines to avoid trial-and-error cycles which would require the actual implementation of a system in order to assess its properties. Engineering disciplines can reason on the base of theoretical models.

Nowadays, engineering approaches are also available for *software* systems. Such approaches for software systems support for example reasoning on software design at an architectural level [WFP07a, Koz10]. These approaches rely on software models and allow a predictable assembly of components at design time *without* actually developing code, deploying applications to execution environments, configuring them, or writing integration code for the integration with existing software systems. Depending on the approach, functional and non-functional properties such as performance, reliability, or maintainability can be estimated from models.

The remainder of this thesis focuses on performance properties of software systems which are well-supported by engineering approaches (e.g. [BKR09, BCdK07, FNNS06, MG00, Kou06]). These approaches enable what-if analyses of software architectures and help answering questions in the following scenarios which are crucial to software performance engineering [SW02]:

1. **Sizing** (e.g. estimate required hardware to handle certain workload situations, reliability after changes in usage profile, or performance on a new target platform)

2. Extensions of **legacy software systems** (estimate quality properties of a software after adding new components and guide design of the extension part)

3. **Reusing** existing components (what is the impact of using an existing component within an application or when designing a new application from partly existing components)

4. **Design optimisation** of software systems (e.g. what performance or reliability can be expected for later implementations)

All these engineering approaches have in common that for *existing* or partially existing software systems, they first need to determine the status quo – i.e. a *model*

1

representation of a software system under study. The above scenarios, which are explained in more detail in Section 1.2, become feasible with the availability of reverse engineered software architecture performance models.

Although model-based reasoning of performance properties is becoming increasingly important (cf. [WFP07b, BDIS04b, Koz10]), no approach exists which is able to reverse engineer the required performance models for component-based software architectures from code. The four above scenarios require parameterised performance models of existing software systems in order to become feasible.

Existing reverse engineering approaches for software architectures (see [CHDP07, MJS+00, TTBS07] for an overview) aim at reverse engineering models with loose semantics, e.g. components possess no explicit interface, have no or incomplete connectors, support no composite structures, the models make no performance properties available for components, or the result models possess no execution semantics. If such models are reverse engineered, they can help humans understanding a software architecture but do not support software performance engineering approaches in the introduced scenarios. Furthermore, the reverse engineered architectures of such approaches often possess little abstractions which makes dealing with large applications cumbersome.

Also for behavioural models no satisfying reverse engineering approach exists. Behaviour models of components need to be highly parameterised to reflect the changing *contexts* a component has to cope with: changing usage (number of users, user interaction, varying amounts of data to be processed), changing assembly (different components connected), and changing execution platforms (fast and slow servers) – Section 2.6 details on component contexts. Existing approaches (e.g. [CDH+00, Ros06]) assume all or at least one of the contexts of a component to be fixed. This assumptions cannot hold for components which, by definition, are a subject of re-composition and reuse.

This thesis focuses on the reverse engineering of component-based software architectures for the design and evaluation of performance properties in early development phases. The reverse engineering approach presented in this thesis enables the application of model-based prediction techniques to real world software systems by overcoming the need for manual reverse engineering. It provides an integrated method for:

- Reconstruction of the static architectures and behaviour specification of component-based software systems and to

- reverse engineer highly parameterised and abstracted performance models which enable reasoning in sizing, legacy software extension, reuse, and design optimisation scenarios.

The *core contributions* are automated approaches for (i) architectural reverse engineering, (ii) reverse engineering behavioural models, iii) reconstruction of model parameterisation (control and data flow), iv) creation of performance abstractions of software systems, and v) an integrating approximation approach for parametric dependencies in models (combining static, dynamic, and statistical analysis). The approach combines static, dynamic, and statistical analysis techniques and machine learning for reverse engineering.

This thesis introduces an integrated approach that deals with reverse engineering of component-based architectures and also reverse engineers behavioural models from code. Source and binary code (for Java: Bytecode) are supported as sources. The Palladio Component Model (PCM) [BKR09] serves as output model as it allows model-based reasoning on software architectures and supports the four introduced scenarios for performance prediction.

Section 1.5 highlights the contributions and goals of this thesis in more detail. Section 1.1 pursues the motivation.

1.1. Motivation

The previous section already introduced the motivation to enable performance predictions for component-based software systems, and the four scenarios on sizing, extension of legacy software systems, reuse of components, and design optimisation (details in Section 1.2) which are desirable for the engineering of software systems.

Whenever different design alternatives of a software system are being analysed, where the software system at least partially comprises existing software, the existing source code must first be translated into a performance model. This model then serves as input to performance prediction approaches like Palladio [BKR09] which allow the evaluation of design alternatives or of the performance scenarios from the introduction (bullets 1 to 4 in Section 1). The creation of performance models can either be performed manually or automated with support of reverse engineering approaches.

Only small portions of software development projects are greenfield projects which do not depend on any existing software system. Existing software systems consequently must be captured by models when aiming at the analysis of the performance of software systems. As models usually grow with the size of applications, it is cumbersome, expensive, and error-prone to manually reverse engineer models for today's software systems which comprise hundreds of thousand of lines of code.

Manually reverse engineering software architectures and performance models implies large effort, error-proneness, potential modelling inconsistencies, oversimplification to handle large software systems, and a lack of parameterisation since parameterisation results in additional effort. With the approach which is developed in this thesis, manual reverse engineering can be replaced by an automated approach which addresses all of these issues. Section 1.4 addresses the issues in more detail.

3

1.1.1. Advantages of model-based Approaches

The proposed approach reverse engineers component-based software performance models of existing software from code. Operating on the base of *models* instead of existing code of software systems helps avoiding efforts in the following areas:

- Estimating the impact of design decisions does not require implementing the design decisions in code. Design alternatives can be modeled and then – based on the model – be evaluated. Thus, it becomes easy to enable what-if analyses of design alternatives.

- No glue code for integration purposes is required. At the model level, no configuration and implementation effort is required for evaluating single design alternatives which incorporate existing software components.

- No deployment effort is required at the model level beyond assigning software to hardware. For instance, no deployment descriptors (such as EJB deployment descriptors) are required and the cumbersome task of setting up execution environments (e.g. application servers and databases) is not needed.

- To answer sizing questions or analyse scalability of a software architecture, it is not necessary to actually buy hardware. Instead, models of hardware are sufficient to predict the impact of hardware.

- Some scalability and sizing questions cannot be answered in practice. For example, it is infeasible to stress a large distributed execution environment (nowadays sometimes called "cloud") at 100%, as hardware resources are really huge and require an equivalent amount of load generators to stress the servers. Furthermore, servers are globally distributed and not fully accessible from a single location (requests are answered locally). Thus, only models can be used in these cases to estimate scalability.

Again, in all of the above cases, models of existing software architectures are required. The next two sections introduce further advantages of having reverse engineering approaches for software performance models available.

1.1.2. Software Architectures for Performance Predictions

Reverse engineering only the static architecture of a software system is not sufficient to predict Quality of Service (QoS, e.g. reliability or performance) properties of that software system. QoS prediction only become feasible if performance specifications of the behaviour of components of the architecture are available. If no behaviour specifications are available, it would be unknown what happens inside of components when calling a certain provided service.

If performance specifications of the behaviour are available, performance prediction approaches like Palladio [BKR09], KLAPER [GMS05], or SOFA [BHP06, BDH+08b] can be applied. Then, for a given component-based software architecture, performance metrics like response time, execution time, or throughput can be predicted based on models which capture the full software architecture.

Since the reverse engineering approach which is presented in this thesis aims at the support of performance predictions for existing software systems, it targets full software architectures which subsume the static architecture, a behavioural model for components, and performance annotations for the behavioural model. Hereafter, the "full" software architecture will simply be referred to as "software architecture".

1.1.3. Automated Reverse Engineering

Reverse engineering approaches can be classified as either quasi-manual, semi-automatic, or quasi-automatic (see classification by [PDP+07, DP09]). Obviously, an automated reverse engineering approach is appreciated for a number of reasons:

- Increased productivity can be expected due to less effort for single reverse engineering tasks

- Reverse engineering can be expected to be less error-prone than manual reverse engineering since sporadic errors typically do not occur in automation.

- Increased precisions can be expected as even for large systems all necessary model details can be captured by automation: Reverse engineering models are not rough estimates of humans but calculated.

- Automated reverse engineering can also reduce complexity if built-in simplification and abstraction mechanisms are made available. Then, analysing even large and complex software systems becomes feasible.

1.1.4. Programme understanding

Through the developed approach, static architecture models and behaviour abstractions of component services become available which can help in programme understanding. Since the developed approach is going to be automated, a tight feedback cycle between software architecture and the actual implementation can be established.

The reverse engineering architecture models of the envisioned reverse engineering approach can help in programme understanding for:

- existing applications that are going to be refactored. Software systems which possibly exist for a long period of time naturally evolve. Gradually, architectural erosion can take place, leading to poorly understood systems, or systems which do not match the requirements for maintainability for other reasons. Before refactoring a software system it first needs to be understood.

- existing applications that are going to be enhanced. To support meaningful enhancements of software, the existing software first should be completely understood. Architecture documentation should actually match the software system it describes. Once up-to-date architecture documents are available, enhancements for the existing system can be planned.

- migration and legacy system support. For example if legacy systems need to be integrated into new software systems, there is a need to understand the basic architecture of legacy systems. The need for integration can originate from the software system's evolution where previously independent software systems need to cooperate from a certain point in time.

  For legacy systems there often is little (up-to-date) documentation available. People involved in the development of the legacy system are no more available. Hence, the architecture of the legacy system is not known and must first be extracted from the code.

All the above cases require the reconstruction of software architectures from given software systems. It can be stated that having an available up-to-date software architecture is a common problem for software development and software engineering.

1.2. Application Scenarios

The developed reverse engineering approach supports four core performance prediction scenarios, which will be presented in detail in the following. Each scenarios involves a number of sub-scenarios which the reverse engineering approach must account for. All of the scenarios require the presence of a up-to-date component-based software performance model of an existing software system to allow the analysis of the scenario.

1.2.1. Sizing

Figure 1.1 visualises typical sizing scenarios. Sizing is the relation between usage of a software systems by users (which can also be other software systems) and the resource environment (servers, network) which executes the software system. Sizing can be further divided into the following sub-scenarios:

- Sizing of hardware: How much server infrastructure is required to support a certain number of concurrent users (e.g. server requirements for 100 concurrent users)?

(a) Resource Sizing   (b) Scalability

Figure 1.1.: Sizing scenarios involve, among others, resource sizing and the scalability for different usage profiles. Images sources: left server by
Craig Spurrier licensed under Creative Commons Attribution 2.5 Generic; right server ©LiquidImage Fotolia.com

- Relocation of running applications: How does a business application perform
  on different servers (e.g. 128 GB main memory instead of 32 GB)?

- Platform selection: Does an application perform better on application server
  A or B (e.g. does a WebSphere application server perform better than a JBoss
  application server for a certain software system)?

- Changes in the usage profile

  – Estimate the impact of changes in the usage profile: For up to how many
    concurrent users does a software system scale until bottlenecks take ef-
    fect?

  – Changes in user behaviour: How much will an application slow down
    if users change their interaction frequency with the system or the kind
    and volume of data (e.g. upload high definition videos instead of low
    resolution ones)?

1.2.2. Extension of Legacy Software Systems

Only few software systems are developed from scratch. Most of today's software
must integrate with existing software systems. The integration can take place on
different detail level: loosely via calling the existing software system or tightly by
actually changing the existing software system. Figure 1.2 illustrates the extension
of a legacy software system.

In both cases, the extension of legacy software systems should be analysed prior
to actually extending the legacy software system on the code level. If changed usage

7

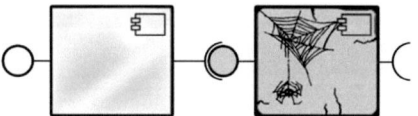

Figure 1.2.: Extension of legacy applications

scenarios due to the extensions are not considered, the extended functionality but also the legacy software system can suffer from poor performance. The sub-scenarios for existing software systems are:

- Investigate the extension of legacy applications: How much will the new front end or business case stress my legacy applications?

- Reuse of existing components: How will an existing component perform on a new execution platform?

1.2.3. Reuse of Components

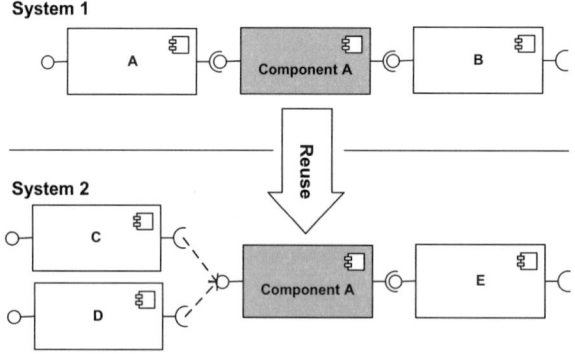

Figure 1.3.: Component reuse

The reuse of a software component (see figure 1.3) implies changes in its contexts. The assembly, allocation, or usage profile of a reused component change although the component itself does not change. In the example, different components (A for System 1; C and D for System 2) access a single Component A which is being reused (changing usage context). In System 1, Component A is connected to B, while in System 2 it is connected to component E (changing assembly context). Furthermore, the allocation of Component A could have changed between System 1 and System 2.

When reusing a component implementation, the implementation remains the same. In the same way, the possibility of reusing a component in different contexts should not be limited on the model level.

1.2.4. Design optimisation

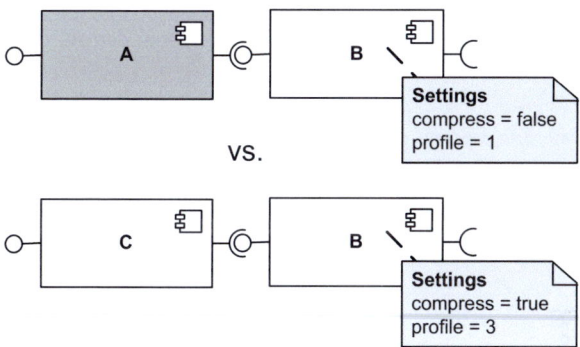

Figure 1.4.: Design optimisation

When designing and engineering new software systems or new components, often at least portions of the employed components are subject to reuse.

Examples for design optimisation scenarios are:

- Design and engineer new applications and new components: Is it worth spending 15,000 EUR for load balancing hardware or will 1,000 EUR for software caching be sufficient?

- Bottleneck avoidance: Does a software system architecture contain a potential bottleneck when using a non-threaded sorting component?

- Design optimisation: Which size should a SQL connection pool have to reach optimal performance for 100 concurrent users?

The availability of parametric performance models for existing components allows to reasons on the quality of a new design more precisely, since the variation of expected performance values for existing components can be reduced. The availability of reliable software performance models (due to relying on existing implementations) of existing components helps reducing the possible design space (values must not be purely guessed) and the likelihood to provide performance results which match the performance of a later implementation of the software system (cf. [Bec08a]).

1.3. Target Model

The Palladio Component Model (PCM, [BKR09]) is the target model of the developed reverse engineering approach. The PCM supports the analysis of all of the scenarios from Section 1.2, if it operates on fully parameterised models (details in Section 2.6).

According to [Sta73], a model posseses a *pragmatism* which defines the goal of a model, *abstraction*, and an *isomorphism* relationship to what is modelled. When analysing the PCM with respect to these model properties, one can identify the model properties which must hold to apply the PCM for the scenarios from Section 1.2. Details of the PCM are presented in Section 2.5.

Figure 1.5 shows an example of the model and an implementation of a software system. There are two design alternatives in the example ("Scenario A" and "Scenario B") which are reflected in the model *and* in the implementation. The design alternatives differ in the usage of the system (two versus six users), the assembly (Component "B" versus component "C"), and the execution environment (four cores versus two cores).

Pragmatism The aim of the PCM is the performance prediction for design alternatives of component-based software architectures.

Abstraction The PCM abstracts software systems to entities of component-based software architecture (e.g. components, interfaces), the execution environment, and the usage profile (i.e. users interaction with a software system). Furthermore, only performance-relevant properties of such system are maintained.

Isomorphism The isomorphism is a very important aspect for reverse engineering. Changes in the implementation of a software system must be reflected in the reverse engineered model (if not abstracted and within the pragmatism) and vice versa changes of the software model must hold for the implementation of the software system.

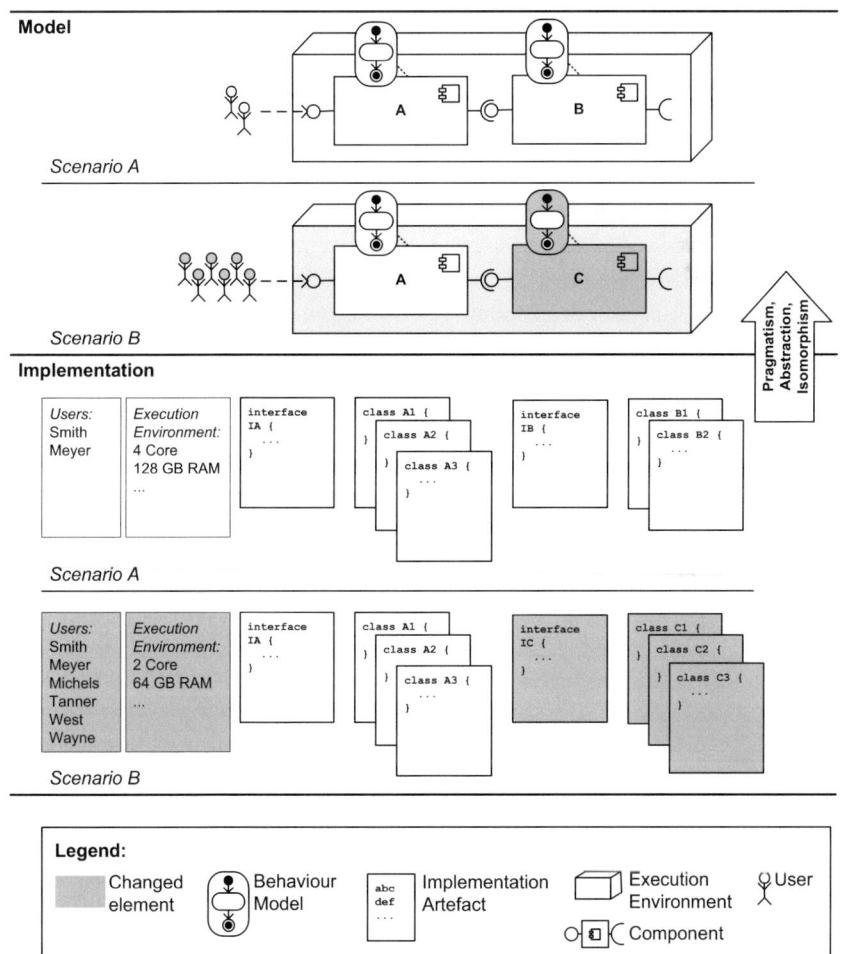

Figure 1.5.: Example: Model pragmatism, abstraction, and isomorphism

If in the example, the number of users of component A changes or users interact differently between "Scenario A" and "Scenario B", the performance implications from the model must be reflected in the implementation and vice versa. Likewise, changes in the execution environment and in the assembly of component A must be isomorph between model and implementation.

The required isomorphism is a driver of *parameterisation* of the model which will be further discussed in Section 2.6 and 2.7. Non-parameterised models cannot account for the isomorphism of implementation and model.

1.4. Problem Statement

This section briefly summarises the problems which can be identified for the current state of the art in reverse engineering when aiming at support of the scenarios from previous sections. Section 4.1 and Section 5.1 will highlight the problems specific to the reverse engineering of static archtitectures and behavioural models. A detailed discussion of the current state of the art is part of the related work in Section 8.

The current state of the art in reverse engineering does not properly support component-based software architectures following a strong component definition – which is required for the scenarios from Section 1.2. The current state of the art lacks support for the reverse engineering of models which i) are suitable for performance predictions, ii) possess execution semantics, iii) have explicit context dependencies and thus allow third party composition at the model-level. iv) A missing parameterisation of the reverse engineered component models makes them hardly usable for changing component contexts (i.e. usage profiles, component assembly, or execution environments are assumed to be fixed in existing approaches).

1.5. Contributions and Goals

This section summarises the contributions and goals of this thesis. The contributions to reverse engineering in general are presented in Section 3.2. More detailed contributions for the reverse engineering of static architectures are presented in Section 4.3 while Section 5.3 details on contributions for the reverse engineering of behavioural models.

Architectural Reverse Engineering This thesis contributes an integrated automated architectural reverse engineering approach for the *static architecture* of component-based software systems and *behavioural models* of individual component services. The following characteristics hold for the approach:

- The reverse engineered component models are fully *parameterised* components over usage profile, assembly context, and execution environment.

- The target model possesses *executions semantics* and is created such that performance analyses can immediately operate on the reverse engineered models.

- The reverse engineered components are *strict components* as defined by Szyperski [SGM02] and form a *hierarchical* component model.

- The reverse engineering approach is *robust* against design and component structure violation and can be adapted to properties which are specific to single software systems.

- The approach is *language-independent* and thus applicable to object-oriented and imperative code (C code).

Reverse Engineering Approach for Parametric Dependencies of Software Components This thesis contributes a reverse engineering approach for *parametric dependencies* which are suitable to parameterise the *control and data flow* of component behaviour. The developed approach contributes as follows:

- It creates *performance abstractions* aligned with the component abstraction level.

- The approach make a component's dependencies to the environment *explicit parameters*.

- The approach provides an analysis method for *complex parametric dependencies* covering possibly thousands of lines of code.

Genetic Programming This thesis contributes the *application of genetic programming* to the field of reverse engineering and provides extensions of genetic programing for the specific requirements of reverse engineering. The adaptations of genetic programming include:

- *Domain knowledge* from the performance analysis and performance modeling is encoded into genetic programming. Special enhancement of genetic programming's mutation, crossover, and fitness function are provided. Adapted gene and chromosome structures and an improved mechanism for generating the initial generation are proposed.

- Static, dynamic and statistical analyses are *integrated* in a genetic programming approach which is able to further evolve and combine the results of each input analysis approach. The reverse engineered models are (by construction) granted to be never worse than models created by the best available static, dynamic, and statistical analysis technique.

1.6. Outline

The remainder of this thesis is organised as follows. Chapter 2 introduces the foundations for this work. The core contribution chapters are Chapters 3 to 5. Chapter 3 first provides an overview of the reverse engineering approach. Chapter 4 then deals with the reverse engineering of static architectures and Chapter 5 deals with the reverse engineering of behavioural models. In Chapter 6 the crosscutting aspect "Traceability" is addressed.

The validation of the reverse engineering approach is presented in Chapter 7, Chapter 8 discusses related work, whereas Chapter 9 details on the results and lessons learned. Finally, Chapter 9.12 briefly summarises and concludes this thesis.

2. Foundations

This section breifly introduces foundations and general terminology which will be used throughout the remainder of this thesis. The topics which are covered by this section are reverse engineering, genetic, component-based software engineering, and the Palladio Component Model. The Palladio Component Model is the central meta-model dealt with in this thesis. Furthermore, basic knowledge on so-called *parametric dependencies* in software component models will be presented.

2.1. Component-Based Software Engineering

Component-based software engineering (CBSE, [SGM02, HC01]) is a software development paradigm. In it, software systems are built from a reusable entity called "software component". The term *software component* was first coined in 1968 at the NATO conference on software engineering [McI69]. Since then, components have resulted in popular implementations and frameworks including Microsoft COM [Cor], Sun EJB [EJB07], OSGi [OSG09], and the Corba Component Model by the OMG [Obj06a].

It must be emphasised that the term "software component" is highly overloaded. Some people see software components as classes or modules while others see it as a high-level entity [LW05, LW07, SGM02]. Section 2.9 presents a short definition of the term "software component" which is used throughout this thesis. The remainder of this thesis assumes CBSE characteristics of software architectures.

CBSE implies a development process (see e.g. [KBHR08]) which enables the division of labour. Multiple developer roles participate in the creation of component-based software systems. The development process is intended to allow for concurrent and distributed work an a component-based software system such that the developer roles' responsibilities do not overlap. For example component developers and software architects interact with component deployers. The division of labour reduces the complexity for individuals (e.g. component developers) and allows the creation of large and complex software systems.

One key idea of software-based software development is the reuse of individual components (see for example [BC88, BR88, BP89, Est95, HC91]). Due to better testing of reused components, a higher quality of single components is expected. Additionally, reuse can lower the costs of software development, if single components of a software system are reused multiple times.

Components are software entities which can be composed from other components. The composite pattern [GHJV95] allows the creation of higher-level components. For example, the components `Accounting`, `Authentification`, and `Reporting` can be composed to a higher-level component `SalesManagement`.

Software components are contractually specified entities. They possess explicit provided and required interfaces which determine pre and post conditions (the required interface determines the pre condition – the services a component needs to operate; the provided interface the post condition – the services a component offers to other components). Systems manufactured from components with contractually specified properties are common to engineering disciplines (e.g. voltage and resistance of components in electrical engineering or the dimension of structural elements in building construction).

Software component models describe or specify the properties of component-based software systems. They are abstractions of implementations of component-based software systems and can highlight aspects like architecture, deployment, performance, reliability, or composition of a software system. A survey on software component models can be found in [LW05, Lau06].

2.2. Performance Prediction

General Performance Prediction Approaches Performance prediction approaches (surveys in [BDIS04a, BJH$^+$05]) estimate the expected performance of software systems from model representations or other formalisations. Common performance formalisations include Petri nets [Rei85, BK96, BK02], queuing networks [BGdMT98], markov chains [Tri01, BGdMT98], and process algebras [HHK02]. Of each formalisation, various extensions exist to overcome limitations of a certain formalisation (e.g. Petri nets [Pet80] as original form, stochastic Petri nets [BK02] which include stochastic timing behaviour, queued Petri nets [Bau93] to account for queuing effects of, for example, resources with contention).

Performance prediction approaches allow reasoning on the performance of software systems (e.g. bottleneck detection, capacity planning) and provide various metrics like response time, throughput, and resource utilisation to estimate the performance. The Software Performance Engineering approach (SPE, [Smi90]) is among the best-known approaches which systematically tackles the design of software systems with respect to performance. SPE aims at equally capturing the software architecture and the resource environment during early design phases. Prior to starting the implementation of a software system, the design is critically evaluated in SPE to identify potential bottlenecks in the design and avoid them in the design phase already. Only designs with promising performance properties are then implemented.

Hence, SPE aims at saving development effort for poorly performing software design alternatives [SW02]. The key idea behind SPE is that fixing the *design* of a software system in early development stages is less costly than optimizing the *implementation*. The effort for fixing implementations includes potentially the re-design, re-implementations, data migration, buying new hardware, and new setup of the execution environment while the effort for the design phase is only the re-design.

Component-Based Performance Prediction Approaches For component-based software systems, special performance prediction approaches (e.g. [WMW03, WW04a, Kou06, EFH04, DMM03, Yac02, BM03, CLGL05]) exist which account for the specifics of component-based software systems (e.g. reuse of components). A recent survey on component-based performance prediction approaches can be found in [Koz10].

Some software component models (e.g. [BKR09, WW04b, BHP06, GMS05, GL03]) allow the analysis (numeric, analytic, or simulation) of properties of a component-based software-system based on the model. Since models are not necessarily related to an implementation, model-based predictions (e.g. performance, reliability) become feasible for component-based software systems. For example, design decisions, architecture evaluations, and the analysis of "what-if-scenarios" for component-based software systems can then be met at the model level when using such approaches.

Depending on the component model, components carry values for the response time of single component services [GMS05], the resource demand of component services is mapped to queuing networks [WW04b], or components include behaviour models for single component services with annotated execution time of single actions of the behaviour [BKR09].

Related Prediction Approaches Beside performance prediction, various approaches exist for the prediction of software reliability (e.g. [MIO87, GWTH98, RSP03, KB09]). These approaches also incorporate a software model. Opposed to performance prediction approaches, these model do not carry timing-related values but transition probabilities and error probabilities of software systems. Based on these models, metrics like the probability of failures on requesting a service are calculated to estimate the overall reliability of a software system.

Performability is the combination of performance and reliability. Performability respects that the residence time of software in faulty components or states that impact the reliability. As for performance and reliability, various performability prediction approaches exist (e.g. [CMST90, HMRT01]).

17

Since software reliability and performability models can have many commonalities with software performance models, the applicability of reliability and performability prediction approaches to the models reverse engineered by the approach which is presented in this thesis, is discussed later (see Section 9.7).

2.3. Reverse Engineering

Reverse engineering is the process of reconstructing properties of a system and creating a higher level of abstraction of that system [CC90]. In the context of software systems, those properties include the architecture, allocation, deployment, and behaviour which are reverse engineered from the source code of a system under study. In a broader scope, reverse engineering is used to create lost documentation, helps understanding software systems, and provides a basis for reviews. Reverse engineering can be considered at the initial step of reengineering [CC90] activities which aims at refactoring a system. For example, in order to refactor the architecture of a system under test, its architecture must first be known and understood. Reverse engineering can help in identifying the software architecture and help understanding the system.

Furthermore, a subset of reverse engineering techniques targets models like the above introduced component models (e.g. [KSRP99, SAG$^+$06]) and performance models (e.g. [CW00, HMWR99]) as primary output (see Section 2.1 and 2.2). Performance predictions are then based on reverse engineering models. When applying (automated) reverse engineering techniques for the creation of these models, the effort for creating performance models can be reduced compared to the manual creation of performance models.

Code Analysis Most reverse engineering approaches itself either rely on static code analysis or dynamic analysis approaches. *Static analysis* approaches analyse code without actually executing the code. Code can either be binary or source code. Static analysis approaches investigate for example class structures, statements, and declarations in the code. Typical results of static analysis are abstract syntax trees (cf. [PE88]) or metrics (e.g. lines of code, number of classes, or code complexity measures).

Dynamic analysis approaches actually execute the code and monitor the code's behaviour an runtime. Therefore, the code is typically executed in a test bed. Test cases or load drivers then run the code and the code execution (e.g. control or data flow) is recorded. To record data, either the code can be instrumented (e.g. via source code instrumentation, bytecode instrumentation, or aspect logging) or recording facilities of the execution environment (e.g. virtual machine or application server monitors) can be used.

Generally, static and dynamic code analysis techniques complement each other (see for example [Ern03, Sys00, RR02, Par93]). Static code analyses generally have a higher precision and partially provide soundness of their results, while dynamic analysis techniques rely on representative test cases to create complete results. Most static code analyses are limited with respect to code complexity and the size of the systems under study while dynamic analysis mostly is able to handle very large systems with hundreds of thousands lines of code. For example, dynamic bindings are hard to handle statically, while at runtime bindings are readily available to dynamic analysis.

Various analysis techniques which complement reverse engineering build on static and dynamic analysis. These techniques include model checking (automatic checking whether a given specification is met by code), data flow analysis (the calculation of possible variables values for various places in code), and symbolic execution (a pseudo execution of code with symbolic values).

2.4. Genetic Programming

Genetic programming (GP, [Koz93, BNKF98]) is a meta-heuristic machine learning technique [WF05] which, by means of evolution, creates a solution to a given search problem, optimised according to a *fitness function*. *Individuals*, representing potential solutions to the search problem, are realised by *genes*.

Genetic programming is a special kind of genetic algorithm (GA, [GH88, Whi04]) with genes forming a tree structure. The original idea of genetic programming was to automate the implementation of code by specifying a problem (requirement) and source code which solves the problem is being generated automatically. In such cases, the genes represent of computer programme. Nowadays, genetic programming is broadly applied as a meta-heuristic optimisation technique (see [VGM+09] for an overview).

Figure 2.1 highlights and relates the most important terms from genetic programming to each other. Genes reside in a *gene repository* which itself is the base for creating a *chromosome repository*. The chromosome repository holds a set of *chromosomes* (also called indididividuals), where each chromosome is realised by a set of genes. Chromosomes represent potential genetic programming solutions, while genes are the "atoms" that are required to express the solutions. A set of chromosomes represents a so-called *generation*.

During genetic programming, multiple generations evolve. A typical genetic programming process, as it will be used in later sections of this thesis, covers multiple steps which are illustrated in Figure 2.2. The steps are repeated in multiple iterations. In the first iteration, a random initial generation is created from individuals in the gene repository ("fill generation"). Next, the so-called crossover and mutation

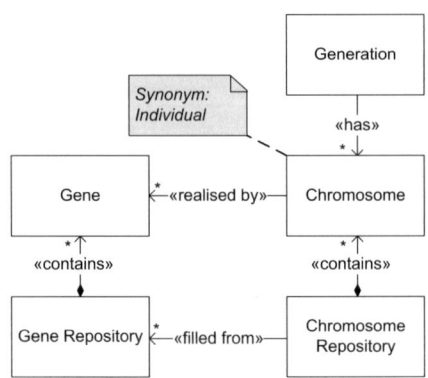

Figure 2.1.: Relations between gene, chromosome, generation, gene repository, and chromosome repository

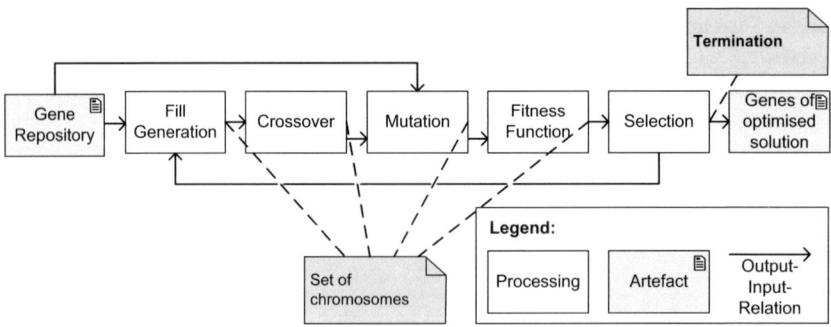

Figure 2.2.: Overview: Steps of genetic programming

take place. During crossover (analogous to reproduction and biological crossover), parent chromosomes are recombined to form new children. Mutation changes single or multiple genes of a chromosome to create genetic diversity. For example, if a gene represents a constant, that constant can be changed.

The fitness function then judges how "good" the solutions represented by the chromosome are. Typically, the fitness function encodes domain knowledge on properties of an expected optimal solution (e.g. small error) to decide how "good" a chromosome is. During selection, a subset of chromosomes is then selected for survival in the next generation. This can for example be the best chromosomes and a number of randomly selected other chromosomes (to ensure diversity). After the selection, genetic programming decides whether to evolve another generation or to stop evolution. Evolution is for example stopped, if an optimal solution has been found or a fixed number of generations has evolved. Usually, the best chromosome (determined again by the fitness function) is the result of a genetic programming run. For the case in which the evolution is not terminated, another generation is evolved. In genetic programming settings where generations possess a fixed population size, prior to evolving, first new individuals are (randomly) generated to fill up the generation until the fixed size is reached. In other cases, the evolution starts again with crossover and mutation.

Genetic algorithms in general, and genetic programming as a special form, are known to be robust machine learning techniques which are suitable for large search space and multi-dimensional optimisation problems (cf. [BNKF98, Su09]). Since genetic algorithms exist since the 1960's, a large variety of genetic algorithm approaches and extensions exist. Many approaches stick with the basic processing steps described above and extend crossover, mutation, selection, and termination for genetic algorithms in general (e.g. [SP94, AGP03]). Other approaches apply genetic algorithm to a certain domain (e.g. [WAW04a, WAW04b, Gar06, Dol01]) or enrich the capabilities of genetic algorithms by domain-specific requirements (e.g. [DMM99, CDPEV05]).

Section 5.11 formalises the above terms and introduces the developed extensions of genetic programming which go beyond the state presented in this section.

2.5. The Palladio Component Model

The Palladio Component Model (PCM, [BKR09]) is a well-validated (e.g. [MBKR08b, KBH07, BDH08a, Bec08b, BKR07, Koz08a, Hap08]) and broadly applied (e.g. [KR08b, RK09, KR08a, HBR$^+$10, CMRT10, BKK09, BKBR10]) software component model for the prediction and evaluation of software performance and reliability at the design level. The PCM enables the analysis of component-based software architectures before actually implementing the software system. For example, for performance prediction, potential bottlenecks can be discovered, resource contention be estimated, response time and throughput be predicted. For reliability, metrics like the probability for failures on demand can be predicted.

To capture a software system, models for the static architecture (components and their connections), component behaviour (comparable to UML activity diagrams [Obj05b]), resource environment (hardware servers, application servers, and network), usage profile (user interaction with the software system and data passed to the system)), and component allocation to the resource environment exist. All of the afore mentioned models are meta-models [Obj05b, Obj06b] for instances which hold properties for a concrete software system.

21

PCM models are performance abstractions of software systems (for models which also carry reliability information: reliability abstractions). Only performance-relevant aspects of a software system are covered by the model. For example, the real implementation of an interface might contain eight parameters. The parameter representation in the PCM component interface could be a subset of only 5 performance-relevant parameters from the source code. Parameters which do not affect the performance of a software system, e.g. a flag which changes the color of a reporting table, can be omitted in the PCM.

Note that the PCM itself does not provide a mapping to source code. To ease understandability, the following sections will point typical relations to source code. A component in the PCM can cover an arbitrary number of source code classes but a class must not belong to multiple components. Further abstractions from source code are: Public methods in the source code do not necessarily correspond to provided component services and interfaces implemented by classes do not necessarily map to provided interfaces of a corresponding component.

Since the PCM is the central model which the reverse engineering approach presented in this thesis targets, its model structures will be briefly discussed in the following. Due to space restrictions, (the PCM contains more than 130 meta-classes) only a subset of the meta-classes which are relevant for the thesis will be presented. For further details refer to [Koz08a, Bec08b]. Names given in a `Typewriter` font describe meta-classes in the following.

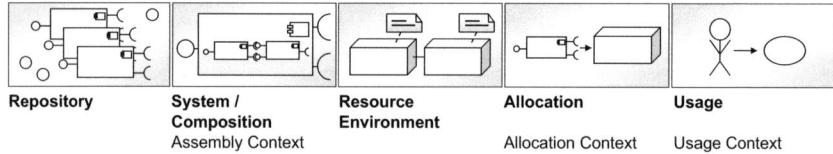

| Repository | System / Composition Assembly Context | Resource Environment | Allocation Allocation Context | Usage Usage Context |

Figure 2.3.: Overview on PCM models and component contexts

2.5.1. Component Contexts

The PCM distinguished three so-called *component contexts* [BDD+06, Koz08b]: assembly, allocation, and usage context. These contexts are generally applicable to component-based software development. Contexts specify different kinds of instances of components. Opposed to object-oriented programming for which mostly only classes (types) and objects (instances) are distinguished, the differentiation for components is more fine-grained. It must be emphasised, that none of the contexts can be assumed to be fixed or known to a component type due to the reuse of components in different contexts – the component contexts instead explicitly capture the variable environment, a component is exposed to. The sections 2.6 and 1.2 further detail on this.

Each component context is captured by a single PCM model. Figure 2.3 provides an overview on the relation between the models and the contexts. The repository and resource environment model are not related to a component context.

Assembly The *assembly context* captures the composition and connections among components. A component in an assembly context are component instances in a system, subsystem, or composite component (see Section 2.5.2). Furthermore, the assembly context determines the binding to other components (the components, a components is connected to). The meta-class `AssemblyContext` captures the assembly context.

Allocation The *allocation context* determines in which execution environment a component is executed. Since components can be reused, the actual execution environment is not known to components. The allocation context binds components to a certain execution environment (e.g. server, application server). The meta-class is `AllocationContext`.

Usage The same software system can be reused in different usage scenarios. For example, once 10 users concurrently interact with the system and upload files to a file sharing application with a size of 10 KB, while in another scenario 100 users upload files with a size of 1 GB. The usage scenario obviously has a strong impact on the performance of a software system. The *allocation context* determines the usage scenarios in which a software system and its components are being executed.

2.5.2. Static Architecture

The static architecture of the PCM comprises components, interfaces, and connectors (cf. Figure 2.4). Interfaces and components are first class entities in the PCM which reside independently in repositories. Components either provide or require interfaces through a `ProvidedRole` and `RequiredRole`, respectively. Each interfaces holds a number of service signatures, which describe the service the provision of an interface implies.

The PCM is a performance abstraction of component implementations. For each parameter of a signature defined in interfaces (e.g. `boolean doSth(List l, MyType mt)`), so-called *parameter characterisations* exist which abstract from

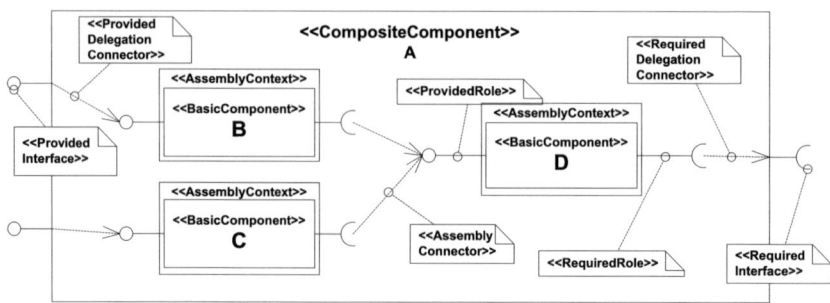

Figure 2.4.: Example: PCM composite component (from [Koz08b])

concrete values and introduce further properties. Parameter characterisations identify performance-relevant characteristics of data types. For example, lists are characterised by their size and own data types ("MyType") can be characterised by specifically defined properties (e.g. value of a flag, their bytesize, etc). The understanding of parameter characterisations is essential for this thesis. Thus, Section 2.7.1 discusses parameter characterisations in the context of model parameterisation.

Connectors can be AssemblyConnector, ProvidedDelegationConnector, or RequiredDelegationsConnector as know from UML2 [Obj05b]. All connectors connect roles of components, since the same interfaces can be shared among multiple components (imagine for example a chain of responsibility [GHJV95] in which all participating components must provide and require the same interface). An AssemblyConnector, for example, connects the tuple (RequiredRole, AssemblyContext) with (ProvidedRole, AssemblyContext), where the AssemblyContext is the above introduced mean to identify component instances in assemblies.

The PCM distinguishes multiple component types. The relevant ones for this thesis are composite component (CompositeComponent) and basic components (BasicComponent). A composite component is realised from further sub-components, while a basic component is an atom component entity which realises its component services via so-called Resource Demanding Service Effect Specifications (RDSEFF, see Section 2.5.3).

Like a composite component, a system (System) is a special kind of composite structure with special semantics. A system is the outer-most structure of a software system and describes the system boundary. All interfaces provided by the system are externally available and can be accessed by users or external systems which are out of scope of a certain PCM analysis. A system itself can also have required interfaces. Calls to the required interfaces of systems are out of scope for PCM analyses. For example, if a database is not going to be analysed, the corresponding interface becomes a required interface of the system. In order to still allow analyses of systems with external dependencies, Quality of Service (QoS) values can be specified for external services. For example, the average response time and throughput of the database component could be specified as QoS values.

2.5.3. Service Effect Specifications

The PCM behaviour model is called Resource Demanding Service Effect Specifications (RDSEFF). Each provided service of a basic component is specified by a RDSEFF. A RDSEFF specifies the behaviour of a component service including its control flow, data flow, and effects on other components (which required services are called in which order and with which parameters). A RDSEFF is comparable to UML activity models, but more powerful with respect to data flow specification and parameterisation. Figure 5.6 on page 115 introduces an example RDSEFF model for the uploadFile(..) service of the component BusinessLogic. Note that Figure 5.6 utilises an abbreviated concrete syntax for RDSEFFs.

As pointed out earlier, the PCM is a performance abstraction of components. Additionally, RDSEFFs abstract details of component source code, which becomes obvious when seeing that components and thus single component services can span multiple classes and methods. The behaviour of component services is intentionally aggregated to as few as possible RDSEFF actions as possible. The formalisation of the RDSEFF abstraction and its relation to source code are pointed out in Section 5.

RDSEFFs consist of sequences of actions (ResourceDemandingBehaviour) which can be nested (e.g. control flow alternatives or parallel executions). Those actions which describe the internals of a component service are *internal control flow actions* and comprise:

- StartAction / StopAction represent the start and stop nodes of a RDSEFF. (Start and stop node in Figure 5.6.)

- InternalAction specifies internal behaviour of a component which does not depend on other components (i.e. the behaviour represented by an Internal-Action does not call required services). An InternalAction can cover an arbitrary amount of internal behaviour of a component service (i.e. multiple classes and methods). (Action "StoreFile" in Figure 5.6.)

- LoopAction captures behaviour which is executed in a loop. The loop body is itself represented by ResourceDemandingBehaviour. For each loop, a loop condition specifies the number of iterations of that loop. For, while, and do-while loops are not distinguished in the PCM. (Not present in Figure 5.6.)

- BranchAction specifies alternatives in the control flow. Each BranchAction has 2..* branches which each are represented by ResourceDemandingBehaviour. Furthermore, each branch has a branch condition associated which

25

specifies when a branch is entered. From source code, if-then-else and switch statements can be mapped to BranchAction. (Branches visualised by the rhombus in Figure 5.6.)

- ForkAction specifies component-internal behaviour which is executed in parallel. If for example, a component service creates multi-threaded behaviour, this is captured by a ForkAction. Each ForkAction holds 2..* Resource-DemandingBehaviours which are executed in parallel. By default, the behaviour of ForkActions is not synchronised (there is no synchronisation point). Optionally, a SynchronisationPoint allows all forked behaviour of a Fork-Action to wait for all other threads to finish until continuing. (Not present in Figure 5.6.)

- AcquireAction / ReleaseAction allow the modelling of the acquire and release of a semaphore (PassiveResources). The behaviour of a RDSEFF stops, until an acquire is successful (the semaphore becomes available). AcquireAction / ReleaseAction allow the specification of mutex logic and enable synchronisations among multiple services of the same component. (Not present in Figure 5.6.)

All of the above internal control flow actions carry resource demands (Parametric-ResourceDemand) which allow the specification of demands to the execution environment underlying a component. For example, accesses to the CPU and hard disks are captured by such resource demands. Resource demands (in general) are not timing values. Instead, they are abstract resource demands like "number of utilised CPU cycles".

Further actions (which are not internal control flow actions and thus have no resource demand directly attached) complement the RDSEFFs:

- ExternalCall is an action which represents the call to a required service of a component. Thus, indirectly, another component is called by an External-Call. Each ExternalCall has a specification of the parameters which are passed to the called service. Vice versa, each ExternalCall specifies how the parameters returned by a called service are handled in the calling RDSEFF (i.e. which local variables result from the return value). (Actions "checkFile" and "compress" in Figure 5.6.)

- SetVariableAction specifies which values a service captured by the RD-SEFF itself returns. (Attached to the stop node in Figure 5.6.)

- InternalCallAction specifies the call of internal behaviour. RDSEFFs can have internal behaviour (comparable to private methods of classes). It must be noted that RDSEFFs allow only one level of internal behaviour to force abstraction (i.e. within internal behaviour no further `InternalCallActions` are allowed). Note that not every method call inside a component in source code results in an `InternalCallAction`. (Not present in Figure 5.6.)

To allow the specification of data flow and parameterise control flow, so-called random variable (`PCMRandomVariable`) allow the specification of branch conditions, loop conditions, resource demands, variables set in `SetVariableActions`, and call parameters of `ExternalCall`. These parameterisations depend on the parameter characterisations introduced above and represent a so-called *parametric dependency*. For example, a RDSEFF can specify that a loop iterates twice as often as elements in an input parameter list exist. Section 2.7.2 further details on the parameterisation options of the PCM.

2.5.4. Further Models

Resource Environment The PCM resource environment captures processing resources (`ResourceType`) which are bundled in resource containers (`ResourceContainer`) and linking resources (`LinkingResource`) which connect resource containers. A resource container covers for example servers and application servers on which components run. Linking resources are for example local area networks.

Resource types have a processing rate (e.g. "1 CPU cylce/s") which allows the conversion of resource demands of internal control flow actions into timing values. Every resource type acts using a configurable scheduling policy to process resource demands (e.g. "first come first serve" or "processor sharing"; cf. [Hap08]).

Allocation The allocation is a mapping between components (the component's `AssemblyContext`) and resource containers. In the allocation, each component is assigned to a resource container, the component is running on. Resource demands of components deploy load on the resource containers they are allocated on.

Usage The usage model describes the interaction of users with a software systems. Users can be human users or other software systems. Usage models specify typical interaction sequences with the software system (i.e. which provided service of the `System` are called in which order). Alternatives can be specified using branches and repeated behaviour can be specified by loops in the usage model. Furthermore, the use model characterises the data (parameter characterisations) which the provided services of the system need to process (e.g. "10 files each of a bytesize of 1 MB" or "2 files each of a bytesize of 10 GB").

Prediction   The *Palladio approach* automatically creates a performance simulation model from instances of the PCM. This thesis does not detail on the performance model and concentrates on the static architecture and RDSEFF behaviour model of the PCM. Reverse engineering of the usage, resource environment, and allocation model are not subject of this thesis and must be complemented manually. The resource environment model is topic of another thesis [Kup10].

2.6. Component Performance Influence Factors

The performance of a component has four major influence factors which are visualised in Figure 2.5. Only if all four factors are known, one can determine the performance of a component. When reverse engineering a performance model, the reverse engineering approach must account for these factors.

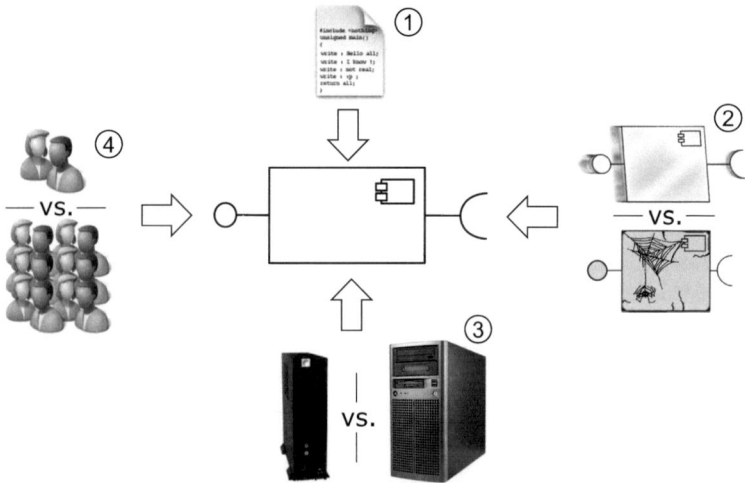

Figure 2.5.: Component performance influence factors. Images sources: left server by Craig Spurrier licensed under Creative Commons Attribution 2.5 Generic; right server ©LiquidImage Fotolia.com

The four performance influence factors are:

1. **Component implementation**. The implementation of a component impacts its performance. Fast or slow algorithms (e.g. quicksort vs. bubblesort), cho-

sen data structures, and the utilisation of resources (e.g. use of multiple cores) result in different performance.

2. **Connected components**. Whether a component is connected to fast responding components which have a high throughput or not, impacts performance. For example, if a component relies or the lookup of names through an name service, being connected to a fast or slow DNS server affects the performance of a component. The corresponding component context is the assembly context.

3. **Execution environment**. A component which is executed on fast hardware will usually serve responses faster than the same component component running on slow hardware. The allocation context corresponds to this factor.

4. **Usage profile**. The way users or other components interact with a component impact the performance. For example, 2 vs. 100 concurrent user requests cause a different load of component. The usage profile can either directly stem from user or be propagated via intermediate components, which pass and transform requests to a component. The usage context captures this factor.

In a component model, all factors should be explicit parameters so that all factors become exchangeable without affecting the component model. If for example, the hardware of the execution environment changes (faster CPU), the component model must not change to reflect the impact of the execution environment on the modeled component.

2.7. Parametric Dependencies in Code

The so-called *parametric dependencies* (see "parameter dependencies" in [Koz08b]) model a relation between input data and a variable. Parametric dependencies parameterise the control and data flow of the Palladio Component Model. They describe for example the number of loop iterations, express branch conditions, and specify how input data of a component is passed to required services of that component.

An example for a parametric dependency of variable a (e.g. describing the number of loop iterations) is IF(b > 5) THEN 3 * b ELSE 2 * c, where b and c are input parameters which stem from either arguments of a method call or return values of method calls. Listing 2.1 shows a corresponding source code example in which a determines the number of executions of the lower loop.

A parametric dependency is a variable which depends on $0..n$ input parameters, where input parameters are input data from method call arguments or return values

```
1  void doSth(int b, int c) {
2    int a = 2 * c;
3    if(b > 5) {
4      a = 3 * b;
5    }
6    // further calculations
7    for(int i = 0; i < a; i++) {
8      // some external call
9    }
10 }
```

Listing 2.1: Source code example for parametric dependencies

of methods. Since 0 input parameters are allowed, a constant is also a valid parametric dependency. Opposed to slices, a parametric dependency qualifies the relation between input parameters and a variable.

Formally, a parametric dependency is mapping of a number of input parameters to a typed value:

$$ParametricDependency := IV \rightarrow v$$

where IV is a set of input parameter (component service arguments, return values of called services) and v is a value of a type in $\{boolean, integer, double, string, enum\}$.

Parametric dependencies follow the grammar of the so-called *Stochastic Expressions* ("StoEx", see [Bec08a, pp. 86] and [Koz08a, pp. 93]), an expression language including stochastic elements introduced for the Palladio Component Model and the Q-ImPrESS EU project [qim09]. They will be used to model the number of iterations of a loop, the values of method call parameters, the return value of methods, the conditions of branches, and the resource demand within InternalActions.

2.7.1. Parameter Characterisations

In the PCM, so-called *parameter characterisations* are used to describe data (parameters, arguments, variables). Instead of using the actual values of data, such as [2, 4, 3, 5, ..] for an integer array, the PCM uses these parameter characterisations to provide additional information for data such as the bytesize while at the same time reducing the amount of data.

For example, a List can often be sufficiently described by its number of contained elements and the bytesize when abstracting it to performance-relevant aspects. Whether the first element of a list is a true or false boolean, usually does not impact the performance, while exchanging the boolean by a double increases the size of the data structure and therefore can impact computation time or network usage. In cases where single data elements are important, they can be modeled nonetheless.

On the one hand, parameter characterisations force abstractions, on the other hand they help lowering the amount of data which needs to be handled during model simulation. Thereby, parameter characterisations help keeping the simulation time low. An additional benefit of parameter characterisations are information which are not directly available from data structure like its bytesize.

The PCM supports the following characterisations out-of-the-box:

- VALUE (the actual value)

- NUMBER_OF_ELEMENTS (size of an array or size of an collection type)

- BYTESIZE (the size of a data structure in bytes)

Accordingly, these parameter characterisations will be dealt with in this thesis.

2.7.2. Parametric Dependencies in the Behaviour Model

For understanding the behavioural reverse engineering part of the thesis, it is crucial to understand the abstraction criteria underlying the control and data flow representation in the PCM, specifically the RDSEFF. Figure 2.6 introduces an example illustrating the various parametric dependencies which must be captured during reverse engineering. Details on parametric dependencies are presented in Section 5.7, page 5.7.

Overall, there are three different types of parametric dependencies which must be captured:

1. Resource demands of internal actions

2. Control flow (branches and loops)

3. Data flow (data passed to other components; "parameter output" and "return value output" in Figure 2.6)

It must be emphasised that parametric dependencies are intended to be approximations of the real dependencies expressed in source code. Parametric dependencies should balance precision and abstractness to allow precise performance predictions

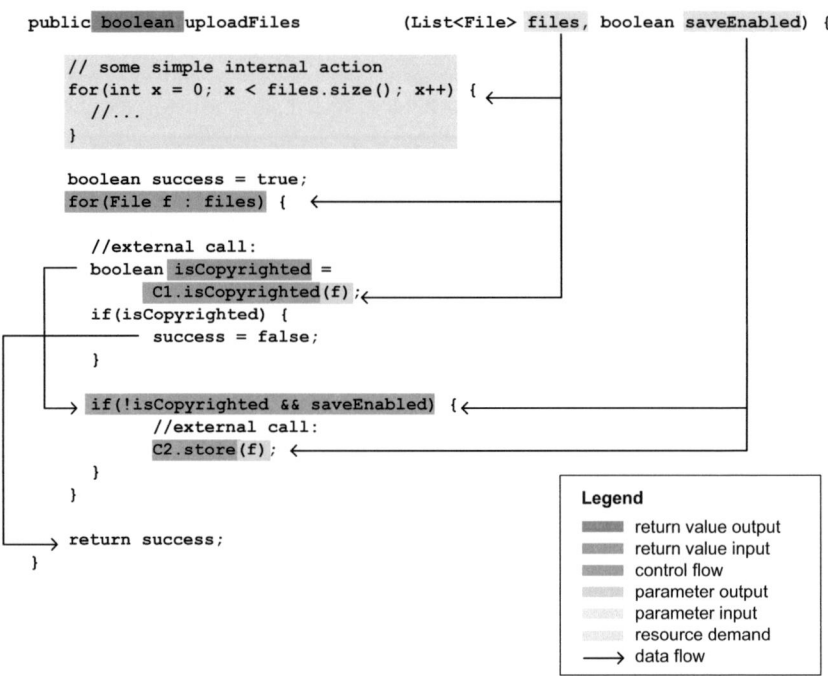

```
public boolean uploadFiles          (List<File> files, boolean saveEnabled) {

    // some simple internal action
    for(int x = 0; x < files.size(); x++) {
        //...
    }

    boolean success = true;
    for(File f : files) {

        //external call:
        boolean isCopyrighted =
            C1.isCopyrighted(f);
        if(isCopyrighted) {
            success = false;
        }

        if(!isCopyrighted && saveEnabled) {
            //external call:
            C2.store(f);
        }
    }

    return success;
}
```

Legend

- return value output
- return value input
- control flow
- parameter output
- parameter input
- resource demand
- → data flow

Figure 2.6.: Parametric dependencies in code at a component abstraction level

based on models but at the same time they should not overly increase analysis complexity due to complex parametric dependency expressions. Thus, parametric dependencies do not need to be sound for all input parameters. This stress field is further discussed in Section 5.11.4.1.

In Figure 2.6, a simple example is given covering all the above dependencies. In the example, a service for uploading files uploadFiles is depicted having two arguments (files and saveEnabled), itself returning a boolean for indicating the success of an execution. The service depends on two components C1 and C2, were C1 offers a lookup service for detecting copyrightes files isCopyrighted and C2 a service to persist files in an external store system through store.

Resource Demand   In the example, the *resource demand* (light grey area) depends on the number of files uploaded, indicated by the for loop iterating over the elements of files. A rough parametric dependency for the CPU demand could be files.NUMBER_OF_ELEMENTS * 0.243 where files.NUMBER_OF_ELEMENTS is the number of elements of the `files` argument and `0.243` an estimate of the CPU demand per element to be processed. The resource demand could also be an estimation of hundreds or thousands lines of code if the covered code section does not contain any call for another component.

Control Flow   *Control flow* (pink areas) has to be determined in two cases in the example as there are calls for external components inside these statements (the criterion for making this control flow statements explicit in the model is thus fulfilled; cf. Section 5.7.2). The first control flow statement `for(File f : files)` has a dependency to the number of files passed as argument to the `uploadFiles` service. The resulting expression for the loop is consequently `files.NUMBER_OF_ELEMENTS`.

The second control flow statement `if(!isCopyrighted && saveEnabled)` has more complicated parametric dependencies. The `isCopyrighted` flag depends on the return value of a previous external call for C1, which is considered as input to the `uploadFiles` service. `saveEnabled` is an input argument of `uploadFiles`. The resulting expression for the branch is consequently `!C1.isCopyrighted().RETURN.VALUE AND saveEnabled.VALUE`. The internal variable `isCopyrighted` is not known to the parametric dependencies and thus replaced by the direct dependency to the return value. Expressing dependencies in terms of input parameters is comparable to symbolic execution [Kin76].

Data Flow   The same argument f is passed the external services of C1 and C2, which consequently must be captured in the *data flow* (orange area). The argument is a single element of the `files` List argument of `uploadFiles`. A possible estimation of the data flow would result in the expression `files.INNER.VALUE`, where `INNER` holds parameter characterisations (`VALUE` in the example) of inner elements of the list. From the `List` input parameter `files`, the expression would care for passing parameter characterisations of single elements of that list to the external services of C1 and C2.

Finally, the return value (green background area) of `uploadFiles` needs to be characterised. The return value depends on the previously chosen control flow statements, i.e. whether the the loop statement is executed at all and what the results of the external call of C1 are. The default value is `true`. If a single copyrighted file is to be uploaded, `isCopyrighted` returns `false`. The resulting expression for the parametric dependency thus must respect the return values of all external calls and concatenate them using logical ANDs. To perform the logic concatenation, an intermediate return value is being updated within the loop in an `SetVariableAction`. The resulting expression for the parametric dependency is thus determining `return.VALUE: isCopyrighted.RETURN.VALUE AND return.VALUE`, where `return.VALUE` is a local variable which is ultimately returned.

When assuming a fixed assembly context (which is limiting the expressiveness and parameterisation; see Section 2.8), the parametric dependency can be simplified. In such a case, an approximation of the return value of `isCopyrighted` can be used (the actual behaviour of a called service can be known with fixed assembly contexts). A probability value indicates the likelihood of a having to return false. This likelihood depends on the number of files uploaded: `files.NUMBER_OF_ELEMENTS * 0.01`, where `0.01` is the probability of a single file being copyrighted.

2.8. Model Parameterisation

Section 2.6 introduced the performance influence factors for components. This section will briefly highlight the importance of making the influence factor explicit parameters in a component performance model. Every influence factor which is not made an explicit parameter limits the prediction capabilities of a software component model since dependencies which exist in the implementation of a components are not reflected on the model level.

If the contexts of a component are assumed to be fixed, neither the use profile, execution environment, nor the assembly can be changed without implying changes to all affecting elements of the model. For example, if the usage profile changes from passing audio files to a provided service of a system to passing video files, all models components which are processing the files must be adapted in the case of non-parameterised models. Changing the execution environment would imply changes to models of all components that are executed on that execution environment for non-parameterised models and changing the assembly context (e.g. exchanging a slow logging service by fast one) would again imply changes to models of all components which directly or indirectly (via transitive calls) access the logging service.

If no global knowledge on a system exist (e.g. multiple component vendors), it is even impossible to change a model consistently if no correct parameterisation exists. Without parameterisation, none of the scenarios in Section 1.1.1 and Section 1.2 would be supported.

For few scenarios in which a certain context is known to be fixed (e.g. a constant execution environment), a model with limited parameterisation can be created. Still, in that case, the model is only valid as long at the fixed context does not change (i.e. the same execution environment). These models generally have no prediction capabilities for changes in contexts which are assumed to be fixed.

2.9. Terminology

This section introduces central terms which are used throughout the remainder of this thesis. Especially for overloaded terms, readers should refer to this section to determine the intended semantics of terms.

Meta-Model   A *meta-model* is a rule set for the construction of an arbitrary number of models (cf. definition in [BBJ⁺08]). In the context of this thesis, the employed meta-models will be

- the Palladio Component Model (PCM) meta-model,

- the Service Architecture Meta Model (SAMM) from the Q-ImPrESS project [qim09],

- the Generalised Abstract Syntax Tree (GAST) meta-model [qim09], and

- the source code decorator meta-model.

For each meta-model there will be multiple instances. If not pointing out that a meta-model is meant, the corresponding model instance (see below) is meant.

Model   A *model* – in the context of this thesis – instantiates an explicit meta-model. Although a meta-model is as well a model, meta-models will be explicitly named meta-model and not model. In figures in the remainder of this thesis, models are visualised as "Artefact" (small file symbol).

Model Integrity   *Model integrity* subsumes that all mandatory attributes and relations which are defined in the meta-model are set in the model and that all constraints defined in the meta-model are fulfiled by the model. Furthermore, in the context of this thesis, model integrity includes that additional constraints defined by analysis approaches (i.e. the Palladio approach) hold for the model. Section 4.9 addresses model integrity in more detail.

Reuse   The *reuse* of a component is the usage of a component in a varying assembly, allocation, or usage contexts. If one of the contexts is changed, a component is being reused. For example, employing the same component in a heavy loaded system and in a little loaded is a reuse due to changes in the usage context.

Optimality   No global optimum is meant by the term *optimality* in the remainder of this thesis. Instead, the quality of a reverse engineered parametric dependency is judged according to a so-called *fitness function*. The fitness function does not only account for precision of results but also for the calculation complexity of a result. For example, a very long and hard to compute expression with high precision is considered worse than a computation-in-intensive short expression. Section 5.11.4 details on further criteria for the optimality of a solution in the context of this thesis.

Parameter   The arguments of a called method will be named "input parameters", while the parameters, when calling another method, will be named "output parameters". Consider the following simple example:

```
1  void doSth(int a, int b) {
2      int c = 0;
3      int d = component.do(c);
4      d = d + 1;
5  }
```

Listing 2.2: Source code example: Input and output parameters

Here, a and b are input parameters and c serves as the output parameter from the perspective of doSth(). Additionally, the return value d is considered as a input parameter for the code starting from line 3 since further calculations can depend on it.

Parametric Dependency   See Section 2.7.

Characteristic Curve   In the context of this thesis, a *characteristic curve*[1] is an approximation of the behaviour of a black-box component. Characteristic curves are know from electrical engineering disciplines to characterise electrical components. A characteristic curve is a parametric dependency, if the parametric dependency describes a black-box component.

Genetic Algorithms   *Genetic programming* is a special form of *genetic algorithms* with a tree chromosome structure, which will be the core *machine learning* technique in this thesis. If statements apply not only the genetic programming but to genetic algorithm in general, the relation to genetic algorithms will be highlighted.

---
[1]German: "Kennlinie"

Chromosome   A *chromosome* is a set of *genes*. A single chromosome is in the developed Beagle approach used to represent a parametric dependency whose language is the stochastic expression language. Figure 2.7 provides an overview on the related terms. Chromosome is a synonym to *individual*.

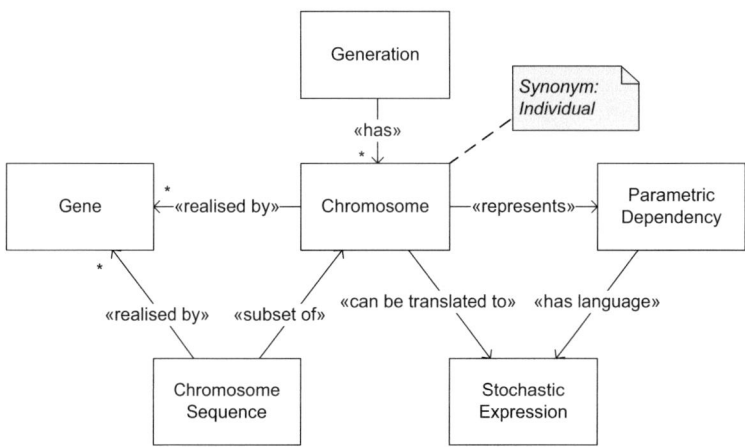

Figure 2.7.: Relation between genes, chromosomes, generations, stochastic expressions, and parametric dependencies

Individual   see Chromosome. *Individual* is a synonym of chromosome which is preferably used in the context of evolution while "chromosome" represent a technical term.

Chromosome sequence   A *chromosome sequence* is a subset of a chromosomes; a set of genes. It is sometimes referred to as *gene sequence*.

Architecture   Comprises static structure (components) and behaviour (component services).

Component   "A software *component* is a unit of composition with contractually specified interfaces and explicit context dependencies only. A software component can be deployed independently and is subject to third-party composition." (Szyperski, [SGM02]). Especially a component – as used in the remainder of this thesis – is not a class, module, or trait (cf. Scala [OSV08]). A component can comprise multiple classes, module, or traits when being realised in a object-oriented language. Components can be composed from other components (referred to as *composite structure* and *composite component*). Figure 2.8 summarises the core properties of components.

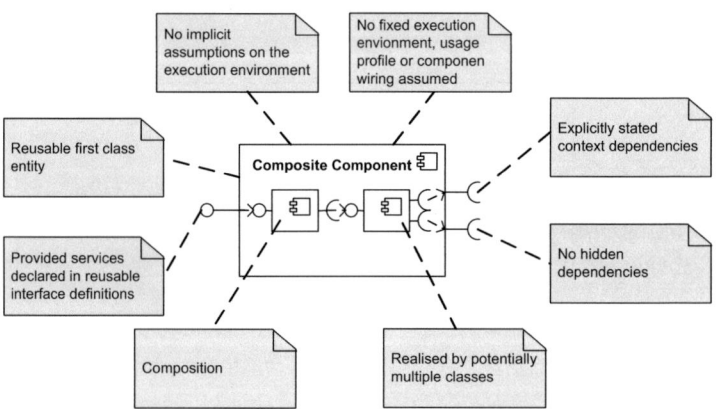

Figure 2.8.: UML representation of the static view of a component with annotated core properties.

Role   The *role* of a component is the association between a component and an interface. In the context of the Service Architecture Meta Model (SAMM) of the Q-ImPrESS project [qim09], it is referred to as *port*.

Provided Interface   The term *provided interface* is the short notion for the provided role with an associated interface of a component.

Required Interface   The term *required interface* is the short notion for the required role with associated interface of a component.

3. Reverse Engineering Approach for Component-Based Software Architectures

The following chapter introduces the reverse engineering approach which is contributed by this thesis. The chapter's purpose is to provide an overview on the approach and to highlight the relations between the two major steps of the approach. Furthermore, the key challenges and contributions related to the overall approach are presented. The Chapters 4 and 5 then detail on the major reverse engineering steps and provide insights to findings which are specific to a single step.

The overall aim of this thesis is the development of an integrated reverse engineering approach for parameterised component-based software performance models. The approach must enable the reverse engineering of the static architecture of a software system and for each identified component of that architecture the reverse engineering of a behaviour model.

The reverse engineered models must be fully *parameterised* models of a component-based architecture to enable analyses using the Palladio performance prediction approach. Only parameterised models enable reasoning on *sizing*, *legacy software extension*, *reuse*, and *design optimisation* scenarios. These scenarios have been briefly introduced in Section 1 and detailed in Section 1.2.

Opposed to parameterised models, conventional monolithic models (e.g. [SKK+01, Obj05a, Obj06c, CLGL05, LFG05]) have limited prediction capabilities for these scenarios. For example, execution environments or component assembly are assumed to be fixed by such models. When exchanging, for example, a database component or the application server of such monolithic models, all of the model or at least large parts of the model need to be revised to account for the changed assembly. If in a shopping system the number of items users buy varies, the way users interact with the system changes, or product videos instead of only product photos become available, the corresponding monolithic models need to be changed to reflect the performance impact.

While many existing reverse engineering approaches claim to reverse engineer software components (e.g. [AL99a, FDE+01, IWF07, KSRP99, MM01a, MOTU93, Sar03]), none of them reverse engineers components which follow a strong component definition comparable to the one of Szyperski (see Section 2.9).

Only when following such a strong definition, components become parameterised (see Section 2.6) and the introduced scenarios become fully analysable. Furthermore, currently no integrated reverse engineering approach for static and dynamic component-based architectures exists.

Models which are reverse engineered by the developed approach are subject to performance prediction. Thus, the reverse engineering approach must be capable of creating models with *execution semantics*. Opposed to various existing reverse engineering approaches which mainly target program understanding of static architectures only (e.g. [AGC02, FDE$^+$01, Kos02, PMT$^+$08, BBT06]), the presented approach is able to deal with strong model semantics – which enable for example performance simulations.

In order to enable performance analyses of large systems, reverse engineered static architecture and behaviour must provide *abstractions* of source code details. Fine-grained models would make the performance analysis infeasible due to long-running analyses, CPU and memory demands. Component performance models must therefore be abstractions of the underlying classes. The behaviour of components must be abstracted in a way which provides sufficient information to analyse the presented performance prediction scenarios but at the same time keeps down analysis complexity. In the presented approach, the reverse engineered behaviour model has the same abstraction level as the identified components to provide a consistent result model with full execution semantics (discussion of the abstraction in Chapter 4 and 5).

Furthermore, the developed reverse engineering approach targets program and component architecture understanding of legacy component-based software applications. The reverse engineered models (static architecture and behaviour abstraction model) assist in investigating a component-based software system starting at a coarse-grained level. Due to component compositions, more detailed model levels are available for coarse-grained components.

The key features of the developed approach are:

- **Model parameterisation**. Models have explicit parameters for external influence factors. They are parameterised over usage, assembly, and allocation context.

  For example, the number of loop iterations of component behaviour is generally not a constant value. Instead, the reverse engineering approach determines the number of loop executions depending on input parameters of a component. If the same component is reused by different components or users interact differently with that component, the reverse engineered model is still valid due to its explicit parameterisations. The component model can be reused like a component.

- **Abstraction**. The static architecture model abstraction is consistent with the behaviour models.

  The developed reverse engineering approach creates a consistent abstraction of the control and data flow of component behaviour and reverse engineers multiple abstraction levels of the static component architecture. The data flow, for example, captures only parameters which are likely to affect the performance of a component. For the static component architecture, for example, multiple classes are merged into a single component to increase the system's level of abstraction.

- **Execution semantics**. The resulting models are direct input for performance analysis.

  The reverse engineered models (instances of the PCM) can be analysed and simulated using the Palladio Component Model approach. Due to full control and data flow of the result models and executions semantics of the result meta model (PCM), it is possible to predict performance metrics like throughput, response time, and resource utilisation based on the reverse engineered PCM models.

The developed approach supports performance predictions for *all* of the scenarios introduced in Section 1.2, page 6. These are the major investigation scenarios for component-based software engineering (cf. [Kru92, Sam97]):

- sizing,

- legacy software extension,

- reuse, and

- design optimisation.

In this introductory section, the scientific challenges, contributions, and the overall process of the reverse engineering approach will be discussed. More detailed discussions follow in the Chapters 4 (Reverse Engineering of Static Architectures, "SoMoX") and 5 (Reverse Engineering of Behavioural Models, "Beagle").

3.1. Scientific Challenges

The main scientific challenges for an integrated reverse engineering approach for component-based software systems lie in the following areas:

- **Integration of reverse engineering for static architectures and component behaviour.** Static and dynamic aspects of a system are going to be reverse engineered in a single approach. Here, it is specifically important to have static and dynamic architecture at the same abstraction level corresponding to the identified components such that static architecture and behaviour model elements talk about the same components and component services.

- **Execution semantics of output model.** The targeted Palladio performance prediction approach requires input models with full execution semantics in order to perform performance analyses. Consequently, the reverse engineering approach must be able to create model instances of the PCM which already proofed to have rich semantics. Such models not only help humans understanding a software system but facilitate performance analysis. For the static architecture and behaviour model, an approach should be developed, which produces fully specified output models.

- **Model parameterisation.** To support the component paradigm, a reverse engineering approach must be developed which ensures context independence of reverse engineered component models (as claimed by Szyperski [SGM02]). To support the performance prediction scenarios introduced in Section 1.2 (sizing, extension of legacy applications, reuse, design optimisation) at the model level, a fully parameterised performance model must be the output of reverse engineering. A non-parameterised performance model could not predict the performance impact of any changes in a component's context due to the absence of calculation rules. The challenge is to reverse engineer components which are parameterised in the static architecture and in the behaviour. Ultimately, all performance impacts listed in Section 2.6 must be explicit parameters in the result model. This implies a component specification with explicit context dependencies, independence from the component usage, independence from connected components, and platform-independence.

- **Abstractions.** The reverse engineered components models must be performance abstractions of component implementations to make large systems analyseable within feasible time. The abstraction requirement is a challenge in two areas: In the static architecture, coarse-grained components must be identified to help performance analysis and to foster program understanding. For component behaviour, analysing large software systems requires abstractions of control and data flow to lower model complexity.

- **Traceability.** In order to interpret performance prediction results correctly (e.g. a certain component service or resource) and derive the right potential architectural changes (e.g. bottleneck avoidance) based on reverse engineered models, all reverse engineered artefacts must be traceable. Traceability must established throughout the whole reverse engineering process in the source code, the reverse engineering steps, and the reverse engineered models.

For more detailed scientific challenges see Section 4.2 and 5.2.

3.2. Contributions in Reverse Engineering

To face the identified scientific challenges and to overcome the named limitations from the introduction, this thesis contributes a novel reverse engineering approach which combines

1. an iterative hierarchical clustering approach based on source code metrics for the reverse engineering of component-based software architectures and

2. reverse engineering for behaviour models based on static, dynamic, and statistical analysis of source code. The approach contributes to genetic programming in finding abstractions for component behaviour.

The resulting reverse engineered models follow the *strong component definition* by Szyperski (cf. Section 2.9) and thus are *fully parameterised* (explicit context dependencies) as introduced in Section 2.6 and thereby enable performance predictions for all of the scenarios introduced in Section 1.2.

The developed reverse engineering approach furthermore has the following major contributions. It is a reverse engineering approach:

- ...which creates fully parameterised component models. These models are parameterised in the static architecture as well as in the control and data flow of reverse-engineered component models.

- ...for abstracted performance models. It transfers genetic programming to the field of reverse engineering of parametric dependencies of component models. The approach extends genetic programming by abstraction capabilities.

- ...for behaviour models, the reverse engineering approach integrates multiple static, dynamic, and statistical analysis approaches.

- ...for component-based software architectures which is capable of identifying components for object-oriented languages. The approach is generally applicable to object-oriented languages. Besides built-in support for Java, C/C++, and Delphi it can be extended to for example EJB or Spring descriptors which use dependency injection.

For detailed contributions see Section 4.3 and Section 5.3.

3.3. Reverse Engineering Process Overview

Before presenting the details of the reverse engineering approach, this section provides an overview on the ideas for the developed reverse engineering approach. The reverse engineering process is divided into two major steps: i) an architecture reverse engineering approach called *SoMoX* and ii) a reverse engineering approach for behavioural models called *Beagle* .

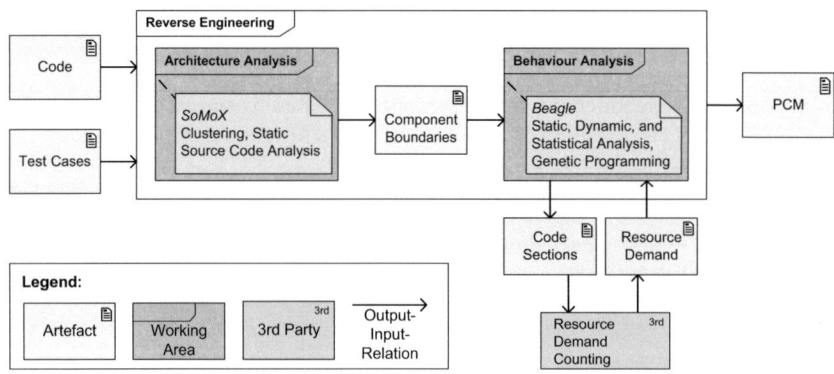

Figure 3.1.: Reverse engineering overview

Figure 3.1 shows the outline of the overall approach. The reverse engineering approach first extracts the software architecture ("Architecture Analysis", SoMoX) and then reconstructs the behaviour model for each component ("Behaviour Analysis", Beagle). While SoMoX is primarily responsible for identifying components and component interfaces, Beagle first reverse engineers the control flow of components and then adds data flow information to the behaviour model. The component boundaries identified by SoMoX, source code, and test cases serve as input for Beagle to find behaviour abstractions which match exactly the component abstraction provided by SoMoX. Therefore, a specification of component boundaries serves as primary interchange artefact for architecture and behaviour reverse engineering.

The reverse engineering process uses source code and test cases (left hand side in Figure 3.1) as primary inputs and creates instances of the Palladio Component Model (PCM, right hand side in Figure 3.1) from these inputs. This output model is a valid instance of the Palladio Component Meta-Model. The output model comprises a PCM repository of basic and composite components. For every provided service of a basic component, a valid RDSEFF serves as behaviour specification of that service.

The RDSEFF is complete with respect to control and data flow and resource demands. In order to estimate the resource demands, the developed approach integrates the raw resource demands of components (counts of resource demands issued during execution of components) delivered by a third-party approach (see Section 5.16).

The reverse engineering does not cover reverse engineering of usage models which represent the interaction of users with a software system. Also, the execution environment of components (application server, virtual machines, operating system, servers, and network) is not reverse engineered by the presented approach. Although the PCM captures usage model, execution environment, and allocation, these sub-models are no software components and consequently left out during reverse engineering. Please note, that the reverse engineered models are nevertheless parameterised over usage and allocation context.

3.3.1. Reverse Engineered Artefacts

Architecture   The reverse engineering approach presented in this thesis covers the reverse engineering of component-based software architectures and component behaviour models. The ultimate goal is to enable, among others, performance predictions based on such models. This requires semantically rich, complete, and consistent models. Otherwise, considerable manual effort would be required to complete the reverse engineered models, which would contradict the idea of a broad use of software performance prediction.

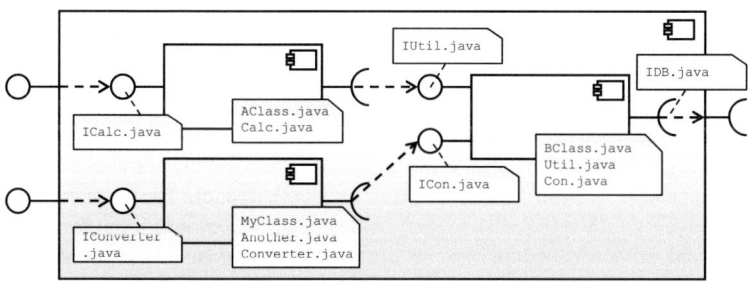

Figure 3.2.: Example for a reverse engineered architecture model

Figure 3.2 illustrates an example instance of a static architecture which SoMoX reverse engineers from source code. Additionally, fragments of the trace model which is created concurrently with the reverse engineering process to establish trace links between original source and result model are indicated. Opposed to Figure 3.2, real result models conform to the meta-model of the PCM and possess no reverse engineered graphical layout.

As Figure 3.2 indicates, the reverse engineered architecture comprises basic components, composite components (outer component), interfaces, assembly contexts (the component "instance" within a composite component), containment relations for the assembly contexts of inner components of a composite component, provided and required roles (the relation between components and interfaces), delegation and assembly connectors. The component architecture can have multiple abstraction levels as composite components can have multiple levels of containment. The trace model associates one class interface or class with each component interface and a number of classes with each component.

Behaviour Model   For the behaviour model parameterised control and data flow are reverse engineered. For `InternalActions` the platform-independent resource demand is estimated. Figure 5.6 on page 115 visualises an example instance of the RDSEFF behaviour model. The reverse engineering approach reconstructs all `Actions` of the RDSEFF (cf. Section 2.5.3) including all `StochasticExpressions` to express parametric dependencies. For each `Action`, its origin is preserved through the trace model.

3.3.2. Independence from Timing Values during Construction of the Architecture and Behaviour Model

Like a car body, a software component has no performance in the sense of response time or throughput. Instead, when a software component is *executed* in an execution environment, performance metrics become measurable. Since a component cannot make assumptions on the actual execution environment, it, per se, possesses no performance expressible in wall clock timing values. It must be highlighted that this is intentionally reflected in the reverse engineering approach and the reverse engineered component models. Both, the architecture and the behaviour model generally have no timing values. To reflect the impact of the execution environment, the execution environment (allocation context) is an explicit parameter in the reverse engineered models.

Imagine a component which offers a compression service. Compression algorithms heavily rely on CPU power. Thus, if the same compression component is once executed in an execution environment with a fast virtual machine and a fast CPU and the next time in a slow execution environment, the response time of the compression service can vary heavily. Without knowing the actual execution environment, the response time (in seconds) cannot be known. The specification of the component and the execution environment hence must be split.

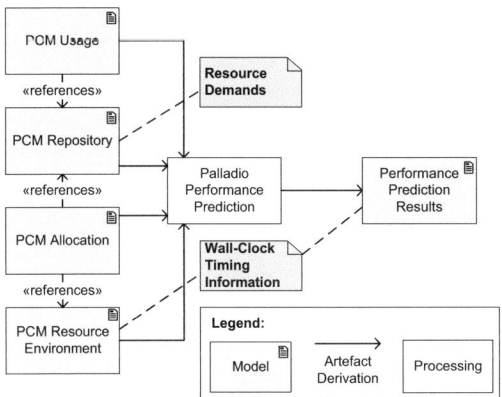

Figure 3.3.: Calculation of timing information from resource demands in the Palladio approach

The relation between components and execution environment is specified through abstract resource demands. Resource demands contain, for example, the number of CPU cycles a component algorithm's computation requires. Timing values are calculated during the performance prediction of the PCM when the execution environment model is available (see Figure 3.3). In the PCM, only the execution environment model introduced in Section 2.6 carries timing values (CPU frequency, HDD throughput, Bytecode instruction execution duration).

Separate approaches [Bec08a, Kup10] which are out of scope for this thesis, are capable of calculating timing values for PCM models. The approach by Kuperberg [Kup10] for example benchmarks timing values of the execution environment and then predicts the execution duration of component services from (reverse engineered) component models based on Java bytecode. In these models, individual bytecode instructions serve as fine-grained resource demands.

The major advantages of splitting timing values from component models are: Component models become reusable across different platforms, a prediction for different platforms can use the same component model, and the reverse engineered component models do not make assumptions real components cannot make (i.e. the concrete execution environment). Section 5.16 details on the integration of resource demands into reverse engineering.

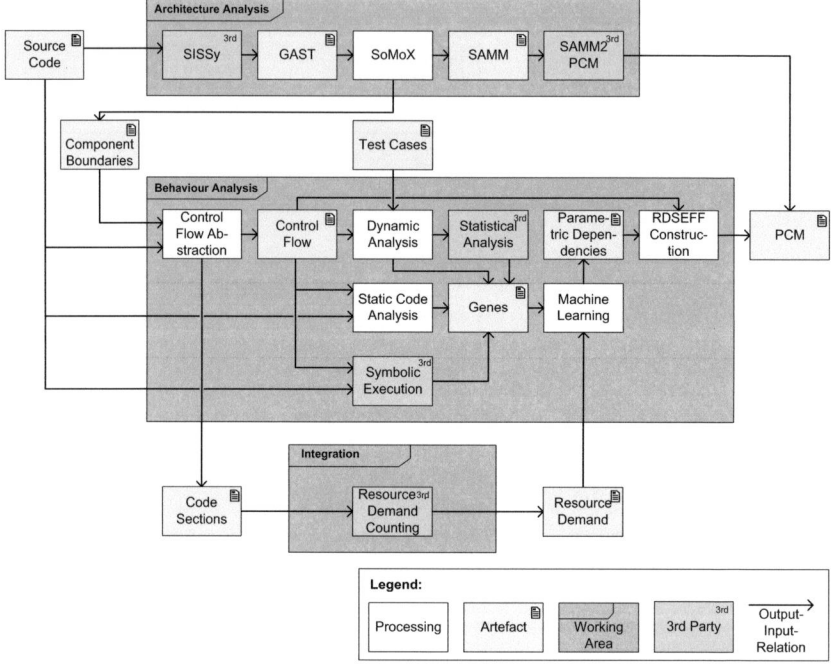

Figure 3.4.: Detailed view on the integrated reverse engineering process

3.4. Realisation Overview

The complementation of reverse engineering for the structural architecture (SoMoX) and the behaviour model (Beagle) is also reflected in the realisation. The main steps of the integrated realisation are depicted in Figure 3.1. The architecture analysis steps provide the component boundaries which are required by the behaviour analysis.

Full details on the architecture and behavioural reverse engineering approach follow in Chapter 4 and 5. The following section emphasises the overview, interaction of processing steps, and integrated third party approaches.

3.4.1. Architecture

The reverse engineering process starts with the architectural step (top-most in Figure 3.4). The major component of this step is the SoMoX tool. It is able to combine various source code metrics to detect components, composite components, component interfaces, and bindings from given code. Metrics can be both static and dynamic, which are then evaluated by SoMoX. SoMoX internally weights the various input metrics and then combines them in detection strategies which ultimately result in a graph-based component detection approach comparable to hierarchical clustering (see [Sch07, Ber06]). SoMoX is kept flexible with respect to the number and kind of input metrics, their weighting, and interdependencies among metrics.

SoMoX utilises SISSy [ABM+06, SSM06, TS05] as a major static code analysis approach. SISSy allows static code analysis for C, C++, and Java code, which is afterwards represented in a language independent format (Generalised Abstract Syntax Tree, GAST). SoMoX implements a number of source code metric plugins (e.g. coupling, name resemblance, and package mapping) which rely on the GAST of SISSy.

The output of SoMox is an instance of the Q-ImPrESS Service Architecture Meta Model (SAMM) [The09]. It is transformed into an instance of the Palladio Component Model (PCM) using the SAMM2PCM transformation [Cia10] which has been developed in the context of the Q-ImPrESS project. The resulting PCM instance comprises a hierarchical static component architecture.

3.4.2. Behaviour

The second major working area (see "Behaviour Analysis" in Figure 3.4) is the reverse engineering of behavioural model for component services. Here, abstractions of component behaviour are gained from source code. These behavioural models, called RDSEFF, include control and data flow information. RDSEFFs are part of the PCM and parameterised over usage, allocation, and assembly context making them reusable for different usage scenarios, changing execution environments, and various connected components.

Component boundaries from the architectural reverse engineering step and source code serve as input, while the result is a RDSEFF. Static and dynamic analysis are combined with machine learning to reverse engineer the RDSEFF to create a performance abstraction of a real component's behaviour.

First a control flow abstraction is created. Only control flow statements affecting other components are kept in this step. This leaves out for example internal loops within which no other components are called. Component boundaries serve as input to judge whether another component is affected by a certain statement. Section 5.8 will detail on this step.

The control flow abstraction is input for dynamic analysis, static code analysis, statistical analysis, and symbolic execution. These three analysis techniques contribute in identifying parametric dependencies, for example, how often a loop is executed depending on an input parameter. The individual results are then translated into "genes" of the machine learning step.

The "Dynamic Analysis" consists of three major steps: first, it instruments given code with monitoring instructions; second, it executes the code in a test bed environment and gathers runtime monitoring data; third, the monitoring data is aggregated. The dynamic analysis uses the control flow abstraction to determine the instrumentation points in code. See Section 5.10 for details.

Machine learning is used to integrate static, statistical, and dynamic analysis and to find abstractions of parametric dependencies in code. The aggregated monitoring data provides information on typical control and data flow observations, which need to be generalised, abstracted to performance-relevant information, and parameterised over the contexts introduced in Section 2.5.1. The learned parametric dependencies are then added to the control flow abstraction of the RDSEFF.

To estimate the resource demand of the RDSEFF for InternalActions based on executed bytecode instructions, the reverse engineering approach integrates By-Counter ([KKR08b]; cf. "Resource Demand Counting" in Figure 3.4). ByCounter is responsible for providing raw resource demand counts for InternalActions (e.g. the number of executed Bytecode instructions). Source code sections representing InternalActions are therefore passed to ByCounter, which then counts executed resource demands for every InternalAction. The "Resource Demand Counting" step outputs raw resource demands along with the input parameters of a component which produced them. The "Machine Learning" step then identifies parametric dependencies between input parameters and executed resource demands and annotates the InternalActions with results.

Based on the reverse engineered model, performance predictions with the Palladio approach can be conducted. Using Palladio together with the reverse engineered models allows to investigate the performance analysis scenarios introduced in Section 1.2.

3.5. Overview Visualisation

Figure 3.5 is used throughout this thesis to visualise to which part of the overall approach a certain step belongs. The upper part of Figure 3.5 symbolises the steps of SoMoX, the bottom part shows the steps of Beagle. Either an excerpt from Figure 3.5 or a bold 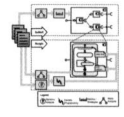 rectangle highlights the step from the overall reverse engineering approach which is presented in a certain section or chapter. Note that the steps in Figure 3.5 are strongly aggregated. Further details are presented in the corresponding sections.

The remainder of this thesis is structured following the steps from Figure 3.5. First in Chapter 4 introduces SoMoX, Chapter 5 details on Beagle, and finally Chapter 6 presents how traceability was ensured for the reverse engineering approach. Chap-

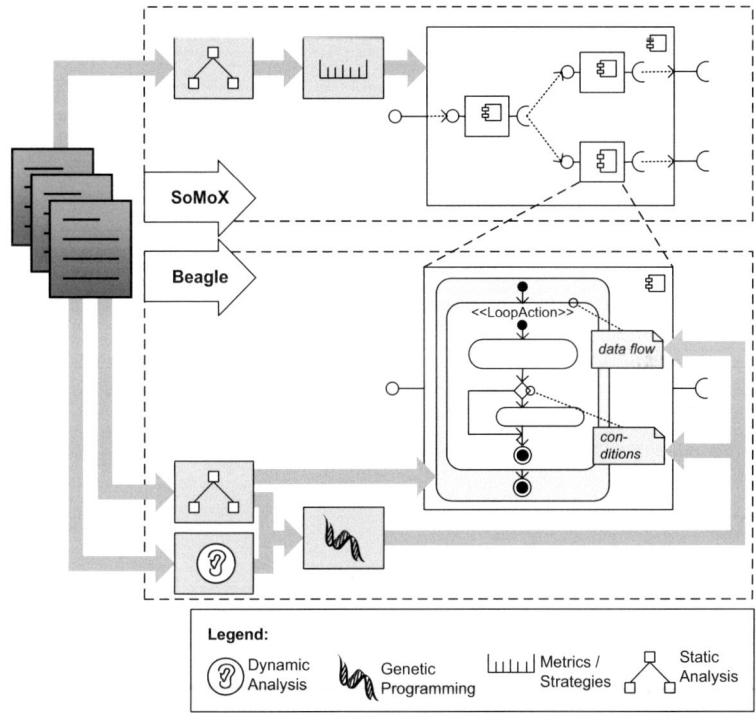

Figure 3.5.: Overview visualisation

ter 7 presents the validation of the appproach, Chaper 8 shows related work, Chapter 9 details on the lessons learned and summarises the thesis, while Chapter 9.12 concludes the work.

4. Reverse Engineering Static Architectures

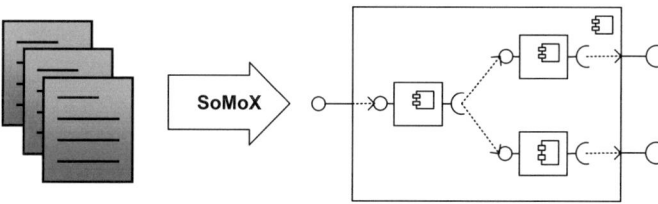

Figure 4.1.: The *SoMoX* approach reverse engineers a static component-based architecture from source code.

The first reverse engineering step in the developed approach is the reconstruction of the static software architecture. In this step, the SoMoX approach extracts the static part of a component-based software architecture (i.e. component, interfaces, and connectors) from source code.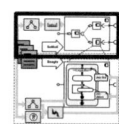

The SoMoX approach is a graph and metric based, multiple abstraction level, component-aware, and integrity keeping reverse engineering approach for software component architectures. It utilises various detection strategies for components, interfaces, and connectors. It is specifically designed for software component architectures and robust against architectural style violations. Metrics can have complex interrelations (e.g. metric A is only valid if the preconditions metric B and C hold with 90%) to enable high-level and complex strategies which are required to check for example a component's communication style.

Opposed to existing reverse engineering approaches (e.g. [AL99a, FDE+01, IWF07, KSRP99, MM01a, MOTU93, Sar03]), SoMoX follows the strong component definition by Szyperski (see Section 2.9). According to this component definition, components must state their context dependencies explicitly. This

53

implies explicitly stated provided and required interfaces. Thereby, components are specifically distinguishable from classes and modules.

SoMoX targets the reverse engineering of component-based software architectures which are subject of later analysis approaches (e.g. performance analysis through simulations). Components are thus required to be reverse engineered with full interfaces and connectors since the inter-component control flow would be incomplete otherwise. If required interfaces are incomplete, control flow which exists in the source code cannot be reflected in the component model. Also if connectors are not reverse engineered completely, communication would lead to undefined callees which makes analyses of such systems impossible. Thus, model integrity is a prerequisite to model analyses.

The lifted abstraction level of components created by SoMoX helps analysis approaches to cope with model complexity. Abstract components imply less model details which helps keeping analysis time short. In addition to analyses, the created high-level components help in program understanding.

Since software systems can follow different implementation styles, design principles, and architectural guidelines, SoMoX can be adapted to the specific needs of a certain software reverse engineering project. For example, one software system might emphasize interface communication, another follows fixed naming schemes, and yet another prescribes a certain package structure for the realisation of a software system. When detecting components, interfaces, and connectors, SoMoX can be adjusted accordingly. Nevertheless, SoMoX is equipped with default settings for C/C++ and Java projects to ease its application.

SoMoX is held extensible with respect to new metrics and strategies. Besides, it has support for multiple so-called "fact extractors" which can for example enable support for further programming languages (e.g. C#) and frameworks (e.g. EJB, Spring). The SoMoX approach does not differentiate among metrics and thus can deal with static and dynamic source code analysis approaches. Therefore, new metrics and strategies can take extra information from further fact extractors into account (cf. Section 4.10).

4.1. Shortcomings of Existing Approaches

This section presents a brief overview of related work. The presented work is a selection of related approaches which are discussed in full detail in Section 8.2. The most distinguishing aspects of the SoMoX approach compared to existing work are highlighted in the following.

Weak Components Many existing approaches [AL99a, FDE+01, IWF07, KSRP99, MM01a, MOTU93, Sar03] follow a weak component definition or reverse engineer modules. Some approaches claim to reverse engineer components but actually reverse engineer detected source code patterns [KSRP99, Sar03]. Other approaches assume components to be classes [SLLL07] or do not support the composition of components [Fav04, FDE+01].

A relaxed component definitions implies limited reuse of reverse engineer models due to implicit context dependencies (i.e. no explicit required interfaces exist or some dependencies are not made explicit in required interfaces). Implicit context dependencies cannot be know to the user of a component, which contradicts the third party reuse of a component (cf. Section 2.9).

Program Understanding   Other approaches focus on program understanding [AGC02, FDE+01, Kos02, PMT+08, BBT06]. The target of these reverse engineered models are human. Thus, there is no requirement of model completeness which is necessary when further approaches (like the developed Beagle approach for reverse engineering of behaviour) use the reverse engineered static architecture model as input.

No Execution Semantics Targeted   Most of the existing reverse engineered approaches for static software architectures do no target models which are subject to later execution (e.g. [Kos05, Kos02, MM06]). Opposed, the presented SoMoX approach is suitable as a base to compute performance analyses of the reverse engineered software system.

Limited Abstraction   Some reverse engineering approach have limited abstraction capabilities [LL03, KSRP99, Sar03]. They purely rely on programming language constructs (e.g. classes, or packages). Thereby, the possible abstractions are a) limited to what has originally been encoded into a software system, and b) limited to the abstraction levels and constructs supported by the programming language.

4.2. Scientific Challenges

The scientific challenges in the field of reverse engineering static component-based software architectures are:

- It must be investigated how to reverse engineer components following a *strong component definition* as introduced in Section 2.9. The reverse engineered static architecture model must be complete and posses full model integrity. Furthermore, the reverse engineering approach must create a model of a static component-based software architecture which lays the foundations for *execution semantics* to enable later model analyses (e.g. performance analysis).

- Reverse engineering of the static architecture

  – It must be clarified how to reverse engineer components from object-oriented languages which have *no explicit language element* "component".

  – It is subject to research how to detect *abstract high-level components.*

  – Composition of components (composite components) should be supported by the approach to achieve multiple abstraction levels of components.

- Realistic reverse engineering scenarios imply mixed component implementation styles (also within a single system). It is subject to research how to cope with *different implementations styles* and implementation techniques in an unified approach.

- A reverse engineering approach should be *generic* and not limited to a narrow subset of technologies. Furthermore, a reverse engineering approach should be held as *extensible* as possible. It must be investigated how to keep the approach *independent from concrete object-oriented languages*, or frameworks of source systems. The developed approach must generally be agnostic to implementation styles and implementation techniques and instead provide means to support arbitrary implementation styles and implementations techniques through extensions.

4.3. Contributions in Reverse Engineering

The SoMoX approach contributes in the following areas of reverse engineering for static component-based architectures:

- SoMoX contributes multiple detection strategies for components, composite components, provided and required interfaces, and connectors. These detection strategies have been developed for C/C++ and Java based systems. SoMoX provides a number of strategies which propose the selection and combination of source code metrics for the reconstruction of component-based software architectures.

- SoMoX is a reverse engineering approach suitable for hierarchical component-based systems and held extensible to support new component implementations styles and techniques.

  – The reverse engineered output models Service Architecture Model (SAMM) and Palladio Component Model (PCM) posses execution semantics and have full model integrity. The reverse engineered models

56

represent the static architecture which the Palladio approach uses for performance simulations.

- Its hierarchical output models enable the navigation through reverse engineered architectures and thus help in program understanding.

• The SoMoX approach helps reverse engineering large-scale software systems. It is scalable for projects of more than 250,000 lines of code.

• The implementation of the approach provides strong automation and minimises the amount of required human interaction. Yet, it is configurable to be adapted for specific project needs (e.g. selection of component detection strategies).

4.4. Requirements for Reverse Engineering of Static Architectures

The following requirements are derived from the scientific challenges and contributions sections.

• *R-Detection Mechanisms* Detection mechanisms for components, composite components, provided and required interfaces, and connectors must be provided.

• *R-Component Abstractions* Component abstractions higher than classes must be reverse engineered. Besides, multiple levels of composite component structures must be supported.

• *R-Completeness* The completeness requirements subsume i) model integrity to have a base for model analyses, ii) the requirement of a complete static architecture which does not miss elements like connectors etc., and iii) the requirements to reverse engineer components which state explicit context dependencies through required interfaces.

• *R-Extensibility* The developed approach must not be limited to a single object-oriented language or an implementation technology (e.g. EJB, Spring).

• *R-Scalability* The approach must be scalable for up to 250,000 lines of code.

• *R-Automation* The approach should be largely automated to make large system analyseable with little effort. Manual interaction should not be needed during a reverse engineering run.

Section 9.1 discusses the realisation of these Requirements.

4.5. Solution Idea: Overview

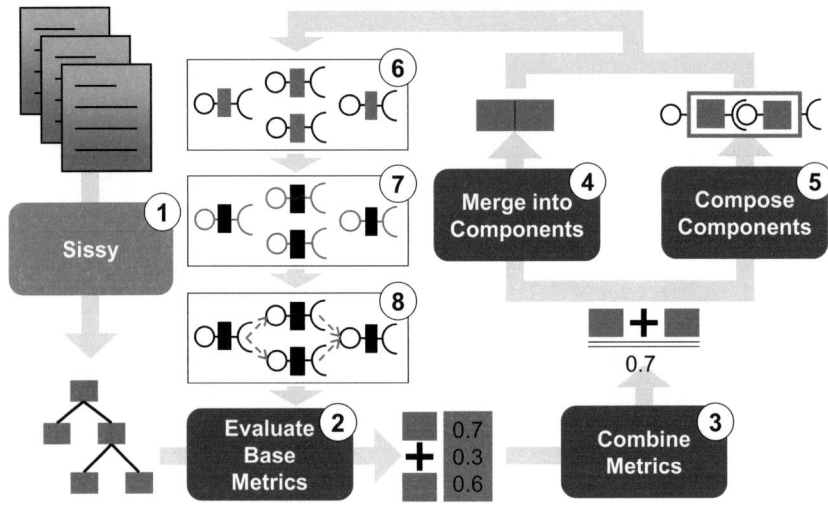

Figure 4.2.: Overview on SoMoX reverse engineering

Figure 4.2 provides a rough overview on the reverse engineering process of SoMoX. The following Listing 4.1 further details on the process of SoMoX. Please note that the original result model of SoMoX is not a number of sets but the instance of a meta-model (SAMM).

```
 1  Inputs:
 2    SC = SourceCode(System) //Set of source code of the system
 3    AllBaseMetrics //Non empty set of all base metrics
 4    //Non empty sets of strategies:
 5    ComponentStrategies, InterfaceStrategies, ConnectorStrategies
 6  Outputs:
 7    Components ← ∅
 8    Connectors ← ∅
 9    Architecture ← ∅
10  // (1) Extract source code information into a language independent representation
```

```
11  GAST = SISSy(SC)
12  do {
13    ComponentCandidates = deriveComponentCandidates(GAST)
14    // (2) Evaluate basic source code metrics
15    for(ComponentCandidate : ComponentCandidates) {
16      for(Metric_n : AllBaseMetrics) {
17        BaseMetricResults.add(Metric_n(ComponentCandidate))
18      }
19    }
20    for(ComponentCandidate : ComponentCandidates) {
21      // (3) Combine a number of base metrics in component detection strategies
22      for(Strategy_n : ComponentStrategies) {
23        ComponentCandidateRatings.add(
24            Strategy_n(ComponentCandidate, BaseMetricResults) )
25      }
26      // (4) Try to merge components
27      if(passingThreshold(ComponentCandidateRatings, ComponentCandidate,
          mergeThreshold)) {
28        Components.add(merge(ComponentCandidateRatings, ComponentCandidate))
29      } else {
30        // (5) Try to compose components
31        if(passingThreshold(ComponentCandidateRatings, ComponentCandidate,
            composteThreshold)) {
32          Components.add(compose(ComponentCandidateRatings, ComponentCandidate)
              )
33        }
34      }
35    }
36    // (6) Integrate results in the architecture model
37    Architecture.add(Components)
38    // (7) Assign component interfaces
39    Interfaces = assignInterfaces(Components, InterfaceStrategies)
40    // (8) Create component connectors
41    Connectors = createConnectors(Interfaces, Components, ConnectorStrategies)
42  } while (components found) // (9) Perform a new iteration starting with (2)
```

59

Listing 4.1: The basic steps which are performed in the SoMoX approach.

The following section focuses on the steps of the component detection approach. Individual steps will be further discussed in later sections.

Extract Source Code Information   The reverse engineering process start with the SISSy (1) approach which extracts a Generalised Abstract Syntax Tree (GAST) from source code. The employed GAST is a language-independent representation of object-oriented source code. This enables SoMoX to reverse engineer any object oriented code which can be mapped to the GAST representation. SISSy [ABM+06] is a third party approach which is reused in the reverse engineering process. The GAST is extracted once per reverse engineering run and is a prerequisite to the reverse engineering run.

Component Detection Approach   In this step, the core of the iterative reverse engineering process of SoMoX is performed. SoMoX starts extracting low abstraction level components which comprise just a few classes. Each iteration builds on the results of the previous iterations and aims at higher abstraction levels of components. Each iteration results in an architecture model which describes the components detected until that iteration. These components associate encapsulated GAST classes through the trace model. The iterations stop if no further component abstractions are found.

Evaluate basic Metrics   In each iteration, first a number of basic source code metrics (2) like coupling, name resemblance, package mapping etc. are evaluated based on the GAST representation. Metrics are always evaluated for so-called *component candidates*. A component candidate is a tuple C_i, C_j of two sets of classes $C_x = \{class_1, class_2, ..\}$. A component candidate is a subject to merge and composition in subsequent steps. Ultimately, sets of component candidates result in new components of a higher abstraction level.

In the first iterations, $C_x, x \in \{i, j\}$ consists of only a single class. In later iterations, C_x contains the classes of previously identified components. For example, C_x of an existing composite component comprises all inner associated classes. Thus, component candidates are a uniform base for the evaluation of metrics, merge, and compose.

Merge and Compose   The next two steps then decide on converting a component candidate into a component. SoMoX first tries to merge (4) component candidates. If merging component candidates is not beneficial because this would result in a poor component quality, SoMoX tries to compose (5) composite components from component candidates. The decision when to convert component candidates will be detailed below.

1. The first step (4) *merges* the component candidate with an existing component. In a first iteration, this results in a basic component comprising the classes $C_i \cup C_j$. The classes of the component candidate are then merged into a single basic component of a higher abstraction level.

   In later iterations, this step can also result in composite components (with the associated set of classes C_{CC}) to which further classes are attached: $C_{CC} \cup C_i \cup C_j$. In that case, C_{CC}, C_i, and C_j represent the classes of components of previous iterations which are merged into a single composite component of a higher abstraction level.

2. The second step (5) *composes* composite components from component candidates. The components represented by C_i and C_j are preserved and encapsulated into a composite component. Later iterations then operate on the resulting composite component which comprises the classes $C_i \cup C_j$.

To decide whether to merge (4) or compose (5) component candidates, a number of detection strategies (3), each representing a component detection heuristic, is responsible for identifying components. There exist two different groups of strategies: One for suggesting merges for step (4) and one for suggesting compositions for step (5). Each strategy group consists of a number of strategies and results in a "recommendation" whether to merge or compose.

The term strategy is used to emphasize that there are possible alternative realisations. The following sections will point out which alternative strategies exist. The term strategy refers to the design pattern listed by Gamma et al. [GHJV95].

Component Detection Strategies Each strategy acts as a mean to identify characteristics of a potential component like interface communication, high coupling, and name resemblance of implementing classes. Component detection strategies operate on component candidates and evaluate whether a component candidate should become a component. The result of a detection strategy is a numeric value in the interval $[0..1]$ where 1 means accepting a component candidate and 0 suggests rejecting a component candidate. Thus, a strategy is mapping from component candidates to a numeric value:

$$Strategy(C_i, C_j) \rightarrow v \in \mathbb{R} \; : \; 0 \leq v \leq 1$$

All strategy evaluations of a component candidate are aggregated into a single value $S_{all}(C_i, C_j)$ which indicates the confidence of having a component represented by the component candidate. The calculation of $S_{all}(C_i, C_j)$ will be explained in detail

61

in Section 4.8. In that section, strategies for component composition and merge will be differentiated.

Intuitively speaking, the aggregated value $S_{all}(C_i, C_j)$ is a kind of weighted sum of strategy results. But strategies itself are composable to express for example inter-dependencies among detection strategies in a higher level strategy.

$$Strategy_{composed}(C_i, C_j) :=$$
$$\{Strategy_a(C_i, C_j), Strategy_b(C_i, C_j), ...\} \rightarrow v \in \mathbb{R} : 0 \leq v \leq 1$$

This allows to express for example, that similar names of classes (e.g. `CustomerAccounting` and `CustomerRelations`) of a component candidate do not indicate a component, when the classes are not at all connected at the code-level.

The decision mechanism whether to merge or compose components from a component candidate operates on a graph structure and reuses existing graph algorithms. Each element of a component candidate (C_i, C_j) is therefore considered as a vertex in a weighted directed graph $G = (V, E)$ with directed edges $e = (v_{start}, v_{end}) \in E : v_{start}, v_{end} \in V$, edge weights $w(e) \in [0..1] \in \mathbb{R}$, and vertices $C_x \rightarrow V$ derived for every set of a component candidate. The set of all evaluations of $S_{all}(C_i, C_j)$ serves as adjacency matrix. For all $S_{all}(C_i, C_j) > 0$ a directed edge with a corresponding weight $w(e) = S_{all}(C_i, C_j) > 0$ is derived.

In a first graph transformation step, edges' weights are merged into weights of a single non-directed edge where the weight of the non directed edge is the sum of the directed edges

$$w_{nd}(e) = w(e_1) + w(e_2) : e_1, e_2 \in E \wedge v_{start}(e_1) = v_{end}(e_2) \wedge v_{end}(e_1) = v_{start}(e_2)$$

with $v_{start}(e)$ being the start vertex and $v_{end}(e)$ being the end vertex of a directed edge. Converting the directed graph into a non-directed graph is necessary since metrics and derived component detection strategies can be directed. A directed graph is not required for component detection but only for deriving connectors.

In the next graph transformation step, all edges whose weights fall below a previously selected threshold ($E_{filtered} = E \setminus \{e \mid w_{nd}(e) < threshold\}$) are removed from the graph. Based on that graph, all *weakly connected components* of the graph structure (cf. [Die05]) are converted into components. While $S_{all}(C_i, C_j)$ is an evaluation of a component candidate of *two* sets of classes, the weakly connected components from the graph can comprise $n \geq 2$ classes which is ensured by the definition of weakly connected components. This intentionally allows the creation of component abstractions with strong aggregation.

Weakly connected components in the graph are first determined for the merge step (4) and then, if (4) does not produce components, for the compose step (5). The steps

(4) and (5) operate with the same graph structure. Only the component detection strategies from which the graph is built (and thus the edge weights) differ.

Integrate Results   After step (5), the detected components of an iteration are integrated in the architecture result model. Component candidates that have been converted into components are therefore removed from the graph structure and a new vertex representing the newly created component is introduced. Next, the base metric are recalculated for the changed parts of the graph, and a new iteration can start.

Dynamic Threshold   SoMoX is using two separate dynamic thresholds: t_{merge} for merging in step (4) and $t_{compose}$ for composition in step (5). These thresholds are dynamically changed from iteration to iteration to reflect the increasing abstraction in later iterations. t_{merge} is increased over the iterations to lower the probability of component merging. While merging is useful for early iteration to build `BasicComponents`, adding classes to `CompositeComponents` in later iterations becomes less important. Instead, in later iterations, composing components of components which exist in that iteration becomes important. For that reason, $t_{compose}$ is decreased over the iterations.

Each threshold t_x (for $x \in \{compose, merge\}$) has a configurable initial value $t_{x,init}$, a decrementation / incrementation stepwidth $t_{x,stepwidth}$, and a final value $t_{x,final}$ associated. The t_x values are changed over the defined interval $[t_{x,init}, t_{x,final}]$.

Large values for $t_{compose,stepwidth}$ result in fewer component abstraction levels (less composite component nesting). $t_{x,init}$ determines the initial abstraction level. Larger values for $t_{compose,init}$ foster smaller composite components, while smaller values for $t_{compose,final}$ determine the maximum abstraction level in later iterations. For merging, the values induce a complementary behaviour: Larger values for $t_{merge,init}$ result in a smaller number of primitive components which have a smaller size. Smaller final values for merging $t_{merge,final}$ limit the overall number of detected primitive components. Small values for $t_{compose,stepwidth}$ increase the chance that existing composite components are merged with existing composite components in the first iterations.

The threshold is only adapted, if in an iteration, no new component has been identified. Since the graph structure is changed by each detected component, the threshold does not need to be lowered after an iteration in which at least one component has been found.

Interface and Connector Creation   After the component detection has run, interfaces are assigned (7) to components and connectors are created (8). Since interface communication can be checked by component detection strategies, interfaces must be created along with components (after each iteration, the component architecture is complete including connectors). For the detection of interfaces there exist separate strategies. These strategies for example decide whether to expose the interfaces of inner components contained in a composite component. Section 4.8 details on these strategies.

SoMoX directly derives component connectors from the graph. Since the original edges are directed, connectors can be derived directly from the graph. Depending on the component types (basic or composite component) which are created from the vertices and the associated interfaces, provided or required delegation connectors and assembly connectors are established. Connectors can only be established if components have interfaces assigned in the previous step.

4.6. Integration of User Feedback

After each iteration, SoMoX results in a valid intermediate instance of the architecture model. This model can be displayed to users to enable interaction with the reverse engineering process. For example, iterations can be stopped (i.e. when the abstraction level is sufficient), or the assignment of component candidate elements to components can be changed by the user. The user is provided with a visualisation of the results of the last iteration using an existing editor for the architecture model.

4.7. Core Assumptions

The core assumptions which must hold for every supported system are:

1. The reverse engineering target must be mappable to a component-based architecture. Only architectures which are created with some notion of component in mind are well-supported. If components are not recognisable from source code structures in some way at all, the reverse engineering approach is not applicable. The internal representation of the reverse engineered system of this approach is fixed to a component-based architecture.

2. Any fact extractor (e.g. SISSy in the above solution) must relate its information to classes represented in the GAST (Generalised Abstract Syntax Tree) representation. Additional input information can be easily supported, but any information must have a mapping to GAST classes. For example, Spring [Spr06] or EJB [EJB07] deployment descriptors are not supported out-of-the box. When supporting them, any bindings among classes, introduced by for example dependency injection, must name the classes they connect. Section 4.10 discusses the extension in more detail.

4.8. Reverse Engineering Strategies

In its core, SoMoX relies on a number of strategies for component recognition, interface assignment, and connector creation. Strategies are responsible for identifying for example components which are implemented following a certain architecture or implementation style (cf. [BMR+96]). Strategies themself comprise a number of base metrics or are built from a number of sub-strategies. They combine base metrics to form higher level recognition mechanisms for architecture elements.

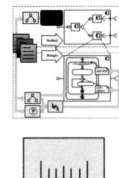

For systems which are implemented with object-oriented techniques, no component terminology exist. Instead, components can only partially be reflected in object-oriented code. Multiple strategies can be applied during reverse engineering, each representing a heuristic, to detect components. Depending on an architectural style and the intended component definition, different strategies must be applied to reflect the expected style and component definition in the reverse engineered architecture. A single strategy usually is not sufficient to reverse engineer a system since a large system might involve different implementation styles. Each implementation style can then be covered by one or multiple strategies.

The following section will first provide an overview on possible reverse engineering strategies. This also covers strategies which have not been realised in SoMoX to illustrate the possible design space for reverse engineering and point out possible alternatives for reverse engineering. To structure the design space, two feature diagrams (Figure 4.3 and 4.4; introduction of feature diagrams in [CE00]) are provided. In these feature diagrams, strategies which have been selected for SoMoX are highlighted ("check symbol") – the so-called *Feature Configuration*. Later, base metrics (Section 4.8.3) and realised strategies will be presented in detail (Section 4.8.5).

4.8.1. Overview on Strategies

The following strategy variation points have been identified, which should be accounted for during reverse engineering. Figure 4.3 provides an overview on possible strategies which complement metrics for component recognition.

At the top level, there are two strategies for dealing with component candidates, namely component merging and component composition represent the most important strategies. Further top level strategies are filtering mechanisms through blacklisting, strategies for creating provided and required interfaces for components, and finally strategies for the creation of composite component structures like connectors and the exposition of composite component interfaces.

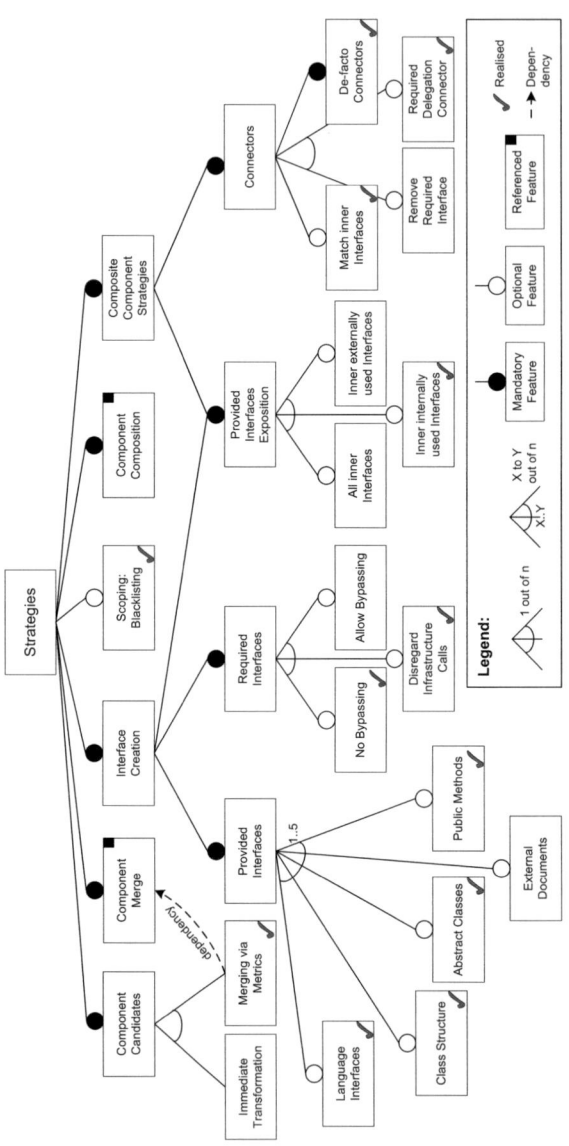

Figure 4.3.: Feature diagram of strategies for the creation of component candidates, interfaces and connectors (capturing only cases for which multiple strategies exist)

Figure 4.4 provides an overview on possible strategies for deciding whether to merge or compose components from a component candidate. The following sections will detail on the features and on the rational of each feature.

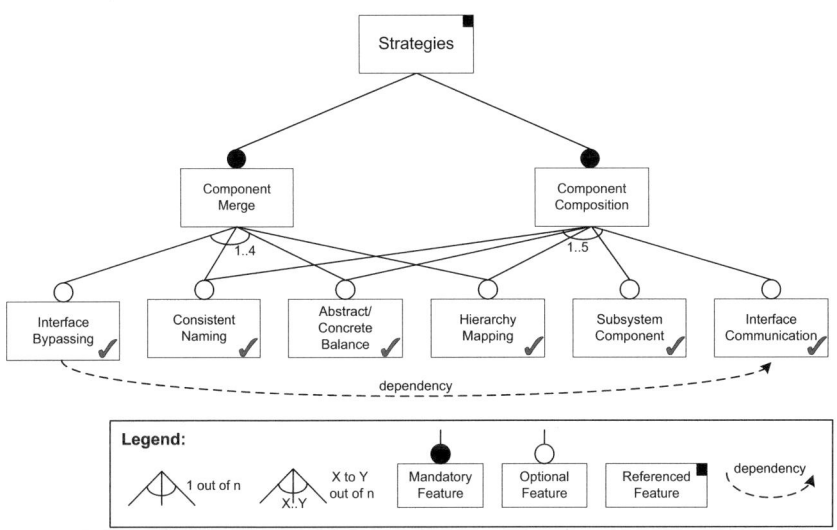

Figure 4.4.: Feature diagram of strategies for merging and composing Components

Every strategy can comprise a number of sub-strategies which contribute to a certain top-level strategy. Component merge and component composition strategies share common sub-strategies. While a component merge strategy indicates when to add classes from a component candidate to an existing component, component composition strategies indicate when to create a composite component from a component candidate.

4.8.2. Process for Selection of Metrics and Strategies

Metrics and strategies for SoMoX have been selected in a demand-driven empirical process. In the process, the reference decompositions of multiple systems under study were compared with reverse engineering results. SoMoX initially started with a small set of metrics and strategies. When comparing the reference architecture of the reverse engineered systems with the output of SoMoX, new metrics and strategies were introduced to make previously unrecognized components identifiable. Therefore, non recognised components were analysed for specific characteristics which had not been identifiable with the existing metrics and strategies. New metrics and strategies were then imagined to capture exactly these characteristics. The process has been repeated until satisfactory results were achieved when comparing reverse engineering results with the reference architecture.

4.8.3. Basic Metrics

In order to understand the strategy explanations in the following, first the employed base metrics will be explained. The basic metrics have been derived purely from the strategies. First the strategies have been identified and only those metrics which are required by the strategies have been integrated into SoMoX.

For components only few metrics are available as Cho et al. [CKK01] point out. Source code metrics from object-oriented programs cannot necessarily be directly reused for components since components comprise sets of classes and associate interfaces. Therefore, basic metrics which are used in this section are adaptions of existing object-oriented metrics where necessary. Of the available component metrics, most are dedicated to special purposes. For example, Washizaki et al. [WYF03] provide a set of metrics to estimate the reusability of black-box software components, Cho et al. [CKK01] evaluate metrics for complexity, customizability, and reusability of software components, and Ko and Park [KP05] present metrics for component architecture redesign.

All of the following metrics are calculated for component candidates. Opposed to pure object-oriented metrics, the required basic metrics must be able to deal with sets of classes, which represent a component candidate. All basic metrics map the evaluation of a component candidate to the interval between 0 and 1: $C(C_i, C_j) \rightarrow v \in \mathbb{R} : 0 \leq v \leq 1$.

A component candidate C_i, C_j can contain classes and class interfaces associated to these classes (i.e. interfaces implemented by classes from C_i or C_j). For example, a basic component could internally use interfaces of data structures which do not necessarily become component interfaces but nevertheless should be associated to components. Basic metrics are not aware of component interfaces, they operate on class interfaces only. Component interfaces are created after the evaluation of basic metrics.

Metrics (and strategies) are evaluated for two set of classes A and B. For the components detection, these two sets of classes originate from a component candidate C_i, C_j.

Coupling The coupling metric reuses the ideas of the afferent coupling (C_a) and efferent coupling (C_e) metrics by Martin [Mar94]. The metrics have been transferred to components. The afferent coupling (C_a) is the number of types outside a component candidate that depend on types within the component candidate. The efferent coupling (C_e) is the number of types inside a component candidate that depend on types that are outside the component candidate.

Coupling, in this context, is the ratio of accesses inside a component candidate to the total number of accesses and thus based on efferent coupling C_e. Opposed to efferent coupling, the number of accesses is counted

$$Coupling(A, B) := \frac{R(A, B)}{R(A, all)} = \frac{\text{InternalAccesses}}{\text{ExternalAccesses}}$$

with $R(A, B)$ the number of accesses of from A to B, where A and B are sets of classes, *all* is the set of all classes of a system. An access subsumes accesses of a type, a method, or a field, each counted separatly. Counting the number of accesses helps quantifying the access relations between two sets of classes. Coupling is a non-commutative normalised metric which composes the raw counts of internal and external accesses.

Name Resemblance The *name resemblance* reflects how the names of classes and interfaces of component candidates resemble each other. The metric counts similar names for each of the classes in the component candidates and relates them to the total number of class names. Prior to comparing the names, common prefixes and suffixes are removed. Common prefixes and suffixes which misleadingly would indicate name resemblance must be specified by the user. For example, EJB components might be prefixed with "EJB" which still does not indicate classes which belong together and thus would let this metric become partially misleading.

The calculation of the name resemblance relies on the *Jaro-Winkler distance* [Win06] $JR(string_1, string_2)$ which calculates the similarity of two names. The similarity N_{SN} of classes and interfaces of a component candidate is then calculated based on the pairwise similarity comparison of the cross product of all classes and interfaces of a component candidate:

$$N_{SN} := \sum_{class_1, class_2}^{A \cup B \times A \cup B} JR(class_1, class_2)$$

with $class_1$ and $class_2$ being individual classes and interfaces of the cross product of all classes and interfaces $A \cup B \times A \cup B$.

The Jaro-Winkler distance metric was chosen since it respects the number of matching characters and the number of transpositions. It is well-suited to compute the similarity of identifying names. Its result value is normalised to the interval $[0..1]$ where 1 is an exact match and 0 states no similarity.

Alternative simplistic distance metrics on strings such as the Hamming distance [Ham50] are tolerant against typing error, but are less meaningful for class naming which often involves common pre and post fixes like in `BusinessLogic`, `Business-View`, and `BusinessFacade`, where "Business" indicates classes belonging together.

Based on N_{SN}, the name resemblance can be calculated as follows:

$$NameResemblance(A, B) := \frac{N_{SN}}{card(N_{all})}$$

where $N_{all} = A \cup B \times A \cup B$ and $card(N_{all})$ is thus the cardinality of the cross product of all classes and interfaces of a component candidate. Name resemblance is a commutative metric.

Interface Violations   The interface violation metric captures the number of accesses between two sets of classes which bypass interfaces (i.e. direct type access).

$$InterfaceVioloation(A, B) := \frac{RI(A, B)}{R(A, all)}$$

where $RI(A, B)$ is the number of accesses from A to B bypassing interfaces, and $R(A, all)$ is as above the number of all accesses. The interface violation metric lays the foundation for detecting a communication style through interfaces. Section 4.8.6 will be dealing with the identification of interfaces as not all programming languages have an explicit notion of interface. Interface violation is a non commutative metric which is 1 if all communication from A to B uses interfaces.

Package Mapping   The package mapping metric indicates that a component candidate is realised by classes that reside in the same package structure. The package structure is therefore mapped to a separate tree structure formed by the package containment relation.

$$PackageMapping(A, B) :=$$
$$NonLinearMapping(\frac{commonRootHeight(A, B)}{maxHeight(A, B) - commonRootHeight(A, B)})$$

where $maxHeight(A, B)$ is the maximum height of elements of A and B in the package tree and $commonRootHeight(A, B)$ is the height of the maximum common tree node for all elements of A and B. $Packagemapping(A, B)$ non-linearly depends on the inner fraction with

$$NonLinearMapping(x) := \begin{cases} x & \text{if } x > 0.2 \\ 0 & \text{else} \end{cases}$$

where $x = [0..1] \in \mathbb{R}$. $NonLinearMapping(x)$ realises a limiter which helps avoiding a component indicator for classes which only share a very top-level package. The limit of 0.2 is a configurable value which proved to be reasonable during the validation of the approach. Package mapping is a commutative metric.

Directory Mapping The directory mapping metric is comparable to the package mapping metric besides its applicability to programming languages which do not support packages or implementations which do not make use of packages. For Java, where directory and package structure are the same, directory and package mapping result in the same value. For C++ namespaces, for example, the directory can deviate from the namespaces structure. Instead of building a package tree from the package containment relation, the directory tree is built from the directory containment relation for the directory mapping metric. Besides, directory mapping is calculated in the same way as package mapping. Directory mapping is a commutative metric.

Although the directory of elements of A or B contain the full file system path, the metric remains independent from where the sources are placed in the file system, since no absolute root element is part of the calculation.

Instability The instability metric by Martin [Mar94] is the ratio of efferent coupling to total coupling. It indicates whether the classes implementing a component candidate have many external dependencies which make a component implementation likely to change if an external class or interface changes.

$$Instability(A, B) := \frac{C_e(A, B)}{C_e(A, B) + C_a(A, B)}$$

Instability indicates a component candidate's resilience to change. 0 indicates a completely stable component candidate, 1 indicates an instable component candidate. Instability is a commutative metric.

Abstractness   When transferring the instability metric by Martin [Mar94] to components, it is the ratio of abstract elements of a component candidate to the total number of elements of a component candidate.

$$Abstractness(A, B) := \frac{card(abstract(A \cup B))}{card(A \cup B)}$$

where $abstract(S) = \{s \in S | s \text{ is abstract}\}$ is the selection of abstract elements of the set S. Abstract elements are abstract classes and interfaces. Abstractness is commutative.

Distance from the Main Sequence   The metric Distance from the Main Sequence (DMS) was first introduced by Martin [Mar94] and indicates a balance between instability and abstractness (see Figure 4.5). The more abstract a component candidate is (involving more internal interfaces), the more stable it should be. Vice versa, it is acceptable for a component candidate to be instable if it is less abstract. Fully instable and abstract component candidates are as unwanted as fully non-abstract and stable ones. The first ones have no realisation and are unreliable from the developer perspective, while the latter ones tend to be little accessible monoliths. For further reading, please refer to [Mar94].

$$DMS(A, B) := 1 - |Abstractness(A, B) + Instability(A, B) - 1|$$

where abstractness and instability are the metrics introduced above. The above formula calculates the distance from the visualised "main sequence". The prefixed $1 - x$ is required to have a value of 1 indicating a good component candidate. DMS is a commutative and composite metric.

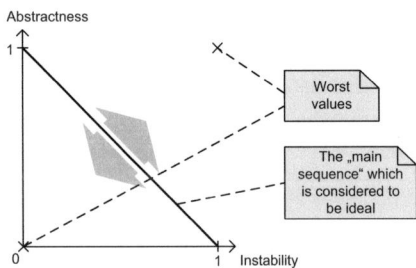

Figure 4.5.: Distance from the Main Sequence visualised

Slice Layer Architecture Quality The Slice Layer Architecture Quality (SLAQ) metric captures how a broadly used architecture style of organising a system in slices and layers is followed. Slices are service oriented cuts of a software system, like for example contracting, billing, and customer data management. Layers are cross-cutting technology induced cuts of a software system, like for example a view layer, a middle-tier, and a database access layer. An element which resides in one layer and one slice is called *natural subsystem*, like the view of the contracting slice in the following example (see Listing 4.2).

The SLAQ metric can be interpreted as the similarity between the slice and layer architecture style and its occurrence in the system under study. It judges to which extend the slice and layer architecture style is followed by the implementation.

SLAQ expects slices and layers to be encoded into package names. For example:

```
1 edu.kit.ipd.mysystem.contracting.view
2 edu.kit.ipd.mysystem.contracting.business
3 edu.kit.ipd.mysystem.contracting.data
4 edu.kit.ipd.mysystem.billing.view
5 edu.kit.ipd.mysystem.billing.business
6 edu.kit.ipd.mysystem.billing.data
7 ...
```

Listing 4.2: Package names example of a project organised in slices and layers

Opposed to previous metrics, SLAQ is not related to a component candidate. It is a basic metric which is reused by the subsystem component metric. SLAQ is the ratio of found and expected natural subsystems.

$$SLAQ := \frac{card(S_{found})}{card(S_{expected})}$$

with S_{found} the set of identified subsystems and $S_{expected}$ the set of expected subsystems. $S_{expected}$ is derived from the package structure. S_{found} contains all natural subsystems of $S_{expected}$ which are present in the package structure. $S_{expected}$ represent the set of all natural subsystems of the system.

The problem of SLAQ is, that neither slices nor layers are know to the metric. Both must be derived from the existing package structure of a software system using a heuristic. Hence, also $S_{expected}$ is unknown. The following pseudo-algorithm in Listing 4.3 calculates $S_{expected}$.

```
1 C ← classes(System) // Set of classes in the system
2 P ← ∅ // Set of packages
3 L ← ∅ // Set of layers
```

```
4   S ← ∅ // Set of (packageSuffix, frequency) tuples
5   S_expected ← ∅ // the result; expected natural subsystems

7   calculateExpectedNaturalSubsystems(C) {
8       //determine the largest common package prefix and remove from package hierarchy:
9       P = packageHierarchy(C) \ commonPackagePrefix(C)
10      //layer identification:
11      L = layersFromPackageHierarchy(P)
12      //determine common package suffixes (e.g. 'data' 3x, 'view' 2x):
13      S = packageSuffixes(C)
14      //minimum number of slice occurrences, at least 2:
15      f_min = min(card(L) * slice_percentage, 2)
16      //calculate the expected subsystems:
17      S_expected = L × {(prefix, frequency) ∈ S|frequency ≥ f_min}
18      return S_expected
19  }
```

Listing 4.3: SLAQ calculation

where $slice_{percentage}$ is the required percentage of occurrences of a slice among all packages (e.g. 5%).

First, the algorithm computes the longest common package prefix of the elements of a software system. The package structure of a software system does not deviate in the hierarchy above the identified package. Then, the layers below the calculated base package and the most common package suffixes and their quantity (e.g. 3x ".data" and 2x ".view") are calculated. From that, a configurable minimum number of occurrences f_{min} of a slice is calculated (line 9). Each slice which is bypassing the minimal frequency f_{min} becomes part of the cross product of identified layers and slices. Each element of the cross product is considered as an expected natural subsystem.

Natural Subsystem The natural subsystem metric indicates how likely a component candidate is representing a natural subsystem identified by SLAQ. Figure 4.6 visualises the natural subsystems of an example system.

$$NaturalSubsystem(A, B) := SLAQ * SubsystemMatch(A, B)$$

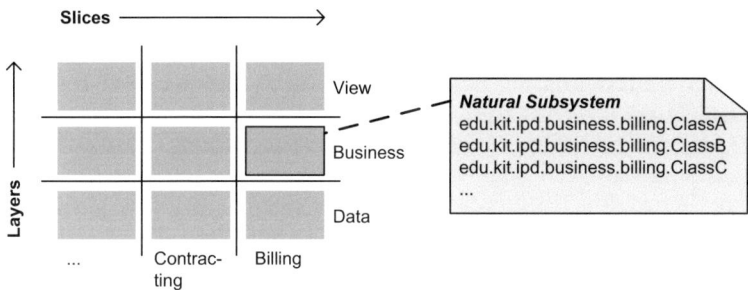

Figure 4.6.: Natural subsystems of a software system

where $SLAQ$ is the previously introduced metric and

$$SubsystemMatch(A, B) := \frac{card(subsystem_{inside}(A \cup B))}{card(subsystem_{outside}(A \cup B))}$$

is a value $[0..1] \in \mathbb{R}$ which is the ratio between classes inside a natural subsystem $subsystem_{inside}$ and classes outside a natural subsystem $subsystem_{outside}$. Since there are multiple natural subsystems, the natural subsystem to check against is the one where the largest number of classes of $A \cap B$ is in:

$$SelectedSubsystem(A, B) := s \in S_{expected} \mid card(s \cap (A \cup B)) =$$
$$fmax(\, card(ns \cap (A \cup B))\,)\, \forall ns \in S_{expected}$$

where $fmax(expression)$ determines the maximum value of $expression$ (in this case the calculation of the cardinality) for all $ns \in S_{expected}$. $subsystem_{inside}$ and $subsystem_{outside}$ are then evaluated on the subsystem selected by $Selected\-Subsystem(A, B)$. The fact that multiple subsystems can have the same maximal cardinality does not harm the result, since only its cardinality is used to calculate the $SubsystemMatch(A, B)$. If $fmax(expression)$ is not resulting in a single unique element, an arbitrary element of the result set is returned.

The maximum value of the subsystem component metric is the SLAQ metric value. For architectures which are not organised in slices and layers, the natural subsystem metric does not apply and results in a value of 0. Natural subsystem is a commutative and composite metric.

4.8.4. Blacklisting and Filtering

All strategies can be combined with an optional *blacklisting* and *filtering* strategy (cf. Figure 4.7). This strategy first of all allows limiting the scope of reverse engineering. For example, infrastructure or system libraries can be excluded from reverse engineering, but reverse engineering can also be focused on specific subsystems of a software. Furthermore, this strategy allows filtering certain classes or data types. For example, primitive data types or classes which are pure data structures with only public fields are not subject of component reverse engineering. They can be part of component interface definitions but should not be contributing to components. When not filtering pure data types, basic metrics like coupling or interface violation could be misleading (they could for example indicate an interface violation and high coupling).

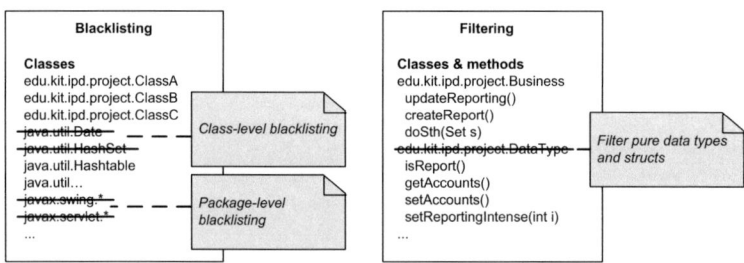

Figure 4.7.: Blacklisting and filtering

The blacklisting is a set projection based on the naming of its elements:

$$Blacklisting(S, names_{blacklisted}) := \{ s \in S \mid s.name \notin names_{blacklisted} \}$$

where S is the set of classes, interfaces, and packages of a system's GAST model and $names_{blacklisted}$ is the set of blacklisted names. For classes and interfaces, the name attribute is the fully qualified name, for packages the name is the full package path name.

Typical applications of blacklisting are the removal of libraries and runtime environment classes. For example, java.* and javax.* are removed in most Java-based scenarios.

While blacklisted classes and interfaces are fully removed from input interpretation, filters can be specific to certain reverse engineering steps (e.g. component detection or interface creation). By default, structs, enumerations, primitive types, and classes with only getters, setters and is*-methods are considered as pure data structures and therefore filtered.

Data structures are filtered from the set of all types by first checking the data type attributes available from the GAST model and then removing those types that represent pure data structures. The latter heuristic is based on regular expression checks. The following term defines the white list filter which bypasses desired types:

$$Filter_{DataStructures}(T) := \{t \in T \mid$$
$$t.isStruct = false \wedge$$
$$t.isPrimitive = false \wedge$$
$$t.isEnum = false\}$$
$$\setminus \{t \in T \mid card(t.methods) = card(\{m \in t.methods \mid$$
$$RegEx("get. * ", m.name) \vee$$
$$RegEx("set. * ", m.name) \vee$$
$$RegEx("is. * ", m.name)\})$$
$$\}$$

where T is the set of types of a system and $isStruct$, $isPrimitive$, $isEnum$, and $methods$ are properties directly available for types from GAST models. Additionally, methods possess a $name$ attribute.

$RegEx$ is a regular pattern matching (cf. [Tho68]):

$$RegEx(pattern, arg) := \begin{cases} true & \text{if } arg \text{ matches the regular} \\ & \text{expression } pattern \\ false & \text{else} \end{cases}$$

4.8.5. Component Detection Strategies

Strategies, among others, help identifying components and interfaces in SoMoX. They rely on the basic metrics which have been introduced in the previous section. Instead of calculating a weighted sum from the basic metrics, strategies allow SoMoX to identify higher level structures of components which are not directly visible from a single metric. Each strategy therefore can combine a number of basic metrics and is able to take interdependencies into account. As explained before, for example the naming of classes by itself is a bad indicator for componentisation, when ignoring the coupling on the code level. If two classes have similar names but no code relation, they form a bad component.

Principles like cohesion and coupling [Mye75] are well-known to be indicators for software modularisation but have been identified to be not the ideal driver for modularisation [AG01]. Furthermore, when dealing with software components instead of modules, cohesion and coupling reflect only a small portion of the component properties which are required by the developed reverse engineering approach. Therefore, various strategies which go beyond cohesion and coupling are responsible for detecting component-based architectures in the SoMoX approach.

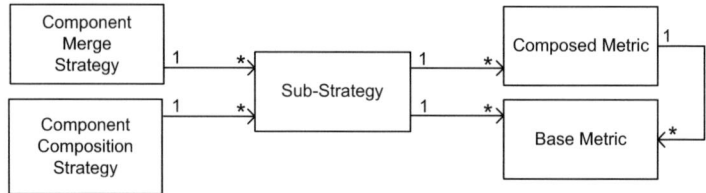

Figure 4.8.: Relations between strategies and metrics visualised an UML class
diagramme

The strategies for component identification (component merge and component composition) are realised as a special form of composite metric. Other strategies which do not rely on metrics will be pointed out separately. In SoMoX, the main strategies component merge and component composition rely on a number of sub-strategies (see Figure 4.8). These sub-strategies themselves rely on basic metrics and composed metrics. Generally, strategies and metrics follow a composite pattern [GHJV95] which does not limit the number of nesting levels. Strategies, sub-strategies, and metrics are separated to clarify the concepts.

The following sections will detail on the strategies from the overview in Figure 4.3 and 4.4.

Component Candidates The GAST representation contains only constructs of object-oriented programming languages. Thus, a strategy is required which turns the constructs into component candidates. There are two different alternative strategies for dealing with the creation of component candidates: The immediate transformation from source code to component candidates and the merging strategy which uses the graph-based component creation as introduced in Section 4.5. The two alternative strategies in detail are:

- *Immediately transform* each initial component candidate into a basic component. Using this strategy, low-level components are preserved since they form the basic entity for creating further composite components. Here, a fixed heuristic is used to identify low level components and directly convert them into basic components. Such heuristics cover the creation of a basic component for every class including its inner classes. The heuristic can be extended by strategies for specific technologies. For example for EJB components, all classes which implement a single EJB component can be transformed into a basic component (the required information on EJBs can for example be derived from deployment descriptors).

- *Merging via metrics.* More advanced strategies make use of metrics for merging classes into basic components. This is the same strategy as for later merging of components (see strategy "Component Merge"). In this step, metrics identifying criteria for merging classes into a component are applied. For example, a helper class which is accessed without interface use by a single other class can be merged into the component of the accessing class. By using the merging strategy, the lowest abstraction level of the reverse engineered components can be significantly lifted.

  High initial abstraction levels help keeping the result model small and assist creating understandable initial component abstractions which can significantly differ from classes. Furthermore, the abstraction level of basic components directly impacts the control flow abstraction level of the later reverse engineering of behaviour models (cf. Section 5). The behaviour abstractions become more fine-grained for smaller components. To increase the control flow abstraction of behaviour models, high-level basic components are required.

In both cases, each class including its inner classes are considered minimal initial component candidates. Component candidates at a sub-class-level (e.g. inner classes or methods) are intentionally not supported by SoMoX for a number of reasons:

i) The selected minimal abstraction level forces abstraction, while sub-class-level components would result in very fine-grained architectures,

ii) the identification of methods or inner classes interface's is unclear, since they do not posses an explicit interface notion, and

iii) such components made from methods or inner classes would not be units of independent deployment since they depend on their outer classes.

Both strategies (immediate transform and merging via metrics) have been realised during the development of SoMoX. Both strategies create reasonable component abstractions but the "merging via metrics" strategy proved to be more flexible. This strategy is configurable and can behave like the immediate transformation when lowering the probability of merging. Especially for larger systems, low abstraction level components help little in understanding a software system and at the same time lower the abstraction level of behaviour reverse engineering. Therefore, the strategy "merging via metrics" was finally selected to best fit the requirements.

Interface Adherence Interface adherence is based on the interface violation metric. Interface adherence highlights component candidates with a clear interface communication style. The interface adherence strategy checks whether components candidates are coupled at the code level prior to indicating interface communication. If a component candidate is not coupled at the code level, from the perspective of interfaces, all communication would use interfaces but no communication can be present. Thus, if no coupling is present, interface adherence also results in a low rating. In all other cases, interface adherence is derived from interface violations.

$$InterfaceAdherence(A, B) :=$$
$$\begin{cases} 1 - max(IV(A, B), IV(B, A)) & \text{if } max(Coupling(A, B), \\ & \quad Coupling(B, A)) > \epsilon \\ 0 & \text{else} \end{cases}$$

with $IV(A, B)$ being $InterfaceViolation(A, B)$ as define above. Coupling is not commutative. Therefore, the maximum coupling value is used which indicates the highest coupling present within the component candidate. The check for coupling is performed using an ϵ environment to overcome numeric limitations.

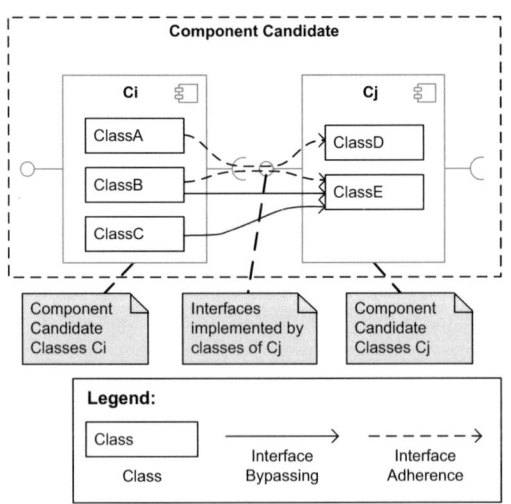

Figure 4.9.: Example: Interface adherence and bypassing

Figure 4.9 visualises a component candidate whose classes partially communicate using interfaces (dashed line). Other communication is bypassing the interfaces (solid line between classes). In the example, the classes A, B, and C on the left hand side access classes on the right hand side (classes D and E).

Interface Bypassing Interface bypassing is based on the interface violation metric. While components should externally communicate through interfaces, internally no interface communication is required. Instead, communication bypassing interfaces indicates the need to merge a component candidate. Interface bypassing indicates when to merge or compose a component. Interface violations are only considered as serious if the classes of a component candidate are coupled at the code level.

$$
InterfaceBypassing(A, B) :=
\begin{cases}
max(IV(A, B), IV(B, A)) & \text{if } max(Coupling(A, B), \\
 & Coupling(B, A)) > \epsilon \\
0 & \text{else}
\end{cases}
$$

with $IV(A, B)$ being $InterfaceViolation(A, B)$ as define above. Interface bypassing should not be mixed up with interface violation as the latter does not respect coupling.

Consistent Naming Consistent naming indicates that the names of classes of a component candidate have similarities. Component developers tend to name classes of components according to naming schemes. For example classes realising an accounting component could be named AccountingInitialisation, AccountingInfrastructure, and AccountingRegistration. Since naming schemes are not necessarily formal, deviations must be handled. The basic metric name resemblance, which is used in this context, is sufficiently flexible to account for loose naming conventions.

$$
CNRaw(A, B) :=
\begin{cases}
NameResemblance(A, B) & \text{if } max(Coupling(A, B), \\
 & Coupling(B, A)) > \epsilon \\
0 & \text{else}
\end{cases}
$$

The consistent naming strategy only applies if A and B from the component candidate are actually coupled at the code level. This avoids seeing classes of a component candidate being related because of accidental naming clashes. For example ContractingInitialisation is not necessarily related to AccountingInitialisation.

The raw consistent naming value is non-linearly mapped to the consistent naming value

$$
ConsistentNaming(A, B) := NonLinearMapping_{naming}(CNRaw(A, B))
$$

with

$$NonLinearMapping_{naming}(x) := \begin{cases} 1.0 & \text{if } 1.0 \geq x > 0.8 \\ 0.9 & \text{if } 0.8 \geq x > 0.6 \\ 0.7 & \text{if } 0.6 \geq x > 0.5 \\ 0 & \text{else} \end{cases}$$

Since names of classes can only be the same in special cases (different packages), the non-linear mapping helps to boost candidates which comprise mostly similar names. At the same time, only partially related names are rejected for identifying components. As the consistent naming metric could be misleading otherwise, the non-linear mapping is important to limit the impact of naming on componentisation. The boundaries and assigned values are kept configurable; the presented values represent defaults. The general guideline when configuring the non-linear mapping is to prefer similarly named classes and reject little similarly named classes as components.

An alternative to the discrete mapping steps would be a continuous function. The disadvantage of a continuous function is the complexity of configuring it as human. When aiming at a certain effect, such continuous functions (e.g. a gamma distribution [Lin93]) have parameters which are hard to guess.

Abstract/Concrete Balance   The abstract/concrete balance strategy reuses the composite basic metric Distance from the Main Sequence (DMS). It is universally applicable to rate the quality of a component. The balance of abstract and concrete elements of a component help ensuring extendability of a component and at the same prohibits components which comprise extension mechanisms only.

$$AbstractConcreteBalance(A, B) := DMS(A, B)$$

Abstract/concrete balance lifts DMS metric to the strategy level. The DMS metric is currently not extended for this.

Hierarchy Mapping   The hierarchy mapping strategy combines the package mapping and directory mapping metrics to gain a language-independent component detection mechanism which evaluates the adherence of component candidates to hierarchies expressed in packages and directories. The idea behind this strategy is that developers tend to place classes of components in a hierarchical structure.

$HierarchyMapping(A, B) :=$

$$\begin{cases} PackageMapping(A, B) & \text{for Java-based systems} \\ DirectoryMapping(A, B) & \text{for C-based systems} \\ \frac{w_{DM} \cdot DirectoryMapping(A,B) + w_{PM} \cdot PackageMapping(A,B)}{2} & \text{C++-based systems/} \\ & \text{systems using} \\ & \text{packages and} \\ & \text{directories} \end{cases}$$

with w_{DM} and w_{PM} in $[0..1]$ being adjustable weights typically set to 1.0 each. As neither package nor directory structure can be preferred in general. For Java-based systems, the evaluation of packages is sufficient since directory and package structure correspond to each other. For other systems, using directory or package structures depends on the information available.

For other implementation technologies, this strategy can be further refined. For example, Python-based systems comprise modules which can be respected during analysis.

Subsystem Component   A subsystem component is identified using the natural subsystem metrics. To recall, the natural subsystem metric checked for a component candidate being placed inside a slice and layer of a software system organised in slices and layers. The aim of the subsystem component strategy is to convert natural subsystems to components of the result model.

$$SubsystemComponent(A, B) := \sqrt{NaturalSubsystem(A, B)}$$

Subsystem component is scaled compared to the natural subsystem metric by using the square root (cf. Figure 4.10). Natural subsystem is a strong indicator for components where also smaller values can contribute in detecting components which are consequently pushed.

The employment of the square root creates a smooth continuous function ($x = 1, y = 2$). Nevertheless, it could be replaced by other continuous functions which push small values further. Steeper functions are for example of the type

$$NaturalSubsystem(A, B)^{\frac{x}{y}}$$

where the parameters $x = 1$ and $y = 4$ are typical parameters which are suitable to steer the scale-up of small values.

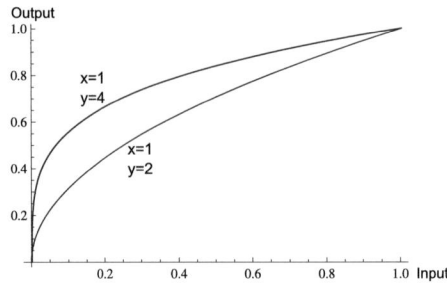

Figure 4.10.: SubsystemComponent scales small values of NaturalSubsystem

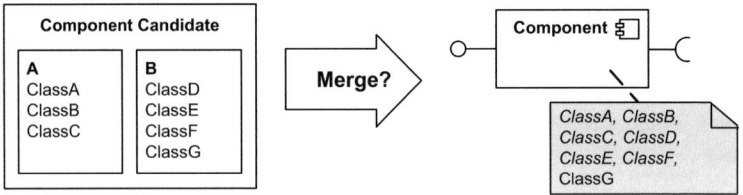

Figure 4.11.: The component merge strategy indicates when to merge the classes of a component candidate into a single component

Component Merge Component merge is a strategy which decides whether to merge the elements of a component candidate to a single component (see Figure 4.11). If applied, the classes of a component candidate become members of *one* component.

Merging is primarily applied in early iterations of reverse engineering to gain a higher abstraction level of basic components. Merging is also meaningful for later iterations, but becomes less important from iteration to iteration. At low levels, merging enables components having a non trivial initial abstraction level. In later iterations, especially helper and utility classes can be merged into existing components.

Imagine a helper class which is shared among only two low-level components. For these two separate components, the helper class cannot be assigned uniquely to one of these components. If in a later iteration these two components are composed into a single composite component, the previously non-assignable helper class would be tangling. In this case, the helper class should be merged into the composite component, since no accesses from other components exist at that abstraction level.

For later iterations, component merge avoids small helper components which comprise only one or very few classes. In early iterations, the base abstraction level can be significantly raised.

Figure 4.4 (page 67) provides an overview on sub-strategies which component merge involves. Component merge comprises *interface bypassing*, *consistent naming*, *hierarchy mapping*, and *abstract/concrete balance*. Of those sub-strategies, consistent naming, hierarchy mapping, and abstract/concrete balance are shared with component composition.

Component merge calculates an adaptable weighted score for every component candidate. If the dynamic "merge" threshold is exceeded, a component candidate is merged as explained in Section 4.5.

Component merge is defined as:

$$\begin{aligned} ComponentMerge(A, B) := (\ & w_{m1} \cdot InterfaceBypassing(A, B) + \\ & w_{m2} \cdot ConsistentNaming(A, B) + \\ & w_{m3} \cdot AbstractConcreteBalance(A, B) + \\ & w_{m4} \cdot HierarchyMapping(A, B) \\ &)/4 \end{aligned}$$

where $w_{m1..4} \in \mathbb{R} \ : \ 0 \leq w_{mx} \leq 1$ represent weights for each sub-strategy. Depending on the weights, the detection strategies can be adapted to system specifics. If for example, the naming of components is not very consistent, the according weight of the strategy can be lowered.

Component merge makes situations identifiable where classes of a component candidate are strongly coupled and internally communicate bypassing interfaces. Additionally, components are preferred which posses a consistent naming and reside in the same area of the system hierarchy.

Component Composition Component composition is the top-level strategy which is responsible for judging whether a component candidate should be converted into a composite component comprising sub-components from A and B (see Figure 4.12). The strategy prefers components which communicate via interfaces. This is the most important difference to the component merge strategy. Besides, as for components resulting from a merge operation, components are identified by naming, a balance of abstract and concrete elements, or alignment with the system hierarchy. In addition to the component merge strategy, the subsystem component strategy is used to identify composition scenarios. Since subsystem components can comprise multiple low-level components, only composite components use this strategy.

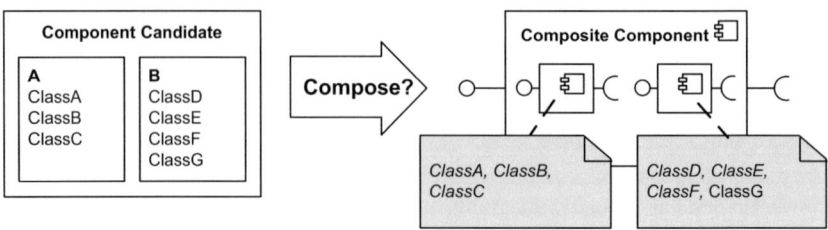

Figure 4.12.: The component composition strategy indicates when to create a new composite component from a component candidate

Figure 4.4 (page 67) provides an overview the sub-strategies which component composition involves. *Interface adherence, consistent naming, hierarchy mapping, abstract/concrete balance*, and *subsystem component* are used in component composition.

$$
\begin{aligned}
ComponentMerge(A, B) := (\ &w_{c1} \cdot InterfaceAdherence(A, B) + \\
&w_{c2} \cdot ConsistentNaming(A, B) + \\
&w_{c3} \cdot AbstractConcreteBalance(A, B) + \\
&w_{c4} \cdot HierarchyMapping(A, B) + \\
&w_{c5} \cdot SubsystemComponent(A, B) \\
&)/5
\end{aligned}
$$

where $w_{c1..5} \in \mathbb{R} : 0 \le w_{cx} \le 1$ represent weights for each sub-strategy. The weights can differ when comparing with the component merge strategy. For example, hierarchy mapping is an important strategy to identify high-level composite components. The hierarchy of a software system can carry information for high abstraction levels. Imagine two top-level components which reside in a common namespace and beyond that only differ in being held in two different source folders in the file system. Those components can be pure design entities which are not directly reflected in the source code. Thus, hints on their existence can be beneficial for high-level component detection.

The dynamic threshold for component composition, which is lowered over the iterations of reverse engineering, helps identifying high-level components which have only a weak manifestation in artefacts. Lower abstraction levels of components are ensured to not be skipped as the threshold is lowered only if no components have been found in an iteration. Hence, adding high-level abstractions does not squeeze lower abstraction levels out.

For high abstraction levels, consistent naming automatically becomes less important since large components with dozens of classes seldomly have a consistent naming scheme.

4.8.6. Interface Detection Strategies

Interface detection in SoMoX is based on a number of strategies which each represent a heuristic to identify component interfaces. SoMoX distinguished between class interfaces (e.g. indicated by the `interface` keyword in Java) and component interfaces (e.g. `ICustomerAccounting` of a business component), which are associated via component roles and represent functionality which is exposed at the component-level.

The strategies which will be presented in the following decide whether to turn a class interface into a component interface. The class interface must not necessarily correspond to a language feature "interface". For example abstract classes can also be interpreted as component interfaces. Vice versa, not every class interface must result in a component interface. Overall, there are four different main strategies (Section 4.8.6.1 to 4.8.6.4) which identify provided and required interfaces for basic components and for composite components. Figure 4.3 (page 66) visualises these strategies.

Generally, the interfaces of basic components are the superset of interfaces which become part of higher abstraction levels of a reverse engineered software architecture. For composite components it must be decided which interfaces shall be exposed as provided interface. This can only be a subset of inner component interfaces. For required interfaces of composite components, no other interfaces are exposed than the actually internally required ones. Since every composite component is ultimately built from basic components, the set of available interfaces is determined by basic components.

The following sections first deal with the recognition of interfaces for basic components. Second, the interface exposition for composite components is being discussed. For basic and composite components, the handling of provided and required interfaces is distuinguished.

4.8.6.1. Provided Interface Recognition for Basic Components

An architecture should be able to provide different abstractions of a software system (cf. [CBB+03]). Accordingly, interface recognition must be adaptable to different granularity levels. Interfaces can capture business aspects (e.g. user management, accounting) or infrastructure aspects (libraries, execution environment). Depending on the settings, it might be desirable to limit interfaces recognition. Vice versa, not every programming language provides means to specify interfaces or interfaces are not used in a certain system. SoMoX must also handle such cases.

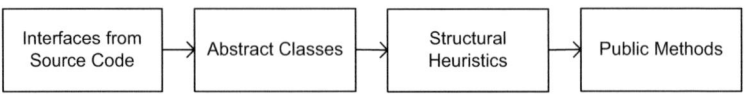

Figure 4.13.: Interface identification fallback strategies

The interface identification of SoMoX comprises multiple strategies which serve as fallback strategies if a major strategy fails. Figure 4.13 illustrates the strategy fallback where strategies on the right hand side serve as fallback for strategies next to them on the left. The strategies are organised as a chain of responsibility [GHJV95]. First, interfaces realised through source code constructs (e.g. Java interfaces) are going to be identified. If none of them are present for a single component, abstract classes are used and after that specific class structures (e.g. only virtual methods) and public methods. These sub-strategies will be discussed below.

Any identified interface is translated into a component interface and a provided role which associates the interface with the corresponding component. Interfaces can be shared among multiple components. SoMoX ensures that no interface is duplicated. If an interface already exists, only the provided role is created.

Language Interfaces In this strategy, interfaces reflected in underlying programming languages (e.g. Java interfaces) are identified as component interfaces. An interface is considered a component interface, if classes of the previously identified components implement it. The language interfaces strategy and all following strategies are binary decisions whether to consider a class interface as component interface.

Abstract Classes Comparable to the language interfaces strategy, the extends relation of source code identifies component interfaces in this strategy. Any abstract parent class of the classes realising a previously identified component is considered as component interface.

Class Structure Heuristics Besides language interfaces and abstract classes, heuristics can identify classes which are structured like interfaces. SoMoX realises a strategy which identifies classes with virtual methods only as component interfaces. Especially for C/C++ based systems, this strategy allows the identification of interface-like structures although no explicit interface notion is present in these languages.

Public Methods   The last fallback strategy is the interpretation of public methods as part of the component interface. This strategy can be applied even if no other interface notion is available. Components should always have provided interfaces, thus having a fallback strategy which ensures a provided interface for all cases like the presented is required.

External Documents   External documents (e.g. information from EJB deployment descriptors) can be used to identify component interfaces among the class interfaces. EJB interfaces can for example be used as component interfaces. The usage of external documents for identifying interfaces is also meaningful for languages such as C/C++ which by default have no explicit interface notion. Here, template libraries can be used to realise interfaces. The corresponding external artefacts then can be analysed to identify interfaces. Besides, interface definition languages (IDL, such as CORBA IDL [Obj07] or WSDL [CCMW01]) become analysable using this strategy. This strategy is currently not carried out by the SoMoX implementation.

Component Interface Service Identification   By default, all methods of a class interface become services of a component interface. Of the above identified elements (interfaces, classes), the identification of component services can differ. Using *all methods* is especially meaningful for interfaces which are declared in source code (e.g. the `interface` keyword) and abstract classes.

An alternative identification strategy is the use of only those methods which are *actually used* in a concrete architecture. This keeps the result model small. The drawback is the reduced genericness of reverse engineered components. Since only portions of the methods become part of the component interface, some services which are provided by a component are left out. In other scenarios, these services could be required but then would not be part of the component interface. This strategy helps reverse engineering the de-factor architecture which comprises only those architecture elements which are actually used in a software system. This is predominantly useful for understanding an architecture since only a limited scope of a system is reverse engineered. Employing only the actually used methods is preferably combined with the public methods strategy which, due to its fallback nature, tends to identify low-level methods as component services.

SoMoX realises the *all methods* strategy to reverse engineer potentially reusable components.

4.8.6.2. Required Interfaces Recognition for Basic Components

For required interfaces it is essential to decide whether to follow a strict interface communication style or to relax this architectural requirement. Additionally, one can distinguish business and infrastructure interfaces as with provided interfaces. The following basic strategies result from these requirements.

No Bypassing Any component-external communication must use component interfaces in this strategy. Bypassing an interface is not allowed. This strategy results in large required interfaces. Any call from classes of the considered component to classes of another component are therefore realised through a required interface.

Disregard Infrastructure Calls Infrastructure calls (calls to libraries and execution environments) are not captured in interfaces in this strategy. Only business interfaces are considered to be component interfaces. This strategy allows focusing on business functionality of components. Business interfaces are distinguished from infrastructure calls via the blacklisting mechanism which has been introduced in Section 4.8.4. Non-blacklisted interfaces are identified as business interfaces.

The aim of SoMoX is reverse engineering for the sake of performance predictions. Although infrastructure calls can be disregarded during architectural reverse engineering, the overall model integrity from the performance perspective can be ensured. The performance impact of infrastructure calls is therefore captured during reverse engineering of behaviour models. Infrastructure calls end up in `InternalActions` of the RDSEFF as will be detailed in see Section 5.16.

Allow Bypassing Using this strategy, bypassing required interfaces (not only infrastructure calls) is accepted. This results in component architectures which intentionally deviate from code. It can be used to reduce complexity and size of interfaces and communication structures. Additional heuristics are required to identify the interfaces which are kept in this strategy. This heuristic is project-specific and could be based on naming conventions or namespaces which are considered to be part/not part of the interface communication. SoMoX does not realise this strategy.

4.8.6.3. Provided Interface Exposition (for Composite Components)

For composite components it is questionable which interfaces of inner components should be exposed to the outside world. The exposed interfaces are a subset of the provided interfaces of the inner components which are contained in the composite component. Only directly contained (not transitively contained) interfaces are subject for exposition. Otherwise, the hierarchy of composite components could be broken.

Expose all inner Interfaces   Following this strategy, all interfaces of inner components of a composite component are exposed as provided interfaces.

Expose used inner Interfaces   This strategy exposes all inner interfaces which are actually used inside the composite component. The idea behind this strategy is that any interface which is successfully used as a component service internally, can also be used from outside the component.

Expose externally used Interfaces   Only interfaces which are actually used from outside a composite component are exposed in this strategy. This strategy helps reverse engineering a de-facto architecture which employs only interfaces which are used in a certain setting. The resulting architectures remain slim and by that can be of benefit for understanding software architectures. Still, the reuse of components which are reverse engineered using this strategy is limited as only portions of the full interface functionality are exposed by composite components. The strategy corresponds to the *actually used* strategy for the identification of component services.

4.8.6.4. Required Interface Exposition (for Composite Components)

To ensure model integrity, all inner required interfaces which are not internally connected *must* be exposed. Otherwise, some call destinations would be undefined in the model. Unlike for provided interfaces, exposing required interfaces which are already connected within a composite component generally is not feasible since it would blow up the required interface.

4.8.7. Connector Strategies

Connectors establish the control and data flow among components and must be established for all composite components. During their creation it is crucial to connect all required interfaces of components to ensure model integrity. Calls for a required service of a component must not end up in non-connected interfaces if a reverse engineered model is subject to performance analysis. Other reverse engineering approaches which aim at program understanding only, can either fully omit connectors or accept "dangling" interfaces without connectors attached. Figure 4.14 provides an overview for the different connector strategies.

De-facto Connectors   Assembly connectors should generally rely on de-facto connections among component interfaces. To establish assembly connectors, they can be derived from the graph structure. Since the graph structure has directed edges, the direction of connectors can be directly derived.

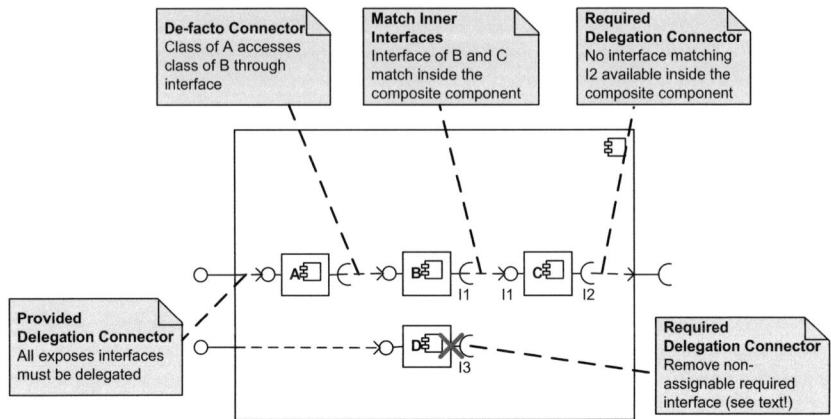

Figure 4.14.: Connector strategies overview

Not all dependencies among classes can be statically analysed (cf. [Ern03, NNH99]). Hence, dependency information of components can be incomplete. Advanced dependency analysis approaches can be of benefit for identifying dependencies which cannot be analysed with the employed SISSy approach which creates the GAST model. The results of these analyses would then be reflected in the graph structure and allow establishing further assembly connectors.

Match Inner Interfaces For cases of dynamic binding, dependency injection, and external connector definitions (e.g. EJB deployment descriptors) where no reliable information on assembly connectors can be made available using a certain tooling, the following heuristic can be used: If a couple of provided and required interfaces within a composite component matches (the interface associated by required and provided role are the same), composite component-internal connectors are preferable. This forces component-internal communication of composite components.

This heuristic might introduce assembly connectors which never occur at runtime. If multiple provided interfaces match for a single required interface, an arbitrarily selected provided interface becomes part of the assembly connector.

An advanced version of this heuristic (the advanced form has not been realised in this thesis), could use standard interface interoperability checks (e.g. [BOR04]) to determine valid matches of interfaces. For example, an required interface $I_{req} = \{service_1, service_2\}$ can be interoperable with an provided interface $I_{prov} = \{service_1, service_2, service_3\}$ although the interfaces are not equal. In the example, every service of the required interface has a counterpart at the provides side.

Required Delegation Connectors If an assembly connector cannot be established *inside* a composite component, a required delegation connector must be established. Thus, any required call will have a determined callee and model consistency is not harmed. For a composite component a required role with the corresponding interface is therefore added (if it has not been present before) and a required delegation connector connects the inner required role with the outer required role of the composite component.

This strategy implies that the outer required role must be bound transitively until either the "match inner interfaces" heuristic applies or the system boundary is reached. In the latter case, inner calls are delegated to required roles at the system boundary. Cases in which calls are delegated to system boundaries can for example happen if the system scope is limited and only portions of a software system have been reverse engineered of if calls of infrastructure services are considered as component services which are realised outside the system scope. To ensure model integrity, measured quality attributes must be specified for the services realised by system-external components (cf. Section 2.5).

Remove Required Interfaces An alternative strategy for required delegation connectors is the removal of required interfaces. If connectors for required interfaces cannot be established successfully, required interfaces can be deleted from components. This strategy ensures model integrity but has the major drawback that a component must account for the performance impact of external calls in `Internal-Actions`. The callees of external calls are generally unknown to components, thus the performance impact of external calls cannot be known in general. Furthermore, explicit dependency statements (the required interface) are neglected when applying this strategy. This strategy can only be applied if the assembly and allocation context of calling component and callee are fixed – and thus *cannot* be known during reverse engineering of reusable components. This strategy has not been realised in SoMoX.

Provided Delegation Connectors All exposed provided interfaces must be mapped to inner provided interfaces of components. Otherwise, model integrity would be violated. Hence, the creation of provided delegation connectors is a fixed mechanism not a strategy. The strategy to not expose all inner provided interfaces is not affected by this mechanism.

4.8.8. Characteristics of Target Components

This section summarises typical characteristics of components which are identified by the previously introduced strategies. Components, which are reversed engineered by SoMoX, have a subset of the following characteristics which are visualised in Figure 4.15:

93

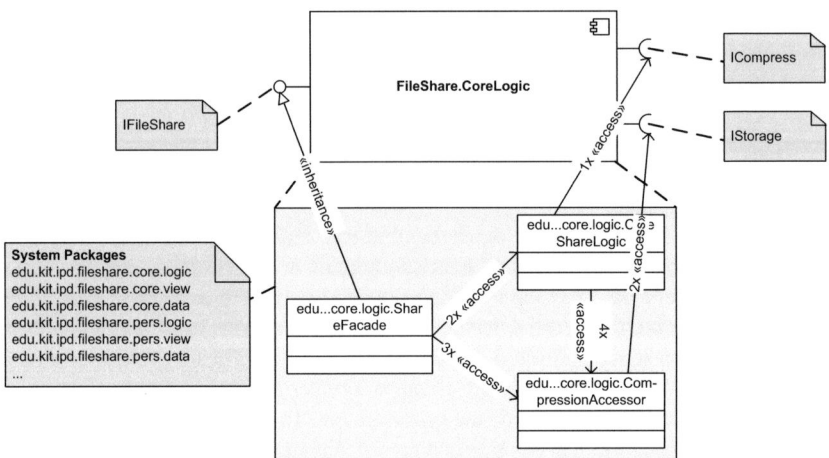

Figure 4.15.: Typical characteristics of a basic component in the source code

- Components communicate with other component using *interfaces*.

- Components possess a consistent *naming* of inner classes.

- Components have a common *code structure*.

- Components follow a component architecture which is organised in *layers and slices*.

- Components are *well-balanced* concerning abstract and concrete realising source code artefacts (i.e. interface, abstract classes, and implementing classes are balanced).

- Components have high *cohesion* in the source code.

4.8.9. Determining Weights

The SoMoX approach requires a number of weights to be calibrated. For example, the weights of the component merge and component composition strategy need to be specified when applying SoMOX. Meaningful weights are hard to guess for unexperienced users. Therefore, SoMoX provides two sets of default weights to ease the applicability of the approach. One set serves as a starting point for Java-based systems, the other for C/C++-based systems. For example the absence of interfaces in C requires an adaption of weights for interface communications strategies.

The default weights have been determined when reverse engineering a number of reference projects. For these projects, the reference architecture was known. During various iterations, the default weights have been adapted to provide a baseline for multiple projects. Weights were adapted until satisfactory results could be achieved (i.e. a large ratio of reference components has been detected when using SoMoX).

For the application of SoMoX, the default weights serve as a starting point. Then, the weights can be optionally adapted to match specific project needs (e.g. no strict interface communication required). By adapting the weights, component detection strategies can be emphasized or neglected. In any case, for every reverse engineering project, a scope and optionally blacklists have to be defined. Furthermore, name pre and post fixes can be set for name resemblance. This makes SoMoX broadly customisable and adaptable to project-specific needs. It must be emphasized that weights do not aim at encoding any static structures to be detected into a reverse engineering run. Weights purely express preferences which strategies to apply and hence what kinds of characteristics the target model is supposed to possess.

The calibration of weights and metrics is part of the validation in Section 7.

4.9. Ensuring Integrity

The architectural reverse engineering approach is explicitly designed to ensure integrity of reverse engineered models. Model integrity subsumes that all mandatory model attributes and relations are set and all constraints defined on the model are fulfiled. The PCM carries a number of built-in constraints. Furthermore, all model constraints defined by the performance simulation (cf. definition in SimuCom [Bec08b]) must hold. Only models with full integrity can be analysed for performance and the reverse engineering of behaviour models (cf. Section 5) is only applicable for valid models. Otherwise, model semantics would be broken, e.g. dangling references prevent interpreting a model as an execution description of a software system. Hence, for the strategies from the previous section, it has been pointed out how model integrity was ensured. SoMoX grants integrity for reverse engineered models.

Model integrity also helps users to understand a software system. Especially, if the control flow and data flow of systems is investigated manually, entities which have just high cohesion and low coupling (cf. [MM06] for an evaluation of cohesion and coupling metrics) are not sufficient. These entities usually do not conform to what is expected to be an *architectural* entity like a component.

4.10. Extendability of the SoMoX Approach

The SoMoX approach is held extensible with respect to metrics, strategies, and input data. When extending SoMoX, source code information must be related to the GAST input model as stated in Section 4.7 but is not limited to the information available in the GAST. Possible extensions include the support of Spring or EJB deployment descriptors.

An extension has two options to enrich input data:

- **Update GAST information.** Following this kind of extension, additional information (e.g. binding among classes established via dependency injection) is used to update GAST class access information. The information on existing and additional GAST classes is represented by the GAST only. Existing metrics and strategies in this case evaluate the additional information such as any other GAST model elements of a non-updated GAST model.

- **Create an GAST decorator model with additional information.** This option requires the creation of a GAST decorator model and corresponding metrics and strategies which evaluate the decorator model. Since for example Spring and EJB have their own notion of components, it can be beneficial to explicitly handle this information on components during metric evaluation and application of strategies. If for example a number of classes is identified as EJB component, the decorator model can hold the information on the classes participating in an EJB component. New metrics and strategies can then prefer EJB components when converting component candidates into components. Comparable extensions are also imaginable for interfaces, which can be identified as EJB interfaces through a decorator. The interface creation strategies could then prefer EJB interfaces as component interfaces.

For both options, metrics and strategies still evaluate component candidates. Thus, their results are first always mapped to the graph structure and then to the SAMM architecture model representation. New metrics and strategies can seamlessly integrate with existing ones.

Generally, the reverse engineering process of SoMoX can start with an (unlimited) number of source code analysis approaches. They operate on input source code and either update the GAST model or create the instance of a GAST decorator. Analyses can be both static or dynamic analysis approaches. The design of the SoMoX approach does not require modifications in order to support further analysis approaches.

Further options for extending the SoMoX approach are presented in Section 9.11. Klatt [Kla08] discusses the general extendability of SoMoX.

4.11. Complexity and Scalability

SoMoX incorporates several performance optimisations and heuristics to improve scalability. Systems with a size of more than 250,000 LOC are supposed to be supported. Please note that there is no strong correlation between LOC and complexity of the reverse engineering, as not the LOC but the number of classes and the number of relations among classes are more important for the execution time. Also, chosen strategies influence the complexity at run time because for example naming-based strategies are more computation intensive than others. Furthermore, due to scoping not all classes of a system are evaluated. Blacklisted classes have no influence on the execution time and thus reduce complexity.

One important optimisation SoMoX applies, is concerned with what is evaluated by metrics. As the calculation of metrics is very time-consuming, metrics within SoMoX are evaluated only for component candidate *tuples* (as already introduced above in Section 4.5). This allows to dramatically reduce the number of required metric and strategy evaluations, while the composition and merge phase can still use transitivity properties of metrics to create components of more than one element. For reasons of brevity, hereafter metrics will subsumed strategies.

Metrics need to be re-calculated from iteration to iteration – but only if a component candidate has changed since the last iteration. Imagine an iteration comprising 10 classes of which two are merged into a new component. Most classes are potentially not affected by the component merge and metrics related to these classes should not be re-calculated non-necessarily. SoMoX determines those vertices of its graph structure which need to be re-calculated. Only graph vertices which are adjacent to changed edges are recalculated in SoMoX.

Dependency Analysis For metrics, interdependencies can also be used for optimisations. In SoMoX, metrics explicitly state their dependencies. A metric which another metric relies on can be seen as a precondition of the depending metric. SoMoX analyses the dependencies (for example multiple metrics can depend on a single basic metric), and calculates in which order to execute them. Depending metrics are then only evaluated if the basic metrics return a non-*null* result. An example for such a case are two classes that are residing in distinct packages without any relation among them. If it is already known for packages that there are no relations, this must not be checked again for classes of these packages.

The metrics themselves decide whether to interpret a result as a *null* result. The decentralisation of termination logic is required as it generally cannot be know how sub-metrics are used by a metric (e.g. name resemblance must only be evaluated if a certain threshold different from *null* holds for coupling). If a termination criterion holds for a sub-metric, the depending metric can return a *null* value as well. Dependency cycles are assumed to be avoided by metric developers.

Parallelisation SoMoX is designed to allow parallelisation. In each iteration, the computation of metrics is largely independent from other metric calculations, besides the stated dependencies. Furthermore, the metrics for each tuple can be calculated fully independently from each other. Systems have a total of n^2 component candidates which need to evaluated, where n is the number of classes after the application of blacklisting and scoping. From iteration to iteration, the number of component candidates gets reduced. Hence, the first iteration is most computation intensive since additionally, *all* metrics for *all* component candidates need to be calculated. The number of component candidates is falling monotonically, while the size of component candidates is monotonically rising.

Synchronisations (which are limiting the parallelisation) are required:

- After each iteration before applying the weakly connected component detection on the graph structure and

- For dependent metrics, sub-metrics which a metric depends on must be finished prior to evaluating the metric.

In the realised parallelisation, all metrics for one component candidate are calculated in parallel. Thus, the metric calculation for *one* component candidate is not split among multiple threads to avoid overly small working units and to reduce synchronisation overhead. The maximum degree of parallelisation is n^2 which makes the calculations parallelisation applicable for many core CPUs. The limited need for sychronisation makes the approach applicable for distributed execution scenarios.

Results of a metric calculation can be written to distinct "cells" (the edges) of the resulting graph structure. Thus, write conflicts cannot occur when building the graph in an adjacent matrix graph data structure which holds only the edges.

The chosen solution requires to have the GAST model and the resulting adjacent matrix in memory to enable fast data accesses. In former versions of SoMoX (see also Section 4.12) database queries were used to access the GAST data structure, which turned out to be heavily limiting the overall performance (due to I/O latency and database query overhead). This solution had enabled holding GAST structures larger than the main memory, but implied very expensive data queries. For nowadays computers, the amount of main memory is sufficient to hold a GAST representation together with the resulting graph structure and the internal architecture model for software projects with much more than 1 MLOC. SoMoX is capable of fully utilising CPU power. The validation Section 7 will further detail on typical execution times.

The calculation of weakly connected components is taken over by a third party library (JGraphT, [Bar10]) which is not included into this scalability discussion. The complexity of this calculation is larger for early iterations since the graph structure only represents the component candidates of the latest iteration.

Overall Complexity Estimation The worst case complexity of a single iteration is

$$O(n^2)$$

with n being the number of classes of a system. The first iteration is the most computation intensive one due to the large number of component candidates. The evaluation of a single iteration is dominated by the computation of metrics.

The validation in Section 7 will further report on the scalability of the SoMoX approach and name typical processing times for case studies.

4.12. Realisation

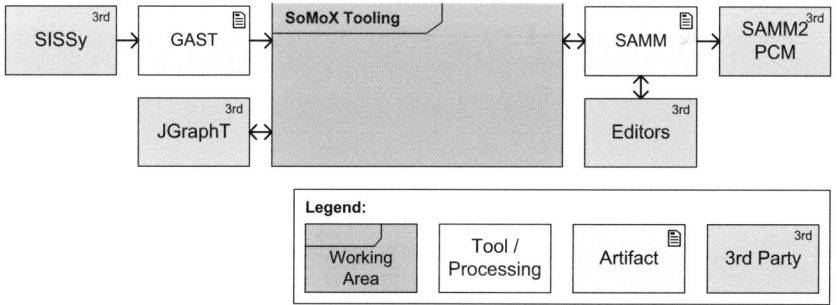

Figure 4.16.: Overview on third party integration of SoMoX

The implementation of the SoMoX (cf. Figure 4.16) approach has been carried out in the context of the EU project Q-ImPrESS. SoMoX is fully integrated in a platform for reverse engineering, performance, maintainability, and reliability prediction of service-oriented and thus component-based software systems. This platform allows to evaluate different design alternatives for their specific advantages and drawbacks. Hence, the results of SoMoX are used as a base for reliability and maintainability predictions, which extends the application scope of SoMoX. Q-ImPrESS contributes graphical and tree-based editors for the SAMM which can be used for SoMoX. The Q-ImPrESS tooling (including SoMoX) is based on Eclipse.

The SoMoX tooling [Som10] is a complete rewrite of an earlier implementation of the approach called ArchiRec [Cho07]. Compared to the SoMoX tooling, ArchiRec was limited with respect to extendability and scalability. Furthermore, ArchiRec relied on the proprietary Sotograph [helc] tool while SoMoX employs the open source tool SISSy [TS05] for source code analysis.

SoMoX is realised as an Eclipse feature comprising various plugins. All plugins are integrated into the Q-ImPrESS tooling. SoMoX contributes its own Eclipse run configuration which integrates into the Q-ImPrESS run dialogs. Design alternatives can be directly selected from the Q-ImPrESS run dialogs.

SoMoX possesses an EMF-based core model (the SAMM), and relies on models being present as EMF models (such as the GAST model and the PCM model). It makes heavy use of scalable EMF-based filters and queries. SoMoX intentionally resigns the use of a database as its predecessor implementation ArchiRec showed performance problems due to the use of a database. All data is held in-memory in SoMoX to allow for fast computations.

JGraphT [Bar10] is used as graph library which holds component candidate weights. Futhermore, it contributes the algorithm for the detection of weakly connected components.

To transform the internal SAMM model into an instance of the PCM, SoMoX employs the so-called "SAMM2PCM" transformation [Cia10] which is based on QVT-O. It converts components, interfaces, and connectors from the SAMM meta-model into the PCM meta-model.

4.13. Limitations and Assumptions

Besides the assumptions listed in Section 4.7 (the target architecture must be a component architecture, the source code must represent a component-based architecture, and input must be mapped to GAST model) a few further assumptions and limitations apply to SoMoX. The remaining limitations are caused by the fact that SoMoX relies on the static analysis performed by SISSy.

4.13.1. Dynamic Binding

The GAST representation is created by SISSy from C/C++, Delphi or Java code. SISSy has no capabilities to deal with dynamic binding. This frequent limitation to many static analysis approaches (see for example [NNH99, Ern03]) is also present for SISSy and thus inherited by SoMoX. If classes are bound dynamically, SISSy will only recognise a dependency to the static type (typically an interface) but not an implementing class bound dynamically. Without extending SoMoX (cf. Section 4.10), required and provided interfaces can be correctly recognised but connectors must be established via heuristics. If the binding is ambiguous (e.g. calls are actually delegated to an external component and not to a component which is providing the same interface inside the analysed software system), heuristics can possibly delegate to the wrong component.

4.13.2. Single Instance per Component Type

SoMoX cannot deal with multiple instances of a single component type. Each component type is assumed to have only a single instance (assembly context). This limitation is induced by the assignment of each class to a single component only and the assumptions that there is a 1:1 relation between component types and component instances.

4.13.3. No Dynamic Architecture

SoMoX assumes a static architecture which does not change at runtime. If architectures are changing at runtime, i) dynamic binding cannot be resolved and ii) potential states of the static architecture are not supported (neither by SISSy, SoMoX nor the SAMM and PCM models).

5. Reverse Engineering Behavioural Models

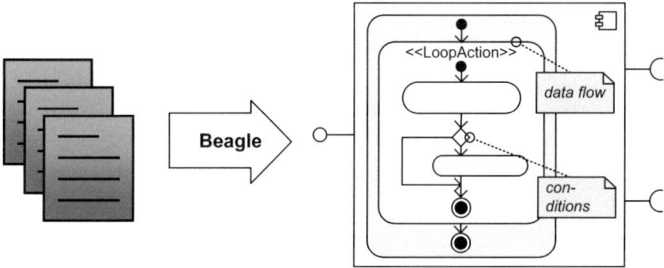

Figure 5.1.: The *Beagle* approach reverse engineers behavioural models of component services

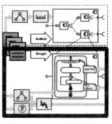

After the static architecture of the system has been reverse engineered, the behaviour of each provided service of a component must be reverse engineered to allow performance predictions. A static architecture without information on behaviour can help understanding a software system. Performance predictions, nevertheless, require a model with execution semantics.

Reverse engineering behaviour models for the sake of later performance simulations and design space exploration requires a semantically rich output model (result model of the reverse engineering approach) with execution semantics. In the context of this thesis, the role of the output model is taken over by RDSEFFs of the Palladio Component Model. Thus, the behaviour model dealt with in this thesis is a design-level performance model for component performance (hereafter referred to simply as *behaviour model*). Design-level means that no low-level performance model such as a queuing network is used. For example, queuing networks represent performance effects at a low level and thus disallow easily recognizing software components. Instead, the targeted behaviour model of the presented approach from this thesis is aware

103

of components to allow reflecting changes in a component's architecture also in the behaviour model. For example, when comparing two design alternatives, the Palladio Component Model allows the selection of that component where internal computations (behaviour) of a component are executed the fastest.

The need of Reverse Engineering Components If reverse engineering does not account for components, the resulting behaviour model does not allow for deriving architectural design decisions. Such a model which is not aware of components becomes fully "fixed" with respect to design decisions which depend on the component structure. Imagine a reverse engineering approach which merges two components, which are running on the same machine, into a single node of a low-level performance model. In such a setting it becomes impossible to exchange a single component by another since each component's performance impact cannot be distinguished from the impact of another component. It becomes obvious that a design-level behaviour model must explicitly deal with components in order to support architectural design decisions. The various influencing factors (see also Section 2.8) which must be respected by a component behaviour model will be discussed further below in the context of reverse engineering.

The need of Parameterisation To understand the requirements for a reverse engineering approach for such behaviour models, one must first understand the shortcomings of a naïve reverse engineering approach for behaviour models. A straightforward naïve reverse engineering approach could first benchmark an application using a test driver, and then create a look-up table containing the average response times for each provided service of that component. For performance prediction, such a model could simply return a measured value from the look-up table (see left part of Figure 5.3). While this model can result in very precise performance values, the prediction capabilities are limited: The resulting model is largely inflexible due to the absence of any parameterisation. Only the setting which has previously been measured can be directly predicted.

If such a model is for example used for a setting where a component under study is connected to a different required component with a lower response time than during the initial measurements for building the model, the performance impact of the newly connected component cannot be predicted. The lookup table could not predict any changes in the model and keeps predicting measured values.

Generally, components must be parameterised over usage, assembly, and execution context as introduced in Section 2.6. After introducing a motivating example which illustrates why parameterisation is required at all, means for parameterisation over all contexts are introduced in the remainder of this chapter.

Figure 5.2 introduces the BusinessLogicComponent of an example file sharing application. The component provides the services uploadFile(..) and requires the

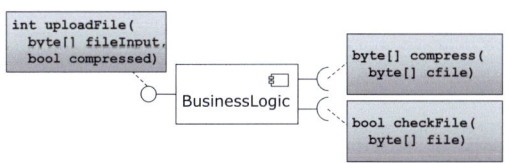

Figure 5.2.: Example: Business logic component

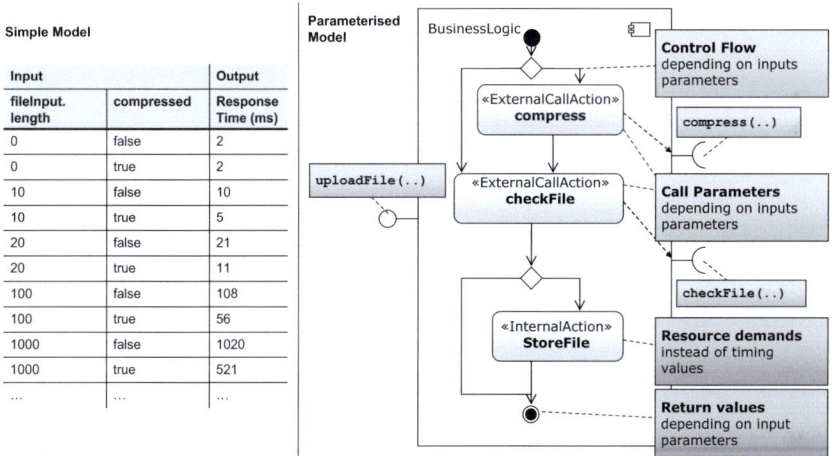

Figure 5.3.: Example: Simple lookup table model (left) vs. parameterised model with explicit control and data flow (right)

two services compress(..) and checkFile(..). When comparing a simple lookup table model and a parameterised model for this component (see Figure 5.3), the advantages of a parameterised model become obvious: The prediction capabilities of the simple model are rather limited. The lookup table can only predict the response time of the uploadFile service for given input parameters. For example, the response time for intermediate values (e.g. byte size fileInput.length = 500) must be approximated from values for a length of 100 and 1000 bytes. Overall, the lookup table would become very large for many input parameters since the cross product of parameter values must be captured.

Further limitations of the simple example model include:

- If the concurrency level or resource contention change (e.g. caused by concurrently active components and concurrently active users on the same hardware), the model does not reflect this impact.

- Which component services (i.e. compress and checkFile) are called, when and how often is not captured. If, for example, the performance of the compress service itself depends on its load (i.e. frequency of calls), the performance of that service cannot be correctly predicted as the load is not part of the simple model.

- Call parameters are not propagated to other components (if users upload larger files, the effects on the compress and checkFile service are not captured).

- The return value of the uploadFile service is not specified. If for example the return value of uploadFile indirectly depends on the return value of check-File, this cannot be expressed in the lookup table.

- As introduced above, when changing the assembly context, the performance impact cannot be predicted (e.g. exchanging the component providing the compress service by a faster one would likely impact the response time of the uploadFile service which the simple model cannot reflect).

Figure 5.6 provides a more detailed view on the behaviour model of the parameterised model.

To not contradict the component definition by Szyperski from Section 2.9, a component behaviour model must be *parameterised*. Otherwise, a component would have implicit context dependencies resulting in limited reusability and third-party composition.

A component behaviour model which acts as surrogate for a component implementation during performance predictions must account for the following parameters which cannot be assumed to be fixed for components (see right hand side of Figure 5.3):

- The impact of changes in the usage context must be reflected since the number of users, the behaviour of users (which services are called in which order), and the usage parameters (e.g. number and size of uploaded files to a file sharing service) can change. A behaviour model must not assume a fixed usage of a component.

- A fixed execution environment (including middleware and hardware environment) cannot be assumed by a behaviour model in order to support sizing and relocation scenarios. In general, a component can only make fundamental assumptions on its execution environment, e.g. the presence of a x86 processor and an implementation of a Java EE middleware. The concrete specification (e.g. processor speed "3.0 GHz" or middleware implementation "JBoss 5") cannot be assumed to be fixed for a component.

- Which actual components are connected to a component is not fixed for a component. Components are units of third party reuse and thus connected components should not be assumed to be fixed.

- Input parameters of component service generally have a continuous range. A reverse engineering approach needs to deal with the full range of input parameter values a component can process.

Since all of the above three contexts (cf. Section 2.8) cannot be assumed to be fixed, the impact of changing them must be explicitly reflected in a behaviour model. A behaviour model of a component should be usable along with a component without implying changes to the model. If one would need to adapt the behaviour model of a component for every change in the context of a component, it would become infeasible to perform model-based performance predictions. Thus, the naïve reverse engineering approach described above is not sufficient for performance prediction. A component behaviour model must be parameterised as pointed out.

5.1. Shortcomings of Existing Approaches

Existing approaches in the field of reverse engineering of behaviour models are limited with respect to a number of aspects which are realised in the Beagle approach:

- No parameterised control and data flow is reverse engineered (e.g. [CDH$^+$00, BLL06, HMWR99, CW00]).

- The output models have no execution semantics (e.g. [BLL06, WAW04b, WAW04a]).

- The resulting models possess no performance abstraction (e.g. [BLL06, WAW04b, WAW04a]).

- No component support. The behaviour model is not a component behaviour model (e.g. [Ros06, HMWR99]).

The following section will briefly summarise the shortcomings of existing approaches and relate the Beagle approach to them. The full related work is covered in Section 8.3.

Pure static analysis approaches [NNH99] like symbolic execution [Kin76, CC77] cannot deal with complex code structures (e.g. variable values which are manipulated inside loops) when determining parametric dependencies. In those cases at most approximations of real parametric dependencies can be reverse engineered. Other programme analysis approaches like slicing (e.g. static [Wei81, Luc01, SRK06] or dynamic [AH90]) do not provide sufficient information for creating stochastic expressions which represent parametric dependencies. Slicing, for example, does not qualify the relation between variables. In its classical form, it only establishes a binary relation, which indicates which programme statements are within one slice, with respect to a slicing criterion (e.g. a variable declaration). While such techniques proved helpful for debugging, information flow control, or maintenance [Luc01] (among others), they cannot directly contribute for parametric dependencies. See Section 9.11 for a further discussion on how to integrate slicing information into the developed approach.

Dynamic analysis approaches like [Rei08, BLL06, ECGN01] can lead to imprecisions due to the naturally limited coverage of control and data flow which can be monitored at runtime with a finite number of test cases and within finite time. Parts of a programme which are not monitored during execution (e.g. seldom execution paths), cannot be found by dynamic analysis approaches. Still, they are well-suited to represent frequent program executions. Cornelissen et al. [CZvD⁺09] provide a summary on dynamic program understanding approaches.

Statistic analyses [HL00] like linear regression [SLS77] often have no support for non-continuous behaviour which results from branches in code (i.e. if-then-else). Only few approaches like multivariate adaptive regression splices [Fri91] support non-continuous behaviour. Furthermore, regression approaches have limited support for steering abstractions. Specifically performance abstractions have limited supported. Jain [Jai91] further discusses regression approaches in the context of performance analysis.

Regression approaches are complemented by machine learning approaches which cover, among others, statistics, neural networks, and fuzzy logic. See [CM98] for a review. Still, these approaches are no software engineering approaches and thus not designed for component support or performance analysis. Yet, they provide a substantial base for the reverse engineering of parametric dependencies which will be utilised in the Beagle approach.

Ernst [Ern03] proposed the integration of static and dynamic analysis in 2003, but no approach currently combines the individual advantages of static, dynamic, and stochastic analysis. The Beagle approach tries to overcome the individual limitations of each analysis field by combining them. The combination is performed by Genetic Programming (GP, [Koz93, BNKF98]). The weaknesses of strength of static, dynamic, and stochastic analysis are balanced in it. If for example static analysis approaches refuse the analysis of certain source code, dynamic and statistical analyses can be used for this source code. Vice versa, if static analysis can provide fast and precise reverse engineering, the convergence speed for a reverse engineering model can be increased.

The individual limitations, the comparison to the Beagle approach, and further related approaches will be discussed in detail in the related work Section 8.3.

5.2. Scientific Challenges

The major scientific challenges for the reverse engineering of behaviour models are:

i) How to reverse engineer parameterised behaviour models of components maintaining usage, assembly, and allocation context independence in the result model?

(This challenge corresponds to requirement *R-Context* and *R-Resource Demands* from Section 5.4.)

ii) How to automatically create software component behaviour models which represent performance abstractions?

(This challenge corresponds to requirement *R-Abstraction* from Section 5.4.)

iii) How to seamlessly integrate static, dynamic, and statistical analysis techniques for reverse engineering to overcome the limitations of each single approach (e.g. data flow analysis for very large systems using static analysis; or the runtime complexity of dynamic approaches)?

(This challenge corresponds to requirement *R-Abstraction* and *R-Integration* from Section 5.4.)

For i) this includes challenges on how to create behaviour models for components instead of low-level constructs like classes or methods. Some additional challenges must also be mastered: how to create behaviour models which balance precision, simulation efficiency, and understandability for humans.

Figure 5.4 illustrates the various inputs the approach for ii) must be able to handle when creating a behaviour model. It is desirable to include existing reverse engineering approaches and combine them.

Further scientific challenges will be discussed in Section 5.11 in the context of genetic programming which was selected as a integration technique for static, dynamic and statistical analysis and also contributes to dynamic analysis.

5.3. Contributions in Reverse Engineering of Behaviour Models

The reverse engineering approach for behaviour models which has been developed in this thesis, fulfills the above stated requirements and thereby contributes to the field of reverse engineering of behaviour models. The developed approach pioneers in reverse engineering software component behaviour models which are independent of usage, assembly, and allocation context and at the same time enable performance predictions without any manual effort for modeling static architecture or component behaviour.

Furthermore, the approach provides a general mechanism for the integration of static, dynamic, and statistical analysis by means of genetic programming. To push the abilities of dynamic analysis further and make dynamic analysis aware of components, a dynamic analysis approach for software component behaviour has been developed. This dynamic analysis allows instrumentation of source code at the level of components to overcome unnecessary low-level monitoring at an object-oriented class level and by that lowers the number of monitoring points. Furthermore, the dynamic analysis supports monitoring of distributed systems, and is capable of capturing parameter characterisations according to the specification of component interfaces.

Genetic programming was extended to allow a seamless combination of static, dynamic, and statistical analyses for creating behaviour models. The developed approach is generally capable to integrate multiple reverse engineering approaches through genetic programming and further optimise the input of each reverse engineering approach. For genetic programming, optimisation criteria have been developed. They support the creation of *abstract* behaviour models.

Through its contributions, this thesis helps answering questions on how to integrate multiple reverse engineering approaches – especially the convergence of static and dynamic analyses – which has been identified as a challenge by Ernst in [Ern03]. Specifically, the presented approach helps to understand how to create parameterised and thus context-independent [BHK06] behaviour models which are at the same time simulatable performance abstractions of components.

The developed reverse engineering approach for behaviour models is called Beagle (BEhaviour Analysis using Genetic Learning and Evolution), named after the sailing ship "HMS Beagle". On a survey voyage from 1831 to 1836, the naturalist Charles Darwin was on board of "HMS Beagle". Darwin's work finally made the Beagle one of the most famous ships in history.

5.4. Requirements for Reverse Engineering of Behaviour Models

For the reverse engineering of component behaviour models, a number of requirements have to be fulfilled, which are derived from the scientific challenges and contributions:

- *R-Integration* The approach should be able to combine the specific advantages of static, dynamic and statistical analysis and hence overcome the limitations of each single approach.

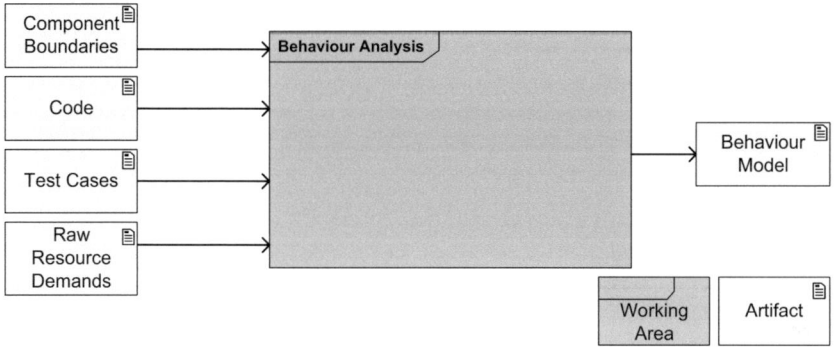

Figure 5.4.: Setting for the reverse engineering of behavioural models

Figure 5.4 visualises the various information sources which should be considered during reverse engineering of behaviour models. In this step, the component boundaries as recognised by the architectural reverse engineering from Section 4 are assumed to be given. The component boundaries determine the desired abstraction level for the behaviour model. Since static and dynamic analysis are to be carried out during this step, the source code of an application and test cases for the application under study must be provided to the behaviour reverse engineering.

- *R-Context* The output model must be parameterised over all three contexts introduced in Section 2.8.

The counterexample of a reverse engineering approach for behaviour models in the previous Section 5 imposes some minimal requirements for an improved approach: A reverse engineering approach for behaviour models which is suitable for performance analysis must account for the varying contexts a component is faced with.

- *R-Resource Demands* The approach must be able to integrate and approximate platform-independent resource demands.

The reverse engineering approach must be able to integrate resource demands of software components (e.g. executed instructions on a CPU or executed instructions of a virtual machine) to parameterise over the execution environment. The resource demand must be expressed in a parameterised form to account for its dependencies to the usage and assembly context. For this thesis, it is assumed that for each "section" of component behaviour raw resource demands are provided by a separate approach which is not covered by this thesis. The

ByCounter [KKR08b] tool is for example capable of counting executed byte code instructions at runtime and can be used for gathering raw resource demands.

- *R-Abstraction* The reverse engineering approach must work on a component abstraction level.

Components can comprise multiple classes. Depending on the component boundaries, the number of classes which must be merged into a single behaviour model of a component deviates. Internally, the control and data flow must therefore be lifted to the component level (component internal behaviour must be abstracted; only behaviour affecting other components should be preserved; cf. Section 5.7.2). The abstraction must be sufficiently strong to not expose implementation internals or disclose intellectual properties.

Section 9.1 discusses the realisation of these Requirements.

5.5. Solution Idea: Overview

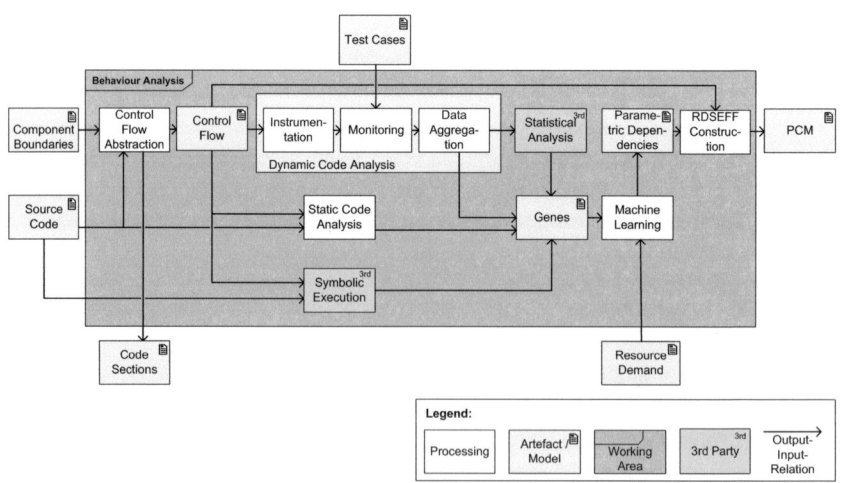

Figure 5.5.: Beagle: Behavioural reverse engineering (extract of Figure 3.4 with further details on dynamic analysis)

After the architectural reverse engineering step is finished, the reverse engineering of the behaviour model (Resource Demanding Service Effect Specification, RD-SEFF) of each previously discovered component starts. The reverse engineered behavioural model is the computation of an abstraction of components. Figure 5.5 depicts an extract of the relevant parts of the reverse engineering process for behavioural reverse engineering.

The main steps for the reverse engineering of behaviour models, are the creation of a control flow abstraction which serves as a skeleton for data flow annotations. Parametric dependencies (parameterised data flow annotations for e.g. loop iteration counts or parameter values passed to other component) are reverse engineered through an combination of dynamic and static code analysis, complemented by statistical analysis approaches for the approximation of dynamic analysis data. Static code analysis includes simple techniques like the extraction of constants from source code and symbolic execution as an advanced technique.

The integration of static, dynamic, and statistical analysis is taken over by genetic programming ("Machine Learning" in Figure 5.5). Furthermore, genetic programming contributes in creating parametric dependencies and finding performance abstractions for them. Besides, genetic programming estimates resource demands (e.g. CPU and HDD) from raw resource demand counts gather during an external dynamic analysis approach.

The reverse engineering approach presented in the following is a reverse engineering approach for grey-box components (cf. [BW99]). It requires source code to be available. Nevertheless, the source code does not need to be understood by humans due to the automation of the Beagle approach. For scenarios in which no source code is available, Section 5.17 presents an extension of the Beagle approach which applicable to black-box components.

In the remainder of Chapter 5, the reverse engineering of Beagle is discussed step by step. First, the control flow abstraction is discussed in Section 5.8, then the dynamic analysis (Section 5.10), machine learning (Section 5.11), the integration of static and statistical analysis approaches (Section 5.12 and later), the integration of resource demands (Section 5.16), and the applicability of the developed approach to black-box components (Section 5.17) are presented. Complexity, scalability and the realisation are discussed in the conclusion of this chapter.

The following section details on the behavioural reverse engineering approach, starting with an example for the reverse engineering model and the abstraction criteria for the RDSEFF. See Figure 2.7 (page 37) for an overview on terms.

5.6. Core Assumptions

Beagle implies two core assumptions which must hold when applying it. These assumptions are briefly introduced in the following. Further assumptions of the Beagle approach are discussed in Section 5.20.

1. Since Beagle is an approach based on static and dynamic analysis, test data (e.g. unit tests) must be available for the dynamic analysis part. The test data must cover relevant parameter inputs of provided component services and vary the input data. For example, if a math service is provided, the input integers should be varied in the input parameter space (cf. Section 5.20).

   Although Beagle targets at creating software performance component behaviour models, load drivers are generally not required as Beagle does not rely on timing values but on abstract resource demands (cf. Section 5.16). Other approaches which target at software performance prediction (e.g. [HMWR99, CW00, ZWL08]), require special load drivers and not just test data.

2. Furthermore, Beagle requires the availability of a test bed in which the software system under study can be executed. This can either be a fully running software system or a software system where mock-ups realise required functionality.

5.7. Abstraction Criteria of the RDSEFF

Resource Demanding Service Effect Specifications (RDSEFF) have specific abstraction criteria for their control and data flow. The following section will first introduce a running example of a RDSEFF and then first introduce the control flow and second the data flow abstraction criteria. How this abstraction is created in the Beagle approach will be detailed in Section 5.8.

5.7.1. Running Example

Figure 5.6 provides an example for a RDSEFF which has been introduced in Section 2.5.3. Each RDSEFF describes a single provided service of a component. It is important to understand how data and control flow are described and what the abstraction criteria of a RDSEFF are. In the example, the component BusinessLogic, its interfaces, and its internal behaviour are shown. The component provides the service uploadFile(fileInput, compressed) and requires the interfaces compress(cfile) and checkFile(file) which specify a single service. BusinessLogic is capable of compressing files, checks the files for being copyrighted, and afterwards stores them on a harddisk.

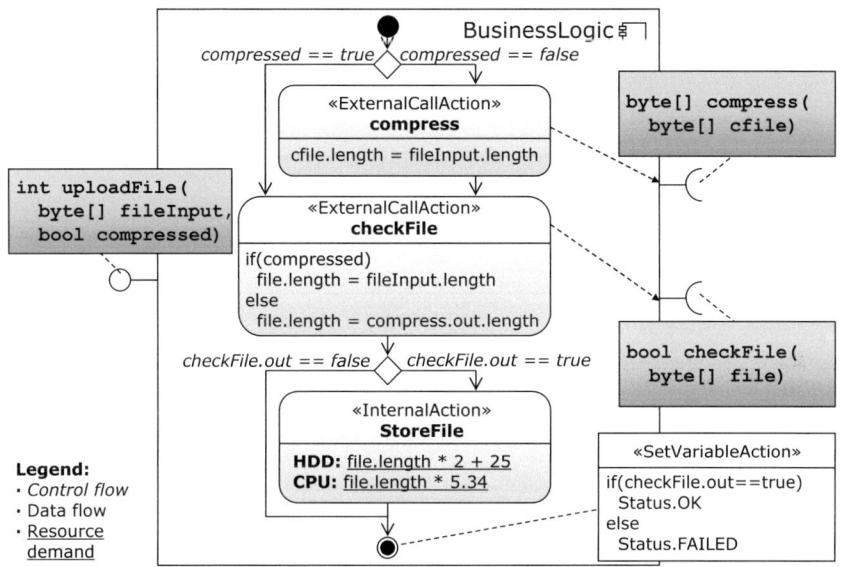

Figure 5.6.: Example RDSEFF for the service uploadFile(..)

The internal behaviour consists of multiple steps, including two branches. First in the behaviour, the flag compressed is checked. If the uploaded file is not compressed, it is passed via an external call action to a compression service (≪Call≫Compress). Otherwise, the file is directly passed to an external service checking for potential copyright violations (≪Call≫checkFile). If the file is not copyright protected, it is then stored on a harddisk (≪Internal≫StoreFile) without utilising other components. Finally, the BusinessLogic component returns its status (whether the uploadFile service was successful or not).

```
1  class Status BusinessLogic implements IFileShare {

2    ICompress compressionComponent;

3    ICopyrightCheck copyrightCheckComponent;


5    public uploadFile(byte[] fileInput, boolean compressed) {

6      if(!compressed) {

7        fileInput = compressionComponent.compress(fileInput);

8      }

9      boolean isFileCopyrighted = copyrightCheckComponent.checkFile(fileInput);

10     if(!isFileCopyrighted) {
```

```
11      // store file on harddisk
12      // ..
13      }
14      if(isFileCopyrighted)) {
15          return Status .FAILED;
16      } else {
17          return Status .OK;
18      }
19   }
20 }
```

Listing 5.1: Source code example of the component BusinessLogic. IFileShare is the provided interface; ICompress and ICopyrightCheck are required interfaces

5.7.2. Control Flow Abstractions of Resource Demanding Service Effect Specifications

RDSEFFs are abstractions at the component-level. They only capture control flow elements of a component that directly affects component-external control flow (see Section 5.8.1 for a definition). Component-internal control flow is merged into InternalActions. The StoreFile action is for example not visible from outside and consequently tagged as InternalAction (cf. Listing 5.1, lines 10 to 13). StoreFile might contain several loop and branch statements and might be using the Java API, middleware service, or other frameworks. As these services are not identified by component interfaces as being component services, they are subsumed in InternalAction to gain a higher abstraction level. Opposed to this, the branch deciding on calling the compress service (see Listing 5.1, line 6) is made explicit because compress is a service provided by another component.

Generally, only non-infrastructure services are considered being component services. In the overall approach, the architectural reverse engineering step determines which interfaces are being considered component interfaces. When reverse engineering for example Java code, not every Java interface is necessarily considered being a component interface. Especially technical interfaces such as messaging (e.g. Java Messaging Service) or security are not represented as component interfaces in PCM models. Instead, their performance impact is captured in resource demands within InternalActions.

The strict explicit handling of external actions arises from the desired assembly context parameterisation (making connected components a parameter). If the same component specification was reused in another assembly, the actually connected component would change. It is therefore important to capture whether an external service is called or not but make no assumptions on the actually connected components. Only the interface of required components (their *component type*) is known to a component. If the performance of an external service was captured in an InternalAction, this would imply a fixed connected component which cannot be known to components at design time. InternalActions by design do not require such a parameterisation as they only depend on component internals.

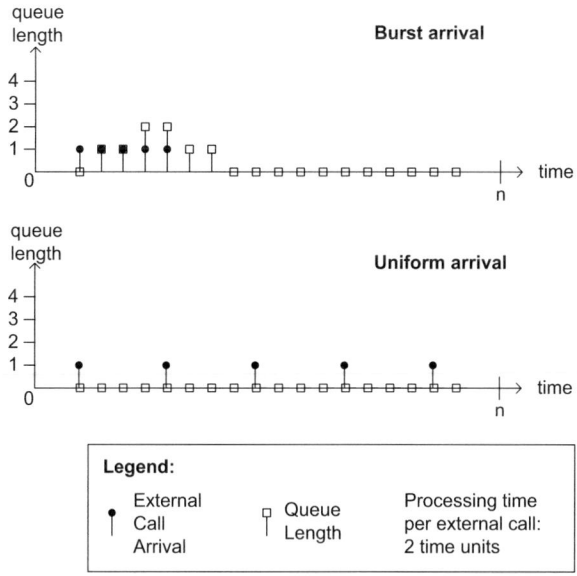

Figure 5.7.: Queue lengths for burst arrivals compared to uniform arrivals

A component's data flow abstraction must not abstract external calls of other components. While a single instance of a component and thus an InternalAction is always running on a single hardware node. Hence, InternalActions have local resource demand which can be accounted for locally. Local execution cannot be assumed for components invoked via external calls. As external calls invoke components which could be deployed for example on remote machines which utilise a network, it makes a difference whether an external service is invoked in a "burst" of calls or with uniform inter arrival times. External calls can result in load of *dis-*

tributed resources. For example, a network which has to handle a burst of calls has a different response time than a network which is processing uniformly distributed request. Figure 5.7 depicts the arrival of external calls in a queue [GSTH08] (e.g. a network queue). The burst (top) increases the response time due to the wait time in the queue. For uniform arrivals (shorter than the processing time), no waiting time is caused (bottom). Thus, opposed to InternalActions, a RDSEFF captures the order of external calls. They are individual elements of a RDSEFF's control flow.

Abstraction Criteria InternalActions imply an abstraction of a component's control flow. Any component-internal control flow is captured within Internal-Actions of the RDSEFF.

- **Only component-external control flow.** Component-internal control flow is abstracted to not expose component-internals. The corresponding performance impact is captured by InternalActions.

- **Execution order.** InternalActions make no assertions on the execution order of internal resource demands or internal method calls. Instead, all internal behaviour is cumulated (e.g. all HDD read accesses can be reduced to the number of accesses).

- **Explicit external calls.** Opposed to component-internal behaviour, external calls must not be abstracted in order to create a reusable component behaviour model which makes no assumptions on connected components.

- **Order of external calls.** As explained above, the order of external calls can have a significant impact on the overall performance of a software system which the abstraction must account for.

Section 5.8 will formalise and further detail the control flow abstraction.

5.7.3. Data Flow Abstractions of Resource Demanding Service Effect Specifications

Data flow information is evaluated in control flow statements such as branches (as branch conditions), in loops (number of executed loops), and for data flow as arguments of external calls, in return values of external calls, and as return value of the service described by the RDSEFF itself. *Resource demands* of internal actions can also depend on data flow. The dependency of control flow on input data, data passed to other components, and resource demands is called *parametric dependency* (cf. Section 2.7). Parametric dependencies can include if-then-else constructs, mathematical expressions, and stochastic expressions.

For example, the return value of `uploadFile` in Listing 5.1 depends on the return value of the required `checkFile` service. It is therefore determined by a parametric dependency.

The definition of parametric dependencies bases on parameter characterisations as introduced in Section 2.7.1 instead of concrete values. Therefore, they can be more abstract than a dependency expressed in source code. For example, if a loop iterates over the elements of a list, the `NUMBER_OF_ELEMENTS` characterisation of a parameter is sufficient for describing a parametric dependency. The concrete elements of the list are abstracted.

Parametric dependencies need not to cover all dependencies in full detail. If for example, for a list with a size of x elements, a loop is executed $x - 1$ times if x is larger than 1000, a parametric dependency stating x loop executions would still be sufficient. A parametric dependency is intended to abstract details since details would tend to increase complexity, endanger abstraction, and contradict the idea of RDSEFFs.

Abstraction Criteria   Abstraction demands of RDSEFF's parametric dependencies are:

- **Simulation speed**. RDSEFFs are behaviour models which serve as input for performance simulations. To keep the simulation time small even for large systems, the computation complexity of each parametric dependency must be small. For example, additions and subtractions are less computation intensive than calculating roots or evaluating if-then-else constructs.

- **Human understanding**. Humans should be able to understand reverse engineered RDSEFFs to either identify performance issues at the model level or for adapting a RDSEFF to create new design alternatives of components. Thus, simple expressions involving only a few arguments are preferable.

- **Intellectual property**. In a distributed development scenario, component developers are forced to provide component models (including RDSEFFs) in the Palladio scenario. This enables performance predictions and meeting design decisions at the model level without requiring to buy and set up every single component just for testing purposes. RDSEFFs should not contradict the protection of intellectual property of component internals. Hence, implementation internals and internal algorithms should not be exposed in models.

5.8. Static Control Flow Analysis for creating RDSEFFs

The first step which is performed during the reverse engineering of behaviour models (RDSEFFs) is the extraction of a control flow model. The control flow is inferred from given source code and abstracted to the component-level (see previous Section 5.7) using given component boundaries, specified as *provided* and *required interfaces* of a component.

The static control flow abstraction is a prerequisite to the later data flow analysis which parameterises the control and data flow. The resulting parametric dependencies characterise those control flow statements identified during the static control flow analysis (i.e. the number of iterations of loops and the branching conditions branches which are identified) which is described in the following.

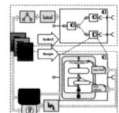

5.8.1. Control Flow Abstraction

As already pointed out in the previous sections, each RDSEFF is representing the behaviour of a single provided service. All component-internal behaviour resulting from that particular provided service is represented by a single RDSEFF.

Definition of Component-External Control Flow Consider the example from Listing 5.1, here the branch statement from line 6 is relevant at the component-level since it comprises an external call to a compression service. When removing the branch during in the abstraction, the resulting behaviour model would include calls of the compression component for *all* files – even those files which are already compressed. Thus, the component source code behaviour and the behaviour model would largely deviate as a compression service can consume a considerable amount of time. *Some* executions of the component source code would not result in the external call, but *all* executions of the behaviour model would. Since the branch statement is affecting the call frequency of the external compress service, it is part of the control flow which must be made explicit in the RDSEFF abstraction.

> **Component-external control flow.** A call to a service which is provided by another component results in *component-external control flow*. A particular control flow statement s of a component A is affecting the component-external control flow of another component B iff the order or frequency of the component-external control flow changes when changing the control flow statement s of component A.

The following formula formalises the definition of component-external control flow. It decides whether a control flow statement s is part of component-external control flow. The algorithm from Listing 5.2 define the computation of the control flow abstraction of a RDSEFF.

$s \in P$ is Component-External Control Flow $\Leftrightarrow$

$(\exists (p_{all} \in P \land p_s \in (P \setminus \{s\}) \land x \in X | freq(p_{all}, x) \neq freq(p_s, x)))$

$\lor (P_{-s} = (P \setminus \{s\}) \land x \in X \Rightarrow order(P, x) \neq order(P_{-s}, x))$

with P being the set of all control flow statements of a component, X a set of sets of the cross product of all possible input parameter combinations of a component, and $freq(p, x)$ the execution frequency of program statement p in an component execution with a set of input parameters x. $order(P, x)$ is the pairwise order of executed control flow statements P for the input parameters x.

$freq(p, x)$ does not respect the reachability of the code statement p. Instead, every statement which is contained in another control flow statement (e.g. a loop or branch) is assumed to be actually executed when executing the surrounding statement. Hence, no control flow statement is eliminated due to missing reachability. As the above formula is the base of the control flow structure but not the parametric dependencies, the actual execution frequencies in the final behaviour model are not affected by this assumption. If an external call is never executed due to missing reachability, the corresponding parametric dependency which determines its execution frequency will specify 0 executions in the final behaviour model.

The definition intentionally neglects data flow transformation effects of s. They are accounted for in later data flow analysis. For example, if the statement s appends an element to a list over which a loop later iterates, such changes of frequency are not considered when deciding on component-external control flow. The parametric dependency which later describes the number of iterations of a loop will be created to account for added elements of a list.

Calculation of the Component Control Flow Abstraction

The control flow abstraction is created in a three phase algorithm (cf. Listing 5.2): The creation of markers for external calls, the transitive marking of resulting relevant control flow statements, and the creation of the RDSEFF control flow structure.

In the **first phase** of the algorithm (cf. Figure 5.8 and Listing 5.3), all provided and required services of the component recognised in the architectural reverse engineering step (cf. Section 4), are marked (*marker relation*) in the Generalised Abstract Syntax Tree (GAST) which is build from the input source code. Since not every public method of a class or every method declared in an interface is a service at the component-level, the marker relation indicates which method declaration or me-

```
1 Inputs
2    gast := A GAST model
3    providedInterfaces := A set of provided interfaces
4    requiredInterface := A set of required interface
5 Outputs
6    rdseff := The resulting RDSEFF model containing the control flow abstraction

8 // 1. marker relation
9 gast = markProvidedAndRequiredServices(gast, providedInterfaces, requiredInterfaces)

11 // 2. transitive identification of parent control flow statements
12 gast = markParentControlFlowStatements(gast)

14 // 3. collect marked control flow statements
15 rdseff = createRDSEFFFromMarkers(gast)
```

Listing 5.2: Pseudo code of the three main phases of the control flow abstraction

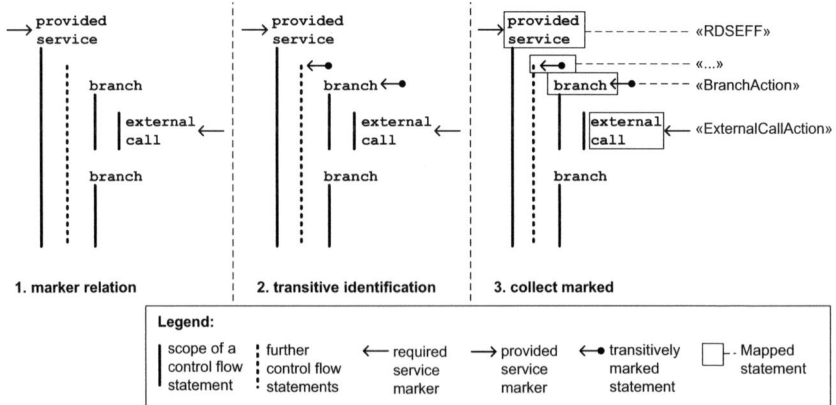

Figure 5.8.: Phases of the control abstraction applied at an abstract example. The depicted phases must be repeated for all calls of required services. The control abstraction then comprises the union of all marked control flow statements of all repetitions.

122

```
 1  Inputs
 2    gast, providedInterfaces, requiredInterfaces // as above
 3  Outputs
 4    gast // with markers for statements relevant for the performance abstraction
 5  markProvidedAndRequiredServices {
 6    forall(Method m ∈ gast.Methods) {
 7      if(m.interface ∈ providedInterfaces) {
 8        markProvided(m); // mark m as a provided component service
 9      }
10    }
11    forall(Call c ∈ gast.Calls) {
12      if(c.interface ∈ requiredInterfaces( {
13        markRequired(c); // mark c as a required component call
14      }
15    }
16  }
```

Listing 5.3: Pseudo code of the marker creation

thod call statement in the GAST is relevant at the class level. Hence, every method identified by the provided interface of the component and every call to the required interface is marked in the GAST.

In the **second phase** of the algorithm (cf. Listings 5.4 and 5.5), a transitive relation (realised as recursion in the implementation) identifies control flow statements which must be preserved at the component-level abstraction. The relation is defined starting from required service calls and then transitively identifies control flow statements which are relevant for the component behaviour model. The relation captures all control flow statements up to the method declaration, starting from the external method calls. When having marked all potential statements of a potential "path" between the required service calls and the provided method, the second phase terminates.

In the example from Listing 5.1 (page 115), for example the method call compress from line 7 would be identified in the first step (marker relation). The second phase would then (i) relate the method call with the surrounding branch statement (lines 6 to 8) and (ii) relate the method declaration from line 5 with the branch statement. Of these statements, the external call, the branch, and the method call would be identified as actions in the component behaviour. The remaining statements would be handled

123

```
1  Inputs
2     gast // marked GAST model
3  Outputs
4     gast // with markers for statements relevant for the performance abstraction
5  markParentControlFlowStatements { // for entrance
6     forall(Statement s ∈ gast.Statements) {
7        if(isMarkedRequired(s)) {
8           markParentControlFlowStatements(s)
9        }
10    }
11 }
```

Listing 5.4: Pseudo code of marking parent statements: Initialisation

```
1  Inputs
2     statement // current GAST statement
3  Outputs
4     gast // with markers for statements relevant for the performance abstraction
5  markParentControlFlowStatements { // for recursion
6     mark(statement) // mark statement as relevant at the component level
7     if(statement.Predecessor ≠ ∅) {
8        markParentControlFlowStatements(statement.Predecessor) // recursion: predecessor
9     } else if(!isMarkedProvided(statement.Parent)) { // check termination
10       markParentControlFlowStatements(statement.Parent) // recursion: parent
11    }
12 }
```

Listing 5.5: Pseudo code of marking parent statements: Recursion

```
1  Inputs
2    gast // marked GAST model
3    providedInterfaces // marked GAST model
4  Outputs
5    rdseff // resulting RDSEFF model
6  createRDSEFFFromMarkers {
7    forall(providedInterface ∈ providedInterfaces) {
8      // top down order of transClosure result
9      forall(gast ∈ transClosure(
10         providedInterface, {'child', 'call', 'isMarked', !'isMarkedRequired'}) ) {
11       map(gast.call → rdseff.ExternalCallAction : isMarkedRequired(gast.call))
12       map(gast.method → rdseff.StartAction : isMarkedProvided(gast.method))
13       map(gast.method → rdseff.StopAction : isMarkedProvided(gast.method))
14       map(gast.branch → rdseff.BranchAction : isMarked(gast.branch))
15       map(gast.loop → rdseff.LoopAction : isMarked(gast.loop))
16       map(gast \ {call,branch,loop} → rdseff.InternalAction : isMarkedRequired(gast \
                {call,branch,loop}))
17       map(gast.containments → rdseff.containments)
18     }
19   }
20   // mapped in the code order: successors can be connected
21   connectSuccessors(rdseff)
22 }
```

Listing 5.6: Pseudo code of marking parent statements: Recursion

in the same way. Here, for example the branch in lines 10 to 13 has no inner external method call and thus is not preserved for the component behaviour abstraction.

Finally, in the **third phase**, the algorithm (cf. Listing 5.6) is collecting all control flow statements which are part of the relation of the second phase and transforms them into the control flow of an RDSEFF model. Overall, the transformation from GAST into RDSEFF follows strict conversion rules and does not make use of any heuristics.

In the listing, $transClosure()$ is extended such that it can also handle attributes ($isMarked$ / $isMarkedRequired$) which are evaluated on the elements of the transitive closure.

```
1  class A : IA {
2    public void providedMethod() {
3      subjectForInlining();
4    }

6    public void subjectForInlining() {
7      // some code
8      // external call
9      anotherComponent.doSth();
10     // further code
11   }
12 }

14 class B : IB {
15   public void providedMethod() {
16     A.subjectForInlining();
17   }
18 }
```

Listing 5.7: Example: Method inlining vs. InternalCallAction

5.8.2. Method Inlining

A single provided service of a component, which is described by a RDSEFF, can span multiple methods and multiple classes. Even a single InternalAction can comprise multiple methods of multiple classes of a component. If a single provided service covers multiple methods and classes, the corresponding code must be handled within a single RDSEFF. For example, the first InternalAction of the service providedMethod() would cover the lines 3 to 8 (see Listing 5.7).

Method inlining is a way to handle such provided services. The object-oriented methods can therefore be inlined at the model level into a single provided service of a component. Method inlining helps for example to increase simulation performance (like compiler function inlining, cf. [CH89]) since less method calls need to be performed during simulation and less overhead for maintaining stackframes for simulated variables in the simulation incur.

However, method inlining can lead to inconsistencies in reverse engineered models if they are later changed manually by humans to explore for example new design alternatives. If the same source code is mapped to multiple sections of a RDSEFFs, changing them consistently in a RDSEFF would become infeasible for humans as argued below. In the simple example from Listing 5.7, the lines 7 to 11 would be inlined for the provided methods of the classes A and B. To change the resulting RDSEFF consistently, humans would first need to look up the original code in order to find all places of inlining. The more classes inline a certain source code section (generally unlimited), the harder it becomes for humans to completely find them.

Therefore, method inlining is only performed if no inconsistencies are being expected. For other cases, so-called ResourceDemandingInternalBehaviour helps avoiding duplicated model sections. ResourceDemandingInternalBehaviour introduces a kind of private method at the component-level which can be called from multiple InternalCallActions of a RDSEFF.

Example In the example shown in Listing 5.7, both, method inlining and explicit internal calls are illustrated. When considering only class A as a single component (ignoring class B for the moment), the method subjectForInlining() (lines 6 to 11) would be inlined at line 3 as only class A is calling that method. If class A and B would be merged into a single component, there would be two calls of subject-ForInlining(). In this case, subjectForInlining() would be translated into ResourceDemandingInternalBehaviour and lines 3 and 16 would result in InternalCallActions.

Inlining Condition If a method declaration is not part of the marker relation, the corresponding method is a potential subject of inlining. Whether to inline or to create a ResourceDemandingInternalBehaviour depends on the usage of the method: *Iff* a method is not called from at least two different control flow blocks within a component, it will be inlined. Otherwise, that method is converted into a ResourceDemandingInternalBehaviour of the provided service of the component and an InternalCallAction calls that internal behaviour.

The binary decision whether to inline or not $Inline(method)$ is:

$$Inline(method) := \begin{cases} true & \text{if } \forall mc_1, mc_2 \in MC(\\ & (mc_1.callee = method \Rightarrow mc_2.callee \neq method) \\ & |mc_1 \neq mc_2) \\ false & \text{else} \end{cases}$$

where MC is the set of all method calls of classes associated to a component for which the RDSEFF is being constructed. Thus, calls of $method$ from multiple RDSEFFs of the same component are explicitly part of MC.

When creating the RDSEFF, the component control flow of all methods which are transitively reachable via the call relations of method calls for which

$Inline(method) = true$ holds, will be inserted at the place of the call statement of that method. For method for which $Inline(method) = false$, the call statement of that method is translated into an `InternalCallAction` and the called method and its component-level control flow itself results in an `ResourceDemandingInternalBehaviour`.

5.8.3. Implementations

Currently, there are two different implementations of this transformation available. Multiple implementations exist, since the transformation implementations use different inputs (e.g. Eclipse JDT vs. SISSy GAST), different transformation technologies with specific advantages and steem from different project contexts.

- Java2PCM [KKKR08] is a transformation approach written in Java based on the Eclipse JDT AST. It runs directly on any Eclipse Java projects. This implementation is not able to deal with `InternalCallActions` and limited to components which span only one class.

- GAST2SEFF [BHT+10] is a transformation written in Java which uses the SISSy GAST (which has been developed in the context of the Q-ImPrESS project [qim09]) as input and thus can handle C/C++, Delphi and Java code. Its implementation is based on EMF visitors which translate node by node of the GAST. GAST2SEFF is the more recent transformation.

5.8.4. Resulting Control Flow Abstraction

After applying the presented algorithm, the GAST representation of source code is translated into the control flow abstraction of a component and represented as RDSEFF. Such a RDSEFF includes the PCM control flow elements internal actions, loops, branches and external calls but no parametric dependencies. All internal methods which have a single fixed caller, are inlined in the component abstraction to ensure a grey-box view of components which helps hiding implementation internals.

This thesis extended the PCM with `InternalCallActions` and `ResourceDemandingInternalBehaviour` to support internal calls within RDSEFFs to avoid model duplications and have an equivalent to coarse-grained private methods at the component-level. Internal calls complement the method inlining concept of RDSEFFs. The introduced extensions of the PCM intentionally allow only one level of internal calls to force model abstraction. This way, the extensions serve as a balance between model abstraction and information hiding on the one hand and the avoidance of model clones and inconsistency issues on the other hand.

5.8.5. Identification of Parametric Dependency Input and Output

Data related to single parametric dependencies (cf. Section 2.7) must be tracked over multiple steps of the Beagle reverse engineering process depicted in Figure 5.5 (page 112). For example, "dynamic code analysis", "static code analysis", "symbolic execution", and "statistic analysis" contribute in determining parametric dependencies. Hence, the individual output of all processing steps must be related to each other, which results in two sub-tasks:

- unique identification of parametric dependencies (*output*) and

- the identification which data serves as *input* for a certain parametric dependency.

The identification of parametric dependency *input* and *output* is thus a preparation step for the required tracking across multiple reverse engineering steps. Furthermore, it is a prerequisite for the later machine learning which relies on this information.

In the following, first a running example for the various kinds of parametric dependencies is introduced. Then, the terms *input* and *output* are defined to lay a foundation to formally state potential dependencies between *input* and *output* for a certain RDSEFF. The set of potential inputs for a certain parametric dependencies one information source for the later base for machine learning step.

5.8.5.1. Inputs

Inputs indicate parameter characterisations and return value characterisations a parametric dependency can potentially depend on. These *inputs* are parameter characterisations of every parameter of a provided service and parameter characterisations of return values of `ExternalCalls`. In Figure 5.9, for example, the parameter characterisations "fileInput.NumberOfElements" ("fileInput.NoE"), "compressed.VALUE" of the described `uploadFile()` service and the return values' "numberOfElements" of the external call to `compress()` are *inputs*.

A single input is a tuple that comprises a unique input "position" represented by an annotated model element of the RDSEFF (i.e. method parameter or return value of an external call) and a parameter characterisation (e.g. "NumberOfElements", "Value") of that parameter:

$$input = (inputposition, parametercharacterisation)$$

where $input \in Inputs$ and $parametercharacterisation$ is a parameter characterisation specified for the input position in the interface of the component which contains the RDSEFF (see Foundation Section 2.7.1).

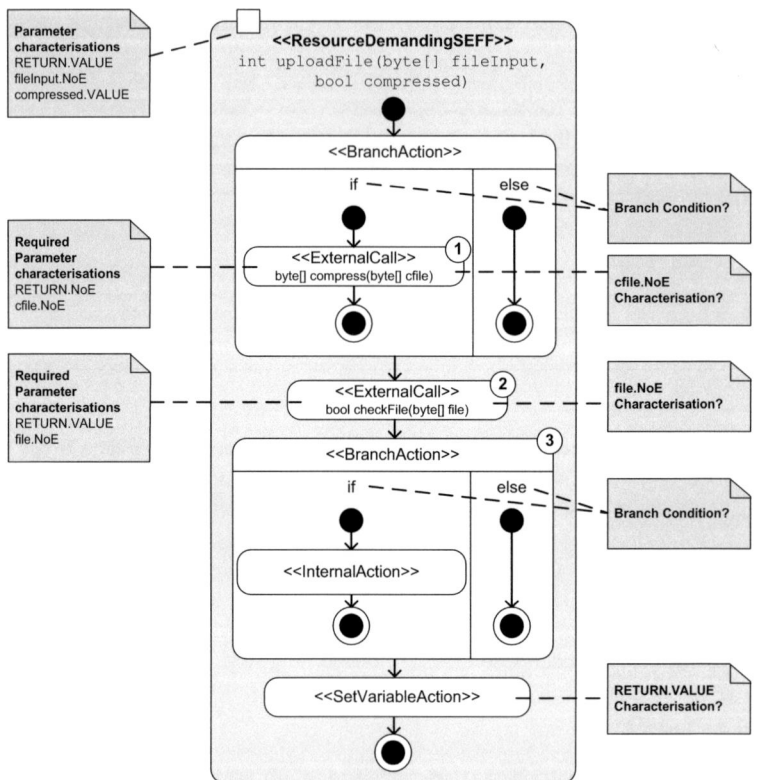

Figure 5.9.: RDSEFF BusinessLogic example showing input and output positions for the service `uploadFile()`

5.8.5.2. Outputs

To ease a later identification of parametric dependencies and model elements of the RDSEFF which require the specification of a parametric dependency, RDSEFFs carry annotations to identify the corresponding model elements. All places which require the specification of a parametric dependency are marked as *outputs*. *outputs* annotate LoopAction (requires a loop iteration number), BranchAction (a selection criterion for branches), and parameters characterisations for each parameter of an ExternalCall. An *output* represents the unique location of a parametric dependency, not a parametric dependency (a concrete relation) itself. An *output* corresponds to a single parametric dependency.

There are two kinds of *outputs* as external calls can have multiple arguments each with multiple parameter characterisations and returns values can have multiple required parameter characterisations:

$$
output = \begin{cases}
(outputposition, & \text{for parameters} \\
\quad parameter\ characterisation & \text{of ExternalCalls} \\
& \text{and Returns} \\
outputposition & \text{for LoopAction} \\
& \text{and BranchAction}
\end{cases}
$$

where $output \in Outputs$ and, for `ExternalCalls`, $parameter characterisation$ is a parameter characterisation specified for a parameter in the interface of the called service.

Outputs and *Inputs* are unique location identifiers for RDSEFFs and the corresponding source code locations represented by the GAST model. Due to the presence in the RDSEFF and in the GAST, one can track data across multiple steps of the reverse engineering process.

5.8.5.3. Potential Inputs Relation: A Model-Level Backward Slice

In order to provide a working base for the later machine learning step of Beagle, the potential inputs of a parametric dependency must be determined (comparable to the data flow analysis for source code). Since machine learning relies on dynamic analysis, it cannot be known which data is input to which *outputs*.

In the example in Figure 5.9 the branching condition (3) is unknown. It can potentially depend on all data of predecessing actions of the RDSEFF. This are the return value of the `ExternalCalls` (1) / (2) and the parameters of the *uploadFile()* service.

The *potentialInputs* relation determines the potential inputs for an *output*. It is a backward slice (see [HH01] for an overview) on the control flow structure of the RDSEFF model. The scope of the backward slice is limited to a single RDSEFF and based on the predecessor relation of RDSEFF control flow statements only. $potentialInputs(output)$ is defined as:

$$potentialInputs(output) :=$$
$$\{x | x \in Input \ :$$
$$(\ x = \{c \in \left(\bigcup_{p \in Predecessors(output)} p.children \right)$$
$$\wedge \ c.type = \ 'ExternalCall' \} \ )$$
$$\vee (\ x = params \in (\bigcup_{p \in Predecessors(output)} p.parent.signature.parameters \ |$$
$$p.parent.type = \ 'ResourceDemandingSEFF' \ )$$
$$) \}$$

where $output \in Outputs$.

For each set $Inputs_{out}$ returned by $potentialInputs(output)$ holds $Inputs_{out} \subseteq Inputs$. $Inputs_{out}$ is a superset of parameters employed in an actual parametric dependency. $Predecessors(output)$ builds upon the transitive closure of the predecessor and parent relation of control flow actions of the RDSEFF and collects the inner `ExternalCall` statements of predecessor actions:

$$Predecessors(output) = transClosure(output, \{'predecessor', 'parent'\}) :$$
$$parent.type \neq 'ResourceDemandingSEFF'$$

where $transClosure(output, \{'predecessor', 'parent'\})$ is the transitive closure containing actions transitively reachable from $output$ via the $predecessor$ and $parent$ relation of any RDSEFF action. 'ResourceDemandingSEFF' represents a boundary of the transitive closure (i.e. the top-most control flow element is reached).

Source code level (backward) slicing [Wei81, HH01] would not help for the determination of inputs, since it, i) is not able to deal with component boundaries, ii) is not aware of component services, and iii) cannot deal with parameter characterisations.

The result set of $potentialInputs(output)$ for a certain output will be referred to $Inputs_{out}$ for reasons of brevity:

$$potentialInputs(output) := Inputs_{out} = \{input_1, input_2, ..\}$$

$Inputs_{out}$ holds a set of all potential input parameter characterisations which can serve as input for parametric dependencies in the position identified by $output$.

5.9. Implications of Component Boundaries on the RDSEFF Abstraction

Discussion: Implications of Component Boundaries on the RDSEFF Abstraction The following section discusses the relation between the abstraction level of components and the resulting abstraction of the behaviour model. The component abstraction level has direct implications for the resulting RDSEFF abstraction.

As the reverse engineered behavioural model is an abstraction at the component-level, it is a pre-requisite to have component boundaries as input. Component boundaries are used for finding the right abstraction level for control flow and also for finding the right places for instrumentation for dynamic analysis (see Section 5.10). Section 5.7 already pointed out how blocks of internal behaviour are abstracted into single InternalActions. Calls through component interfaces are used to identify component boundaries in the behaviour analysis. If calls bypass the explicitly stated interfaces, they are considered to be *infrastructure calls* which are merged into InternalActions (for example calls to the Java API if the Java API is not considered as component interface). Thus, the distinction of infrastructure calls and calls to other components (ExternalCall) contributes directly to the abstraction of SEFFs. A single InternalAction can comprise hundreds of lines of code (e.g. a sorting or compression algorithm) and span multiple classes and packages.

5.9.1. Interface Selection and Granularity

Recognised required interfaces of architectural reverse engineering impact the abstraction level of component behaviour since the interfaces help to distinguish InternalActions and ExternalCalls. The more required interfaces a component has and the more services an interfaces has, the more fine-grained the resulting components tend to become. If for example a logger is part of the required interface of a component, each logger statement results in an ExternalCall. When the logger is instead considered as part of the component (and not part of the required interface), the size of the resulting behaviour model decreases as the logger statements are covered by InternalActions. Consequently, the selection of component interfaces and the quantity of contained services guides the possible abstraction level during reverse engineering of behaviour models. The behaviour model of large coarse-grained components can have a reduced complexity in relation to the overall lines of code covered by a component compared to a small fine-grained component – which at first glance might sound counterintuitive.

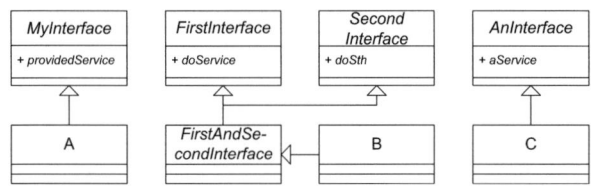

Figure 5.10.: Classes and interfaces from Listing 5.8

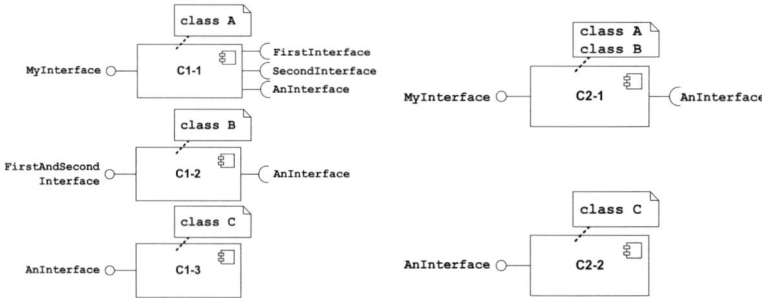

(a) Classes A, B, and C as separate components (b) Classes A and B merged into a single component

Figure 5.11.: Resulting components of classes A, B, and C before (a) and after (b) merging classes A and B into a single component

5.9.2. Example

Listing 5.8 provides an example illustrating why the behaviour abstraction level of coarse grained components is increasing for the components from Figure 5.11. The inheritance relations at the class level are visualised in Figure 5.10. The example covers interface selection, component boundaries, and sizes of the resulting RDSEFFs for the code- and the component-level.

When considering each of the classes A, B, and C as separate *fine-grained* components (named "C1-1" to "C1-3"; see Figure 5.11 (a), the control flow statements in the lines 5 and 9 would be translated into control flow elements of the RDSEFF (cf. Figure 5.12). Additionally, line 8 would become an InternalAction and line 12 would be translated into an ExternalCall. Of class B, line 19 would be translated into a LoopAction, line 20 would become an ExternalCall and the lines 24 to 26 result in an InternalAction. aService of class C would result in a single InternalAction in this simplified example. A **total of 10** control flow statements would result from the three classes. In this case, MyInterface would be the provided inter-

```
1   class A implements MyInterface {
2     FirstAndSecondInterface classB = ..; // FirstAndSecondInterface implements
          FirstInterface and SecondInterface
3     AnInterface classC = ..;
4     public void providedService(int a) {
5       for(..) {
6         classB.providedService(a);
7       }
8       // some internal calculation
9       if(..) {
10        classB.doSth();
11      }
12      classC.aService(a);
13    }
14  }

16  class B implements FirstAndSecondInterface {
17    AnInterface classC = ..;
18    public void doService(int a) { // declared in FirstInterface
19      for(..) {
20        classC.aService(a);
21      }
22    }
23    public void doSth() { // declared in SecondInterface
24      if(..) {
25        // some mathematical operations
26      }
27    }
28  }

30  class C implements AnInterface {
31    public void aService(int a) {
32      //some calculations
33    }
34  }
```

Listing 5.8: Source code example demonstrating the increasing behaviour abstraction for large components

135

face of the component formed by class A, FirstInterface, SecondInterface and AnInterface would be the required interfaces. For class B, FirstInterface and SecondInterface are provided interfaces for the corresponding component, AnInterface the required interface and class C would only have the provided interface AnInterface.

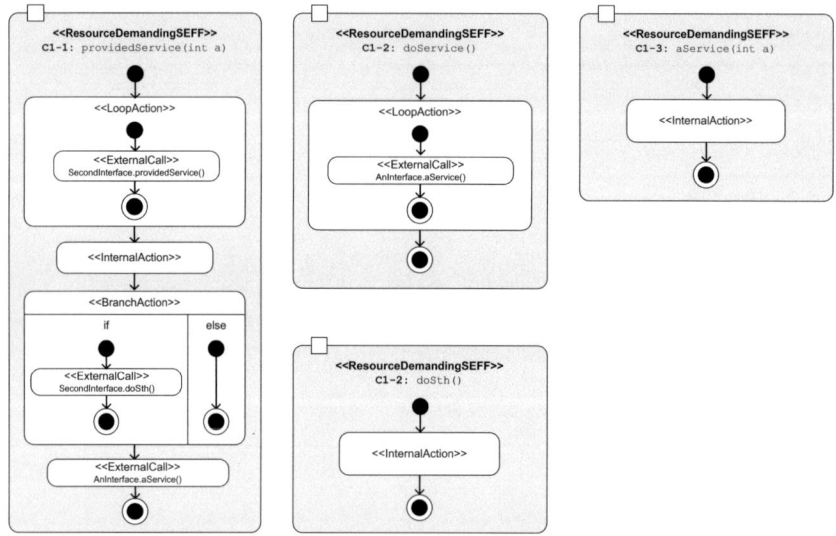

Figure 5.12.: RDSEFFs for the fine-grained components C1-1, C1-2, and C1-3

When instead considering the classes A and B as a merged *coarse-grained* component "C2-1" (Figure 5.11) which only accesses the external component formed by class C "C2-2", the number of control flow statements would be reduced to **6 statements in total** (see Figure 5.13). Of class A, lines 9 to 11 would be eliminated and merged with the InternalAction from line 8. A RDSEFF does not allow two subsequent InternalActions. They must be merged into a single InternalAction. The InternalAction of the method doSth of class B (lines 23 to 26) would also be merged into this InternalAction. Due to the merge of class A and B, the provided interface SecondInterface of class B could be removed from "C2-1" which eliminates doSth from the list of provided services.

The ExternalCall in line 6 would be removed as class B is now component-internal and the loop from lines 19 to 21 would be inlined. The ExternalCall in line 20 would be preserved. The remaining behaviour model would stay the same including the component representing class C. This lowers the number of control flow statements by 5 compared to the previous version where the classes A and B where separated into different components.

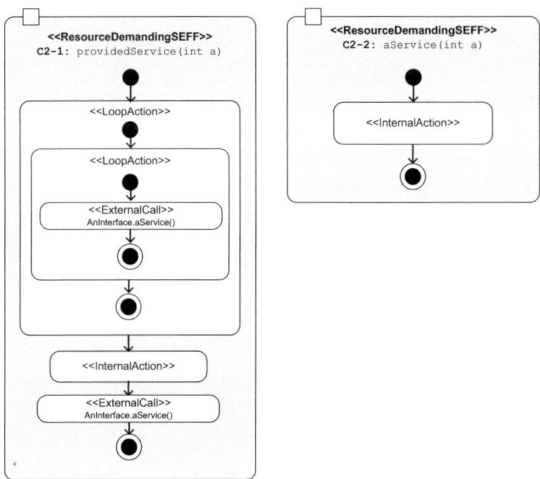

Figure 5.13.: RDSEFFs for the coarse-grained components C2-1 and C2-2

5.9.3. Size of the Resulting Control Flow

The example illustrates how larger coarse-grained components can result in stronger abstractions (with less complexity in total) although more lines of code are covered. Generally, also counterexamples can be found. In the worst case, the number of control flow statements of two classes ($Ctrl_1$ and $Ctrl_2$) which are merged into a single component is the sum of both control flow statements. Compared to separate components for each class, no additional statements can originate from merging classes into larger components:

$$card(Ctrl_{max}) \leq card(Ctrl_1) + card(Ctrl_2)$$

with $card(x)$ being the cardinality of a set x. In the worst case:

- No two consecutive `InternalActions` result from method inlining (the are no two consecutive class methods that end and start with an `InternalAction`) and

- no `ExternalCall` can be removed as no two classes exist in the merged component that access each other ($Ctrl_n$ has no direct call invoking $Ctrl_m$, with $m \neq n$).

Most complexity is generally removed due to method inlining and merging consecutive `InternalActions` which are not allowed in a sequence. If the control flow of a class' method ends with an `InternalAction` and the control flow of the next class' method starts with an `InternalAction`, both `InternalActions` are merged into a single one. Hence, the selection of component boundaries is suitable to steer the abstraction level of behaviour models.

Generally, the number of control flow elements (`InternalActions`, `Branches`, `Loops`, `ExternalCalls`, ...) of two merged classes is

$$
\begin{aligned}
card(Ctrl_{merged}) = \; & card(Ctrl_1) + card(Ctrl_2) \\
& - card(consecutiveInternalActions(Ctrl_1, Ctrl_2))/2 \\
& - card(callsBecomingInternal(Ctrl_1, Ctrl_2)) \\
& - card(transitivelyDependingOn(\\
& \quad callsBecomingInternal(Ctrl_1, Ctrl_2)))
\end{aligned}
$$

where all of the above methods are applied to classes as if they where components, with:

- $consecutiveInternalActions(Ctrl_1, Ctrl_2)$ returns those `Internal-Actions` which after merging $Ctrl_1$ and $Ctrl_2$ are directly successive.

- The set of method calls which become internal is:

$$
\begin{aligned}
callsBecomingInternal(Ctrl_1, Ctrl_2) = \; & p(Ctrl_1, ExternalCall) \\
& + p(Ctrl_2, ExternalCall) \\
& - p(Ctrl_1 \cup Ctrl_2, \\
& \quad ExternalCall)
\end{aligned}
$$

is the selection of all `ExternalCalls` which are considered component-internal due to the merge, with the projection $p(A, t) := \{a \in A \mid typeof(a) = t\}$. $typeof(a)$ determines the types of element a as introduced earlier. $Ctrl_1 \cup Ctrl_2$ is the merged control flow. $callsBecomingInternal(Ctrl_1, Ctrl_2)$ directly depends on a component's interfaces and thus on component granularity.

- *transitivelyDependingOn(Ctrl)* are all control flow statements transitively selected by the second phase of the algorithm described in Section 5.8.1. Due to the transitive selection, the selection applies to multiple recursion levels.

5.9.4. Conclusion: Increasing the Abstraction Level

Since the **control flow** abstraction of RDSEFFs follows fixed rules, the only way to increase the abstraction in the control flow of RDSEFFs is to use coarse-grained components which comprise a large number of classes. As this section showed, in general, the control flow size of coarse-grained components is smaller than for fine-grained components.

Scalability and time complexity of the static control flow analysis will be discussed in Section 5.18 together with the dynamic analysis.

The dynamic analysis which is presented in the next section, operates directly on the reverse engineered control flow structures and uses the RSEFF control flow to find instrumentation points. An increased control flow abstraction is thus suitable to reduce the number of instrumentation point and by that lowers the effort of dynamic analysis. The **data flow** can be abstracted further without needing to increase the granularity of components, as will be pointed out in the next sections.

5.10. Dynamic analysis for creating RDSEFFs

Dynamic program analysis means executing a program and monitoring its behaviour at runtime (cf. [NNH99]). When monitoring for example two classes A and B, from the data captured at runtime, typical dynamic analysis approaches can derive the number of calls from A to B which occur at runtime. Using static analysis approaches, the number of method invocations between two classes is hard to analyse [Ern03]. If for example A calls B within a loop, the number of iterations for which that loop is executed, must be 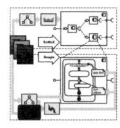 calculated from code. Opposed to static analysis, dynamic analysis can monitor the number of executions of a loop or the number of invocation of a certain method instead of performing complex static analyses like symbolic execution [Kin76].

Besides call relations and the number of executions of control flow statements, the propagated usage profile of an application is available at runtime. If an application is executed, parameter values can be monitored along with the program execution. The propagated usage profile are the input parameters of a component or software system after their transformation through methods executed before entering those sections of a software system which are under study. In static code analysis, parameter values, except for constants cannot be known. Parameter values are only a property of executed code since the usage profile of a software system which determines the parameter values generally is not fixed.

The remainder of this section first introduces dynamic analysis in the context of the developed Beagle approach and presents the purpose of dynamic analysis in the approach. This introduction is accompanied by a discussion of the execution test bed and specialties of dynamic analysis in Beagle. Then, in Section 5.10.2, instrumentation points which are derived from the RDSEFF control flow structure are presented, before Section 5.10.3 details on captured data and Section5.10.4 introduces heuristics for data capturing. Section 5.10.5 discusses how data is uniquely captured across space and time, Section5.10.6 briefly introduces the instrumentation strategy, Section 5.10.7 shows the data recording infrastructure, while Section 5.10.8 concludes with the aggregation of monitoring data.

5.10.1. Dynamic Analysis in the Beagle Approach

Beagle uses dynamic analysis as a base to reverse engineer parametric dependencies. Opposed to the previous static analysis step, the dynamic analysis does not directly result in a reverse engineered model element, instead it forms the base for further analyses (machine learning, statistical analysis). The ultimate goal of dynamic analysis in the Beagle approach is to reverse engineered parametric dependencies (i.e. parameterised data flow and parameterisation of control flow; see Section 2.7 for the definition).

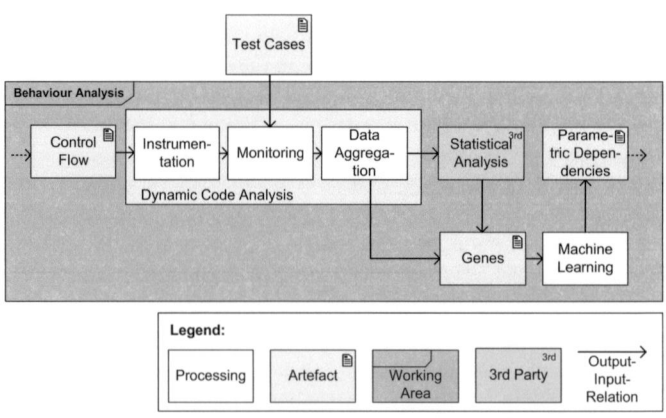

Figure 5.14.: Dynamic analysis: Excerpt of behaviour analysis

Figure 5.14 highlights the relevant parts of dynamic analysis in the overall approach. The control flow abstraction introduced in the previous Section 5.8 is a precondition to dynamic analysis as it identifies the control and data flow elements for which parametric dependencies must be reverse engineering during dynamic analysis.

In the Beagle approach, dynamic analysis serves two purposes:

- **Base for Statistical Analysis.** Monitoring results serve as input of the *statistical analysis*, which approximates parametric dependencies. Statistical analysis is used to complement the results from static and dynamic analysis. So-called Multivariate Adaptive Regression Splines (MARS, [Fri91]) are used to approximate the parametric dependencies between input and output values. Section 5.14 will detail on MARS.

  MARS contributes rapidly computable approximations of parametric dependencies which improve the initial generation of machine learning. Precedent statistical analysis increases the convergence speed of machine learning. Section 5.11 details on machine learning.

- **Judge Precision.** Monitoring results serve as "reference" to judge on the *precision* of the later machine learning step. At runtime the developed dynamic analysis approach monitors the input and call parameter values, selected branches, and the number of loop executions (cf. Section 2.7). The monitored results are fed into the machine learning approach which from these values judges on the quality of its results by comparing predicted values and monitored values.

  If, for example, the parameter a of `providedService(int a)` in Listing 5.8 is monitored as 5 which results in a call parameter of value 15 in line 6 but a parametric dependency created during machine learning results in a value of 14, the deviation is used to estimate the precision of the machine learning results. Details will be discussed further in Section 5.11.4.

To enable dynamic analysis, the executed code or the execution environment need to be instrumented to capture data (cf. Figure 5.15, "Instrumentation "). This implies a certain overhead compared to execution without instrumentation. As the approach presented in this thesis does not rely on timing values during the creation of its model (cf. discussion in Section 3.3.2), monitoring overhead does not impact the precision of the approach. The envisioned dynamic analysis is precise by construction, since monitored values are non-timing values and can be measured without disturbance. For example, the input parameters of a provided service or the call arguments of an external call can be directly measured opposed to response time or throughput which would be impacted by any overhead of monitoring.

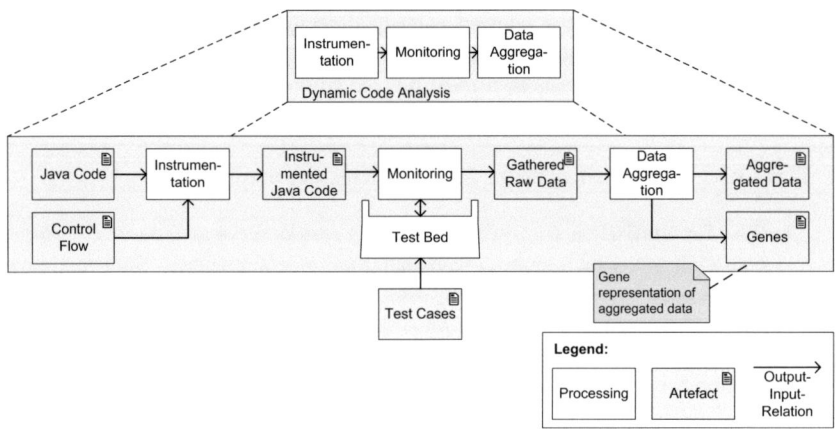

Figure 5.15.: Dynamic code analysis

Performing dynamic analyses requires a program to be executed. Load drivers or unit tests [ZHM97, MPP07, CL02] can serve for driving the execution (cf. Figure 5.15, "Test Cases" and "Test Bed") . To gain discriminative values, the execution should result in a simple branch coverage (cf. [MBTS04]) plus each loop being executed with at least two different numbers of iterations. Discriminative values are required to make parametric dependencies identifiable. If for example input integer values of a method in the range from 0 to 10 always result in the selection of an if branch and any other values in execution of the else branch, unit tests must contain values larger and smaller than the threshold of the if branch. Otherwise, the else branch would not become identifiable for the dynamic analysis approach. For this approach, we assume unit tests to be available (see for example the corresponding approaches for deriving test cases from source code in [BALS08, TS06, PV09, McM04, LMS+99]). This will be discussed further in the limitations and assumptions Section 9.10.

If the application under study has been successfully executed in the test bed, the raw data gathered at runtime is being aggregated (cf. Figure 5.15, "Data Aggregation"). Besides the aggregated data, a gene representation of the aggregated data is created which can be handled by the machine learning approach.

The dynamic analysis of Beagle assumes to deal with oblivious algorithms which have a deterministic behaviour and do not possess an internal state. Further limitations and assumptions are discussed in Section 9.10.

The following sections will detail on the dynamic analysis of Beagle.

5.10.2. Instrumentation Points

Before monitoring data can be captured, the code needs to be instrumented. During dynamic analysis, sufficient information needs to be captured to enable the reverse engineering of parametric dependencies for control and data flow. Too few instrumentation points prevent reverse engineering the full behaviour of a component. At the same time, it is desirable to avoid unnecessary instrumentation points to limit the measuring overhead. The places where to instrument the source code depend on the abstraction level and thus on the component boundaries. For example, any control flow which is inside an `InternalAction` (including private method calls at the class level) results in just a single node. Hence, any internals should not be considered during monitoring. No corresponding instrumentation for such control flow elements is required. The performance impact of `InternalAction` is accounted for by a separate approach which is presented in Section 5.16.

To facilitate an instrumentation which is aligned with the component abstraction level, the static control flow analysis from Section 5.8 is a prerequisite. From the control flow abstraction produced in static analysis, the required instrumentation points can be directly derived. For example, those loops (`for` or `while`) which result in a `LoopAction` are identified. Only points identified in the static analysis as component-level control flow are instrumented in this step.

To recapitulate, the component-level control flow of RDSEFFs identifies `ExternalCalls` and differentiates them from method calls to API or private (component-internal) methods, `LoopActions` which are relevant at the component-level (i.e., they recursively contain `ExternalCalls`), and `BranchActions` which are relevant at the component-level.

At the class-level, this results in a number of instrumentation points to capture the full control and data flow at runtime. The monitoring is then, in a second step, inserted at the following places, $PositionTypes$:

- *MethodCall.* At the beginning of each provided component service the input parameters are captured. For each input parameter its parameter characterisations are recorded. Furthermore, the fact that a method is entered is recorded. This helps in a later stage to uniquely identify call traces within components.

- *InIteratorStatement.* Inside each loop identified in the RDSEFF. Here, the number of loop executions is captured. No further data is captured.

- *InBranchStatement.* In each branch to record selected branches. For if-then-else constructs, `if` and `else` branches are distinguished. For switch statements or multiple if-then-else statements, also each case is identified uniquely.

143

- *BeforeReturn.* Before the return statement of a provided component service the fact that a method is exited is recorded. For non void methods, the parameter characterisations of the return values are recorded.

- *BeforeExternalCall.* Before every `ExternalCall` to capture input data for external services. For each input parameter of that method the parameter characterisation are captured.

- *AfterExternalCall.* After every `ExternalCall` to capture the return data of an external service as that data serves as input data to the monitored method. The return value of that method is captured in terms of its parameter characterisations as specified in the component interface.

All other loops, branches and method calls are omitted for the monitoring step. This also keeps the later monitoring overhead exactly at the level required for a RDSEFF reconstruction.

5.10.3. Captured data per measuring point

The Beagle approach intentionally does not capture the full data flow in detail to avoid unnecessary instrumentation overhead. For performance, often strong data abstractions are sufficient to capture the performance behaviour of a component. For example, in general the second byte of a list does not determine the remainder of the control flow and thus impact the performance. Instead, the number of elements of a list in most cases is determining the performance as each iteration over that list consumes computation power. These parameter characterisations were first introduced by Koziolek [Koz08a].

At each instrumentation point, the monitoring captures those parameter characterisations (cf. Section 2.7.1) which have been identified as performance-relevant in the component interface. If for example a `List` input parameter of a method is passed to another component (`ExternalCall`), most likely the NUMBER_OF_ELEMENTS attribute is identified as performance relevant in the interface and consequently captured during monitoring. For each instrumentation point, the parameter characterisations which must be monitored are derived from the component's interfaces.

Apart from the parameter characterisations specified in the component interfaces, a number of heuristics is available with the approach. These heuristics identify parameter characterisations which can be recorded in addition to the interfaces or can be applied as a fallback if no parameter characterisations are specified in interfaces. Section 5.10.4 will further detail on these heuristics.

5.10.4. Heuristics for Parameter Characterisations of Interfaces

Parameter characterisations can either be manually specified in the component interface as described above or heuristically derived. In cases where enriched component interfaces (holding information on performance-relevant parameter characterisations) are not available, the heuristics presented in this section can serve as helper and fallback mechanisms (see Figure 5.16). For reverse engineering scenarios, these heuristics can complement the specified parameter characterisations. Users do not have to specify all parameter characterisations but select from a number of parameter characterisation proposed by heuristics and add further self-defined characterisations for complex cases where heuristics cannot propose the right parameter characterisations. This lowers the overall effort for reverse engineering component-based models and complements the reverse engineering capabilities of interfaces introduced in Section 4.8.6.

As any for parameter, performance-relevant characteristics are captured by the parameter characterisations and for more complex cases by complex data types which both belong to the component interfaces (cf. Section 2.5). Hence, manually specified interfaces and heuristically identified parameter properties are both translated into regular structures of PCM component interfaces.

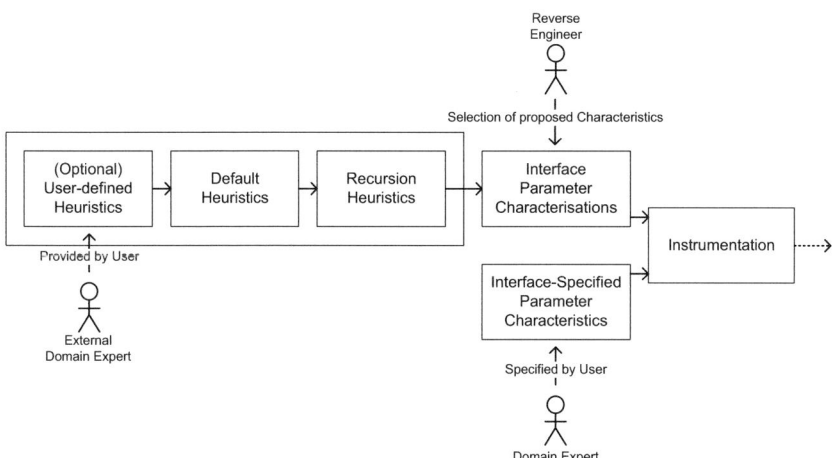

Figure 5.16.: Heuristics for selection of parameter characterisations

Generally, it cannot be decided which data properties are of importance for the reverse engineered models. During monitoring, heuristics are used to identify important parameter characterisations. These heuristics capture best effort rules for potentially important performance characteristics. Please note that these properties are optimised for capturing performance effects and intentionally leave out functional aspects.

Heuristics The heuristics for the parameter characterisations indicate which data properties to monitor. The application of heuristic depends on the type of the parameter. The **heuristics** are:

- For **primitive types** (i.e. int, float, boolean etc.): their actual values (VALUE characterisation). The value of primitive data types can for example directly impact the number of executions of a loop or decide on executing an if or else branch and are thus likely to impact the performance of a component.

- For all *one*-**dimensional arrays** (e.g. int[], String[]), Collection, or Map types: the number of their elements (NUMBER_OF_ ELEMENTS characterisation). As already pointed out in the examples above, arrays and collection types are often subject for iterations. Iterations per se are subject for impacting the performance. Opposed to that, the concrete content of the array is often not impacting performance since the calculation time does only vary little from element to element.

- For **one-dimensional arrays of primitive type** (e.g. int[], boolean[]), additionally aggregated data, such as number of occurrences of specific values in an array (e.g. the number of '0's and '1's in an int[]) is proposed by the heuristics. A PCM ComplexDataType is therefore derived which specifies for example the VALUE characterisation of INNER.one/INNER.zero. The idea behind the heuristic is that when for example filtering a data structures, this is decided based on primitive data types for performance reasons to allow fast element comparison. If filtering is based on primitive types, counting the number of occurrences gives hints on the size of a filtered array (of less size; e.g. an array of zeros) which is then further processed.

- For a *multi*-**dimensional array** (e.g. String[][]): its size, plus results of individual recording of each included array (as described above) are proposed. The above heuristics can be applied to the elements of the array which itself represent an array type. A PCM ComplexDataType is derived for the multi-dimensional array which holds the properties of the inner array (INNER property of the complex data type).

The described heuristics can be applied to component interfaces without a-priori knowledge about their semantics. In general, supporting complex data types (e.g. objects, structs, or any self-defined type) requires domain knowledge to identify important performance properties of these data types. Still, generic data types are used very often, and the presented approach can support the selection of parameter characterisations or even handle these cases automatically through heuristics. The validation in Section 7 will investigate the applicability of the presented heuristics.

Complex Data Type Heuristics To complement heuristics for primitive data types, a heuristic for the handling **complex data types** is proposed: A default heuristic for complex data types is to traverse all public fields and getters of an object recursively. In a transitive query, fields and getters of a data type are queried until finding primitive data types or data types for which the above listed data properties can be captured. For each recursion step, all primitive and collection data type properties are recorded.

$$complexDataTypeProperties = transClosure(t,$$
$$\{t_{sub} \in t.fields \mid t_{sub}.visibility = \text{``public''}\}$$
$$\cup \ getters(t)$$
$$)$$

where t is a data type of a parameter for which to apply the complex data type heuristic, $getters(t)$ are getter methods of type t, and, as earlier, $transClosure(t, Attributes)$ is the transitive closure, starting from t for the attributes of the set $Attributes$.

To avoid infinite or unwanted complex recursion, additional stop criteria can be applied:

- This approach can also be limited to either public fields or getters, by reducing the set $Attributes$ to the first or second element.

- The recursion underlying the transitive closure computation can be stopped after a certain depth n.

The approach is held extensible. Users can add own type-specific heuristics (cf. Figure 5.16) to describe important (performance-relevant) parameter characterisation of a data structure. For each data type a chain of responsibility is applied: First user-defined heuristics, then default heuristics (as described above), and finally a full recursion (for complex data types) can be applied. The PCM supports parameter characterisations for an unlimited number of properties of ComplexDataTypes and adding additional information does not harm the dynamic analysis. Thus additional heuristics cannot conflict with each other. The user has to limit the number of heuristics only for limiting the monitoring overhead associated with extensive instrumentation.

Manually specified Information   If users input information on parameter characterisations for a certain data type to the approach (cf. Figure 5.16, "specified by user"), this information is directly translated into the PCM interfaces. Such information is especially valuable for complex self-defined data types. No further heuristics need to be applied in this cases – still, heuristics can be used for complementing parameter characterisations.

For standard libraries (e.g. Middleware), corresponding PCM components and interfaces can be created. These interfaces can be offered from a repository and include pre-defined parameter characterisations. This reduces the effort of dealing with software which uses standard libraries since the procedure of identifying parameter characterisations is required only once.

Combining Information Sources   All parameter characterisations identified by heuristics are ultimately proposed to the user (cf. Figure 5.16, "Selection of proposed Characteristics"), selected heuristics are translated into parameter characterisations of component interfaces. Hence, the selected parameter characteristics identified via heuristics extend the previously specified component interfaces contributed by SoMoX. Both sources of parameter characterisations (heuristics and specified ones) are combined to have an unique and consistent model representation of required parameter characterisations. Performance affecting properties of parameters are thus formally captured in the model. The instrumentation phase can then look up the parameter characterisations in the components interfaces.

For scenarios which aim at full automation, the manual selection of parameter characterisations can be omitted. In these cases, all parameter characterisations proposed by the heuristics are used during dynamic analysis.

Applications of Static Analysis   In the existing implementation of Beagle, heuristics for the identification of parameter characterisations are not based on static analysis techniques. Still, it would be beneficial to employ techniques such as slicing. If an input parameter is part of the same slice as an output parameter, the parameter should be respected in the corresponding component interface – otherwise the parameter should not be monitored at all.

For future work a more complex heuristic could statically analyse the methods or classes under investigation (which are being monitoring at runtime after instrumentation) and find out the fields and getters that are accessed directly. Then monitoring can limit recording to attributes of data structures that are actually used. For these fields and getters the above heuristics can be applied again. For example, a public field which is additionally available via a getter should not be monitored twice.

5.10.5. Uniqueness of Captured Data

During monitoring, each call to the system and each logging position in the system must be uniquely identifiable to enable later analysis of monitored data. If a user requests a provided service of a component, control and data flow which is issued by that request should be traceable throughout the component to allow to relate monitoring statements to each other. For example, an input parameter of type List over which a loop iterates can only be traced in dynamic analysis, if the request can be uniquely identified at the time of the method call and in the loop iterations. The unique identifier of a request is hereafter referred to as *LoggingTraceID*. LoggingTraceID is unique for a request. If systems have multiple requests (even in parallel) this ID remains unique.

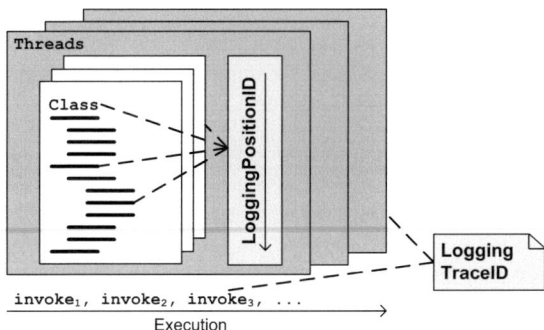

Figure 5.17.: LoggingTraceID and LoggingPositionID

Besides the trace of monitored data, the position of single instrumentation points must be captured to later match multiple runs of the same event type (e.g. method call, loop entrance, etc.) to each other. Such a position must be unique across a whole software project and have a resolution of a single line. This position identifier is referred to as *LoggingPositionID*. The LoggingPositionID is unique for the logger position which means being identifyable across all classes, methods, lines and control flow statements of a software system.

Both, LoggingTraceID and LoggingPositionID together, allow tracing calls over time and space in software systems. Figure 5.17 illustrates the two IDs. Horizontally, the trace and vertically the position is visualised.

For each execution of a instrumentation point, a tuple the following data is monitored and logged:

$$datapoint := (pt \in PositionTypes, \quad \text{e.g. } MethodCall \text{ or } BeforeExternalCall$$
$$datatype, \quad \text{e.g. Integer, Boolean}$$
$$datavalue, \quad \text{e.g. '1' or 'true'}$$
$$LoggingTraceID,$$
$$LoggingPositionID)$$

$LoggingTraceID$ and $LoggingPositionID$ are defined below, $datatype$ is the fully qualified name of the data type. The data value itself is stored as a string to enable a unique database representation which. Since the data type is available from the recorded data, type safety is ensured.

Logging TraceID   LoggingTraceID ensures an unique identification of each request within the provided services of a component, i.e. the logging intentionally does not distinguish component-internal method calls:

$$LoggingTraceID := hash(t_{id}, run, method_{provided}, class_{fqn}, count, logger_{id})$$

where: t_{id} the current thread id, run the test run number maintained by the developed monitoring (cf. Section 5.10.7), $method_{provided}$ the name of the provided method, $class_{fqn}$ the fully qualified name of the class holding the provided method, $logger_{id}$ the local instance name of the logger, and $hash()$ a hash function. $count$ is the count of the provided method's invocations. It is only increased for method invocations of the provided method from the component interface.

Logging PositionID   For the LoggingPositionID less information is required to uniquely identify a position in the source code:

$$LoggingPositionID := hash(class_{fqn}, method_{fqn}, line)$$

where $class_{fqn}$ is the fully qualified class name of the encapsulated statement, $method_{fqn}$ the fully qualified name of the encapsulating method (e.g., void doSth(int, long)), and $line$ the line number in the code (original line number before instrumentation).

This allows a distinction of the logging position at the line level. No further lower granularity (e.g. token number) is required for the presented approach, but could be easily integrated. If a program is written in a "single-line-style" (do   a=a++; b=b++;   while(..)), the code is first unrolled to multiple code lines prior to instrumentation. Otherwise, the line number of LoggingPositionID would not be unique for a logging position. Alternatively, the LoggingPositionID calculation could be extended by the token number to support a unique LoggingPositionID for such a code style.

5.10.6. Instrumentation

During instrumentation, for each measurement point identified in Section 5.10.2, a logger statement is inserted into the source code. The logger statement is responsible for monitoring the code execution. An aspect-based solution (e.g. based on AspectJ [Ecl09]), is not sufficient, since AspectJ cannot insert aspects into control flow statements (e.g., in a loop), which is required in this approach. Only method caller / callee granularity is supported by AspectJ. Unlike Briand et al. [BLL05, BLL06], the approach presented in this thesis, does not introduce artificial method calls at control flow statements to overcome the limitations of AspectJ, but directly manipulates the abstract syntax tree of Java programs through the Eclipse Java Development Tools (JDT).

To ensure limited overhead at runtime, the logging is fully unrolled at instrumentation time, i.e., all parameters are named explicitly and the corresponding parameter characterisations are fixed after instrumentation time. Specifically, no reflection mechanisms etc. are required by the logging. Calculating the LoggingPositionID requires line numbers to be available. Any Java-based approach which needs to access line numbers at runtime must throw an exception, parse the stack trace and only then can infer the line number (cf. [Apa09], documentation on the class LocationInfo). This results in a high overhead. Although the developed logging supports the inference of line numbers via the stack trace (in the same way Apache log4j [Apa09] does), the approach by default intentionally writes the line numbers to the logger statements at instrumentation time to lower the measurement overhead at runtime (i.e. the line number do not need to determined at runtime in the developed approach). When writing the line numbers, the original line numbers (before inserting logger statements) are preserved to ensure traceability.

5.10.7. Data Recording Infrastructure

Collecting measuring data during the execution of a component-based application requires a corresponding data recording infrastructure. Measurement data should be centrally available to ease data aggregation. The storage and integration of data in a database eases the data aggregation since data can be easily accessed by formulating data queries. Due to the nature of the target applications, the recording infrastructure must support distributes scenarios, run with application servers which might have restrictive security policies, and support concurrent executions. For convenience reasons, the infrastructure should be easily set up and perform well. The infrastructure should also help keeping LoggingTraceIDs (cf. Section 5.10.5) unique across multiple analysis runs.

Specific Requirements to the Monitoring Framework The required monitoring framework has to deal with a number of specific requirements, which are not all covered by any single existing monitoring framework. Nevertheless, a large number of monitoring frameworks exist (e.g. [Apa09, RvHG+08, KLM+06]) which cover a subset of the required aspects. Unfortunately, no framework exists which exactly fits the requirements:

- Distribution. Systems running in distributed environments must be supported.

- Concurrency. Systems Under Test (SUT) are potentially installed within environments that are concurrently accessed and might contain additional internal concurrency (threading).

- Parameter Characterisations. Method and constructor parameter characterisations must be tracked instead of only parameter values. Heuristics for the identification of parameter characterisations should be supported.

- No class loader control. The monitoring framework must not rely on load time changes to classes. As for example application servers need to be supported as environment for SUTs, no control over class loading etc. is generally available. Communication and multi threading must conform to the specific requirements of application servers.

- Request tracking. Single user request should be able to be related to each other. Multiple calls of the same provided service need to be distinguishable (introduced before as LoggingTraceID).

- Location identification. The class, method, code line and parameter originating in a monitoring log must be tracked. If there are multiple monitors in the same code section, they must be uniquely and individually tracked back to positions in code (introduced before as LoggingPositionID).

Developed Solution Figure 5.18 gives an overview on the facilities required for recording data in a distributed environment. The Beagle approach uses this infrastructure to also support distributed execution. Control facilities (upper left box) can be separated from the database server (lower left box) and deal with arbitrarily distributed sensors. The initialisation and configuration still is centralised as the sensors first contact the control facilities to set up themselves. Also the configuration is responsible for setting up the database. The dynamical configuration of sensors

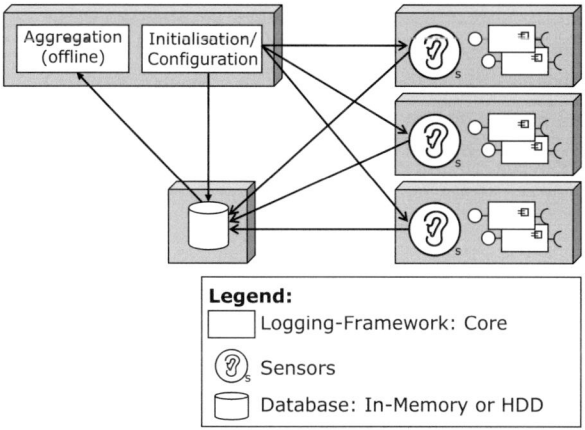

Figure 5.18.: Monitoring infrastructure in distributed scenarios

allows to install sensors with identical configurations but unique IDs. If for example the database server is to be exchanged, the database access data can be configured centrally.

For performance reasons, in this approach, collecting data is strictly separated from aggregating and analysing data. First, all required data is collected with as little overhead as possible; afterwards, time-consuming processing is applied.

To further enhance performance of the data recording framework, monitoring data is locally cached for each sensor node. After a test run has finished, it then can be transferred to the central node asynchronously. This reduces the runtime overhead while performing the monitoring step, enables batch data transfers and thus results in less overall runtime.

The developed data recording infrastructure is not tied to the RDSEFF control flow structures. Instead, it is generally applicable to capture control and data flow of source code elements identified via instrumentation points.

5.10.8. Data aggregation

After all data has been collected through the data recording infrastructure, data resides in a database. At that stage, only raw data is present. For example, loop counts are not available, as only "ticks" for each loop execution exists. In the data aggregation phase, the raw data is converted to, for example, loop execution counts which ease the later interpretation in the machine learning step.

During data aggregation, three basic actions are performed (see Listing 5.9). The first steps aggregates loop counts, the second step aggregated data from multiple executions (i.e. multiple traces), and the third step provides the set of all inputs across all traces for a certain output position.

---

1 **Inputs**

2 Ticks := Set of all monitored single loop executions

3 ExecutedBranches := Set of all monitored branch executions

4 ExternalCallParameters, ReturnValues := Sets of monitored data values

5 $Inputs_{out}$:= Result set of the *potentialInputs* relation

6 Traces := Set of all traces

8 *// 1) Loop execution ''ticks'' are aggregated to loop counts, branch executions are transferred to non–executed branches (only the executed branch is ''aware'' of its execution; the fact that a branch has not been executed is not recorded and must therefore be calculated for other branches)*

9 *// Set of (outputPositionId, aggregatedOutputData) tuples:*

10 AggregatedDataPerPosition ← ∅

11 AggregatedDataPerPosition = aggregateLoops(Ticks) ∪ aggregateBranches(ExecutedBranches) ∪ ExternalCallParameters ∪ ReturnValues

13 *// 2) Data is aggregated over multiple execution runs such that the measured results of multiple runs for the same LoggingPositionID become available. This data serves as a base for the following machine learning and statistical analysis steps.*

14 *// Set of (traceId, outputPositionId, aggregatedOutputData) tuples:*

15 AggregatedDataPerPositionAndTrace ← ∅

16 AggregatedDataPerPositionAndTrace = aggregateTraces(AggregatedDataPerPosition, Traces)

18 *// 3) Provide trace–specific input data for output position data.*

19 *// Set of (traceId, inputPositionId, inputData, outputPositionId, outputData) tuples:*

20 InputOutputRelatedTraceData ← ∅

21 InputOutputRelatedTraceData = aggregateInputOutput(AggregatedDataPerPositionAndTrace, $Inputs_{out}$)

Listing 5.9: Data aggregation steps

The data aggregation relies on the *potentialInputs* relation which has been introduced in Section 5.8.5.3. *potentialInputs* relates input and output data to each other, i.e. for each output LoggingPositionID (return value, method call arguments, loop execution numbers, branch conditions) the valid input LoggingPositionIDs are calculated.

154

5.11. Machine Learning

Machine learning is central to the Beagle reverse engineering approach. It serves two purposes:

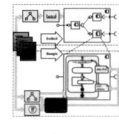

1. the calculation of parametric dependencies from dynamic analysis data and

2. the integration of static, dynamic, and statistical analysis approaches; optimising the results of a single reverse engineering approach.

Thereby, the developed approach

- provides *automated abstraction* capabilities of parametric dependencies and

- allows a seamless *integration* of multiple reverse engineering approaches for parametric dependencies.

For reverse engineering, multiple approaches exist, which have individual advantages and disadvantages. As Ernst [Ern03] points out, static analyses are mostly sound and precise but lack support of large-scale applications or are insufficient when dealing with complex code (e.g. loops which have breaking conditions manipulated inside the loop). Dynamic analysis approaches require the execution of broad parameter ranges of an application to be representative and can be time-consuming. But, if they are applied at the right granularity, they can cover large and complex applications and for example deal with dynamic binding and runtime state. Statistical analyses often can only provide approximations of parametric dependencies but are robust and applicable to large amounts of data.

Generally, little approaches exist which integrate multiple reverse engineering approaches [BLL06, BLL05, WSH08]. Of these, none supports parametric dependencies, performance abstractions, or integrate static, dynamic, statistical analyses. Only few approaches claim component support (e.g. [WW04a]) of which most approaches mean modules and clusters when saying "component" ([Kos02, MM06], cf. Section 8), conflicting with the context independence of components presented in Section 2.6.

Scientific Challenges of Abstract Performance Specifications There are multiple scientific challenges in the field of reverse engineering which must be solved by the presented approach. First of all, the approach must enable the integration of multiple analysis approaches (static, dynamic, and statistical) for the purpose of reverse engineering. To be extensible, a seamless integration of analysis approaches is required. To contribute to the field of reverse engineering, the integrated reverse engineering approach should exceed the capabilities of each single approach and the optimality (cf. Section 2.9) of the results of the integrated approach should outperform the results of each single approach.

Since the approach is using machine learning as a form of meta-heuristics, the optimisation criteria (e.g. abstractness and precision) need to be captured and the optimisation problem (i.e. the search space and the search problem) needs to be formulated. The key challenge for the field of reverse engineering performance models is finding a performance abstraction from given input data provided by static, dynamic, and statistical analysis. Related challenges arise from the field of genetic programming [BNKF98] which is the selected machine learning technique in this thesis. Genetic programming must be adapted for reverse engineering of behaviour models.

Challenges and Contributed Concepts The three major research questions and the corresponding concepts which Beagle contributes to the field of research of machine learning are:

1. $Chall_{Abstraction}$: How to automatically provide abstractions for software performance models?

   $Contrib_{Abstraction}$ is a model abstraction approach which handles the abstraction requirements of performance models (e.g. computation costs, precision, understandability). The approach automates the finding of abstractions for software performance models. The identification and formalisation of domain knowledge on performance abstractions enable the automatic finding of performance abstractions for model parameters which depend on a number of other parameters.

   Given an input model, the approach can create more abstract representations of that model. The developed approach can also be used for manually created models. If it is applied to manually created models, fine-grained details in parametric dependencies of the performance models which contradict analysability are automatically abstracted. The automation increases the usability of performance modeling approaches and their applicability to large-scale systems.

   Simple example: If a parametric dependency depends on 10 variables, covers 10 lines of text representation, and includes terms like $1 \cdot 10^{-50} \cdot x$ where x is a variable, that parametric dependency is missing abstraction. In this case, the abstraction capabilities of the Beagle approach could for example identify the 5 most influential variables, reduce the length of the text representation to 2 lines, and remove the cited term to increase abstraction.

2. $Chall_{Combination}$: How to integrate and combine existing reverse engineering approaches for the purpose of reverse engineering parametric dependencies?

$Contrib_{Combination}$ is a general approach for the integration of multiple source code analyses (e.g. static and dynamic analyses). Furthermore, the approach enables the optimisations of the outputs of these source code analysis approaches with respect to a given fitness function which expresses optimisation criteria (e.g. performance abstraction). The approach shows how to integrate partial, faulty, and contradicting knowledge on approximations of parametric dependencies.

The developed approach is agnostic of the original source of information (e.g. static or dynamic analysis) and only relies on a common representation. For a different approach of each field, a translation of input information to the common representation is exemplarily shown. Through the general problem representation and the optimisation approaches based on that problem representation, this thesis contributes bringing static and dynamic analysis together as claimed by Ernst [Ern03]. The developed approach even goes one step further by allowing the optimisation of each single input.

Simple example: If the static analysis approach a is capable of identifying the number of iterations of a loop to be dependent on parameter x and y, static analysis approach b states the dependency to be $y + z$ for that loop, while a dynamic approach c claims that parameter y is invariant during execution of the method surrounding the loop, this represents partial and contradicting knowledge on a parametric dependency. The real parametric dependency determining the number of loop executions could for example be $y + 2 * z$. The Beagle approach uses the combination of the inputs from a, b, and c to determine an abstraction of the real parametric dependency.

3. $Chall_{CharCurves}$: How to approximate software performance behaviour via abstract models with multi-dimensional influence factors?

$Contrib_{CharCurves}$ is a reverse engineering approach for performance behaviour models through genetic programming. Multi dimensional approximation problems of large search spaces can be effectively searched without a priori knowledge.

The approach can also be used to estimate characteristic curves[1] for multi dimensional performance behaviour approximation problems. Genetic programming has been extended in such a way that it is applicable to performance approximation problems which have multiple input parameters. The resulting performance approximations are able to describe software components and systems based on black box performance data [KKR08a].

---

[1]German: "Kennlinien"; cf. Section 2.9

Simple example: Components have a large number of parameters, their performance could potentially depend on (e.g. all input parameters and all return values of called components). In order to establish a characteristic curve, relevant dimensions must be identified in the search space. Imagine a simple component with 7 provided and 6 required interfaces, each containing 5 services with 4 parameters. Assume that only 2 parameter characterisations for each parameter are available (e.g. NUMBER_OF_ELEMENTS, BYTESIZE). Each required service has a return value and is called from 3 different places in the component. The number of potentially relevant parameters is then $7 \cdot 5 \cdot 4 \cdot 2 + 6 \cdot 5 \cdot 3 \cdot 2 = 280 + 180 = 460$.

If no a priori knowledge is available internals (i.e. control flow structure and parameter propagation), the combination of the 460 parameters forms a large search space. Imagine simple control flow with just one branch with the condition $p_{23} > 123$ && $p_{24} > 123$, which is surrounding an ExternalCall. To estimate when the ExternalCall is triggered, the parameters p_{23} and p_{24} need to have a value larger than 123. This could be specified by a characteristic curve. The Beagle approach is able to create characteristic curves for large search problems.

The following sections present details of the solutions which realise the contributions.

Solution Idea The solution idea to the above sketched challenges $Chall_{Abstraction}$, $Chall_{Combination}$, $Chall_{CharCurves}$ is to use genetic programming, formulate the abstraction and optimisation needs in the genetic programming's fitness function, and capture the performance model in the genetic programming's data structure. A unified representation of the results of each analysis approach as genes of genetic programming enables further optimisations of the reverse engineering results. Furthermore, domain knowledge is encoded into the means of genetic programming (e.g. mutation, crossover, and fitness function) to improve the reverse engineering results. Genetic programming serves well in the desired scenarios since both, the abstract syntax tree of the Stochastic Expressions language of parametric dependencies and the genes of genetic programming are tree structures.

5.11.1. Overview and Introduction

A major contribution of this thesis is the application of machine learning to the reverse engineering of parametric dependencies of behavioural models. The application of machine learning is handled at different levels in the following section. It will be pointed out how the algorithm it set up, what the genes, fitness function etc. are, which specific improvements were made to the field of machine learning (specifically genetic programming), how the abstraction level of RDSEFFs is handled, and how parametric dependencies are calculated.

To recall the importance of parametric dependencies (see Section 2.7 for a definition) which are reverse engineered through machine learning, consider Figure 5.6 from page 115. Parametric dependencies describe resource demands, parameter characterisations of parameters passed to other components, return values, loop iterations, and branch conditions. Any parameterisation of RDSEFFs that depends on data flow is realised via parametric dependencies.

Genetic Programming   The Beagle approach uses *genetic programming* as machine learning approach – a specific form of *genetic algorithms* (cf. [Koz93]) supporting tree-like structured genes. Here, genes are a data structure to capture information. Genetic programming is a heuristic optimisation technique which is applicate to a large problem space which is present in the shown setting (cf. Section 5.11 and Section 2.4 for an introduction).

Genetic programming is in the Beagle approach used to reengineer parametric dependencies. Control and data flow are parameterised over input parameters of a provided service. Learned dependencies parameterise for example the number of times a loop is executed, when a certain control flow branch is executed (the branching condition), which data is passed to other components and how this data is related to the input parameters.

Genetic programming is able to select appropriate input values and reject those that are not relevant for a parametric dependency. This is especially important for estimating control and data flow as the potential input space is large due to multiple data characteristics monitored, of which not all need to be important. The following sections will detail on the chosen genetic programming approach.

Extensions of Genetic Programming   Figure 5.19 provides an overview on genetic programming as applied in the Beagle approach. It combines inputs from static, dynamic, and statistical analyses (left hand side) and creates optimised approximations of parametric dependencies ("Genes of optimised solution", right hand side) from them. The optimisation criteria are summarised in the next Section 5.11.2.

The contributed genetic programming approach is structurally equivalent to commonly used genetic programming [Koz93] as introduced in Section 2.4, but incorporates various extensions and adaptations. These extension and adaptations are necessary to address $Chall_{Abstraction}$, $Chall_{Combination}$, and $Chall_{CharCurves}$.

The specific enhancements are in summary:

- A gene repository which is filled with genes which encode *domain knowledge*. So-called *pre-configured genes* represent knowledge which helps in reverse engineering software performance models.

159

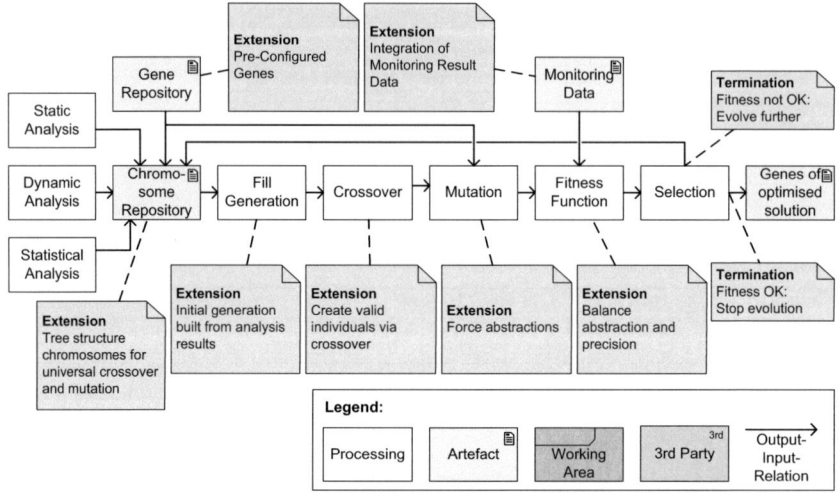

Figure 5.19.: Genetic programming overview

- A chromosome repository which holds individuals which represent *results from static, dynamic, and statistical analysis* for the reverse engineering of a single parametric dependency.

- Tree genes possess evaluation rules for determination of their value which allow *arbitrary subtrees* resulting from mutation and crossover.

- Crossover and mutation operators are designed to *foreclose the creation of structurally invalid individuals*.

- Mutations and fitness function are *supporting abstraction*.

- The fitness function is extended to *balance abstraction and precision* of results.

- If, due to the selection operator, a generation is incomplete, missing individuals of that generations are *filled by special strategies* from the gene repository.

- *Monitoring data* from dynamic analysis is integrated into genetic programming to estimate the precision of results.

Each step of genetic programming will be detailed in the following. The transferred data between all steps from Figure 5.19 are genes; except for an additional fitness value between the "Fitness Function" and "Selection" step.

5.11.2. Abstraction Criteria

All of the following steps are designed to force strong component abstractions to fulfill the aim of reverse engineering: a model which is a performance abstraction of component behaviour. A good abstraction enables analyses of complex software systems with hundreds of thousands of lines of code as case studies show [HBR$^+$10, BKR09, Bec08b]. Additionally, abstract models tend to be easier to understand for humans, if also readability and understandability are abstraction criteria.

In this point, the presented approach especially overcomes the limitations of existing analysis approaches, which are generally not designed to generate *performance abstractions* of component behaviour. Existing approaches from the field of static analysis [CC77, Kin76] mostly emphasize correctness and soundness for their analyses. Dynamic analysis approaches mostly focus on completeness (coverage of executed programs) [EPG$^+$07, NE02]. Statistical approaches provide means of abstractions [Fri91, Lin93], but are not designed to provide performance abstractions.

Abstraction criteria for parametric dependencies include (details in Section 5.11.4.1):

- Computation complexity

- Number of arguments

- Length of expressions

The following example illustrates parametric dependencies of different abstractions levels. In the following example, the If-Then-Else constructs of the expression have only very limited impact on the precision of the results:

$1000.0 * X.\text{VALUE} * \text{EXP}(Z.\text{VALUE}) +$

$\text{IF}(Y.\text{VALUE} > 0) \text{ THEN } (0.001 * X.\text{VALUE}) \text{ ELSE } (0.002 * X.\text{VALUE})$

Here, both branches of the If-Then-Else construct add less than $2 \cdot 10^{-4}$ percent to the overall result of the expression and therefore can be omitted without loosing much precision. Furthermore, the parameter Y could be removed since, independent of its value, the overall expression is not changed much. Hence, a typical abstraction of the above example could result in the following expression:

$$1000.0 * X.\text{VALUE} * \text{EXP}(Z.\text{VALUE})$$

This expression can be computer faster, involves less dimensions (Y is removed), and has a smaller length which human would need to understand when reading the expression. Still, in this example the introduced error due to the abstraction is less than $2 \cdot 10^{-4}$ percent. Section 5.11.4 presents the details of abstraction criteria.

5.11.3. Genes and Chromosomes

The approach combines genes, each representing mathematical functions, to express parametric dependencies of the RDSEFF model. As introduced in Section 2.4, the genes in genetic programming are organised in a tree structure which represents a *chromosome*. Each chromosome is an *individual*. In the following example, a simple chromosome called $Individual_A$ is shown in a linearised form. $Individual_A$ could for example specify the value of a parameter of an `ExternalCall`. It will be used as a running example.

$$Individual_A = 0.001 * X.\text{VALUE} + \text{IF}(Y.\text{VALUE} > 0) \text{ THEN } 1$$

The same chromosome has the following tree structure visible from Figure 5.20. In the example, the ">" comparison is encoded into the IF-THEN gene and thus not an argument.

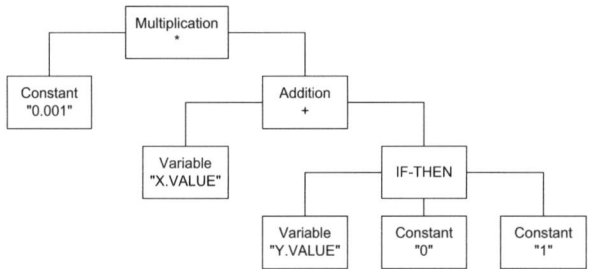

Figure 5.20.: Tree structure of the genes

It can be seen that the gene tree structure of $Individual_A$ is comparable to the abstract syntax tree of parsed source code. Since parametric dependencies ultimately must abstract parametric dependencies from source code (e.g. the one from Listing 5.10), the chosen gene structure basically has the same form like source code structures.

Individuals which are composed from these genes can have a varying length in the developed approach. As the length and tree structure (binary tree vs. trees with arbitrarily many children) of the parametric dependency, which is going to be reverse engineered, are unknown at the beginning of a genetic programming run, neither length nor tree structure can be fixed.

```
1  boolean calculateTax(int x, int y, List<Person> z) {
2      double tax = 0.001 * x;
3      if(y > 0) {
4          tax = tax + 1;
5      }
6      boolean result = C2.persistTax(tax, z); // external call
7      return result;
8  }
```

Listing 5.10: Source code example: The parametric dependency expressed by $Individual_A$ calculates the value of tax in persistTax(..)

The following sections introduce the different kinds of genes which are available in the developed genetic programming approach, discuss characteristics of the chosen genes, and reflect the design of genes and chromosomes.

5.11.3.1. Variable Genes for Input Parameters

For every input parameter characterisation of a provided service (e.g. size of an input array, or value of a primitive type; in the example X.VALUE and Y.VALUE), a gene representing that parameter characterisation in the resulting model is introduced. It is representing that parameter as a variable. The input parameter characterisations are available from the interface specification and have previously also been respected during monitoring (monitoring data is available for them).

The mapping from parameter characterisations to genes results in symbolic representations of parameter characterisations. Each parameter characterisation pc is represented by a tuple:

$$gene(pc) := (pc.\text{parameter.name}, pc.\text{characterisation})$$

Such a "variable gene" is abbreviated to e.g. "X.VALUE" in textual representations.

The resulting set of genes representing input parameter charactersations is:

$$Genes_{inputs} := \{gene(pc) \mid pc \in Param_{char}\}$$

where $Param_{char}$ are all parameter characterisations which are available for potential input parameters of a parametric dependency ($output$) which is to be reverse engineered:

$$Param_{char} := \bigcup_{i \in potentialInputs(output)} i.collect(\text{"characterisations"})$$

where $potentialInputs(output)$ is as defined in Section 5.8.5.3 and $collect$-("characterisations") collects the set of parameter characterisations for an potential input parameter available via the "characterisations" attribute of parameters. For example, consider the parameter z from Listing 5.10 and assume that the two parameter characterisations are defined for z: NUMBER_OF_ELEMENTS and BYTESIZE. Both parameter characterisations would result from $collect(..)$ if it is applied to z.

5.11.3.2. Constants Genes

To increase the convergence speed of the search, special constants genes $Genes_{constants}$ that have a predefined set of possible values $Values_{CG}$ or ranges of allowed values ($lower \leq value \leq upper$ either integer or float) have been introduced to genetic programming. The $value$ of a constant gene $constantGene \in Genes_{constants}$ is defined as:

$$constantGene_{value} :=$$

$$\begin{cases} v \; : \; v = random(Values_{CG}) & \text{for discrete} \\ & \text{values} \\ v \in [lower, upper] \; : \; v, lower, upper \in \mathbb{R} \wedge lower < upper & \text{if } !integer \\ v \in [lower, upper] \; : \; v, lower, upper \in \mathbb{Z} \wedge lower < upper & \text{if } integer \end{cases}$$

where v is a random but constant value per instance of that gene, $integer$ is a boolean flag which indicates integer values if set to true, and $random(Set)$ selects a random element of Set.

These constants genes reside by default in the set $Genes$ and can be used independently of prior analysis approaches. For example, float values in between 0.0 and 1.0 (e.g. $Values_{scaleDown} = \{0.1, 0.5, ..\}$) can be used instead of the full float range to scale values down (e.g. $0.1 \cdot x$ scales down x). Integer sets like $Values_{scaleUp} = \{10, 100, 10000, ..\}$ can be used to scale up values (e.g. $100 \cdot x$) and then can be refined by mutations (e.g. $102.3 \cdot x$). Although these kinds of genes could be randomly created during mutations from a constant gene, the availability of "out-of-the-box" genes with such values increases the chances of selecting them. Besides using these genes as predefined constants, they can also be used for

```
1  float y;
2  if(x < 0.4 || x > 0.8) {
3    y = 0.5 * x;
4  } else {
5    y = 0.5 * x + 0.2;
6  }
7  for(i = 0; i < y * 1000; i++) {
8    //..
9  }
```

Listing 5.11: Example: Non-continuous behaviour

the initial generation and be initialised with data from static or statistical analysis $Values_{statisticalAnalysis}$. The resulting set of pre-defined values is thus specific to a certain reverse engineering task:

$$Values_{CG} := Values_{scaleUp} \cup Values_{scaleDown} \cup Values_{statisticalAnalysis}$$

The creation of the initial generation will be further discussed in Section 5.11.10.2.

5.11.3.3. Mathematical Operators

In addition to variables and constants, mathematical operations are used as genes. Additionally, genes are made available for inequations ($a \leq b$), if-then, and if-then-else to support non-continuous behaviour (e.g. to reflect jumps caused by "if-then-else" in the code). The support of non-continuous behaviour is especially important due to the nature of calculations in source code.

Consider the example from Listing 5.11. Here, the calculation of a parametric dependency is split into two branches. Hence, the function to be expressed by the parametric dependency needs to be non-continuous. The number of iterations of the for loop non-continuously depends on the value of x. The resulting values of y are scattered (see Figure 5.21 for an visualisation).

In order to correctly approximate parametric dependencies from source code, corresponding genes are introduced. The set of mathematical operators genes is:

$$\begin{aligned} Genes_{math} = \{ &power, multiplication, multiplication3, addition, addition3, \\ &subtraction, subtraction3, division, sine, exponential function, \\ &inequations, if-then, if-then-else \} \end{aligned}$$

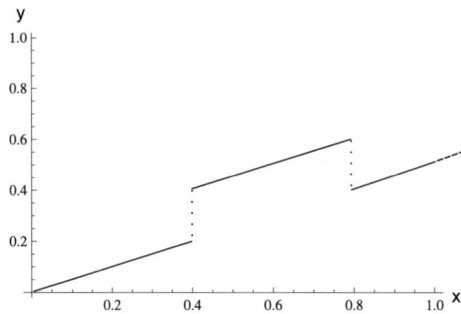

Figure 5.21.: Example: Non-continuous function values introduced by branched calculations depending on the value of X.

where genes ending with "3" are mathematical operators with three arguments (e.g.
$addition3$: $a+b+c$, $subtraction3$: $a-b-c$). The explanation of further semantics
of these genes is omitted here for brevity. More complex genes like $if - then$ and
$if - then - else$ are explained in the context of the fitness function in Section 5.11.4.
The varying number of arguments for each gene is discussed below together with the
definition of genes.

The precedence of gene arguments for their evaluation is encoded into the genes
themselves. Each gene states explicit precedence rules. Hence, the evaluation of
chromosomes is never ambiguous.

5.11.3.4. Characteristics of Genes

Genes have different numbers of arguments as can be seen from Figure 5.20. While
the multiplication has two arguments (sub nodes in the tree), if-then-else has three. To
ease later mutations of genes (the number of arguments must fit for valid mutations;
cf. Section 5.11.7), multiple versions of some genes exits. For example, multiplication is also available as a three argument version which multiplies three numbers.
Hence, each gene with three arguments (e.g. addition with three arguments) can be
replaced by that version of the multiplication gene during mutation.

A (non-variable) $gene \in Genes_{math} \cup Genes_{constants}$ is a triple:

$$gene := (value, numberOfArguments, SubGenes) \ :$$
$$card(SubGenes) = numberOfArguments \land$$
$$numberOfArguments \in \mathbb{N}^0 \land$$
$$value \in \mathbb{R} \tag{5.1}$$

where $value$ is the represented value (e.g. for an addition the value $arg_1 + arg_2$), $numberOfArguments$ is the integer number of sub-genes, and $SubGenes$ is an ordered set of sub-genes which contribute in the calculation of $value$. In the case of mathematic genes $gene \in Genes_{math}$, the $value$ can be calculated from the arguments ($numberOfArguments > 0$). For constant genes $gene \in Genes_{constants}$, the $value$ is fixed.

A variable gene $gene \in Genes_{inputs}$ has only a variable value, which is assigned by $variableValue$ with values recorded during monitoring (cf. Section 5.10):

$$variableValue := gene \rightarrow v \in \mathbb{R}$$

Section 5.11.4 details on the evaluation of variable genes.

The overall set of genes on which Beagle operates is:

$$Genes := Genes_{inputs} \cup Genes_{constants} \cup Genes_{math}$$

The different genes (variables, constants, mathematical operator) presented before, represent the set of available gene *types*, while $Genes$ holds *instances* of genes. For reasons of compactness, the following sections deal with instances of genes only. Gene types are only discussed where necessary.

5.11.3.5. Design of Genes and Chromosomes

In the developed approach which is based on JGAP [Mef], each gene must return a floating point number as its result. This unifies the type of arguments and return types. The unification allows to omit type inference (resulting in reduced calculation time for genetic programming) and simplifies mutation and crossover. Due to the unification of type arguments, mutation can change single genes without affecting whole individuals (e.g. replace an $if - then$ gene by an $addition3$ gene; cf. Section 5.11.7). Furthermore, crossover can interbreed arbitrary sequences of genes (e.g. the condition of a $if - then$ gene can be cut and replaced by arbitrary other genes; cf. Section 5.11.6).

In order to map all arguments and return types to floating point numbers, the $inequation$ gene is for example returning 1 (representing `true`) or 0 (representing `false`) when comparing two arguments. To avoid floating point arithmetic problems, the comparison employs an ϵ environment.

Type inference, although being generally desirable in programming languages, for a number of reasons is not supported in genetic programming.

i) Mutation would be strongly limited when using different types for arguments. Due to the usage of a single result type, genes with the same number of arguments can be replaced by each other without further overhead. If static analysis approaches would provide an integer, using the integer in a if-then-else gene would not be possible straight forward as an argument in the condition which would require a boolean argument. With the chosen unified representation, an integer can be used directly in two different ways: as a constant argument in the condition (IF(integer) THEN) or in an inequation (integer < X or integer > X). Thus, every gene can replace every other gene.

ii) Without type inference, crossover and mutation cannot result in invalid individuals. This helps avoiding runtime overhead for the recognition of invalid individuals. Usual genetic algorithms create individuals through crossover and mutations, then perform a validity check, throw away invalid individuals (cf. [Mef]), re-apply crossover and mutation until a valid individual arises. Hence, avoiding invalid individuals by design helps saving computation time.

The arbitrary combination possibilities of genes ease the creation of diversity among individuals. Diversity is required for genetic programming to overcome local minima and cover the search space. If some points in the search space could only be reached via "small paths", it would become unlikely that they are explored during evolution. Imagine a gene which had three typed arguments of a certain type (e.g. string, boolean, and integer). If there are five incompatible types in total, the chance of picking the right one during evolution is $\frac{1}{5}$. For the combination of all three arguments, the chance of creating a valid chromosome would be $\frac{1}{5} \cdot \frac{1}{5} \cdot \frac{1}{5} = \frac{1}{125}$. Thus, further means would be required to ensure valid individuals. With the chosen design of genes, these means are not necessary.

iii) Chromosomes are not written manually by humans. Programming errors (errors in the gene structure) are therefore not possible and do not need to be recognisable based on the chromosome structure.

iv) The genetic algorithm framework JGAP which is used for the implementation does not support type inference.

5.11.3.6. Gene Subsets

Ultimately, all genes can be made available for genetic programming. Genes are used for the initial generation and the later evolution of individuals. During evolution, mutations can exchange genes by others (with the same number of arguments).

For each genetic programming run, the number of available genes can be limited. If static analysis states for example that there is no branching to be covered by a parametric dependency, all if-then and if-then-else genes could be deactivated. This could potentially increase the convergence speed due to less options in the solution space. Still, in the approach used in this thesis, the full set of genes is used to not artificially limit the expressiveness. The two reasons are:

- The *selection* applied during genetic programming forms "natural" subsets of genes after evolving a certain number of generations. Only genes which are actively present in individuals are used often in crossover. Mutation only brings in a small portion of remaining genes. Thus, genetic programming is working on a problem-specific subset of genes which does does not require a subset of genes.

- Reducing genes to a subset can also be conflicting with the required expressiveness. If for example static analysis indicates that there are no branches in the source code, jump statements can still be present in the code. A loop with labels might require to have branches in the reverse engineered parametric dependencies.

5.11.4. Fitness Function

The fitness function in the Beagle approach is used as a central element to find and evaluate abstractions of component behaviour. A number of measures is taken to provide abilities to deal with abstractions. The fitness function is always evaluated for a whole individual. Since the fitness function is steering the evolution process, it must provide gradual differences in the fitness evaluations of individuals to ensure guidance. If for example two individuals only differ in a single gene which affects the desired results (e.g. the first individual $Individual_A$ is a little more abstract than the second one $Individual_B$), this difference should be expressed by the fitness function. During selection, those individuals with better fitness can be preferred.

Consider the following individuals of which $Individual_A$ is from the running example:

$$Individual_A := 0.001 * X.\text{VALUE} \quad + \text{ IF}(Y.\text{VALUE} > 0) \text{ THEN } 1$$
$$Individual_B := 0.001 * 0.9 \quad\quad\quad + \text{ IF}(Y.\text{VALUE} > 0) \text{ THEN } 1$$

Here, $Individual_A$ and $Individual_B$ are nearly identical, except for $X.\text{VALUE}$ being exchanged by 0.9. $Individual_A$ involves two variables (X and Y) while $Individual_B$ has only one variable Y. Thus, from the perspective of "abstraction", $Individual_B$ is preferable over $Individual_A$. The fitness function should express that $Individual_B$ is more abstract.

The fitness of individuals is judged according to two basic criteria: The precision and abstractness (cf. Figure 5.22). The precision is given by the deviation between monitored values (see Section 5.10) and values predicted by the mathematical expression found by genetic programming. Abstraction is captured by the inverse of complexity of expressions represented by individuals. Complexity should be lowered so that expressions are understandable for humans if possible; low complexity of expressions also increases the abstraction level provided by the overall expression. A number of complexity criteria is therefore evaluated to judge on the abstractness of individuals and balanced with abstraction through weighted sums. Section 5.11.4.1 details how precision and abstractness are balanced.

In the above example, $Individual_B$ was considered to be more abstract than $Individual_A$ but $Individual_A$ could be more precise than $Individual_B$. Imagine that $X.VALUE$ would be a variable with a constant value of 10,000. Then, the values calculated by $Individual_B$ would be off. The precision of $Individual_B$ would be lower than the one of $Individual_A$. As a consequence, precision and abstractness must be balanced.

The fitness function maps an chromosome c to a numerical fitness value:

$$FitnessFunction(c) := c \rightarrow fitness \in \mathbb{R}$$

where $c \in Generation$ is a chromosome of a $Generation$:

$$Generation = \{c_1, c_2, ..\}$$

and a chromosome $c \in Chromosomes$ is a set of genes $c \subseteq Genes$ which must include all transitively reachable sub-genes of each a gene:

$$\forall \, gene \in c \, : \, g \in transClosure(gene, \{\text{'subGenes'}\} \,) \Rightarrow g \in c$$

where $transClosure(..)$ is applied to a set of a single element with semantics as defined before.

5.11.4.1. Balancing Precision and Abstractness

Figure 5.22 visualises the stress field between precision and abstractness. Both, precision and abstractness, summarise a number of sub-criteria like expression computations costs or depth of chromosomes. The trade-off between precision and abstractness cannot generally be decided since neither precision dominates abstraction nor vice versa. As the example of $Individual_A$ and $Individual_B$ shows, various cases are imaginable which require and a trade-off decision between precision and abstractness.

In Beagle, the trade-off decision must be met automatically (without user interaction), since every individual of genetic programming is evaluated in every generation. Thousands of fitness function evaluations result from a single genetic programming run which makes user interaction infeasible.

The developed fitness function employs weights for precision and abstractness which proved to successfully balance precision and abstractness during evaluation. Nevertheless, if more computation complexity resulting in longer simulation time

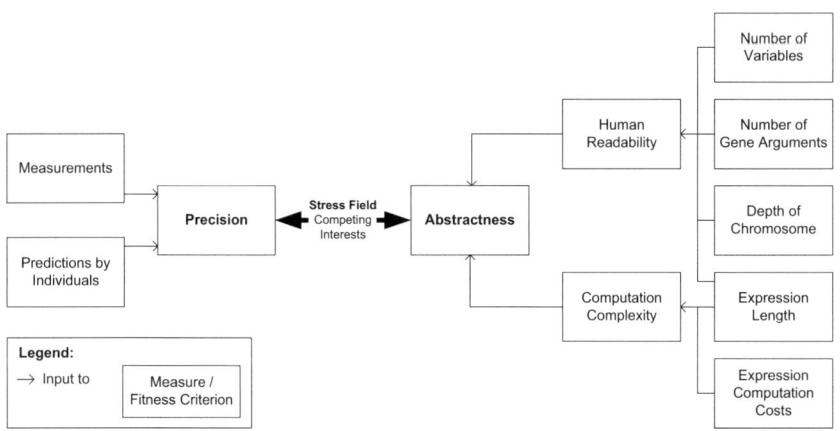

Figure 5.22.: Stress field of the fitness function: Precision vs. abstractness

and reduced human readability of parametric dependency expressions are acceptable in a certain scenario, the weights can be adapted to prefer precision.

The weights have been balanced with respect to the application scenarios of the Palladio approach. For precision, human readability, and computation complexity (the latter are input to abstractness) *boundaries* have been derived for typical application scenarios of Palladio. For example, human readability of expressions drops if expression become to long and complex. An expression covering more than one line is unlikely to be understandable. Furthermore, simulation of the reverse engineered Palladio models should not last more than 10 minutes for quick response scenarios which shall allow interaction with the PCM model performance simulation. These boundaries helped in identifying default weights. The weights were determined for multiple example systems such that the boundaries are not hit. Precision and abstraction are equally balanced. Precision has a default weight of $w_{precision} = 50\%$ and abstractness $w_{abstractness} = 50\%$ in the fitness function results.

Section 5.11.4.3 will further detail on all weights employed in the fitness function. The conceptual elements of the fitness function are intentionally presented separate from the concrete values. The calculation of the fitness function and criteria for precision and abstraction will be presented in the following.

5.11.4.2. Fitness Criteria and Fitness Criteria Calculation

The presented fitness function picks up the ideas of the Generalized Cross Validation (GCV) (cf. [Sta09]) error measure which also incorporates model complexity. It overcomes the limitations of error measures like least square error and generalises the problem of balancing model complexity and precision. As GCV is a general error measure, it does not include domain knowledge. The introduced fitness functions transfers GCV to the field of genetic programming and adds domain knowledge represented as specialised abstraction criteria.

To compute for example the expression complexity, the fitness function considers, among others, the depth of the tree of genes and the length of the resulting mathematical expression. If a certain threshold is passed, the fitness of individuals is reduced. For example, if the length of an expression exceeds a certain number of genes, the fitness of the evaluated individual representing the expression is reduced (Section 5.11.4.3 presents an overview the values of thresholds). Beyond this, a parametric dependency should conform to a number of additional criteria to provide better abstractions. The following metrics evaluate the abstraction criteria of a single individual (see also Figure 5.22) and its precision:

- For each mathematic expression, its **computation complexity** is determined. For example, additions, subtractions and multiplications are less computation intensive than square roots. Thus, easy to evaluate expressions are preferred. The computation costs also depend on the number of terms in the expressions. Each mathematical operation has costs attached. The computation costs for an individual are the sum of costs of all its operations.

  - The *length of an expression* is calculated from the individual string lengths of each gene

  $$m_{ExpressionLength}(c) := \sum_{gene \in c} StringLength(gene)$$

  where $StringLength(gene)$ determines the length of the string representation of each gene. For example, the introduction of Section 5.11.3 and $Individual_A$ show the string representation of chromosomes. The length $m_{ExpressionLength}(Individual_A)$ is 32.

  - The *expression computation costs* depend on the type of genes a chromosome comprises. In order to determine the computation costs of a gene, the gene definition is extended by $computationCosts$:

  $$gene := (value, numberOfArguments, SubGenes,$$
  $$computationCosts) \; : \; computationCosts \in \mathbb{R}$$
  $$\text{other arguments as introduced in Equation 5.1}$$

The constraints on the previously introduced attributes of the gene remain the same. Using this extended definition, the *expression computation costs* are determined by:

$$m_{ExpressionComputationCosts}(c) := \sum_{gene \in c} (gene.computationCosts)$$

For example, in general, the addition in $Individual_A$ can be calculated faster than the conditional branch (if-then-else). Hence, addition has lower computation costs associated than conditional branches. Section 5.11.4.3 will detail on the costs per gene.

– The *computation complexity* is impacted by $m_{ExpressionLength}(c)$ and $m_{ExpressionComputationCosts}(c)$ (see Figure 5.22). Small computation complexity is considered to be more optimal than large computation complexity. The calculation of the overall fitness will be detailed below. Computation complexity is not calculated separately, but together with the fitness function.

• Since the parametric dependencies which are learned in genetic programming are a potential subject for later manual editing during architecture refactoring at the model level, they should be understandable to humans. Longer expressions become hard to grasp for human.

The **human readability** of expressions represented by chromosomes relates to the length of expressions, the number of involved variables, the number of gene arguments, and is indirectly reflected by the depth of chromosomes, i.e. the depth of nesting of expressions.

When comparing $Individual_A$ with the following two examples, it becomes obvious that the length of expressions is a major impact factor for readability (variable characterisations are omitted for brevity reasons):

$$Individual_{Complex} := 0.00001 + 0.005 * X *$$
$$(Y + \text{ IF}(Z > A) \text{ THEN } (0.002 * B) \text{ ELSE}$$
$$(0.0004 * C + 0.00001 * D * \text{EXP}(E)))$$
$$Individual_{Simple} := 0.001 * X$$

The meaning of $Individual_{Simple}$ is much easier to understand than $Individual_{Complex}$ while the complexity of $Individual_A$ ranges in the middle. Variables imply additional complexity since their values can change and thus impact the overall value of a chromosome. Furthermore, constants (with no arguments) are easier to understand than conditional branches with many arguments which must be understood separately. Higher depths of chromosomes results in brackets where pairs of opening and closing brackets are hard to map for humans (see $Individual_{Complex}$).

- The *depth of the chromosome* is derived from the tree formed by its genes. For example, Figure 5.20 illustrates a typical tree structure of a chromosome. In the example, the depth of the chromosome is 3.

  First the top most gene of a chromosome has to be calculated since a chromosome is a flat set which does not indicate the root gene of the tree structure formed by the gene's "SubGenes" relation:

$$TopGene(c) := gene \in c :$$
$$fmax(\ card(transClosure(gene,\ \{\text{'SubGenes'}\})))$$
$$\forall gene \in c$$

  where $fmax(expression)$ (as introduced before; returns a single representative if the expression is maximal for multiple elements) determines the maximum value of $expression$ and thus in this case determines the largest transitive closure for all genes in c. Then for the top most gene of c, the maximum tree height can be calculated:

$$m_{ChromosomeDepth}(c) := maxTreeHeight(TopGene(c),$$
$$\{\ \text{'SubGenes'}\ \})$$

  where $maxTreeHeight(gene, attribute) \rightarrow height \in \mathbb{R}$ is an algorithm which determines the maximum height of a tree data structure for the root element $gene$ and the child node attribute $attribute$. An algorithm for the determination of the maximum tree height is for example documented by Edmonds [Edm08, p. 136].

- The *number of involved variables* and the *number of arguments* of used genes are evaluated to prefer more simple expressions over those involving dozens of arguments. Expressions with just a few arguments make it more likely that removing a dimension (parameter or variable) during mutation is successful without side effects.

- The *number of involved variables* is defined as:

$$m_{Variables}(c) := \sum_{gene \in c} \begin{cases} 1 & \text{if } type(gene) = \text{'variable'} \\ 0 & \text{else} \end{cases}$$

  where $type(gene)$ determines the type of a gene.

- The *number of arguments* is defined as:

$$m_{Arguments}(c) := \sum_{gene \in c} gene.numberOfArguments$$

For example, an addition has two operands, whereas an if-then-else has four (two for the condition and two for the branches).

- The metric for the *length of the expression* $m_{ExpressionLength}(c)$ is used as defined above.

- *Human readability* is impacted by $m_{ChromosomeDepth}(c)$, $m_{ChromosomeDepth}(c)$, $m_{Variables}(c)$, $m_{Arguments}(c)$, and $m_{ExpressionLength}(c)$ (see Figure 5.22). Lower values of the metrics mentioned above indicate increased human readability of a chromosome. Thus, lower values are more optimal than larger ones. The calculation of the overall fitness will be detailed below, since the metric values are transformed prior to calculating the overall fitness from them.

- The **precision** of a chromosome is determined by the deviation between measured and predicted values for a parametric dependency. The error measure is the mean squared error of values (cf. [LC98]):

$$m_{error}(c) := \frac{1}{n} \sum_{i=1}^{n} e_i^2$$

with $e_i = pred_i - meas_i$ being the predicted minus the measured values. $meas_i$ stems from results during monitoring, $pred_i$ is the value predicted by the individual for which the fitness is evaluated. Every individual must predict every measured value. The input data (input parameter values) stems from monitoring. $i = 1..n$ indexes each single pair of measured and predicted values.

Consider the example chromosome $Individual_A$ which depends on the parameter characterisations X.VALUE and Y.VALUE. The first columns of Table 5.1 show measured values which might have been gathered during the execution of code for which a certain parametric dependency (e.g. characterisation of the parameter of an ExternalCall) must be reverse engineered. The real parametric dependency PD_{real} represents an optimal solution.

$$Individual_A = 0.001 * X.\text{VALUE} + \text{IF}(Y.\text{VALUE} > 0) \text{ THEN } 1$$
$$PD_{real} = 0.05 * X.\text{VALUE} + \text{IF}(Y.\text{VALUE} > 1) \text{ THEN } 2$$

i	Measured Input			Measured Value	Predicted Value
	X.VALUE	Y.VALUE	Z.NoE	(Output, $meas_i$)	(Output, $pred_i$)
1	0	-3	2	0	0
2	1	0	5	0.001	0.05
3	2	2	4	1.002	2.1
4	3	1	7	1.003	0.15
5	4	-1	-3	0.004	0.2
6	5	4	-2	1.005	2.25
..	..	..	..	..	..

Table 5.1.: Measured and predicted values for a single parametric dependency

In the table, "NoE" abbreviates the NumberOfElements variable characterisation. The Z.NoE variable characterisation was measured but does not impact the measured output value. An optimal solution like PD_{real} thus can omit Z.NoE. Hence, PD_{real} does not comprise Z.NoE while another parametric dependency, for example a branch condition, can nevertheless depend on Z.NoE.

Prior to judging the complexity of mathematic expressions, the expression itself can be *simplified*. Genetic programming allows having redundant expressions like $+1 - 1 \cdot 1$, which would make the previous two measures ineffective and sometimes misleading. Mathematic simplification is thus a precondition before evaluating the fitness of individuals. The $Simplify$ function creates new simplified chromosomes from an input chromosome:

$$Simplify := c \rightarrow c_{simplified} \ : \ card(c_{simplified}) \leq card(c)$$

The implementation of the according functionality can be taken over by commercial applications like Mathematica [Wol] or Maple [Map].

Fitness Value Range   Generally, fitness functions are desirable which have a well-known range of fitness values. If the range of fitness values is well-known, fitness values become more intuitive. For example, the best individuals have a fitness values of 1 and the worst individuals have a fitness value of 0. For the present genetic programming scenario, nevertheless, no such fitness function can be established as will be explained in the following. Instead, the created fitness function, which is presented in the following, returns 0 for the best individuals and larger values for worse individuals. Although the presented fitness function might appear to be counter intuitive, it does not limit the genetic programming approach itself.

The fitness values of the presented fitness function cannot have an upper bound as its input parameters have no defined limit: i) Precision is measured by the error which has not defined upper limit, thus the error can be very high, ii) computation complexity can be very high as none of the involved metrics has an upper limit, and iii) human readability expressed by metrics which rise for low readability have no upper limit as well.

The chosen fitness function maps a chromosome c to a positive floating point value for which only the lower boundary is known:

$$fitness := c \to x \in \mathbb{R} \mid x \geq 0$$

The fitness function is designed to indicate *relative* fitness instead of absolute fitness values. When comparing two individuals c_1 and c_2, the fitness function indicates which one is better, but a difference of the factor of 2 between the fitness value of c_1 and c_2 does *not* indicate a twice as good individual. For the later selection operator, a relative fitness values is perfectly acceptable since only binary decisions (keep or reject an individual) need to be met.

As the theoretically optimal fitness value of individuals ("0") is known, it allows to immediately terminate genetic programming if an individual with a fitness value of "0" has been found. In such cases, the fitness function thus increases convergence speed of genetic search.

Nevertheless, individuals with optimal fitness are not always reachable due to missing abstractness of fully precise individuals. For example, individuals with no prediction error (e.g. $Individual_{Complex}$) tend to be large and complex expressions with limited abstractness. If such an individual depends on multiple variables, no optimal fitness can be reached due to $m_{Variables}(c)$. The following section discusses counter measures to limit the impact of abstractness on the fitness function.

Thresholds Every computation of a parametric dependency involves some costs and no high precision can be expected from very short expressions (e.g. $Individual_{Simple}$). Therefore, after calculating the above metrics, thresholds are applied to each metric before feeding the result into the overall fitness function. Only metric values exceeding the thresholds result in *penalties* for the fitness function.

Further examples illustrate the need for thresholds:

- Variables: A parametric dependencies is likely to depend on a minimum number of variables. Otherwise it would represent a constant. $Individual_A$, for example, depends on two variable characterisations like the real parametric dependencies PD_{real}. Thus, a minimum number of variables should be allowed for all individuals.

177

- Length: Even the real parametric dependency PD_{real} has a certain length, which should be accepted for every individual.

- Chromosome depth: Every non-trivial parametric dependency requires nesting of chromosomes which increase the chromosome depth. Thus, a non-null minimum depth is desirable for all individuals.

Corresponding reasons for introducing thresholds of all other metrics become obvious for $Individual_A$ and PD_{real}.

Since the optimal solution for a parametric dependency cannot be known in advance (because genetic programming searches for it), the thresholds need to be fixed independent of a concrete parametric dependency. Neither the number of arguments, variables, computation complexity nor the length of an optimal real parametric dependency can be known in general. The default thresholds for all metrics will be presented in Section 5.11.4.3.

Penalties, which count for the fitness function, are derived from metric values and the threshold of that metric. Compared to the pure metric values, penalties increase the values of metrics which are considered to be minimally acceptable. The penalties p_i linearly depend on the metric results m_i and the associated thresholds t_i and are responsible for increasing the fitness value of a chromosome (indicating less optimal fitness):

$$p_j(c) := \begin{cases} m_j(c) - t_j & \text{if } m_j(c) > t_j \\ 0 & \text{else} \end{cases}$$

where t_j is an individual threshold and $m_j(c)$ is an individual result of a chromosome for a fitness metric of $FitnessMetrics$:

$$FitnessMetrics := \{m_{ExpressionLength}(c), m_{ExpressionComputationCosts}(c),$$
$$m_{ChromosomeDepth}(c), m_{Variables}(c), m_{Arguments}(c)\}$$

Normalisation The metric weights are normalised prior to becoming part of the fitness function to account for the fact that all metric values are of a different scale (e.g. "length in characters" vs. "chromosome depth in hierarchy levels"). For example, the expression length $m_{ExpressionLength}$ for the example $Individual_A$ has a value of "30" characters while the corresponding chromosome depth $m_{ChromosomeDepth}$ is just "4".

The aim of normalisation is to have a value of 1 after normalisation. As none of the metrics has a fixed upper limit, "typical large" metric values must be retrieved from experiments. The size of "typical large" values is expressed by the variable $normScale_j$. The default $normScale_j$ values for all metrics are discussed in Section 5.11.4.3.

To normalise metric values after applying the penalty, they are simply divided by a $normScale_j$ value which is specific to each metric from $FitnessMetrics$:

$$norm_j(c) := \frac{p_j(c)}{normScale_j - t_j}$$

where p_j is an individual result of a metric from $FitnessMetrics$ after applying the penalty function. t_j is subtracted so that the $normScale_j$ value can be specified according to the original metric value.

Fitness Value Calculation   The **fitness function** which determines the fitness of a chromosome c is the weighted sum of error and penalties derived from abstractness metrics:

$$fitness(c) := w_e \cdot m_{error}(c) + \sum_{j=1}^{card(FitnessMetrics)} w_j \cdot norm_j(c)$$

with $m_{error}(c)$ the above error metric, w_e the weight of the error, w_j the weight associated to metric j, $norm_j(c)$ as defined above, and $c \in Chromosomes$. The weights balance precision (weight w_e) and abstractness (cf. Figure 5.22) and within the abstractness metrics the individual weights w_j.

The weights in the fitness function are required for two reasons: i) the value ranges of error and metrics differ (the mean squared error (which is not normalised) can have values of 1000 and more while the normalised metrics values have a target value of 1 (after normalisation) and ii) the weights allow to flexibly adapt the approach to the desired abstraction level: Whether more precision or more abstractness are preferred can be adapted using the weights, illustrated by the "stress field" of Figure 5.22. Furthermore, human readability and computation complexity can be balanced.

The error metric $m_{error}(c)$ is intentionally used directly (without threshold), as a no prediction error is desirable in any case. Thresholding is thus not required.

5.11.4.3. Determining Weights, Thresholds, and Normalisation

Overall, threshold and normalisation complement each other. The threshold t_j determines the lower boundary of values, while the $normScale_j$ values determine typical upper values and intend to make values comparable (cf. Figure 5.23). The weights balance the impact of precision, abstractness and the individual metrics on the fitness value.

To infer default weights, thresholds and normalisation values, limits for precision, human readability, and computation time where defined with respect to the application scenarios of the Palladio approach. The thresholds represent minimal accep-

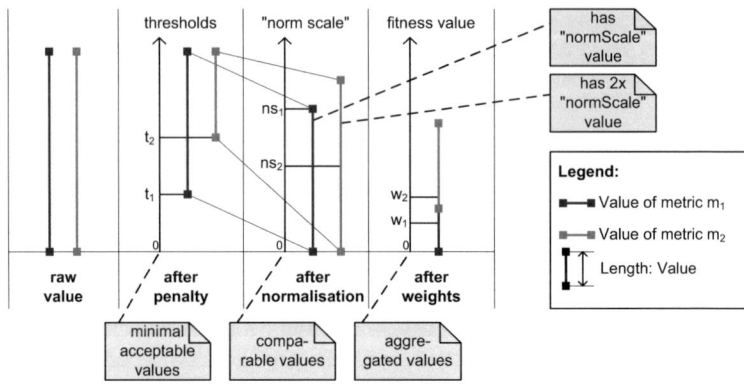

Figure 5.23.: Thresholds reflect lower boundaries; normalisation reflects typical upper values; the fitness value aggregates multiple metrics after weighting them

table complexity for *all* individuals. The thresholds must not be set too high since otherwise for simple parametric dependencies, individuals become indistinguishable from the perspective of their fitness. For example, if the threshold is too large (e.g. "100" for all metrics), $Individual_A$, $Individual_B$, and $Individual_{Complex}$ would all have the same values for abstractness metrics. Since none of the metric values would exceed 100, all metrics values would be considered optimal and thus the fitness functions would result in a fitness value of "0" for *all* individuals.

The weights, thresholds, and normalisation values are based on experiences gained during validation (see Section 7). Still, the values remain rough estimates as no separate experiments have been performed during the validation in order to gain precise weights, thresholds, and normalisation values. Nevertheless, the overall prediction results, presented in the validation, implicitly capture the quality of values selected for the fitness function.

- The *length* of expressions should support human readability. Expressions longer than one line become harder to read. Thus, the threshold was set to 80 (one line of characters). Typical larger expressions have length of two lines, corresponding to a $normScale$ value of 160. The weight is set to 0.1 since the length of an expression is a major impact factor for understandability and also affects the computation complexity.

affected metric	threshold (t_j)	norm scale ($normScale_j$)	weight (w_j)
$m_{ExpressionLength}$	80	160	0.1

- The number of *variables* in an individual should be low to limit the dimensionality of expressions and aid understandability. More than three dimensions are hard to imagine for humans, thus the threshold is set to 3. Nevertheless, parametric dependencies usually depend on a number of parameter characterisation in real settings. Thus, $normScale$ is set to 9 which is a typical memorisation limit for humans (cf. Miller's Law [Mil56]). The weight is set to 0.1 as reducing dimensionality is a major driver of abstraction.

For the *arguments*, the threshold was set to 2 (most mathematic operator have two arguments; e.g. addition). The most complex genes (if-then-else) have 4 arguments. The $normScale$ is set to 10 – a typical value for an expression of two lines. The weights are set to 0.05.

affected metric	threshold (t_j)	norm scale $(normScale_j)$	weight (w_j)
$m_{Variables}$	3	9	0.1
$m_{Arguments}$	2	10	0.05

- Large chromosome *depth* implies large nesting structures of genes which first need to be understood in order to understand a whole individual. Typical representatives of low complexity (e.g. $Individual_A$) has a depth of three, which is used as threshold. Chromosome depths of more then 9 seldom occur ($normScale$). The metric has a higher weight of 0.1 since it impacts computation complexity and understandability.

affected metric	threshold (t_j)	norm scale $(normScale_j)$	weight (w_j)
$m_{ChromosomeDepth}$	3	9	0.05

- *Computation costs* are set such that large models become quickly analysable. A simulation time of less than 5 minutes is desired to allow interaction with model, simulation, and prediction results. For the calculation of computations costs, costs must be associated to every gene. To understand computation complexity, the major drivers for model simulation time in the Palladio approach must be identified:

  - The stochastic expression language for parametric dependencies is interpreted at runtime.

  - Additions, subtractions, multiplications, divisions, power, and exponential functions can be quickly calculated. They have a limited number of arguments and their execution is directly mapped to single Java instructions of the simulation execution environment. The associated costs are 1.

  - Each variable implies the calculation of a random number, each time a stochastic expression is evaluated during simulation. Since the calculation of random numbers is a very expensive computation, the associated costs are 100.

- Inequation and sine genes cannot be calculated in a single processor cycle. Hence, the associated costs are 10.

- If-then-else and if-then genes require the evaluation of a branching condition and a jump to the corresponding branches. Branches are not directly mapped to processor statements in the simulation (due to the interpretation). Thus, the calculation requires multiple processor cycles. The associated costs are 20.

One line of expression has computation costs of at least 8 (threshold). $normScale_j$ is derived from the number of random variables. 9 variables typically occur in expressions (see above), which result in costs of $9 \cdot 100 = 900$.

affected metric	threshold (t_j)	norm scale ($normScale_j$)	weight (w_j)
$m_{ExpressionCC..}$	8	900	0.1

- As explained above, no penalty is applied to the *error*. Still, the error needs to be normalised. Opposed to the other metrics, this is taken over by the weight w_e which in the case of the error combines penalty and weight since no normalisation is applied to the error.

  Typical large error values are 10,000. Thus, the weight of the error is: $w_e = 0.6 \cdot \frac{1}{10,000}$.

It is not expected that the above weights, threshold, and normalisation values represent optimal configurations of the fitness function (see Section 5.11.13 for a discussion). Still, no major imprecision can arise from the chosen values: Individuals in direct comparison remain distinguishable as the same fitness function is applied to all individuals. The fitness function then equally punishes or prefers individuals. Thus, absolute values of the fitness function might be off, but the selection operator (Section 5.11.5) of genetic programming is based the *relative comparison* of individuals of a generation which is not affected by absolute values.

5.11.5. Selection Operator

The selection operator applied in the presented approach is a combination of standard selection operators for genetic algorithms. It derives a generation G_{x+1} from a generation G_x. To select the individuals surviving a generation, the n percent of the fittest individuals are always preserved (step 1, Listing 5.12), and the worst m percent are preserved (step 2). The remainder is selected using the "roulette" strategy (step 3) – a random selection strategy (see [BNKF98, pp. 132] and [Koz93, pp. 604] for an overview on selection strategies).

The size of each generation is fixed to keep computation power and memory consumption for the calculation of genetic programming limited and constant per generation. Since only a subset of individuals of a generation is selected for survival, but a full set is required for the next generation in order to have a constant generation size $generationSize$, the remainder is filled up by randomly selected replicates of the previously selected individuals (step 5). This increases the chance of crossover for selected individuals in the next generation and thus increases the chance of further improving the fitness of resulting individuals. Optionally, the diversity can be enhanced by adding fully randomly generated individuals (step 6).

The following pseudo code Listing 5.12 summarises the process steps:

```
 1  Inputs
 2    G_x // Generation x
 3  Outputs
 4    G_{x+1} // Successor generation of generation x

 6  generationSelection(Generation G_x) {
 7    G_x = SelectFittest(G_x, n) // 1.
 8    G_x = SelectWorst(G_x, m) // 2.
 9    G_x = RouletteSelection(G_x) // 3.
10    G_{x+1} = ReplicateSelected(G_x) // 4. new generation foundation
11    G_{x+1} = ReplicateIndividuals(G_{x+1}, numberOfReplicates) // 5.
12    if(card(G_{x+1}) < generationSize) {
13      G_{x+1} = FillUpWithRandom(G_{x+1}) // 6.
14    }
15    return G_x + 1
16  }
```

Listing 5.12: Selection process

$ReplicateSelected(G_x)$ in step 4 replicates all individuals which are in G_x to form a new generation. Opposed to step 4, step 5 replicates single randomly selected individuals of a generation with the aim of increasing the chance that these individuals participate in crossover or mutation, where $numberOfReplicates$ is the number of individuals to replicate.

Figure 5.24 illustrates the selection process for a generation with a fixed size of six individuals. In the example both, the creation of random individuals (step 6) and the filling of the generation with replicated individuals (step 5) are performed.

For Beagle, m was set to 5% (worst) and n to 50% (best). The $generationSize$ is 100. Crossover and mutation are applied to the individuals as next steps (Section 5.11.6 and 5.11.7).

5.11.6. Crossover

The crossover grants variability of individuals and enables evolutionary changes. In the presented approach, the crossover operator is applied to pairs of individuals. As the individual's chromosomes have a tree structure, subtrees are randomly selected, cut, and then merged for a new individual. The chromosome's genes are constructed

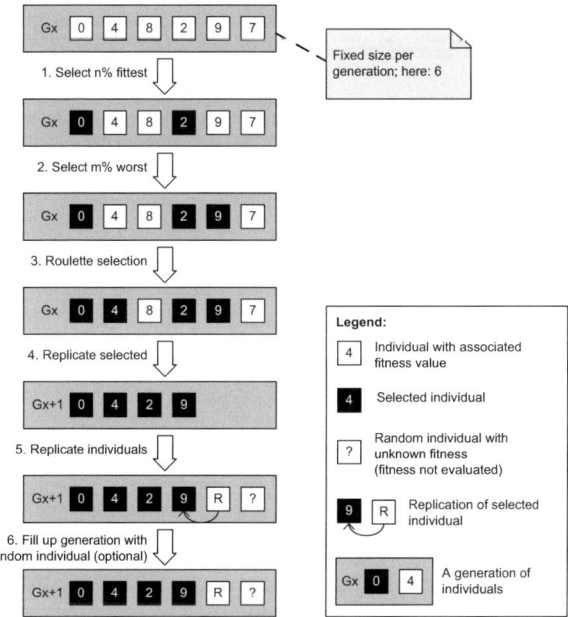

Figure 5.24.: Example: Selection process (lower fitness values are better)

in a way that all subtrees can be exchanged by any other (cf. Section 5.11.3) since they use float as both, input arguments and result type.

If-then-else genes, for example, can take float values as input for the condition statement. Values larger than or equal to zero are then interpreted as a logical "true", negative values are interpreted as "false". In the following example, the if statement evaluates to true if X.VALUE ≥ 0. Note that the utilised if-then-else gene in the following example deviates from the one in $Individual_A$ which has two arguments.

IF(X.VALUE) THEN .. ELSE ..

Due to the chosen design of genes, each chromosome can be split at any cut point. The split of two chromosomes results in four split chromosomes (two for the inter-bred pair and two for the split chromosomes per individual). Two of these chromosomes have dangling $SubGene$ relations (cf. Equation 5.1) but otherwise remain valid chromosome sequences. The dangling $SubGene$ relations can be replaced by any other chromosome sequence from splitting during crossover. There are only two dangling relations since the opposite direction of $SubGene$, "$SuperGene$", is nei-

185

ther made explicit nor required. The $SubGene$ relation is sufficient for building a tree structure (parent nodes reference child nodes; not vice versa).

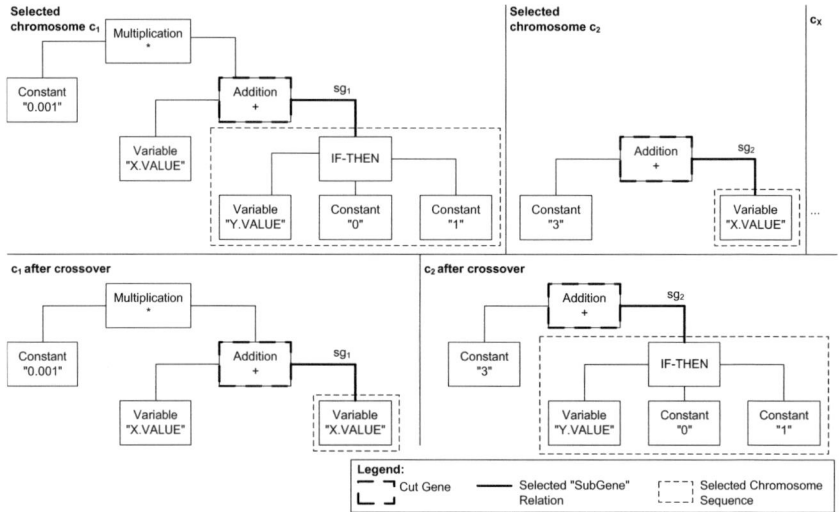

Figure 5.25.: Example: Crossover

Figure 5.25 continues the example introduced in Figure 5.20. First, the chromosomes c_1 and c_2 are randomly selected for crossover from the current generation. For each of them, a gene is randomly determined, which serves as "cut point" for the crossover (dashed box). Next, an element from the $SubGene$ relation of that gene is randomly selected for c_1 and c_2, resulting in chromosome sequences associated via to top-most genes sg_1 and sg_2. The chromosome sequences associated via sg_1 ("IF-THEN") and sg_2 ("Addition") are then exchanged and recomposed with the parent gene in the dashed box. The bottom area of Figure 5.25 visualises the results after the crossover.

The pseudo-code in Listing 5.13 formalises the crossover, where G_x is the current generation, $numberOfCuts$ the number of cuts per individual, $random(Set, number, probability)$ selects $number$ random elements from Set with a given probability $probability$. If Set is empty or no element is returned due to the probability, "null" is returned. The crossover steps are only performed if $random$ returned non-null genes. $p_{ChromSel}$ is the probability of selecting a chromosome, $p_{GeneSel}$ is the probability of selecting a gene.

186

```
 1  Inputs
 2    G_x // Original generation created by the selection operator
 3  Outputs
 4    G_x // Interbred generation
 5  Crossover(G_x) {
 6    for(maxNumberOfCrossovers) {
 7      // Determine selected chromosomes:
 8      {c_1, c_2} = random(G_x, 2, p_ChromSel) : c_1 ≠ c_2 {
 9        for(maxNumberOfCuts) {   //per Individual
10          sg_1 = random(g.SubGene, 1, 1) : g = random(c_1, 1, p_GeneSel)
11          sg_2 = random(g.SubGene, 1, 1) : g = random(c_2, 1, p_GeneSel)

13          if(sg_1 ≠ null ∧ sg_2 ≠ null ∧ sg_2 ≠ sg_1) {
14            // crossover of subgenes:
15            sg_tmp = sg_2
16            sg_2 = sg_1
17            sg_1 = sg_tmp
18  } } } } }
```

Listing 5.13: Crossover

The number of crossovers per individual ("at how many places to cut an individual") and the probability for a crossover correspond to typical values from literature (cf. [SP94]). In Beagle, the probability for an crossover is set to $0.9 = p_{ChromSel} = p_{GeneSel}$. To not end up in nearly random individuals which are made from dozens of other individuals, only a few cuts (1 to 2 = $maxNumberOfCuts = maxNumberOfCrossovers$) are useful to promote a straight evolution. A lot of cut points for crossover would result in largely mixed individuals and thus contradict short and abstract parametric dependencies. If a single individual is cut $maxNumberOfCuts$ times and the number of crossovers per generation is set to $maxNumberOfCrossovers$, the crossover is performed repeatedly for a maximum of $maxNumberOfCuts \cdot maxNumberOfCrossovers$ times, since the chance of a crossover further depends on the chosen crossover probabilities $p_{ChromSel}$ and $p_{GeneSel}$.

Srinvas and Patnaik [SP94] discuss the selection of crossover and mutation probabilities in detail. For the presented approach, the crossover probability is not crucial since it is mostly affecting the convergence speed. Section 5.11.13 further discusses the selection of probabilities for the genetic programming configuration.

5.11.7. Mutation

Mutation is another mean to avoid local minima by evolutionary diversity. Mutation is generally applied to single genes. *Simple mutations* include changing the value of a constant to a new random number (for example a 10 can become a 12). For reverse engineering and aligned with the genes described above, specific enhancements have been realised for the mutation operator. These enhancements are designed to force abstraction and ensure diversity. The following sections present the mutation operators which have been created for Beagle.

5.11.7.1. Mutation: Deleting genes

A primitive mutation is the deletion of genes, which is nevertheless promising to raise the abstraction level by erasing non-important details expressed in genes. This mutation has to ensure the integrity of chromosomes.

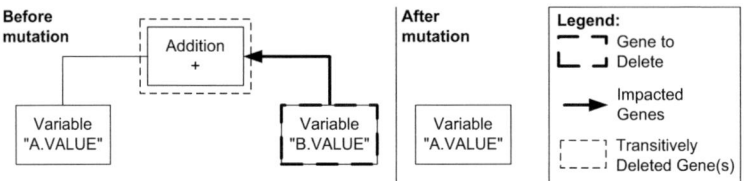

Figure 5.26.: Mutation: Deletion of a gene at the leaf of the chromosome tree

If for example in an addition one argument is deleted (see the bold dashed gene in Figure 5.26), the resulting chromosome would be invalid. Thus, for a chromosome like A.VALUE$+B$.VALUE (an addition gene with two summands, each a sub-tree), not only the argument (summand) would need to be deleted but also the parent addition gene (see the thin dashed line in Figure 5.26). In the example, effectively, a sum is replaced by a single summand.

A different case is illustrated in Figure 5.27. Here, a gene at an intermediate tree level is being deleted from a chromosome. While a leaf gene affects parent genes as in the previous example, an gene at an intermediate tree level affects child genes as visualised by the bold arrow. Only one of the child sub-trees of the selected gene ("Addition") can be preserved in the example, since otherwise the chrommsome consistence would be validated. The actually chosen sub-tree is selected randomly.

The algorithm $DeleteGene(c, g)$ (Listing 5.14) has to differentiate between leaf level genes ($SubGenes = \emptyset$) and intermediate level genes ($SubGenes \neq \emptyset$) as it

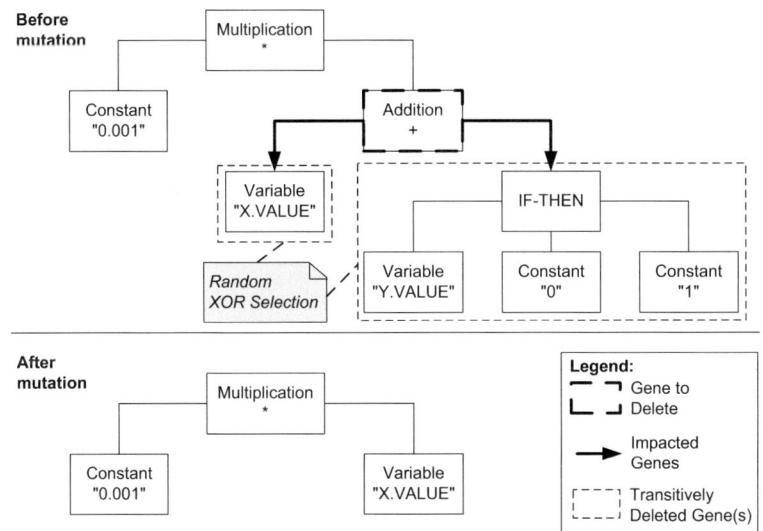

Figure 5.27.: Mutation: Deletion of a gene at an intermediate level of the chromosome tree

must use a different mechanism to ensure chromosome consistency. The basic steps for both cases are:

i) the selection of the gene to delete $geneToDelete$,

ii) determination of preserved genes,

iii) the deletion of a chromosome's sub-tree ($GenesToDelete$) which cannot be references by the chromosome any more due to the deletion of the gene $GenesToDelete$, and

iv) the connection of the preserved sub-trees with the remainder of the chromosome through the $SubGenes$ relation of a parent gene.

Besides, the special case of a chromosome comprising a single gene is handled. The delete gene mutation is applied to a chromosome c: $DeleteGene(c, \emptyset)$.

```
 1  Inputs
 2    c // Chromosome to apply mutation to
 3    g // A gene (see next mutation variant),
 4  Outputs
 5    c // Mutated chromosome
 6  DeleteGene(c, g) {
 7    if(g == ∅) { // support for other mutations (see below)
 8      geneToDelete = random(c, 1, 1) // i) random gene selection
 9    }

11    if(geneToDelete.SubGenes == ∅) { // leaf level
12      parentGene = parent(geneToDelete)
13      // ii) randomly select preserved sibling gene:
14      siblingPreservedGene = random(parentGene.SubGenes, 1, 1)
15      // iii) delete tree of genes:
16      GenesToDelete = transClosure(parentGene, {'SubGenes'}) \
                  {siblingPreservedGene}
17      c = c \ GenesToDelete

19      // iv) connect to upper chromosome tree if possible:
20      superParGene = parent(parentGene)
21      if(superParGene ≠ ∅) { // parent pf parent exists
22        superParGene.SubGenes = superParGene.SubGenes \ {parentGene}
23        superParGene.SubGenes = superParGene.SubGenes ∪ {siblingPreservedGene}
24      }
25    } else if(parent(geneToDelete) ≠ ∅) { // intermediate level
26      // ii) randomly select preserved sub gene:
27      childPreservedGene = random(geneToDelete.SubGenes, 1, 1)
28      // iii) delete tree of genes:
29      GenesToDelete = transClosure(geneToDelete, {'SubGenes'}) \
                  {childPreservedGene}
30      c = c \ GenesToDelete

32      // iv) connect to parent gene:
33      ParentSubGenes = parent(geneToDelete).SubGenes
```

```
34      ParentSubGenes = ParentSubGenes \ {geneToDelete}

35      ParentSubGenes = ParentSubGenes ∪ {childPreservedGene}

36    } else { // delete the single gene

37      c = ∅

38    }

39  }
```

Listing 5.14: Mutation: Deleting genes

where c is a chromosome, g a gene (for use in the next mutation), and $parent(gene)$ is the inverse function of the $SubGene$ relation. The empty set resulting from the last case for the chromosome built from a single gene will be removed by the selection operator.

Generally, of n sub-trees of a chromosome $n - 1$ sub-trees are removed when removing a single gene to ensure integrity. The remaining sub-tree is used to replace the original gene. Which sub-tree is therefore preserved is selected randomly to give a chance that all kinds of arguments can survive. For example in an if-then-else gene, it makes a difference whether the condition or the body is preserved.

5.11.7.2. Mutation: Reducing dimensionality

To reduce the number of involved dimensions and thus to increase abstraction and reduce complexity, another mutation operator is able to reduce the number of variables. For each parameter characterisation a variable exists. This results in a large amount of variables and complex expressions represented by chromosomes. The presented mutation operator removes a single arbitrarily selected variable from a chromosome. Opposed to traditional mutations, which usually affect only *one* gene, this mutation is applied to the *whole* chromosome to effectively remove a certain dimension.

Consider a modified version of the $Individual_A$ example expression which illustrates the problem:

$$Individual_{A'} = 0.00001 * X.\text{VALUE} * X.\text{VALUE}$$
$$+ \text{ IF}(Y.\text{VALUE} > 0) \text{ THEN } 1 + Y.\text{VALUE}$$

where $X.\text{VALUE}$ and $Y.\text{VALUE}$ represent variable characterisations and 0.00001 is a constant gene. $X.\text{VALUE}$ and $Y.\text{VALUE}$ both occur two times in the genes which makes it unlikely, that usual mutation operators remove both occurrences of a variable characterisations in subsequent steps. $m_{Variables}(c)$ allows improved fitness values only if *all* occurrences of a parameter characterisation are removed. The reduction of dimensions thus immediately benefits for the $m_{Variables}(c)$ fitness metric.

In the expression of $Individual_{A'}$, X.VALUE has only a very limited effect on component behaviour due to the small constant prefix. Still, it is present in the chromosome and increases complexity, resulting in a lower fitness. If only small values for X.VALUE are monitored at runtime, the gene representing X.VALUE can be removed. The remaining constant 0.00001 could be removed by the "deleting genes" mutation operation in a successive step. The resulting chromosome would have a much better fitness. Also examples are imaginable where the measured values of Y.VALUE are always less than 0. In this case, the if-then-else gene would have no impact. Thus, removing the variable characterisation Y.VALUE benefits for the required abstraction.

The algorithm for reducing dimensionality is defined for a chromosome c:

```
 1  Inputs
 2    c // Chromosome to apply mutation to
 3  Outputs
 4    c // Mutated chromosome
 5  ReduceDim(c) {
 6    gene = random(c, 1, 1) : type(gene) = 'variable'
 7    GVar = {g_cur ∈ c | ( pc(g_cur) = pc(gene) ∧ pc(g_cur) ≠ ∅ )}
 8    for(variableGene ∈ GVar) {
 9      if(type(parent(variableGene)) ∈ {'Addition' , 'Subtraction'}) {
10        variableGene = ConstantGene('0') // replace by neutral element
11      } else if(type(parent(variableGene)) ∈ {'Multiplication' , 'Division'}) {
12        variableGene = ConstantGene('1') // replace by neutral element
13      } else if(variableGene ∈ c) {
14        // check whether gene present after application of DeleteGene(..)
15        DeleteGene(c, variableGene)
16      }
17    }
18  }
```

Listing 5.15: Mutation: Reducing dimensionality

where $pc(gene)$ returns the parameter characterisation for genes which represent variables and an empty set for other genes and $ConstantGene(arg)$ creates a constant gene g with $g.value = arg$.

First, a randomly selected gene representing a variable is determined. Then all gene instances of the same variable are collected in the set $GVar$. Next, all occurrences of that variable are removed from the chromosome. The removal process depends on the parent of the deleted variable gene since the application of

$DeleteGene(..)$ can result in the deletion of a sub-tree of a chromosome. The removal of a sub-tree could yield unwanted side effects, e.g. the overall fitness of a chromosome could decrease. Thus, variables with a parent operation for which a neutral elements exists, are replaced by the neutral element (i.e. '0' for addition and subtraction, and '1' for multiplication and division). All other parents are handled by the $DeleteGene(..)$ function where the variable gene is specified for deletion. Here, it is first checked, whether a $variableGene$ is still present in the chromosome. Due to the application of $DeleteGene(..)$ in prior iterations of the loop of the algorithm, a variable instance could have been removed together with a sub-tree.

The deletion of large sub-trees through $DeleteGene(..)$ is less likely compared to the application of $DeleteGene(..)$ to genes with multiple arguments. As variables always represent leafs in the tree of genes of a chromosome (they do not have arguments), sibling sub-trees are preserved for parent genes with two arguments.

The result, if $ReduceDim(c)$ would be applied to X.VALUE of $Individual_{A'}$, is:

$$ReduceDim(Individual_{A'}) =$$
$$0.00001 * 1 * 1 + \text{ IF}(Y.\text{VALUE} > 0) \text{ THEN } 1 + Y.\text{VALUE}$$

The desired deletion of a single variable on a whole chromosome would also be possible by means of pure crossover (without this specialised mutation operator), but the probability of removing multiple occurrences of the same gene via crossover is very limited. Each sub-tree enclosing a variable would need to be selected by crossover and replaced by an sub-tree not containing that variable. This is very unlikely for a whole chromosome (cf. discussion in Section 5.11.8).

5.11.7.3. Mutation: Changing Operators

The idea of this mutation is to exchange one gene by another. Additions can for example be exchanged by subtractions. As the mathematic operators defined by the genes have a fixed number of arguments (usually two or more) also the sub-tree of such a gene has two or more branches. Only mathematic operators with the same number of arguments can be exchanged by each other; see Listing 5.16:

```
1  Inputs
2    c  // Chromosome to apply mutation to
3  Outputs
4    c  // Mutated chromosome
5  ChangeOp(c) {
6    gene_old = random(c, 1, 1)  :  gene_old.arguments > 0
7    gene_old = gene_new  :  gene_old.arguments = gene_new.arguments ∧ gene_new ∈ Genes
8  }
```

Listing 5.16: Mutation: Change operator

To increase the exchangeability, for example for additions and subtractions also genes are defined which have three arguments (three summands / subtrahends; e.g. "$(a + b + c)$" where a, b and c are arguments of a *single* gene), which thus can be exchanged for three argument operators like if-then-else. The validity of exchanging genes can be decided depending on the number of arguments only, since the genes are designed to be exchangeable as has been explained in Section 5.11.3.

5.11.8. Application of Crossover and Mutation

The construction of the fitness function, crossover, and mutation operator intentionally match each other. The mutation and crossover are designed to produce individuals which have a high fitness. A general genetic programming approach which is only equipped with the presented fitness function could result in individuals with a high fitness likewise, but the convergence speed would be much lower due to the decreased probability of evolving the way the fitness function rewards.

To illustrate the need for *specialised mutation operators* which are able to create individuals with improved fitness values, consider the following example: In the above example of $Individual_{A'}$, the probability of removing both occurrences of X.VALUE in a single crossover would be very low: Assume the probability of a crossover for a single individual of a generation to be $p_c = 0.75$ (example value), then the probability of two crossovers of a single individual in two generations is $p_c \cdot 2 = 0.5625$. $Individual_{A'}$ consists of 12 genes. The probability of selecting X.VALUE during crossover is $\frac{2}{12}$ for the first time and $\frac{1}{11}$ for the second time; in total 0.0152. Combined with the probability of two crossovers in a single generation, an overall probability of only

$$p_{c\_overall} = 0.0085 \text{ (probability of a crossover eliminating a single dimension}$$
$$\text{in two consecutive generations in the example)}$$

exists for the evolution which is realised by the "reducing dimensionality" mutation when using only crossover.

When comparing the overall probability of such a crossover with a scenario where the "reducing dimensionality" mutation is available demonstrates the benefit of specialised mutation operators: The probability of a mutation of an individual in a single generation p_m is assumed to also be 0.75 (like p_c for crossover). Then one of the four mutation operators (including "simple mutation") is selected with a probability of $\frac{1}{4}$. Selecting X.VALUE has a probability of $\frac{1}{2}$ due to the two variables in the term. The probability of a "reducing dimensionality" mutation is thus $\frac{1}{4} \cdot \frac{1}{2} \cdot 0.75 = 0.094$. Using the "reducing dimensionality" mutation in the above example raises the total probability ("reduce dimensionality" and crossover) of the desired elimination of a single dimension to

$p_{m\_overall} = 0.1$ (probability of the "reduce dimensionality" mutation

   eliminating a single dimension in two consecutive generations in the)

   example)

and therefore improves the creation of the desired abstraction. For scenarios with more than two occurrences of the same variable, the difference between optimised ($p_{m\_overall}$) and non-optimised ($p_{c\_overall}$) evolution would become even more obvious.

5.11.9. Termination

Beagle uses a simple rule as the break condition for stopping further evolution. Either when the fitness function (Section 5.11.4) indicates an optimal solution or when a fixed number of generations has been evaluated, the evolution stops. The break condition of a generation $generation$ is

$$
break(generation) = \begin{cases} true & \exists c \in Generation : \\ & \quad FitnessFunction(c) - \epsilon \leq 0 \\ & \quad \vee\, if(\text{number of generations passed} > g_{max}) \\ & \quad \vee\, if(\text{time passed} > t_{max}) \\ & \quad \vee\, if(RelImprovement(generation)) \\ & \quad \vee\, if(\text{user decides for further evolution}) \\ false & else \end{cases}
$$

where g_{max} is the maximum number of generations to be evolved, t_{max} is the maximum computing time to spent on evolution, and $Improvement(generation)$ as defined below.

Optimal Solution   The optimality of the solution is judged by the fitness function, where an optimal solution has a fitness value of 0 (see Section 5.11.4 for the discussion on the fitness function). To compensate possible numeric errors, the stop condition checks for fitness values in an ϵ environment around 0.

As the fitness function includes thresholds for length and depth of the trees of expressions, optimal solutions are for example not required to have a tree depth of just 1 to have optimal fitness. Depending on the complexity of the reverse engineering task, it is realistic to find an optimal solution. The evaluation Section 7 will further detail on the break condition in practice.

Break after g_{max} Generations or t_{max} Time   As discussed in the Section 5.11.4 on the fitness function, optimal fitness values cannot be expected for all parametric dependencies. The creation of a certain parametric dependencies can be a very complex multi-dimensional optimisation problem for which no solution with an optimal fitness value exists. An optimal solution must be optimal with respect to abstractness and precision at the same time. For example, an expression with no prediction error which involves only few variables and does not span more than one line, for a parametric dependency which actually depends on 10 input variables and due to a piecewise function must have 15 branch conditions, cannot have a fitness value of 0.

For such cases where no solution with an optimal fitness value of 0 can be found, a fixed number of generations g_{max} is evaluated or a maximum of t_{max} is spent to avoid an infinite run time. In this case a "good-enough" solution (ratio of computation effort and result improvement) is the result of genetic programming. The fitness of solutions found after g_{max} generations can usually be further improved when spending more computation time, but the increase of fitness per time becomes smaller from generation to generation.

Statistic Characteristics   To automate the break criterion evaluation in a more sophisticated way, statistic characteristics can be checked automatically, too. If for example the best individual is not improving its fitness with more than x percent over ig_{max} generations, individuals with a higher fitness become unlikely and the evolution can be stopped automatically.

$RelImprovements(generation)$ checks whether a generation has improved its fitness compared to past generations:

```
 1  Inputs
 2    generation // latest generation
 3  Outputs
 4    boolean // flag showing whether the latest generation had improved fitness values
 5  RelImprovement(generation) {
 6    return !(
 7      ∃FitnessValue(c_cur) < FitnessValue(c_old) * (1 + x)  : //relative improvements
 8      FitnessValue(c_cur) = max(FitnessValue(c_x) ∀c_x ∈ generation) //best individuals
 9      ∧ FitnessValue(c_old) = max(FitnessValue(c_y) ∀c_y ∈ generation_old ∈ Generations
10        ∧ generation(c_old) < generation(c_cur) + ig_range) // range of generations
11    )
12  }
```

Listing 5.17: Termination: Relative improvements

where $generation(c)$ determines the generation of a chromosome c, ig_{range} is the range of generations to check for improvements, $Generations$ is the set of all generations until the evolution of the $generation$ argument, and x is the required relative improvement of the fitness value.

User Feedback The strategy to stop after g_{max} generations or t_{max} time can also be relaxed, when active user feedback can be included. Then, users are asked to have a look at the solutions found after g_{max} generations / t_{max} time and can decide whether to extend the search time, so that more generations are evaluated. The user can be provided with feedback on the evolution by statistical characteristics like the best fitness value, a fitness value of the best and worst quantile of each generation, and the standard deviation of fitness values. These statistic means allow the user to judge whether further computation effort should be spent on a continued evolution.

5.11.10. Integration with Static and Statistical Analysis

To contribute to the convergence of dynamic, static, and statistical analysis, a base must be provided which enables a seamless integration of multiple approaches. The basic idea of the Beagle approach to integrate multiple analysis approaches, is to represent static and statistical analysis results as chromosomes and chromosome sequences of genetic programming (see Figure 5.28). These individuals are used in the initial generation and as pre-configured genes in the repository of available genes. The output of each analysis approach is thus uniquely represented by chromosomes and chromosome sequences. Due to the unique representation by means of genetic

197

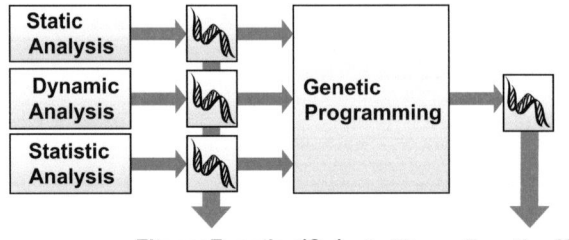

FitnessFunction(C$_{i.j}$) ≤ FitnessFunction(C$_f$)

Figure 5.28.: Overview: Integration   of   analysis   approaches   into   genetic
programming

programming, the individual analysis results can be further optimised like other individuals and automatically integrate with dynamic analysis. Generally, an arbitrary
number of static and statistic analysis approaches is supported as long as the results
can be mapped to chromosomes. Each analysis approach contributes to the initial
generation and adds chromosome sequences to the repository.

Section 9.5 further discusses and generalises the integration capabilities of the
Beagle approach while this section focuses on the integration with genetic programming.

5.11.10.1. Benefits of using Static and Statistical Analyses

Even partial results from static analysis or sub-optimal approximations from statistical analysis can help improving the overall reverse engineering results as will be
pointed out in the following. Genetic programming is robust against incorrect results
(cf. [Koz93]). During selection, it automatically rejects individuals of a generation
with poor fitness. Thus, when ensuring that through mutation and crossover new
individuals can be created from multiple analysis results which represent solutions
with improved fitness, the overall reverse engineering benefits from additional input
through static and statistical analyses.

Consider the following simplified example from Listing 5.18 in which it is hard
to statically analyse the number of executions of the loop in lines 11 to 13. Due to
the manipulation of the preceding loop's counter which depends on the modulo function applied to the parameters a and b, it is hard to infer numberOfExternalCalls.
Assume that a static analysis would calculate the size of numberOfExternalCalls
as $a * b$, neglecting the impact of $a\%b$ which results in a decreased value of numberOfExternalCalls. As $a * b$ is the result of static analysis, it would be translated
into a chromosome. During evolution of $a * b$, further improved individuals can be
created which reflect the impact of $a\%b$.

```
1  void doSth(int a, int b) {
2    int numberOfExternalCalls = 0;

4    for(int x = 0; x < a * b; x++) {
5      numberOfExternalCalls++;
6      if(a % b == 0) {
7        x++;
8      }
9    }

11   for(int x = 0; x < numberOfExternalCalls; x++) {
12     C.doService(a); // external call
13   }
14 }
```

Listing 5.18: Example: Source code which is likely to lead to partial static analysis
results

As the example illustrates, it is beneficial to derive (even incomplete) information
on control and data flow from static code analysis. In this example, the antecedent
static code analysis could have increased the convergence speed and fitness of results
of genetic programming. Using information from antecedent analysis approaches in
genetic programming can help decreasing the time needed for search and aids finding
more optimal solutions.

5.11.10.2. Generating an initial population

The initial population of most genetic algorithms is generated randomly. This is a
valid strategy, if no or little knowledge on the problem to solve is available. In such
a strategy, from the available genes, random initial individuals are created, usually
combining several genes for one individual. Opposed to this, in the presented approach, the initial generation is created systematically.

For the reverse engineering of behavioural models, information from static analysis can be used to enrich the initial generation. As all later generations base on the
initial generation (new individuals can be created randomly also for later generations
to increase diversity), additional knowledge can be encoded into the initial population to increase efficiency and effectiveness (convergence speed). If for example
static analysis is able to determine basic parametric dependencies which only miss

abstraction, or do only cover 95% of all observered cases during monitoring, genetic programming can use these discovered parametric dependencies in the initial generation. Further evolution steps then can improve the initial generation and benefit from knowledge of static analysis.

Due to the design of genetic programming, the fitness of the best individual in the integrated approach can never be worse than the fitness of individuals from static or statistical analysis (see Figure 5.28). The best individual is always kept for the next generation (cf. selection operator in Section 5.11.5). If static or statistical analysis provides a solution, the selection operator preserves the solution from generation to generation unless genetic programming finds individuals with improved fitness. Static, dynamic, and statistical analysis are complementing each other in each genetic programming step.

The are two dimensions in which static analyses can be incomplete. Static analysis results vary over the entire range of these dimensions:

- Of the set of all parametric dependencies in the source code PD only a subset can be handled $PD_{handled} \subset PD$. Of the two parametric dependencies in the example from Listing 5.18, the number of loops might be covered but not the value of a in line 12.

- The quality of recovered parametric dependencies can be limited in three ways:
  - The parametric dependency is fully correct but provides no abstraction. In this case no deviation between measurement results and predicted values exists but the expression is complex ($predicted = measured$ but $FitnessFunction(c) > 0$ and thus not optimal).
  - There is an error or deviation in the dependency ($predicted = measured \pm error$ and $FitnessFunction(c) \gg 0$) but the error is small.
  - The dependency is not recovered at all ($predicted = measured \pm error$, with $error \to \infty$ and $FitnessFunction(c) \gg 0$).

Examples Even multiple results from static analysis which are conflicting at first glance can be beneficial. Individuals of later generations are created from previous generations. The crossover combines different individuals. If for example one of the parent individuals is the result of a static analysis technique that is good in finding abstractions of parameters, and another one is good in reverse engineering algorithmic expression, a combination of both can result in an improved combined individual. Then, each individual from the initial generation is contributing for a later combination of higher fitness. Consequently, it is worth also having individuals in the initial generation that have a low fitness themselves but which are potentially good for later generations.

Consider the following example with results from two static analysis and one statistical analysis for numberOfExternalCalls. $static_1$, $static_2$, and $statistical$ can be translated into individuals of the initial generation.

$$static_1 = a * b - a$$
$$static_2 = \text{IF}(a\%b == 0) \text{ THEN } a$$
$$statistical = 0.9 + a * b/2$$
$$pd_{real} = a * b - (\text{IF}(a\%b == 0) \text{ THEN } (a * b/2))$$

The real parametric dependency pd_{real} is a complex expression. Nevertheless, it can be derived from $static_1$, $static_2$, and $statistical$ by crossover only, since all chromosome sequences of pd_{real} are present in the analysis results already. The chance of creating pd_{real} during evolution is thus increased and the convergence speed can raise due to the use of an initial generation based on prior analysis results.

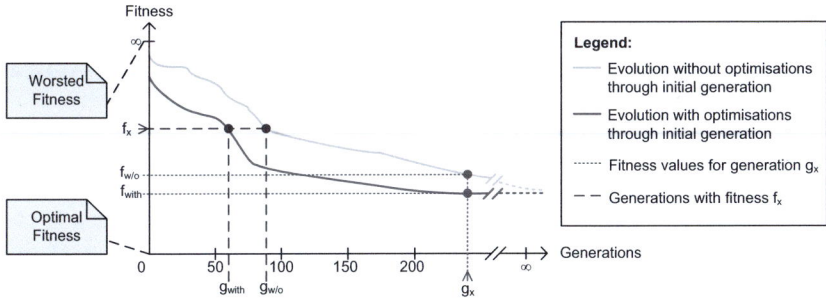

Figure 5.29.: Example: Fitness of the best individuals of an evolution. Evolutions with and without optimisations through the initial generation.

Improving Convergence Speed and Fitness Results from static and statistic analysis approaches are integrated into the initial generation of the Beagle approach for two reasons:

- **Increased convergence speed.** Individuals with high fitness values have an increased chance to be created in earlier generations. The fitness of individuals of the initial generation can be higher than in fully random initial generation which aids finding individuals with high fitness in earlier generations.

201

- **Improved fitness of individuals.** The maximum fitness value can be improved when using an initial generation based on prior analyses. For example, the boundaries of branching conditions can be off when randomly guessed by genetic programming and thus result in reduced precision (e.g. a boundary $x < 10$ instead of $x < 5$).

As Figure 5.29 illustrates, when using optimisations through the initial generation, the same fitness value (f_X) is generally expected to be reached earlier for evolutions with an optimised initial generation (g_{with}) than for evolutions with fully random evolutions ($g_{w/o}$). Vice versa, after a certain number of generations (g_x), the fitness for evolutions with optimisations is expected to be more optimal (f_{with}) than for evolutions without optimisations ($f_{w/o}$). Even for the first generation, an initial generation based on prior analyses, generally should have more optimal fitness than an initial generation of fully random individuals.

When evolving a very large number of generations, the fitness of individuals in evolutions with and without optimised evolutions will converge (dashed lines on the right hand side of Figure 5.29). For an infinite number of generations, the fitness values will become the same, as every random change (mutation, crossover) will have been applied to every individual of both evolutions. Then, the full search space is explored and the optimal solutions are present in the optimised and non-optimised evolutions. Hence, the optimisations of the initial generation are not required to gain optimal results, but reaching satisfactory results within limited time become more likely when using the optimised initial generation.

Since the evolution of genetic programming and the creation of the initial generation always depend on chance, evolutions are imaginable where the fitness of an evolution based an a non-optimised initial generation is always better than the fitness of the optimised case (evolution graphs switched in Figure 5.29). The validation Section 7 will further investigate the improvements of an optimised initial generation.

Improvements of the Initial Generation   To create the initial generation from static analysis, a combination of the following means is used. Each mean represents a guess on a partial parametric dependency.

- **Input parameters** of a provided service can be easily determined by static analysis. For each parameter characterisation, an individual is created assuming that there is a direct (negative) correlation between that parameter and a parametric dependency to be learned. The resulting set of chromosomes is:

$$Chromosomes_{inputParameters} = \{c1, c2, ..\} \; :$$
$$g \in c_x \in Chromosomes_{inputParameters} \wedge$$
$$g \in Genes_{inputs}$$

where the chromosomes are made from a subset of genes from $Genes_{inputs}$. Note that chromosomes in this cases can comprise just a single gene. The chromosome in this case representes only a single input parameter.

- If **constants** are present in code that is reverse engineered, static analysis can find them. For the initial generation, each constant is translated into an individual, making it more likely to have that constant used in more complex expressions. As constants are also utilised in the original code, the reverse engineered behaviour is likely to benefit from them.

  The resulting set of chromosomes is $Chromosomes_{constants}$. Note that $Chromosomes_{constants}$ has nothing to do with $Genes_{constants}$, although the values of the expressed constants can be overlapping by chance. $Chromosomes_{constants}$ complements the set of constant genes $Genes_{constants}$ by constants specific to a certain parametric dependency.

  If there is for example a branch condition in a file processing service, the behaviour can depend on the file size. If a constant (e.g. 2048 Byte) is used in the branch, using the constant as an individual helps finding the correct boundary. When executing the file processing service with only very few different file sizes (e.g. 10, 100, 1.000, 10.000 bytes) during monitoring, genetic programming cannot precisely infer the exact branch condition. Any constant between 1001 and 10.000 matches the observations and thus is not rejected due to a deviation between measurement and prediction. Using the constant from static analysis increases the probability of finding the correct branching condition.

  While the above proposed constants recognition is very simplistic, advanced code analysis techniques such as slicing [Wei81] can be used to increase the precision of constants recognition. As Section 5.10.4 points out, only those constants which are in the backward slice like the output parameter which is determined by the parametric dependencies which is being reverse engineered, can be used as constants of the initial generation. The application of slicing would thus decrease the size of the initial generation.

- Constants can also be **combined** with parameters (e.g. $const * param$), where $param \in Genes_{inputs}$. As parameters are likely to be scaled up or down with constants (e.g. a loop being executed for every second element of an input list), it is beneficial encoding this into the initial generation. Pre-defined constant genes ($const \in Genes_{constants}$) here serve as constants. The resulting set of chromosomes is $Chromosomes_{combined}$:

$$CrossProduct = \bigcup_{(const,param) \,\in\, Genes_{constants} \times Genes_{inputs}} multiplication(const, param)$$

$$Chromosomes_{combined} = random(CrossProduct, x, 1)$$

where $multiplication(arg_1, arg_2)$ creates a chromosome representing a multiplication of arg_1 and arg_2. x is a number of randomly selected chromosomes. To not exceed the size of the initial generation, a limitation is needed when many constants or parameters are available.

- Often, iterations are **"off by one"** in the code. Thus, $param+1$ and $param-1$ are made available in the initial generation. The resulting set of chromosomes is $Chromosomes_{ofbyone}$:

$$CrossProduct = \bigcup_{param \in Genes_{inputs}} (\, addition(param, \text{`1'}) \cup subtraction(param, \text{`1'}) \,)$$

$$Chromosomes_{ofbyone} = random(CrossProduct, x, 1)$$

where x again is a number of randomly selected chromosomes, $addition(arg_1, arg_2)$ creates a chromosome representing the addition $arg_1 + arg_2$, and $subtraction(arg_1, arg_2)$ creates a chromosome representing the subtraction $arg_1 - arg_2$.

- To describe **polynomial** dependencies, a polynomial can be pre-configured for the initial generation, such as $ax + by + cz + \dots$ with $a, b, c, ..$ being coefficients and $x, y, z, ...$ being parameters. This ensures, that all parameters are covered by the polynomial. The resulting set of chromosomes is $Chromosomes_{polynomial}$:

$$Chromosomes_{polynomial} = polynomial(Genes_{inputs})$$

where $polynomial(Set)$ creates a chromosome representing a polynomial with $card(Set)$ variables, each representing elements of $Genes_{inputs}$ and random coefficients.

- The polynomial from the previous bullet can also be pre-defined in a more advanced way. If standard **regression approaches** are used to determine coefficients for the polynomial, the starting point for genetic programming can even be more improved. Besides polynomial regression, linear, logarithmic, or multiple regression approaches can be used to generate initial individuals based on statistical fitting. The resulting set of chromosomes is $Chromosomes_{regression}$.

  In this thesis, Multivariate Adaptive Regression Splines (MARS, [Fri91]) are used for statistical regression. Results from MARS are therefore translated into a section-wise defined function, which is represented as an individual of genetic programming. No special genes are required for representing MARS results in chromosomes. MARS must be seen as an example for integrating statistical approaches into the Beagle reverse engineering approach.Due to the section-wise definition of results, MARS serves well for approximating non-continuous behaviour. Non-continuous behaviour results from branches in source code and must therefore be handled. Simple regression approaches (linear or polynomial) are thus not well-suited for the approximation of component behaviour. Polynomials for example have limited precision for function values near approximated jumps and tend to result to complex expressions when approximation with higher precision. Section 5.14 will provide further details on the integration of MARS.

- More **complex initial individuals** can be formed, if advanced static analysis techniques like **symbolic execution** [Kin76, Cow88, DLR06, HC88, Lee06, Hua08] or **abstract interpretation** [CC77] are used. Such techniques are partially able to determine parametric dependencies from code. As these dependencies are expressed with standard genes, genetic programming can further improve findings of such techniques. The resulting set of chromosomes is $Chromosomes_{complex}$.

  For this thesis, the Wala [IBM] and KeY [BHS07] approaches have been analysed for their applicability for reverse engineering parametric dependencies. Ultimately, for testing purposes, Wala has been integrated as advanced symbolic execution technique. Section 5.12 will detail on the integration.

Most of the individuals (especially the first simple ones) proposed above for the initial generation are likely to have a very poor fitness which makes it probable for them being removed directly after the first generation. Still, it is desirable to have them available for recombination in crossover for later generations. To increase the probability that individuals from the first generation survive – and consequently improve usage of the results from static analysis – the same individuals are created multiple times in the first generation.

In the first generations, this increases the probability of recombinations of initial generation individuals, later generations are affected only by individuals that in fact are beneficial. So, later generations are not suffering from overhead of the initial generation, but nevertheless profit from an improved starting point.

Formally, the $InitialGeneration$ is the union of the above sets of chromosomes:

$$
\begin{aligned}
InitialGeneration := &\ Chromosomes_{combined} \cup Chromosomes_{ofbyone} \cup \\
& Chromosomes_{polynomial} \cup Chromosomes_{regression} \cup \\
& Chromosomes_{complex} \cup Chromosomes_{inputParameters} \cup \\
& Chromosomes_{constants}
\end{aligned}
$$

5.11.10.3. Deriving Genes and Chromosomes

Deriving $ChromosomeRepository$ Section 5.11.1 introduced the term *chromosome repository* as a set of chromosomes which is instantiated for a specific parametric dependency. Chromosomes from the chromosome repository are used when creating random individuals for filling up a generation after selection. While the initial generation affects only the first generations of evolution, chromosomes are available from the chromosome repository throughout the whole evolution. If new random individuals are generated for later generations, chromosomes available from the repository are likely to be chosen. They are influencing also *later* generations. Hence, they contribute equally to *all* generations opposed to the initial generation individuals which predominantly contribute to the first generations of evolution.

The $ChromosomeRepository$ is a set of chromosomes:

$$
\begin{aligned}
ChromosomeRepository := &\ Chromosomes_{combined} \cup Chromosomes_{ofbyone} \cup \\
& Chromosomes_{polynomial} \cup \\
& Chromosomes_{regression} \cup \\
& Chromosomes_{complex}
\end{aligned}
$$

The chromosome repository is derived from the initial generation, where $ChromosomeRepository \subset InitialGeneration$. Constants ($Chromosomes_{constants}$) and input parameters ($Chromosomes_{inputParameters}$) are intentionally not part of $ChromosomeRepository$ as the elimination of unimportant parameters and constants from the evolution is intentionally desired.

Adapting the $Genes$ **Set** Besides configuring the initial population in genetic programming, static analysis can be used to adapt *available* genes (set $Genes$). On the one hand, a selection (subset) of default genes can be used to limit the search space, if static analysis suggests to have a certain kind of dependency (for example, linear dependency plus some branching). On the other hand, special genes can be introduced to reflect a specific problem space using information from static analysis. As already discussed in Section 5.11.3.6, limiting the available genes is not necessary when using genetic programming.

When adapting the set of available genes $Genes$, also mutation is affected since the "changing operators" mutation operator selects from the available genes. Like the use of the $Chromosome Repository$, the adaption of $Genes$ is capable of influencing *all* generations of genetic programming.

5.11.11. Static Code Analysis of Byte Code

The presented approach does not rely on readability of source code or naming of variables, which makes it broadly applicable. When provided with Java byte code, the approach first runs a decompiler to extract Java source code from the binary files. The source code provided by standard decompilers (e.g. JAD or JDEC), is a sufficient base for any further analysis of the approach. In the PCM's RDSEFF, loops and branches are not distinguished like it is the case in decompiled source code. Thus, the missing uniqueness of the mapping of for / while loops and if / switch statements back to source code is not impacting the approach.

Obfuscation The Beagle approach is robust against obfuscation. During obfuscation only naming and non-functional aspects (e.g. order of instructions) can be changed. RDSEFFs are abstractions of the control and data flow. An obfuscator cannot change the order of instructions at the level of an RDSEFF. For a component its assembly context is generally not known at compile time when an obfuscator runs. Hence, the control flow can only change within internal actions of a component. Otherwise, an obfuscator would need to be able to guess the assembly context since the order of component calls can have impact on a component's state.

Consider the following example from Listing 5.19. In the example, the lines 3-5 can be re-ordererd but the order of calling C1 and C2 must be preserved as calling C1 could affect the state of C2 (and potentially break the required-side protocol of the component offering doSth()). When semantically analysing the source code, any internal actions can be reordered (e.g. the internal action after calling C1 and C2. Still, this does not impact the performance model, since the order of the executed code would also be the order of the obfuscated code. Obfuscated code and decompiled code would show the same performance behaviour; only the original source code would be different. Parametric dependencies for internal actions make no assump-

```
1  void int doSth() {
2      // internal action start
3      int i = 0;
4      int y = 0;
5      i++;
6      // internal action end

8      C1.doSth2(); // external component call 1

10     C2.doSth3(); // external component call 2

12     return i + y;
13  }
```

Listing 5.19: Source code example: Obfuscation options

tions on the execution order of covered instructions and consequently are not affected by obfuscation.

Direct Processing of Byte Code   The previous section discussed the availability of *information* in byte code. The *tooling* of the Beagle approach could also work directly on byte code during control flow abstraction (cf. Section 5.8), instrumentation (cf. Section 5.10.6), and monitoring (cf. Section 5.10.7), using byte code engineering tools such as BCEL [Dah01] and Javassist [Chi]. Control and data flow are present in the byte code as well as in source code (see previous section). To limit the effort of developing the Beagle approach, it has only been implemented for Java source code. For Java source code the broadest tooling support and most convenience is available which reduced the development effort. Still, conceptually, any reverse engineering activity could be applied to Java byte code.

5.11.12. Numeric Precision

In the previous sections, for if-then-else genes and for the stop condition ϵ environments have been introduced to overcome numeric limitations when dealing with floating point numbers. This section will briefly discuss the numeric precision of the genetic programming step. The fitness function (cf. Section 5.11.4) is responsible for evaluating individuals. To evaluate the fitness of an individual, the expression represented by the chromosome is calculated for the input values gathered at runtime by monitoring. The mean squared error of deviation between measurement and prediction for all input is then one input to the fitness function. For the calculation of the fitness of each individual, the original values from monitoring are used. Thus, there cannot be a "drift" of precision when evolving over large numbers of generations. Each generation accesses the same values.

To calculate the predicted value of each individual, genetic programming internally performs Java double calculations. For more complex calculations, this might involve numeric imprecisions which are then intercepted by the mentioned ϵ environments. After translating chromosomes into RDSEFF stochastic expressions (see Section 5.15), hence, the approach must account for the ϵ environments. The execution of stochastic expressions is taken over by Java again during the PCM simulation which ensures that the expressions are interpreted in the same way as during genetic programming.

When choosing an overly small ϵ, this does not result in imprecision in the developed approach. The fitness function and the stochastic expression would make the same error when evaluating them. The selection operator of genetic programming would hinder imprecise individuals to survive. The worst impact of choosing an overly small ϵ is an unsteady behaviour of genes. Imagine an if-then-else gene which evolves for several generations. In a first generation an individual might contain for example:

$$\text{IF}(a < 3 \pm \epsilon) \text{ THEN ... ELSE}$$

If a is de-facto an integer value in this individual, the condition will be unambiguously decided. When in a later generation replacing (crossover or mutation) the a by an expression like $a + X$, where X is nearly a constant calculated in a way that it for some input values results in 0.001 instead of 0.0, the result of the IF statement is affected:

$$\text{IF}((a + X) < 3 \pm \epsilon) \text{ THEN ... ELSE}$$

For the same input values, the expression would suddenly return the value of the ELSE branch instead of the value of the IF branch when selecting a small ϵ (e.g. $\epsilon = 10^{-5}$). Assume that the individual has been close to the optimal solution before the last mutation or crossover which introduced $a + X$. Genetic programming could then reject the individual of the next generation due to the numeric problem and the search would have to restart from much worse individuals. If the selection operator has not created of copy of the individual, the unsteady behaviour would artificially extend the search time.

5.11.13. Genetic Programming Configuration as Optimisation Problem

The configuration of genetic algorithms is an optimisation problem on its own. Genetic algorithms (and thus genetic programming) possess a large configuration space which affects first of all the convergence speed but also the possible fitness of the best results. In this thesis, the configuration space has been optimised manually through trial and error, based on configuration values from literature [SP94]. Nevertheless, a full optimisation could be a subsequent project which has not been performed in the context of this thesis. In this section, the chosen configuration and the possible configuration space will be roughly sketched.

The configuration space covers:

- Mutation probability. High mutations rates hinder a convergence of the search process while low rates avoid required diversity. (Selected probability: $p_c = 0.85$)

- Crossover probability. High crossover probabilities result in individuals which are likely to be created from multiple individuals (the chance of two crossovers per individual increases). Such individuals are very diverse. Especially when being close to optimal solutions, only minor changes e.g. constant mutations should be dominating. (Selected probability: $p_m = 0.9$)

- Population size. The population size determines the diversity each generation of genetic programming has. Small populations can lead to local minima but increase the convergence speed. (Selected size: $generationSize = 100$ individuals)

- Termination condition: The number of generations to evolve determines the overall runtime of genetic programming but also impacts the fitness of the best individuals. Another configuration option is choosing whether to stop on sub-optimal solutions (and which fitness they should have) or only on perfectly fit solutions. (Selected generations: $g_{max} = 750$; for more complex problems: $g_{max} = 1250$; $t_{max} = 5\ minutes$; stopping when fitness equals 0)

- Selection of genes. From a set of available gene types (e.g. addition, substraction, constants, etc.) subsets can be selected to lower the solution space (set of all possible chromosomes) if limitations are known for the problem space (parametric dependency reverse engineering problem). (Selected to use all genes plus those contributed by static and statistical analysis)

- Fitness function. For the presented fitness function, weights, considered complexity metrics and the error function have to be selected. (The selected weights are discussed in Section 5.11.4.3.)

For the above configuration space, it is assumed that the superset of available genes, the problem representation, and the population size are fixed and that the basic form of the fitness function is decided.

Srinvas and Patnaik [SP94] discuss the selection of crossover and mutation probabilities in detail. They propose adaptive probabilities for crossover and mutation, which change over subsequent generations. Focusing on the two goals of maintaining diversity and convergence speed, crossover and mutation probabilities depend on the fitness value in their approach.

In the Beagle approach, there is an "adaptiveness" comparable the adjustment of crossover and mutation probabilities: The probability of influence of static and statistic analysis results is higher for the first generations (due to the initial population) and automatically lowered through the selection of individuals in later generations.

5.12. Static Analysis of Parametric Dependencies: Symbolic Execution

In the developed approach, the static analysis technique of symbolic execution [Kin76, CC77] complements dynamic and statistical analysis. Symbolic execution (sometimes referred to as "abstraction interpretation") is well-suited for the reverse engineering of parametric dependencies. Opposed to other static analysis techniques like slicing [Wei81], Symbolic execution "quantifies" the relation between input and output parameters. Hence, as required for parametric dependencies, stochastic expressions can be directly derived from symbolic execution results.

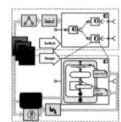

Limitations of Symbolic Execution in General   Section 5.1 already discussed general limitations of static analysis techniques which also apply to symbolic execution. Furthermore, symbolic execution is not able to deal with parameter characterisations, which are specific to performance models. Only the VALUE characterisation of primitive data types is supported. Generally, symbolic execution targets primitive data types. Collection data structures like Lists lack general support (e.g. when adding elements to lists over which is iterated or which are passed to other components, the list size is neither supported out of the box by the well-known approaches KeY [BHS07] nor Wala [IBM]). Yet, the KeY approach can be manually extended with support for arbitrary data structure. Nevertheless, each data structure would require specific extensions of the KeY implementation.

Symbolic Execution Implementations   Symbolic execution, namely the KeY [BHS07] and Wala [IBM] implementation have been evaluated in [Kna10, Chi08] (cf. Table 5.2. Ultimately, an implementation based on Wala was integrated into the Beagle approach. The reasons for selecting Wala and a discussions of the advantages and disadvantages of symbolic execution follow next. It must be emphasised that symbolic execution has various extensions and variations (see [PV09] for an overview). Basically, the KeY and Wala implementation are discussed but it is pointed out which arguments apply to symbolic execution in general.

The main purpose, KeY has been developed for, is the prove of correctness of source code. Wala is a framework for static analysis and provides various static analysis capabilities like slicing, class hierarchy analysis, pointer analysis, among others. To apply KeY, the source code must necessarily be annotated, while Wala can deal with Java bytecode out of the box. Due to the required annotations, KeY cannot deal with source code in an automated approach, which is impractical for Beagle. Concerning the built-in symbolic execution features, KeY provides full symbolic execution,

Criterion	KeY	Wala
Main purpose	Proving correctness of source code	Static analysis framework; abstract bytecode representation
Effort	High: Annotations required	Low: Robust
Automation	No	Yes
Full symbolic execution	Yes	No
Parametric dependency base	Yes	Partial
Primitive date types	Yes	No
Collections / Complex data types	No	No

Table 5.2.: Comparison: Symbolic execution and its implementations

while Wala only provides a base for the implementation of symbolic execution. The symbolic execution of KeY is mainly able to deal with primitive data types; for collection data types and other complex data types, symbolic execution does not work in the way the Beagle approach requires.

The symbolic execution which has been developed in the context of [Kna10] uses Wala as base framework. It is able to create stochastic expressions for given symbolic execution problems. For cases which result in ambiguities for possible parametric dependencies, multiple stochastic expressions are returned by the approach. For example, if two branches manipulate an output parameter (due to phi nodes), both branches are analysed separately and result in separate stochastic expressions. Still, the partial results are beneficial for reverse engineering of Beagle approach (cf. Section 5.11.10).

The results of the developed symbolic execution are translated into individuals of the initial generation of genetic programming and handled like all other results from static, dynamic, and statistical analysis approaches: $InitialGeneration = InitialGeneration \cup Wala_{SymbExec}$, where $Wala_{SymbExec}$ is the set of chromosomes created by the above symbolic execution approach.

5.13. Static Analysis of Parametric Dependencies: Other Approaches

Apart from symbolic execution, further static analysis approaches can be integrated into the Beagle approach. Among the most suitable is slicing [Wei81].

The results of slicing approaches are not sufficient to establish parametric dependencies. Slicing can at most provide a binary relation between input and output parameters but no exact specification how output parameters depend on input parameters (for the classic form of slicing). Furthermore, slicing approaches are not designed to create abstractions, but instead focus on soundness.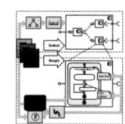

Still, slicing results can be beneficial since it can be known from slicing results which parameters influence a certain parametric dependencie and which do not. For example, the $Genes_{Inputs}$ set can be reduced based on slicing results. If the slice criterion is set to a output parameter $o \in Outputs$, the set of variable genes $Genes_{Inputs}$ can be reduced to inputs which are recognised by slicing:

$$\{gene.parameter \mid gene \in Genes_{Inputs}\} \cap BackwardSlice(o)$$

where $BackwardSlice(o)$ returns the backward slice of statements affecting o. If the utilised slicing approach can guarantee that a certain input parameter cannot impact an output parameter for which a parametric dependencies has to be determined, the input parameter can be safely deleted from the set of genes. Due to the reduced set of variables, the convergence speed can be increased.

```
1  int doSth(int a, List list, boolean b) {
2    for(int i = 0; i < a; i++) {
3      list.add(new Integer());
4    }
5    if(b) {
6      a++;
7    }
8    C.processList(list); // external call

10   return a;
11 }
```

Listing 5.20: Example source code: Slicing of source code

Consider the simple example source code in Listing 5.20. In this example, the `list` parameter characterisation NUMBER_OF_ELEMENTS (NoE) of the external call `processList(..)` is subject of reverse engineering of a parametric dependency. The backward slice would be starting for the `list` parameter in line 8 and include all statements that affect that parameter. The set of statements that is returned by the backward slice would be (informally) $\{``list.add(newInteger)", ``for(int\ i\ =\ 0; i\ <\ a; i\ +\ +)", List\ list, int\ a\}$ which includes the input parameters `list` and a but omits parameter b. The set $Genes_{Inputs}$ would in this case be $\{a.\text{VALUE}, list.\text{NoE}, b.\text{VALUE}\}$. Thus, the "important" parameters `list` and a would be correctly included in the intersection of backward slice and $Gene_{inputs}$. As the example points out, whole parameters and not only single parameter characterisations can be excluded from genetic programming when using slicing.

No slicing approach is currently integrated into the implementation of the Beagle approach.

5.14. Multivariate Adaptive Regression Splines

Statistical Analysis of Parametric Dependencies: Multivariate Adaptive Regression Splines Statistical analysis approaches are known for their abilities in approximation. Woodside et al. [WVCB01], for example, discuss regression approaches in the context of so-called "resource functions" [CW00]. Resource functions approximate, for example, the CPU usage of a software for a single execution environment.

The idea of using statistic regression approaches in the context of this thesis, is to embed approximation abilities of state-of-the art approximation approaches and then to further evolve the findings of statistic regression approaches using genetic programming. The approximations delivered by the statistic regression approach are therefore translated into individuals of the initial generation of genetic programming and can be further optimised. This is especially important since the developed fitness function of genetic programming forces abstraction and therefore implies slightly different optimisation criteria which are not reflected by any existing regression approach.

Regression approaches can be simple linear regressions, which approximate a given dependency by a linear function, or more advanced regression like polynomial regressions. A general problem when dealing with such regression approaches is the selection of an appropriate one which matches the original kind of dependency. Therefore, more advanced approaches based on regression splines have been developed which, depending on the approach, can approximate multiple kinds of dependencies without a priori knowledge. Additionally, regression splines can be defined piecewise.

In previous papers, Woodside et al. [CW00, ZWL08, WVCB01] highlight the use of the Multivariate Adaptive Regression Splines approach (MARS) which has been introduced by Friedman [Fri91]: "MARS-based representation appears to be ideal for nonlinear resource functions fitted to empirical data, as it does not require a hypothesis about the functional form" [WVCB01, p. 252].

For a number of reasons, MARS is well-suitable to the class of data which must be approximated:

- MARS is able to deal with multi-dimensional problems which depend on a number of input variables,

- MARS results in a piecewise defined function which fits the input data and thus is applicable to non-continuous data which is present due to branches in the monitored source code,

- MARS limits the complexity of resulting expressions (e.g. number of nodes; number of selected variables). This helps abstracting expressions during statistic analysis already. MARS uses Generalized Cross Validation (GCV, cf. [Sta09]) to balance model complexity and precision of function fitting. GCV punishes a large number of knots (see below) to overcome the limitation of simplified error measures like the least squared error which does not incorporate any complexity measure and would result in large expressions.

An example for a MARS result expression is (visualised in Figure 5.30):

$$
\begin{array}{ll}
z = 0.92 & \text{constant} \\
+\,0.39 \cdot h(x, 4.3) & \text{knot 1} \\
+\,0.85 \cdot h(x, 27.9) & \text{knot 2} \\
-\,2.27 \cdot h(y, 35.2) & \text{knot 3}
\end{array}
$$

MARS expressions are a product of piecewise defined linear functions. Generally, a function fitted by MARS is expressed as a sum of terms of the following form:

$$
\begin{aligned}
value := {} & const \\
& \pm\, a_1 \cdot h(b_1, c_1) \\
& \pm\, a_2 \cdot h(b_2, c_2) \\
& \pm\, ..
\end{aligned}
$$

with $const$ and a_n constants, b_n and c_n a pair of constant and variable where each pair must have a constant and a variable.

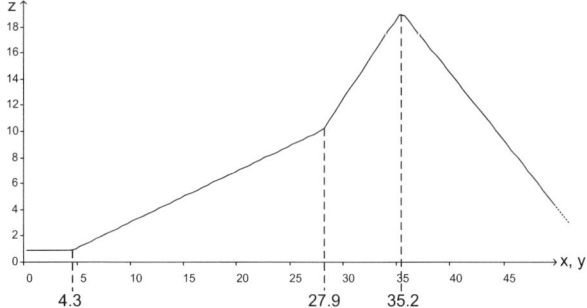

Figure 5.30.: Example: Plot of a MARS function

$h(..) \to v \in \mathbb{R} : 0 \le v < \infty$ is the *hinge function* which must be either of the form $h(const, x)$ (cf. [Fri91]):

$$max(0, const - x)$$

or $h(x, const)$:

$$max(0, x - const)$$

where $x \in \mathbb{R}$ represents a variable and $const \in \mathbb{R}$ is a constant. Each hinge function forms a so-called *knot* contributing to the piecewise function definition.

In the Beagle approach, the result of MARS is translated to an individual of the initial generation. The PCM stochastic expressions do not support the max operator. Therefore, each knot of the hinge function is translated into

$$value := max(a, b) \text{ with } a = 0$$
$$= \begin{cases} 0 & if(0 > b) \\ b & else \end{cases}$$

which can directly be represented in genes and stochastic expressions using a branch condition.

Realisation In the thesis, the R (see for example [Cra07]) implementation of MARS is used. The corresponding package is named EARTH.

217

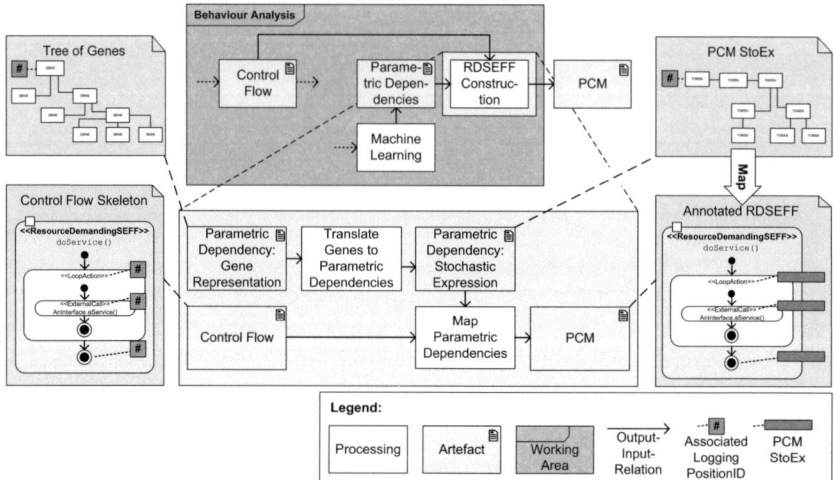

Figure 5.31.: Adding learned parametric dependencies to the RDSEFF: *Translation from trees of genes to stochastic expressions of the PCM and mapping of stochastic expression to the control flow skeleton.*

5.15. Adding Learned Parametric Dependencies to the RDSEFF

After all parametric dependencies (each *output* LoggingPositionID of the control flow; cf. Section 5.8.5) are learned using genetic programming, the parametric dependencies are added to the control flow skeleton of the RDSEFF. Therefore, first the learned dependencies must be mapped back to the control flow skeleton and second, the parametric dependencies represented as genes of genetic programming must be translated into PCM RandomVariables which own a StochasticExpression attribute. Figure 5.31 visualises the steps in the context of the overall process and highlights the translation and mapping step including the input and output artefacts.

For the first step, parametric dependencies are mapped back to the control flow skeleton using the LoggingPositionID introduced in Section 5.10.5. The Logging-PositionID is added to the control flow skeleton when building it from code and maintained during all the dynamic analysis and genetic programming steps. Hence, for each parametric dependency, the corresponding LoggingPositionID is available. In the control flow skeleton of the RDSEFF, the LoggingPositionID can be simply looked up via the trace model decorator (a mapping between source code artefacts and PCM model elements; see Section 6 and Figure 5.31 "Associated PositionID") within constant time. A parametric dependency can then be added for each Logging-PositionID.

The second step comprises a conversion of genes to `StochasticExpressions`. For the `StochasticExpressions`, the PCM provides a parser that converts a text representation into the syntax tree of that text. Genes are therefore converted into a text representation which then by the parser is converted into the syntax tree. Since the gene structure is not visitable (cf. "visitor pattern", [GHJV95]), the stochastic expression cannot be created directly from the gene structure. Each gene is capable of emitting a text representation of itself which can be read by the parser. The text representation is derived by a recursive walk on the gene structure.

The hinge function of learned parametric dependencies resulting from the MARS approach is converted as described in the previous Section 5.14.

5.16. Integrate Resource Demands

While internal actions have been omitted in previous sections, they will be handled in the following to complement the Beagle reverse engineering approach. The RDSEFF models, which are reverse engineered so far, are complete behaviour models except for the specification of resource demands.

As a reminder: In Palladio, no direct timing values are being specified the internal actions of RDSEFFs. Instead, abstract instructions are used to describe resource demands. Timing values are calculated in a later model performance prediction step (which is out of scope of this thesis; see [Bec08a, Koz08b, BKR09]) to allow for exchanging the resource environment at the model level without affecting other parts of the model. A more detailed discussion on the specification of abstract resource consumptions was presented in Section 2.6.

For the estimation of resource demands, basically the same machine learning approach as for estimating parametric dependencies can be used (see Section 5.11). Figure 5.32 provides an overview on the general integration.

Generally, information on arbitrary resource demands (e.g. CPU, memory, Bytecode instructions) is supported by Beagle. Beagle does not require other information than raw resource utilisation counts (e.g. resource demands issued per input parameters) per `InternalAction`. For every `InternalAction`, a dependency between input parameters of the surrounding RDSEFF and resource demands is then calculated through genetic programming. This will be further discussed below.

Bytecode The following section deals with the integration of raw bytecode counts with the behaviour model. Again, genetic programming will serve as a central element for integration.

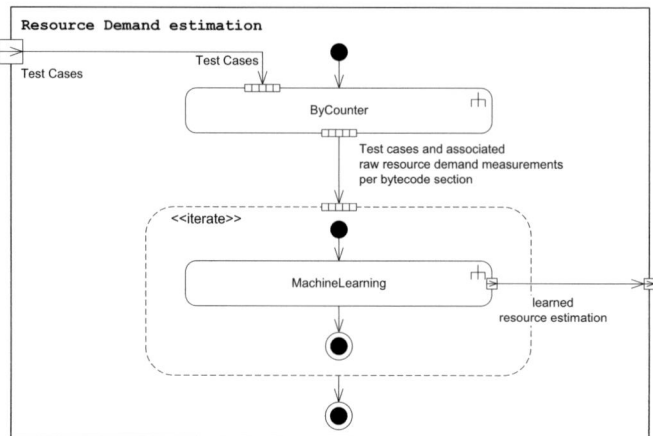

Figure 5.32.: UML activity diagramm: Integration of resource demand counting
("ByCounter") in the reverse engineering process of behavioural
models

A detailed way of capturing resource demands which are not specific for a single
execution environment (cf. Requirement *R-Resource Demands*), is the handling of
low level instructions. For Java, these instructions are formed from bytecode. Bytecode instructions are executed within a virtual machine and thus are not specific to a
single execution environment.

A previous successful combination of the RDSEFF behaviour models and Bytecode resource demands has been shown in [KKR10, KKR08a]. In this approach,
Beagle adds resource demands (e.g. CPU and HDD demand) for all internal actions based on the *raw resource demand counts* delivered by the ByCounter tool
[KKR08b]. ByCounter provides counts of executed bytecode instructions for InternalActions. Therefore, ByCounter is executed using test cases and counts the
resulting bytecode instructions executed at runtime for each parameter input.

Bytecode instructions cover load, store, arithmetical, and method execution instructions, among others. ByCounter captures bytecode counts for each so-called
"building-blocks" in the code. A building-block is a non-branched (if-then-else, for,
or while free) sequence of instructions (see the simplified example in Figure 5.33).

ByCounter results in tupels of the form:

$$ByCounterResult := \{bc_1, bc_2, ..\} ,$$
$$bc := (bytecodeInstruction, buildingBlock, Inputs, count)$$
$$\in ByCounterResult$$

where $Inputs$ itself is again a set of tuples:

$$Inputs := \{input_1, input_2, ..\},$$
$$input := (inputsymbol, inputvalue) \in Inputs$$

which is present for each input from the executed test cases. A $bytecodeInstruction$ is a unique identifier for a bytecode instruction, $count \in \mathbb{Z}$ is a number representing the number of executions of a $bytecodeInstruction$ within a $buildingBlock$, and a $buildingBlock$ is an unique identifier corresponding to an Internal-Action; the bijective mapping between InternalAction and $BuildingBlocks$ is $BuildingBlocksMapping$:

$$BuildingBlocksMapping := InternalAction \rightarrow BuildingBlocks$$
$$BuildingBlocksMapping^{-1} := BuildingBlocks \rightarrow InternalAction$$

This mapping and its inverse mapping allow the processing of ByCounter data and the required annotation of RDSEFFs with resulting resource demands. The set $BuildingBlocks$ holds a number of building blocks:

$$BuildingBlocks := \{buildingBlock_1, buildingBlock_2, ..\}$$

Each single tuple $bc \in ByCounterResult$ is subject to genetic programming. Thus, for every bytecode instruction and building block, the input parameters $Inputs$ and monitored output $count$ (bytecode counts per instructions) are fed into genetic programming. At an abstract level, the task for genetic programming remains the same as for other parametric dependencies. While for parametric dependencies loop execution numbers, branching conditions, and parameter values are calculated, for resource demands pure counts which can depend on input parameters, need to be calculated. Solely, the source of input information is different.

The example shown in Figure 5.33 illustrates the ByCounter integration. For each building block (visually aggregated by curly brackets), ByCounter provides counting results per bytecode instruction and for each measured combination of input data (resulting from test cases). In the example, there are two control flow statements (loop and branch). Each body of such a statement results in a building block (3) and (4). Additionally, there are building blocks for the constant overhead of control flow statements (1) and (2). For example, a loop requires the calculation of initial variable values (1) and a branch has a constant overhead for checking its condition (2). These overheads result in additional building blocks which are considered explicitly and returned by ByCounter.

Prior to genetic programming, the building block representing the constant overhead of a loop is merged with a InternalAction preceding the LoopAction.

```
public void uploadFiles (List<File> files, boolean saveEnabled) {
```

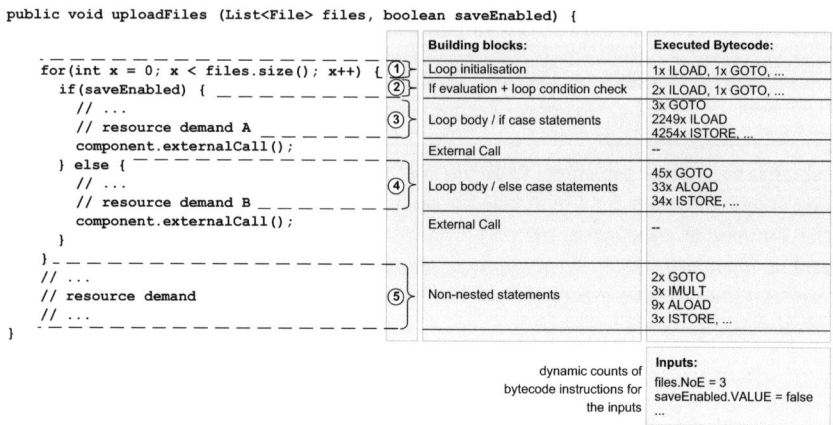

Figure 5.33.: Building blocks example

Hence, each `InternalAction` can correspond to a number of building blocks. Constant overheads of control flow statements (e.g. initialisation of loop statements or condition check of a branch statement) are merged with `InternalActions` predecessing the described control flow element. Building blocks representing static overhead (e.g. condition checks or incrementation) are merged with `Internal-Action` contained in those control flow statements. The condition check of loops is merged into the first `InternalAction` of a `LoopAction` and the incrementation part is merged into the last `InternalAction` of a `LoopAction`.

Adding Resource Demands to the RDSEFF   After learning dependencies between input data and the resulting executed bytecode instructions, these parametric dependencies can be annotated as `ResourceDemands` to the reverse engineered RD-SEFF. Such `ResourceDemands` can be for example ("resource demand A" from Figure 5.33):

$$files.\text{NUMBER\_OF\_ELEMENTS} * (saveEnabled == true ? 1 : 0) * 3$$

for the GOTO bytecode instruction.

To enable matching internal actions in the RDSEFF with the bytecode estimations of genetic programming, unique IDs are used to tag internal actions and corresponding building blocks. The resulting IDs are then matched when creating the RDSEFF.

5.17. Black-Box Components

In some reverse engineering scenarios, coarse-grained component behaviour models might be sufficient for rough performance predictions if the reverse engineering effort can be lowered. Other reverse engineering scenarios might forbid any grey-box view[2] (cf. [BW99]) of components in reverse engineered models which exhibit internals of components. In these scenarios, further limitations of the prediction capabilities of reverse engineered models might be acceptable. In order to support scenarios where either no source code is available, rough models are sufficient, or where no model details are wanted (e.g. protection of intellectual property), a black-box reverse engineering approach [KKR08a, KKR10] has been developed in the scope of this thesis. In a black-box reverse engineering scenario, the control flow of a component is considered as a black-box which is not subject to reverse engineering.

Instead, a black-box behaviour model in the developed approach comprises a single InternalAction covering all internal behaviour of a component and a number of LoopActions each containing an ExternalCall cumulatively representing all calls to a required role of the reverse engineered component. The reverse engineered model uses the LoopAction to express multiple calls to another component. In such a black-box model, first the required roles of a component must be identified, then for each required role the number of calls, the corresponding call parameters of the ExternalCall, and finally, the resource demand of the InternalAction must be approximated.

To facilitate the reverse engineering while maintaining the black-box principle, component behaviour is monitored at the interface-level. Frequency and parameters of incoming and outgoing calls are recorded during the execution of a component. The component can be either executed in a testbed or in an existing installation. Like in the grey-box approach presented in the previous chapters, the approach does not rely on timing values during monitoring. Only frequencies and parameter characterisations are recorded during monitoring. Therefore, the overhead of measurements does not impact the results. Timing information is, as before, added during performance prediction, which is out of scope of this thesis.

The reverse engineered model is comparable to *characteristic curves*[3] as used in electrical engineering, but in contrast to them parameterised over potentially multiple dimensions. As the approach again applies genetic programming for estimating resource demands of the InternalAction, for approximating the LoopAction's executions counts, and the parameters of ExternalCalls. The resulting model can be parameterised over multiple dimensions. The single InternalAction of the reverse engineered model is comparable to a very large internal action for grey-box models

---

[2]The approach presented in the previous chapters is a grey-box approach.
[3]German: "Kennlinien"

in the previous chapters which makes the genetic programming approach well applicable in the black-box scenario.

Assumptions The black-box approach results in a simplified behaviour model which implies a number of limitations and assumptions, primarily concerning order effects:

- A performance impact of the order among external calls to different required roles is neglected. For example, the sequence $CS_{example} = ABACCBA$ of external calls in Listing 5.21 would become an unordered set $A^*B^*C^*$ where $*$ represents an arbitrary number of calls. Thus, the call sequences $ABACCBA$ and $ABCABCA$ become indistinguishable. The reduction may be less accurate due to missing expressiveness of "bursts" of calls as discussed in Section 5.7.2 in the context of `InternalActions`.

    ordered set of external calls $\rightarrow$ unordered set of external calls

- Multiple calls of external services in a single sequence are assumed to have the same performance impact like calling them during a longer period of time. For example, $CS_{example}$ would become the unordered set of $(call, frequency)$ tuples: $A^3B^2C^2$.

    temporal distribution of external calls
    $\rightarrow$ single frequency for external calls

- The same approximation of parameter characterisations for all calls of a required service are assumed. This is due to a single `ExternalCall` for all calls of a required role. In the example from Listing 5.21, instead of specifying *separate* parameter characterisations for x in the lines 3 and 6, the parameter characterisations for x are specified only *once*.

    individual parameter characterisations per LoggingPositionID of an
    external call
    $\rightarrow$ parameter characterisations for *all* calls of a required service

- Any performance impact of order among internal actions is neglected. Thus, resource demands are issued at a single point in time without any delay. For example, $I_1AI_2B..$ could first utilise the CPU in the `InternalAction` I_1 and then utilise the HDD in I_2 after calling A. In the blackbox model, the set would be $IAB..$ where I covers *all* `InternalActions` of a component; including the CPU and HDD resource demands in a single `InternalAction`. This might

```
1  doSth() {
2    /* .. internal action I₁, CPU demand */
3    A(x)
4    /* .. internal action I₂, HDD demand */
5    B()
6    A(x)
7    C()
8    C()
9    B()
10   A(x, y)
11 }
```

Listing 5.21: Example: Sequences of internal actions and external calls

result in bursts of contention in the simulated CPU and HDD which increases the response time, lowers the throughput, and wrongly indicates peak loads of resources (again see Section 5.7.2 for further discussions).

ordered set of internal actions $\rightarrow$ unordered set of external actions

A(x), B(), and C() are external calls of another component in Listing 5.21.

Implications Genetic programming must learn the control flow from black-box monitoring data. For example, for each InternalAction, resource demands can depend on branch and loop execution within an InternalAction which must be reflected in the resource demand specification. Imagine resource demands within a branch which is inside a loop. To exactly express these resource demands, the outer control flow of the resource demands must be approximated. Since this is also true for InternalAction in the grey-box approach, the developed genetic programming approach can be reused. A parametric dependency for the described example could be

$list.$NUMBER_OF_ELEMENTS $*$ (IF(X.VALUE $>$ 1024) THEN 10 ELSE 0)

where $list.NUMBER\_OF\_ELEMENTS$ reflects a loop iterating over the elements of a list and $IF(X.VALUE > 1024)$ is a branch only causing resource demands (10) for values of X larger than 1024.

225

Furthermore, in the black-box approach call frequencies of ExternalCalls are approximated per required role instead of for whole loops in the grey-box approach. The complexity remains the same as in the grey-box approach.

Realisation For the estimation of parametric dependencies, genetic programming from the grey-box approach is reused without modifications. The monitoring framework presented in Section 5.10 can also be reused without major modifications. The main difference lies in changed instrumentation points. For the black-box approach, the instrumentation points lie outside a component under study at the sides of caller (for provided interfaces) and callee (for required interfaces). This places are determined by component interfaces and can be derived from the static architecture description. In order to monitor the resource demands, again ByCounter is used. Instead of counting executed bytecode for building blocks, whole components are monitored.

5.18. Complexity and Scalability

The creation of the control flow abstraction is carried out in a two pass algorithm implemented in GAST2SEFF. The worst case complexity is x^2, where x is the number of control flow statements in the GAST. In the worst case, each node is visited for every other node. In the implementation, if a subtree can be cut off (i.e. it is marked as having no transitively reachable external call actions), the second pass fully omits the subtree and converts it to a single internal action. Thus, for real-world scenarios, the complexity is even lower.

Each node of the GAST structure is held in memory. For the marker, only two additional bits per node (input / external call) are required. Thus, the memory consumptions linearly depends on the number of nodes in the GAST model.

For the genetic programming part, the approach has linear complexity when a fixed number of generations is evolved. For each parametric dependency, the approach demands a constant time. Another linear computation complexity arises from the fitness function. Depending on the amount of monitored data, the fitness function must check against that monitored data to determine the fitness of an individual. The fitness function complexity depends linearly on the amount of monitored data.

Section 7.12 discusses the scalability in the context of case studies which have been performed in the validation.

5.19. Realisation

The following section provides a brief overview on the realisation of the Beagle approach and highlights the core techniques applied. Details can be found on the Beagle website[4].

The Beagle reverse engineering approach is fully implemented in Java. The monitoring infrastructure is partially based on log4j and utilises a MySQL database for data persistence. The instrumentation is based on the Eclipse JDT (Java Development Tools). For transforming the GAST source code representation into the control flow structure of the RDSEFF, Java is used. The source code decorator model which allows traceability between GAST and RDSEFF is generated using Eclipse EMF (Eclipse Modeling Framework). Beagle integrates and extends the JGAP (Java Genetic Algorithms Package, [Mef]) library as base genetic programming implementation.

5.20. Limitations and Assumptions of Reverse Engineering Behaviour Models

In the following section, the limitations and assumptions of the Beagle approach will be discussed.

5.20.1. Handling of Exceptions

One of the core assumptions of Beagle is that exceptions do not affect the control flow across components and that any exceptions thrown at runtime do either not critically affect performance or if they are affecting performance, represent a really exceptional situation which rarely occurs and does not represent regular behaviour.

There are basically two ways of using exceptions in languages like Java: i) to handle really *exceptional* error situations (as recommended [NK05, pp. 104], [Ora10]) or ii) in an *irregular* way to ii.a) introduce additional return values to a method or to ii.b) realise jump statements to break the regular control flow.

Case i) Case i) represents situations, which only rarely occur and are not expected to happen. Such situations are intentionally ignored during reverse engineering of behaviour models as for such situations no meaningful performance behaviour can be expected. Thus, performance prediction is also not meaningful for such cases. Consequently, these cases are not supported by Beagle.

---

[4]http://sdqweb.ipd.kit.edu/wiki/Beagle

227

Case ii) Situations of case ii) in which Java exceptions have mistakenly been used for simulating special return values are only supported by Beagle if the control flow changed by an exception does not cover more than a single InternalAction. In this case, the performance impact of the exception is approximated by the Inter-nalAction. The exception itself is then abstracted by the InternalAction. In all other cases, the exception affects component-external control flow (by definition of an InternalAction) and is not supported by Beagle.

It is generally hard to decide which exceptions have been used for case ii) as the exceptions itself look the same in case i) and ii). Even the distinction between checked and unchecked exceptions, which is known from Java, does not help as even checked exceptions are sometimes used to simulate special return values. Nevertheless, dynamic analysis is able to give hints on case ii) exceptions: If such exceptions are thrown in virtually every request (which can be checked by ByCounter), Beagle can show a warning to the user. If the component-external control flow is changed by such misused exceptions, explicit control flow structures in the SEFF can be introduced manually.

One could introduce distinct support for exceptions by adding separate BranchAc-tions for exception cases. Then Beagle could learn the conditions for entering an exception case. This kind of exception support has intentionally not been realised to the lower complexity of the resulting control flow structure. Since exceptions break the regular control flow structure and escalate until they are caught, every exception would introduce branches in parallel to the regular control flow. Ultimately, the control flow structure could become confusing when including every potential exception.

5.20.2. Availability of a Test Bed

The dynamic analysis step of Beagle relies on the availability of a test bed. The test bed must provide an execution environment of the component(s) under study and test cases which can be executed. Beagle does, opposed to other approaches (cf. [AW96]), *not* require a load driver to be available since timing values are not measured during monitoring. The test cases can be automated unit tests, replay tests of recorded productive component usage, and can also be manual test for the component(s) under study.

Test case data must possess a representative coverage of input parameter space in order to ensure optimal results. Therefore, test cases should possess a good path coverage (C_2c, cf. [Bei90]). Opposed to requirements for unit tests, the path coverage is only needed for control flow statements which are present in the RDSEFF. Control flow statements which are contained in InternalActions do not need coverage during dynamic analysis as they are merged into a single node which is not monitored.

Monitoring the execution of InternalActions is not subject of this thesis. Requirements for test cases to monitor them can be found in the work of Kuperberg [Kup10].

Each branch represented in the RDSEFF should be executed and all loops represented in the RDSEFF should be executed with 0, 1 and n iterations. As for good test cases, minimal, maximal, and boundary values should be included in test case data (cf. [Bei90, GG75]).

Still, genetic programming is robust against less representative test cases. Less representative test cases result in poorer input parameter coverage which in turn make it harder to learn parametric dependencies. Genetic programming, which is part of Beagle, in any case finds parametric dependencies. If no test cases are provided to produce certain component behaviour (e.g. a loop is executed more often if a boolean input flag is set), the corresponding behaviour will not be represented in the parametric dependencies of the resulting RDSEFF. Only behaviour which is shown by test cases can be discovered by genetic programming. Generally, a small number of input parameter variations is sufficient which makes the behaviour of different executions distinctive (deviations in behaviour can be monitored). The number of required input parameter variations is discussed in the validation Section 7.9.

Test cases also influence the precision of parametric dependencies. Imagine the branch condition $x < 3141$. If only 3,000 and 3,500 are part of the test case input, while the real branching condition switches at 3,141, any guess between 3,000 and 3,500 would be considered precise by the fitness function. As long as test cases do not result in a counter example, guesses of genetic programming are considered to have full precision. Thus, test cases which exactly check a branching condition (in the sense of condition coverage; C_3c, cf. [Bei90]) help improving the precision of genetic programming.

Edvarsson [Edv99] surveys a number of automatic test data generation approaches which could be suitable to generate the required test cases. Other test data generation approaches include [LMS$^+$99, FK96, GCL01, Ori05] and address the generation of test data itself as well as the generation of test beds for distributed software systems. Approaches like the one by Cadar et al. [CDE08] fully automatically generate tests. The survey of McMinn [McM04] details on search-based test data generation which includes genetic algorithm-based approaches.

5.20.3. Monitored Data Properties

It is assumed that parameters and parameter characterisations which impact the performance are specified in the interfaces of reverse engineered components. Dynamic analysis relies on parameter characterisations to be available. A domain expert should be able to identify performance-relevant parameters and parameter characterisations based on an interface description. To reduce the manual effort for the specification, Section 5.10.4 presented heuristics which automatically identify performance-relevant parameter characterisations. For scenarios which employ only primitive and collection data types, the available heuristics are sufficient to fully automatically identify performance-relevant parameter characterisations. In other scenarios, a domain expert should complement the heuristically identified parameter characterisations.

5.20.4. Component State

The Beagle approach assumes that the system under test is a component-based system following the component paradigm. The reverse engineering approach is not intended to work for non-component scenarios. This implies that components should not have an externally visible state, according to the component definition of Szyperski et al.: [SGM02, p. 36]: "The characteristic properties of a component are that it [..] has no (externally) visible state."

The cited component definition relates to component types. As the Beagle approach reverse engineers behaviour models which are intentionally independent from a specific component instance, the component behaviour relates to the type level as well. At runtime, component services behave the same way for all calls of that service. Yet, the absence of an (externally) visible state does not imply that components do not possess a state at runtime (e.g. parameters).

Kapova et al. [KZM+10] discuss the potential impact of state on performance evaluations of component-based systems. Possible support of stateful components in the presented reverse engineering approach is discussed below.

State in the PCM Stateful elements of a system are considered to be out of the scope of the reverse engineering approach and out of the system scope of the PCM. When a system involves stateful elements, they are annotated as QosAnnotations to a PCM System. For example, a database can be approximated by its average response time for different kinds of requests (e.g. select, update, insert). Additionally, QosAnnotations can specify return values for called services. Opposed to RDSEFFs, QosAnnotations cannot be parameterised over input values. Instead, they can use general probability distribution functions for QoS attributes and return values.

Generally, the PCM does not support persistent or session state which lasts for more than one request. The PCM supports request state formed by data flow parameters (i.e. request data), state based on semaphors, and state based on per assembly context configurations, only. The Beagle approach shares the state limitation of the PCM.

During simulation, the PCM has advanced support for state which is introduced by the simulation environment. The simulated scheduler can realise arbitrary kinds of states below the application component layer. State complexity is intentionally hidden from the application component layer which is subject of reverse engineering. For example, the scheduler can reflect complex state-dependent performance effects arising from scheduling of an operating system or a Java virtual machine. A detailed discussion of scheduling in the context of the PCM can be found in the dissertation of Happe [Hap08].

Obviously, components like databases have an (externally) visible state. Still, they are supported by the developed approach, as long as changes of the state at runtime do not impact the performance. For example, if files are stored in a database, the files represent a state of the database component. If these files are then transferred over a network, only their byte size impacts the performance. In that case, the file sizes of files stored in the database can be approximated by the database component. When files are requested, file size approximations based on the approximations can then be passed as parameters. Such approximations do not harm the assumptions of the PCM. Yet, the size of files stored in the database must not change over time to fulfill the assumptions of the PCM (steady state).

Hence, persistent state has a limited impact on performance in the target domain of the PCM. Furthermore, databases and storage systems are usually considered to be out of scope of the PCM's components which primarily reflect application-level components. Typical business applications, which are in the focus of PCM, use databases for persisting data and not for business logic.

To nevertheless support different persistent states of components (e.g. full storage vs. empty storage system), components can be parameterised over persisted data which is processed during execution of a component. Thus, a component can depend on state (through parametric dependencies) but itself does not persist state which can change at simulation time from request to request.

Being able to specify `QosAnnotations` for system-external elements of an architecture such as databases, is assumed since the persistent state of a software system mostly is a steady state: The amount of data does not change largely during execution periods of a days which are typical scopes of performance analysis. During performance prediction, usually time frames of less than one day are simulated for which the steady state assumption holds. If the persistent state changes in shorter time frames, prediction results will become imprecise.

Impact of State on Reverse Engineering If a reverse engineered component actually has a persistent or session state, the precision of Beagle is affected. During monitoring in the dynamic analysis phase, pseudo-random behaviour can be monitored in these cases: For the same input values different result values can be monitored. In those cases, Beagle approximates parametric dependencies which perform best according to the fitness function which includes to minimise the mean squared error (cf. Section 5.11.4).

One of the following two conditions must hold to affect reverse engineering by component state: i) the monitored data flow values changes or ii) call frequencies of monitored statements (loops, branchs) change. If not data flow or call frequencies at the component-level (as captured in the RDSEFF and monitored during dynamic analysis) are changed, the reverse engineering precision is not affected through component state. In these cases, for example, functional behaviour might change which is not captured in RDSEFFs. The performance behaviour is not affected in these cases.

If a reverse engineered component has a persistent state which changes over a long-term period (longer than the simulated time), so-called ComponentParameters can be used to explicitly parameterise a component. ComponentParameters are specific to an assembly context of a component and can be changed manually to reflect changes of state. Beagle does support ComponentParameters.

5.20.5. Passive Resources

The PCM supports so-called PassiveResources which realise semaphores. Acquire and Release actions of the RDSEFF allow for modelling of blocking behaviour, synchronisation, mutex etc. behaviour. Beagle does not support the automated recognition of Acquire and Release in source code. Technically, many different semaphore realisations are imaginable which would require a strong semantic analysis in order to be automatically "reverse engineerable".

Often, semaphores are realised and encapsulated in frameworks and middleware which are not considered to be application components. Those kinds of semaphores do not directly affect the behaviour model of components and thus must not be represented in RDSEFFs. For other cases, Beagle requires a user to manually add Acquire and Release actions if needed.

5.20.6. Fork Behaviour

Beagle has only limited support for component control flow forks which thread the behaviour of components. If components actively fork threads which call other components, this must be reflected in the RDSEFF in so-called Fork actions. Beagle is able to recognise the basic thread starting construct for Java Thread.start(). If such a statement is found in the source code, a Fork action is introduced into in the RDSEFF. Still, the behaviour which is executed upon invoking the start() method is currently not reverse engineered, which is not a limitation of the approach but of the realisation. Users need to manually specify the thread behaviour of such explicit threads, e.g. by using InternalCalls to point to the actually executed thread behaviour.

Nevertheless, request- or session-based parallelism is supported by the PCM. In typical application server scenarios, multi-threading is taken over by the infrastructure.

Application components must not explicitly initiate concurrency (i.e. fork threads and instantiate processes). This kind of parallelism is supported by the performance prediction approaches of the PCM and must not be reflected in RDSEFFs. The major concurrency tasks of application components are for example concerned with transactions and data structures (e.g. synchronised methods).

Multi-threading which is completely included in a single InternalAction does not affect the RDSEFF since internal parallelism is not made explicit in the control flow structure of the RDSEFF. InternalActions with internal parallelism are handled like usual InternalActions.

Nowadays, multi-threading, if present within application components, is complemented by complex frameworks such as the one available in Java (java.util.concurrent). Each threading framework would require separate support by Beagle in order to capture the specifics of each framework. An automated semantic analysis of existing multi-threading frameworks is not covered by static program analysis (cf. [Rin01]). For example, such semantic analysis approaches would need to identify the degree of parallelism (pooling etc. affect this value), thread starting time, and thread join conditions, which each require a complex semantic analysis.

5.20.7. Dynamic Binding

Beagle relies on the GAST representation created by SISSy from C/C++, Delphi or Java code. SISSy has no capabilities to deal with dynamic binding. Beagle inherits these limitations. Especially components which comprise multiple classes could have dynamic binding among these classes which Beagle consequently is not able to deal with. In those cases, for example a behaviour model for the wrong class (the static type) could be created.

Again, consider the example from Section 5.9.2 on page 134, which was used to discuss the implications of selected component boundaries. If the classes A, B and C would all belong to the same component Comp, the lines 2 and 3 in Listing 5.8 would decide which behaviour is included into the RDSEFF of providedService of Comp. If instead of the used classes B and C other classes implementing the interfaces FirstAndSecondInterface and AnInterface would be instantiated, the behaviour implemented in those classes would be the correct behaviour to reflect in the RDSEFF.

There are three possible implications from the missing support of dynamic binding for the Beagle approach:

1. The behaviour model becomes wrong. The behaviour of the wrong class is included into the RDSEFF. Due to the use of static analysis only, the binding can be instantiated differently at runtime than analysed statically.

2. The behaviour model becomes incomplete. The concrete bound class cannot be determined at all. The corresponding RDSEFF is thus incomplete. In these cases, the GAST model of SISSy must first be fixed manually such that the concrete bound class is specified in the GAST model.

3. The behaviour model is temporarily wrong and incomplete. If the binding changes at runtime, the actual behaviour differs over time. SISSy cannot deal with behaviour which changes at runtime. The statically analysed behaviour in these cases becomes part of the RDSEFF.

Nevertheless, if the change of behaviour is indicated by any component parameter, the RDSEFF model can be manually adapted to switch its behaviour upon specific input parameters. In such a case, the behaviour introduced by the different classes would reside in a Branch of the RDSEFF which is selected if the input parameters indicate so.

6. Traceability

Traceability aims at linking activities in different phases of software development together. In the approach presented in this thesis, to allow users to follow and evaluate reverse engineering results, traces are stored along the whole reverse engineering process. These trace links bring together sources of reverse engineering and its results in the final PCM instance. Thereby, artefacts from reverse engineering can be mapped though having completely different abstraction levels in the source and target models of the reverse engineering. For an overview on traceability models see for example [GG07, RJ01].

Traceability is for example important in the presented approach, to map performance prediction results to the original source code. When aiming at optimising an existing software architecture, without trace links being available, it would be hard to interpret the performance prediction results and draw conclusions for the existing architecture. For example, if the response time of a certain service is too high, or a single internal action seems to contribute to a performance bottleneck, the corresponding source code artefacts can be easily identified following trace links. If no trace links are available, the "back-mapping" of performance prediction results becomes ambiguous. In a similar manner, all intermediate artefacts which participate in the reverse engineering process, can be mapping along the trace links.

Since traceability is a cross-cutting concern which should be respected throughout the whole reverse engineered process, it is discussed in a separate chapter.

In the presented approach, a decorator model (*PCM source code decorator*, cf. Figure 6.1) realises trace links at the model level. The decorator links model elements from the GAST to model elements in the PCM. Due to the usage of a decorator model, the GAST and PCM can remain untouched and trace link concerns are not mixed with the domain specific languages of GAST and PCM. The source code decorator models are typed trace link models which reference single model element types (opposed to generic trace link models which reference EObjects and thus are not type safe).

Each element in the GAST model has a source code position attached in the GAST already. Hence, each model element of the GAST model can be traced back to its exact source code position. The source code position comprises, among other information, file paths, files, lines of code, and tokens covered by a model element. Thus, linking model elements from the GAST is sufficient to uniquely trace back model elements from reverse engineering results. The presented reverse engineering

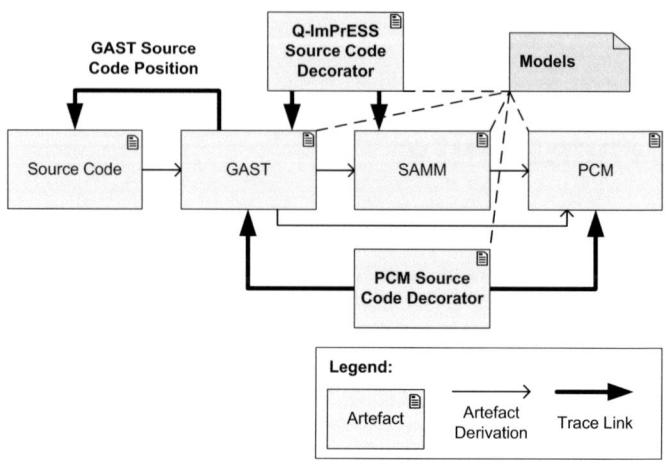

Figure 6.1.: Overview on artefacts referenced from trace links

approach builds up the source code decorator in parallel with the other target models of reverse engineering.

The presence of trace links allows, for example, the tracking of a single source code class on its way to a component. The steps for a source code class are: Source code class > GASTClass > SAMM Component > PCM Component. The links between model elements do not need to be binary as Figure 6.1 suggests. For example, a SAMM Component can result from multiple GASTClasses.

Like the GAST, the source code decorator established language-independent trace links. GAST and PCM are language-independent. Thus, the source code decorator model does not need to be adapted in order to support further object-oriented languages.

Trace Links A trace link generally is a relation between *source* and *target*:

$$TraceLink := (source, target, type)$$

where *source* and *target* are sets of elements of the models involved in the reverse engineering approach (for the developed approach holds: $source, target \subseteq instances(GAST \cup SAMM \cup PCM)$; $instances()$ collects all instance elements of a meta-model). Trace links can have different *types* to distinguish for example the traces from classes to component from the traces from control flow statements to RDSEFF actions. If the *type* of a trace link is set, further constraints on *source* and *target* must hold, i.e. elements in *source* and *target* must be instances of specific meta-model elements and the cardinality of *source* and *target* can be constrained. A trace *type* is defined as:

$$type := (sourceType, sourceCardinality, targetType, targetCardinality)$$

where for a $TraceLink$ of type *type* must hold:

$$\forall s \in TraceLink.source : type(s) = sourceType \wedge$$
$$sourceCardinality = card(TraceLink.source) \wedge$$
$$\forall t \in TraceLink.target : type(t) = targetType \wedge$$
$$targetCardinality = card(TraceLink.target)$$

In the SoMoX and Beagle approach, trace links are realised using trace models which are decorators of GAST, SAMM, and PCM. Each trace links covers only one processing step (e.g. from GAST to component) instead of tracing for example a single GAST class from its creation to the final PCM model. To trace an artefact over multiple steps, multiple trace links can be transitively followed.

Alternative realisations of trace links (which are not realised in this thesis) are:

- N-ary trace links link all elements participating in a trace starting from a start element to a final element. This solution has the drawback that all steps must be known in advance (otherwise the trace links would be needed to adapted to any new reverse engineering step)

- Trace links are realised via embedded trace IDs which remain unique across multiple reverse engineering steps and serve as an identifying "marker" (e.g. a class has a trace ID x which also appears for components derived from that class). This kinds of trace link realisation was chosen for portions of the Beagle approach.

6.1. Architectural Reverse Engineering

The lowest level of entities, architectural reverse engineering uses, are classes. For gaining components, no lower abstraction than "class = component" is supported (especially a component is not a number of class methods). Potentially, multiple classes are forming one component. Thus, it must be traced, which classes result in which component. Classes can belong to one `BasicComponent` and multiple `CompositeComponents` (all `CompositeComponents` which are part of the closure of the `BasicComponent` defined by the *contains* relation in the result model). In Java and C# (currently not supported by SISSy but neither a limitation of GAST nor SoMoX) one file can contain multiple classes. Additionally, in C# one class can be split across multiple files. Thus, tracing on file-level only is not meaningful.

SoMoX creates Q-ImPrESS SAMM models as primary result artefacts. The SAMM2PCM transformation then creates instances of the PCM from SAMM models. For the Q-ImPrESS SAMM model, a separate Q-ImPrESS source code decorator model (cf. Figure 6.1) exists which is comparable to the source code decorator used for the PCM. The content which is hold in the Q-ImPrESS source code decorator is comparable to the content of the PCM source code decorator, only the associated component types belong to a different meta model (the SAMM). The SAMM2PCM transformation is responsible for creating a PCM source code decorator from the Q-ImPrESS source code decorator.

Ultimately, the (PCM) source code decorator establishes $n : m$ links between GAST classes and PCM components (BasicComponent and CompositeComponent). Since any source code files are mapped to GAST files, the trace links are also valid for C/C++/C# code. PCM Interfaces are linked $1 : 1$ to the realising GAST classes.

For the sake of brevity, the trace link types will be presented in a tabular form below. A cardinality (sC: $sourceCardinality$; tC: $targetCardinality$) of "*" indicates no constraint on the cardinality.

$type$	$sourceType$	sC	$targetType$	tC
ComponentLink	GASTClass	*	ImplementationComponentType	1
InterfaceLink	GASTClass	1	Interface	1

6.2. Reverse Engineering Behavioural Models

Tracing the reverse engineering of behavioural models requires much more fine-grained trace links at the source code side. Each action of the RDSEFF must be mappable to source code. The GAST model supports this level of granularity. The PCM source code decorator links a number of GAST statements to a single action of the RDSEFF. The trace links from the PCM source code decorator represent the overall reverse engineering results of Beagle.

Additionally, these trace links are supported by IDs which are internally used to coordinate instrumentation, monitoring, data aggregation, assignment of learned dependencies, static analysis, symbolic execution, determination of resource demands, and integration of benchmarking results. Artefacts must be traced across all steps of the reverse engineering process (see Figure 3.4), which is ensured by maintaining IDs throughout all steps.

The control flow abstraction (see Section 5.8) is responsible for assigning unique IDs to all actions of the RDSEFF and to each corresponding source code section in the very first reverse engineering step. A code section is a section in the control flow (for example an internal action, the body of a loop, or the loop-skeleton itself). To match code sections during the different steps of behavioural reverse engineering, only IDs must be matched.

Trace links established for RDSEFFs:

$type$	$sourceType$	sC	$targetType$	tC
InternalAction-GastLink	Statement	1	InternalAction	*
LoopActionGastLink	LoopStatement	1	LoopAction	*
BranchAction-GastLink	BranchStatement	1	BranchAction	*
AbstractBranch-TransitionGastLink	BranchStatement	1	AbstractBranch-Transition	1
ExternalCallAction-GastLink	FunctionAccess	1	ExternalCallAction	1
SetVariableAction-GastLink	Statement	1	SetVariableAction	1
VariableUsage-GastLink	Statement	1	VariableUsage	1
ResourceDemanding-SEFFGastLink	Method	1	ResourceDemanding SEFF	1
ParameterGastLink	FormalParameter	1	Parameter	1

7. Validation

The developed approaches SoMoX and Beagle are capable of reverse engineering the static architecture and behaviour of individual provided component services of component-based software systems. The resulting models enable the prediction of performance properties based on the simulation of the Palladio approach (cf. [Bec08a]). Each part of the reverse engineered models and the overall performance predictions enabled by the approach are subject to validation.

Figure 7.1 provides an overview on the validations performed for this thesis. On the left hand side, the reverse engineering covered by this thesis is shown, on the right hand side, the existing and already validated Palladio performance prediction approach is shown. Validations of both approaches complement each other. While for the reverse engineering (left) it must be checked that the output models (A) conform to a reference model (B), the performance prediction validation (right) must check whether for a system under test, the prediction results (D) fit to measurements of the real system (G).

7.1. Validation Scenarios

The SoMoX and Beagle approach can be validated in various ways. Case studies are used to show the applicability of the approach to real-world application.

To answer the validity of the developed approaches, a so-called *Type 1 validation* (cf. [BR08]) has been performed. Here, for a single or multiple case studies, reference decomposition models are compared to models reverse engineered automatically by the approach (C). Then, the resulting reverse engineered model is compared to the reference decomposition.

It is also possible to compare the reverse engineered model with the reference model based on performance predictions (I). Then, it is validated, whether both models result in the same performance abstraction. This is especially useful, if both models differ structurally, but are equivalent with respect to the abstraction target "performance". A pure structural test would not be sufficient in that case to judge on the quality of the performance abstraction.

Generally, architectural and behavioural reverse engineering can be validated independently. An overall case study is still preferable to show the integration capabilities of the combined approach.

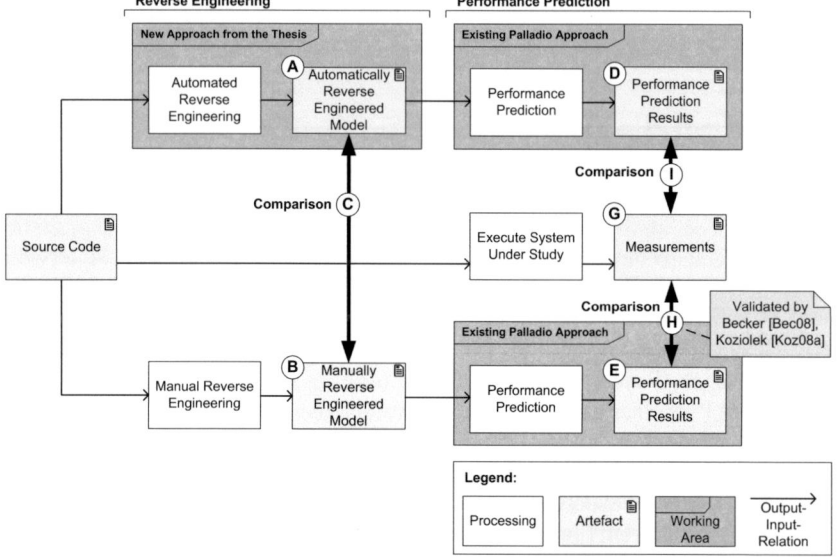

Figure 7.1.: Overview on the validation purposes in the Palladio context: Reverse engineering (left), performance prediction (right)

7.2. Goals and Questions

The validation performed in this thesis follows the Goal Question Metric (GQM) approach [BCR94] by Basili. First, the validation goals are identified, then appropriate questions which are suitable to answer whether the goal has been reached are posed, and finally metrics which provide (preferable quantifiable) answers to the questions are derived.

General questions which are going to be answered in the validation are:

- Q-g-1 Of what quality are the reverse engineered models (architecture and behaviour)?

- Q-g-2 How accurately does a PCM performance prediction based on reverse engineered models perform?

- Q-g-3 How does the approach deal with real-world large-scale applications?

- Q-g-4 How well does the approach scale?

- Optionally, it could be investigated, how well the approach can be applied by ordinary software architects.

For the reverse engineering approach on the left hand side it is checked whether the automatically reverse engineered model (A) matches a manually reverse engineered model (B), comprising of a reference decomposition and a reference behaviour model. The reference decomposition is ideally based on existing up-to-date architecture documentation. If no reliable reference architecture is available (i.e. the existing architecture is outdated or not available at all), a reference architecture must be created. To not bias the results, in the validation of SoMoX and Beagle, such kind of reference architecture was created in interaction with the developers of the corresponding software systems. It will be pointed out in the discussions of the case studies (Sections 7.7 to 7.9) where a reference architecture stems from.

Specific questions per "Comparison" (C, I, H in Figure 7.1) are listed in the following.

(C) Criteria which are being evaluated in (C) are guided by the following questions:

- Q-C-1 What is the quality (consistency, precision, completeness) of the reverse engineered models?

- Q-C-2 How good are the approximations of parametric dependencies compared to parametric dependencies in the models?

- Q-C-3 How much time and effort can be saved compared to the manual creation of models?

Validation step (C) provides insights to specific and systematic errors in the reverse engineered models. It furthermore identifies what the limitations of the reverse engineering approach are with respect to completeness of the result models.

(I) In (I) performance prediction results based on automatically reverse engineered models are compared with measurements of the executed system under test. This validation step checks the suitability of the reverse engineered models for performance prediction with the Palladio approach. Opposed to step (A), the whole reverse engineering approach including the Palladio performance prediction are validated in this step.

Checking the whole reverse engineering and prediction chain implies uncertainties: Errors in (A) and (D) could either boost or annul each other. The results do not make obvious where in the prediction chain possible errors occurred or whether some canceled each other. Hence, this validation step must be complemented by the validation step (C) to identify potential cancellation effects.

The main validation questions for (I) are:

- Q-I-1 Can the reverse engineered models be executed in a Palladio simulation run?

- Q-I-2 Do the reverse engineered models possess the required execution semantics?

- Q-I-3 How much do the predicted performance results deviate from measurements of the actually executed system?

(H) The comparison between manually reverse engineered models (B) and performance prediction results resulting from those models (E) has been successfully performed in previous work. The validation of (H) for different kinds of systems is covered by a number of publications [Bec08a, Hap08, Koz08b, BKR09]. The Palladio performance prediction approach – as a single separate research subject – is not subject to validation in this thesis. Instead, the end-to-end validation of the overall reverse engineering approach includes the validation of the Palladio approach in (I).

The Palladio performance prediction has been successfully checked for its prediction accuracy and its ability to recommend the right design decisions before. For the Type I validation (cf. [BR08]), an ideal performance model was assumed to be given (B). The predictions based on this model (E) where then compared (H) against measurements of the executed system under study (G) [Bec08a, Hap08, Koz08b, BKR09].

In a separate Type II (cf. [BR08]) validation step, the applicability of the Palladio performance prediction approach has been investigated in empirical experiments [MBKR08b, MBKR08a, Mar07, Mar05]. Due to the setting of the empirical experiment, which covered the whole application of the Palladio approach from manual model creation to performing performance predictions and evaluating them, the experiment also investigated the manual creation of performance models (with respect to effort and error-proneness). Thus, the effort for the manual creation of performance models can be derived from these experiments to compare them with the effort when applying the automated reverse engineering approach.

Provided Insights Depending on the validation step (C, I, H), different insights on the validity of SoMoX and Beagle can be gained. Step (C) is suitable to judge on the structural deviation between the reference decomposition and the reverse engineered model for both, static architecture and behaviour. Step (I) allows to validate the quality of the performance model which the reverse engineering results represent. Step (H) validates the quality of the performance prediction approach itself.

Step (C) is meaningful on its own since it validates only a distinct reverse engineering step. If the reverse engineering results in step (C) deviate, the reverse engineering approach obviously has limitations if the reference decomposition (B) can be assumed to be valid. Step (I) provides precise insights only together with step (C): If the performance prediction results in (I) deviate, this can be either caused by the reverse engineering or the performance prediction. Thus, validating step (I) always implies step (C) to be present. When validating only (I), the overall reverse engineering and performance prediction approach can only be falsified; it per-se provides no insights into the root cause (either reverse engineering or performance prediction) without step (C).

Due to the presence of the existing validations in step (H), validating step (I) and step (C) can be seen as a double-check of the performance prediction results, since in both cases the same performance prediction approach (results (D) and (E)) is being validated against the same measurements (G) which are used for validation step (H). Thus, the combination of step (C) and (I) can reveal possible errors in former validations of step (H).

Lessons Learned   Lessons learned are highlighted as (*LL*-) throughout this section and the conclusion Section 9.

7.3. Validation Criteria – Metrics

In order to judge the reverse engineering results of step (C) and (I), the metrics introduced in the following are used. Each metric is associated to one or several questions – according to the GQM paradigm. The metrics cover the static architecture, the behaviour model, and the performance prediction. Metrics themselves can be grouped in the following since they answer multiple questions. The following paragraphs highlight the relation between questions and groups of metrics.

Static Architecture and Behaviour Model (Structure)   Model elements which are checked in the validation cover the whole reverse engineered models. Metrics defined on the following model elements are suited to answer the questions Q-g-1 and Q-C-1:

- Basic components, composite components, connectors, interfaces, service signatures

- Control flow structure of the behaviour models

- Data flow and parametric dependencies in the behaviour models

- Resource demands

Performance Predicting the performance based on the models and comparing the prediction capabilities of reverse engineered models with measured performance values helps answering the question Q-g-2, Q-C-2, Q-I-1, Q-I-2, Q-I-3.

Other For the remaining questions, metrics gained in the following scenarios are used for validation:

- Time saving based on experiences from manual reverse engineerings (Q-C-3)

- Apply the reverse engineering approach to real world application (Q-g-3, Q-g-4)

7.3.1. Static Architecture

To judge on the quality of the static structure of the reverse engineered models, precision and recall [OD08] metrics are being used. Precision and recall are used for components, interfaces, ports, and connectors to identify how complete and precise models have been reverse engineered. Precision and recall are used to compare the reverse engineered model with the reference decomposition.

Precision and recall are common metrics (see for example [Kos02, Kos00, AL99a, AL99b]) to compare a reference or manual decomposition with an automatic decomposition. In their validation, Anquetil and Lethbridge [AL99a] accept meaningful alternative decompositions besides the reference decomposition. In this thesis, only a single third-party reference decomposition is preferred to avoid personal effects which could impact the case study results.

Koschke [KE00] provides a "framework" for the evaluation of clustering techniques which also incorporates reference decompositions. Mitchell and Macoridis [MM01b] discuss the evaluation of software clustering results if reference decompositions are not available. In the present validation, only for a subset of case studies no reference decomposition is available (this will be highlighted in the corresponding sections).

In another paper, Mitchell and Macoridis [MM01a] compare different similarity measures for clusters and propose their own measure. As they emphasize, it is important to not only check the correct assignment of classes to clusters but to also include for example connectors. Hence, the following validation does not limit itself to components but also checks provided and required interfaces and connectors. In [AL99b], different software cluster similarity metrics are discussed. Tzerpos and Holt [TH99] propose the "MoJo" distance metrics for clusters which judged the similarity of clusters based on move and join operation which are required to get from one clustering to another one. The "MoJo" metric has the drawback that it focuses on pure clusters and neglects the importance of other structural properties (e.g. interfaces, compositions, and connectors) of software architectures.

The completeness of the architecture is judged using the following definitions of precision and recall (here for components):

$$ComponentPrecision :=$$
$$\frac{card(\{designcomponents\} \cap \{reverseengineeredcomponents\})}{card(\{reverseengineeredcomponents\})}$$

$$ComponentRecall :=$$
$$\frac{card(\{designcomponents\} \cap \{reverseengineeredcomponents\})}{card(\{designcomponents\})}$$

where $card()$ is the set cardinality introduced earlier in this thesis.

Since design components and reverse engineered components cannot have the same identity (they stem from different identification processes and models), the intersection cannot be based on element identity. Instead, components A and B are considered to intersect, if the classes associated to the components match to more than 80%, i.e. $ComponentIdentity(A, B) > 0.8$ (cf. "Good Match" and "partial subset relationship" in [KE00]):

$$ComponentIdentity(A, B) := \frac{card(classes(A) \cap classes(B))}{card(classes(A) \cup classes(B))}$$

where $classes(A)$ yields the classes associated to component A. In the case studies, for each component that was considered to be successfully reverse engineered, the $ComponentIdentity$ was checked to be larger than 0.8.

Analogously, precision and recall are defined for provided and required interfaces and connectors.

7.3.2. Behavioural Models

The behaviour models have to deal with subsequent errors from static analysis. If component interfaces or component boundaries are wrongly identified during static analysis, the behaviour model must still be consistent with the static analysis results. Whether the behaviour model exactly fits to the interfaces stated by the static architecture will be checked.

Completeness   Since a high accuracy of the reverse engineered models is expected, except for the performance metrics, binary metrics (success/fail) are used to judge the behavioural model. Only if all criteria are met, the model is considered complete. The validation criteria for behaviour models comprise:

- Are all control flow statements correctly identified (loop, branch, external call) when comparing with a manually created reference model.

- Are all conditions (branch, loop) present (precision judged via performance prediction results)

- Are all passed parameters (call actions and return value) present (precision judged via performance prediction results)

$$Completeness(M) := M \mapsto b \in \{true, false\} \qquad (7.1)$$

where M is a model which is being judged for completeness (true if the above question are answered with yes in all cases).

Model Semantics   A precondition to the conduction of performance simulations is the reverse engineering of a model which is complete such that, according to the model semantics, all information for a performance simulation are available. Hence, the description of execution semantics must be complete. This includes the absence of unreachable branches (e.g. contradicting branch conditions) and loops which cannot be executed (e.g. loop condition invalid). The build-in validations of the PCM models, precondition checks of the PCM simulation, and runtime consistency and validity checks of the PCM simulation take over these checks. The results metric is binary: Either the simulation can be conducted successfully or not.

$$SimulationSemantics(M) := M \mapsto b \in \{true, false\} \qquad (7.2)$$

where M is a model which is being judged for its capability and validity to be simulated.

7.3.3. Performance

To check the quality of the reverse engineered model for performance predictions, the relative deviation between the predicted and measured response time is used. The deviation is the quotient of measured and predicted response time based on the mean value to be more robust against outliers. The performance prediction is done by the Palladio SimuCom Framework which uses PCM models as input.

$$Performance(M) := \frac{Prediction(M)}{Measurement(M)} \qquad (7.3)$$

where M is a model, $Prediction(M)$ is the predicted median response time for a provided service of M, and $Measurement(M)$ the corresponding measure response time value.

7.3.4. Other Metrics

To judge on the time savings when using the reverse engineering approach, the time for manually reverse engineering a model is compared to the application of the automated approach.

$$Effort(M) := \frac{AutomatedReverseEngineering(M)}{ManualReverseEngineering(M)} \quad (7.4)$$

where $AutomatedReverseEngineering(M)$ and $ManualReverseEngineering(M)$ are the effort in person hours for creating Model M.

The applicability of SoMoX and Beagle to real world applications is measured by two metrics: The binary metric whether the reverse engineering could be performed to a large-scale system $Running$ at all and the duration of a reverse engineering run $ReverseEngineeringDuration$ in wall clock time. Values for $Effort(M)$ which are < 1 are considered to be good; values ≥ 1 are considered to be poor.

7.4. Type 2 Validation

To complement the Type 1 validation, an optional Type 2 validation (cf. [BR08]) could be performed to check the applicability of the approach for subjects not involved in the development (no Type 2 validation has been performed in the context of this thesis). Therefore, a controlled experiment with two groups of subjects could be set up. One group would apply the SoMoX and Beagle approach and a second group would manually reverse engineer a software system. Then the results of both groups could be compared to judge on the applicability of the approach. Koschke [KE00] proposes a detailled framework for the experimental evaluation of clustering techniques which could – with some adjustments – be applied to the presented reverse engineering approach.

Another scaled-down version of the Type 2 validation could be a small number of case studies were single subjects apply the approach. The qualitative feedback of the case studies could then be used to improve the approach and to get a feeling for its strengths and weaknesses in third party application scenarios.

7.5. Case Study Selection

For the case studies it is important to have applications from different application domains which should at least include business information systems and algorithm-intensive applications. The use of different domains increases the external validity of the overall validation, as applicability to different kinds of problems is shown. Business information systems often utilise dozens of frameworks, application servers, and distributed environments but have comparably little algorithm complexity, while algorithm-intensive applications lead to complex parametric dependencies. As monitoring data usually is not capturing the whole state space of an application, even contradicting monitoring data might be observed in such cases. For example, imagine an algorithm whose behaviour depends on its internal state. If then the internal state is not monitored, observations can be contradicting as first glance (the same input results in different output). Generally, algorithm-intensive applications are computationally expensive, hardly statically analysable and sometimes hard to predict with respect to the observable execution time distributions.

Typical business information systems are distinguished from algorithm-intensive applications as follows: While it is predominantly important to capture which data is passed to which components (control and data flow) at an "inter component level" for business information systems, for algorithm-intensive applications the necessity for more fine-grained observations at the level of internal control flow are expected. Business information systems tend to have more interactions across component boundaries, while algorithm-intensive applications are mostly dealing with component-internal control and data flow. It is worth noting that calls to API are not considered to be calls to other components, which means algorithm-intensive applications have in fact mostly internal complexity. There is no strict borderline between business information systems and algorithm-intensive applications.

For the case studies it is envisioned to have at least one representative for each domain in order to capture the problem space.

7.6. Case Study Candidates

The following section first lists the performed case study software systems. Of the overall eleven case studies, three are "end-to-end" case studies for which all steps of the reverse engineering approach have been applied. The remainder of the case studies were performed to separately validate either SoMoX or Beagle.

7.6.1. Case Study Overview

Software System	SoMoX	Beagle	Remark
CoCoME	✓	✓	Component benchmark system
SPECjbb2005	✓	✓	Industry standard
Palladio FileShare	✓	✓	IEEE TSE [KKR10]
Ohioedge CRM	✓		EJB-based
Rubis	✓		EJB-based
openArchitectureWare	⊘		non-component-based system
LZW Compression		✓	Bytecode estimation
SPECjvm2008 Compress		✓	Industry standard, bytecode estimation
HSQLDB	✓		Scalability analysis, >150 KLOC
ABB OPC	✓		C/C++ system; core "components" found; real architecture unknown
ABB Demonstrator Subsystem	✓		C/C++ system, Scalability analysis, 250 KLOC

Table 7.1.: Overview on case studies

Legend for Table 7.1:

- ✓: Successful validation

- ⊘: Non-successful validation

- No symbol: System not validated for the approach

Various case studies have been performed in order to validate SoMoX and Beagle (see Table 7.1). Each system has specific characteristics which will be briefly highlighted in the following:

- CoCoME, the COmmon COmponent Modelling Example [RRMF08], is a reference system for component-based software engineering research. CoCoME realises a distributed point-of-sale system and includes a business information system of stores and enterprise infrastructure as well as the embedded systems part of cashdesks.

- SPECjbb2005 [Sta05] is an industry standard performance benchmark application which realises a typical client server application. It is designed to benchmark the performance of Java virtual machines. Users of SPECjbb2005 include Apple, Cisco Systems, Dell, Sun Microsystems, Hewlett-Packard, IBM and many others.

- Palladio FileShare is a Java-based software system which realises a server-based file sharing platform. Users can upload files to the application to share them with other users.

- Ohioedge CRM is an open source customer relationship management system which is based on Enterprise Java Beans (EJB).

- Rubis is a Java-based online auction platform, offering a number of online bidding functionality. The implementation is based on EJBs.

- LZW Compression is a Lempel-Zip-Welch compression algorithm written in Java. It has been implemented at the Institute for Program Structures and Data Organization at the Karlsruhe Institute of Technology (KIT). LZW Compression realises a single component of a component-based software architecture.

- SPECjvm2008 Compress [Sta08] is the compression component of the SPEC-jvm2008 industry benchmark. It is implemented in Java.

- openArchitectureWare is an open source model to text framework, nowadays available in the Eclipse modeling project. openArchitectureWare is implemented in Java but possesses no component-based software architecture. It is used as a software system to check the ability of the reverse engineering approach to deal with non component-based systems. As the presence of a component-based software architecture is claimed to be present for reverse engineering subject systems, this assumption for input software systems is checked with openArchitectureWare.

- HSQLDB is a large open source relational SQL database implemented in Java. It comprises a total of more than 158,000 lines of code and is thus used to check the scalability of the developed reverse engineering approach.

- ABB OPC is a software system realised in C and contributed by ABB. ABB OPC allows to discuss the reverse engineering capabilities for C/C++-based software system when applying the SoMoX approach.

- ABB Demonstrator Subsystem is a software subsystem realised in C/C++ and contributed by ABB. The ABB Demonstrator Subsystem allows to discuss the scalability of the SoMoX approach for large-scale software systems (250,000 lines of code).

Either SoMoX or Beagle have been applied to the above software systems. For three of the software systems, a full "end-to-end" validation was performed to show the applicability of the overall approach. Reasons for selecting these systems are discussed in Section 7.6.2.

Table 7.1 points out which software system was used for which kind of validation and notes remarkable properties of those software system. Of the eleven software systems, only one (openArchitectureWare; not component-based) lead to weak reverse engineering results. The quality of the reverse engineering results will be discussed in the following Section 7.7 and further.

7.6.2. End-to-End Case Studies

The software systems selected for the "end-to-end" case studies are intended to cover a broad scope of component-based software systems. Among the major requirements for selecting the below software systems, were the availability of test cases or load drivers, open source software systems, access to architecture documentation or architecture descriptions. Furthermore, the systems should be component-based software systems implemented in a supported programming language (Java, C/C++, Delphi). Since the underlying performance prediction approach Palladio [BKR09] focuses on business information systems, representatives from this domain are preferred. The overall size of the systems should be large enough to show the application of the developed approach to real software systems but could not be overly large since a manual inspection of the reverse engineering results would then become infeasible.

The selected "end-to-end" case studies cover business information systems and embedded systems, synchronous and asynchronous communication, complex and business logic algorithms, client-server scenarios and hierarchically distributed systems, resource demand and business-focused application. Therefore, it can be claimed that the "end-to-end" case studies cover a representative set of software systems.

The "end-to-end" case studies are CoCoME, SPECjbb2005, and Palladio File-Share. These case studies will be presented in detail in Section 7.7 to 7.9.

CoCoME combines a business information system and an embedded systems part within a single system. The implementations supports a distributed deployment on three hierarchy levels (stores, enterprise, cashdeks). To enable the configuration of the system, CoCoME partially employs dependency injection mechanisms. CoCoME involves typical business logic like reporting and accounting but also has complex algorithms which solve optimisation problems. Hence, control and data flow are of varying complexity. The persistence in CoCoME is taken over by a persistence layer based on the Java persistence API. Internally, synchronous and asynchronous (event-based over an event channel) communication are employed.

SPECjbb2005 is an industry performance benchmark for Java virtual machines. SPEC aimed at creating a representative Java server application when designing the benchmark. Partners from industry were involved in the development of SPEC-jbb2005 to ensure creating a balanced and representative benchmark application. SPECjbb2005 is a representative for the business information system domain and realises a typical client-server workload scenario. Due to its benchmark nature, it focuses on representative resource demands (Java virtual machine utilisation).

Palladio FileShare is a typical representative for business information systems. It has a parts with typical business logic and an algorithm-intensive part. Overall Palladio FileShare possesses many parametric dependencies and architecture alternatives which make it suitable to investigate the predictability of the parameterisation of the reverse engineered models. Its architecture and control flow are well-documented and ease the check of consistency between automated and manual reverse engineering.

7.7. CoCoME

CoCoME – the COmmon COmponent Modelling Example [RRMF08] is a reference system for component-based software architectures which aims at providing a base for comparing different research approaches on component-based software. CoCoME provides a detailed architecture description, a fully running implementation, and a specification of reference values for extra-functional properties (i.e. performance and reliability).

The software system realised by CoCoME is a distributed point of sale system with support for house keeping of single stores, central facilities of the whole enterprise, and the embedded system cash desk software of the single points of sale. Furthermore, CoCoME realises complex business logic which includes the optimisation of the exchange of goods among stores to equally distribute low running goods among stores in the same region.

The reverse engineering concentrates on the business information system part of CoCoME. The static architecture of the embedded part of the system was reverse engineered to check the component detection capabilities for embedded systems with event-based communication.

LOC	9,521
Classes	126
Interfaces	21
Prefixes	none
Suffix	.*TO .*Event
Reference decomposition	(non cashdesk; no database)
System level	1
Sub-system level	2
Components	11
Reverse engineered	
Detected primitive components	8
Detected composite components	4
Performed iterations:	11
Execution time	<3 sec

Table 7.2.: SoMoX results for CoCoME

7.7.1. Static Architecture

7.7.1.1. Components

Both, the reverse engineered and the reference decomposition had a total of 16 components (including system and subsystem level components) when applying SoMoX to the business information part of CoCoME. Overall, the reverse engineered architecture and the reference decomposition were mostly the same. Nevertheless, the reverse engineered architecture partially deviated. The reverse engineering focuses on the business information system part of CoCoME for which the Palladio approach is designed. To highlight how SoMoX could handle the embedded systems part, these results are discussed separately.

The reverse engineering results are discussed in detail in the following starting from the top level. Section A.1.1, page 324, visualises the reference architecture. Figure 7.2 and A.7 visualise excerpts from the reverse engineered model.

- At the system level, the reverse engineered architecture was deviating from the design architecture. The reference architecture lists only two components, while in the the reverse engineered system had three components of which one was a primitive component from the embedded systems part which was not correctly merged into the remaining cashdesk line component.

- At the subsystem level, the reverse engineered architecture contains two components as the design architecture does. Still, one of the components, the cashdeskline, contains an inventory component in the reverse engineered architecture while it does not in the reference decomposition.

255

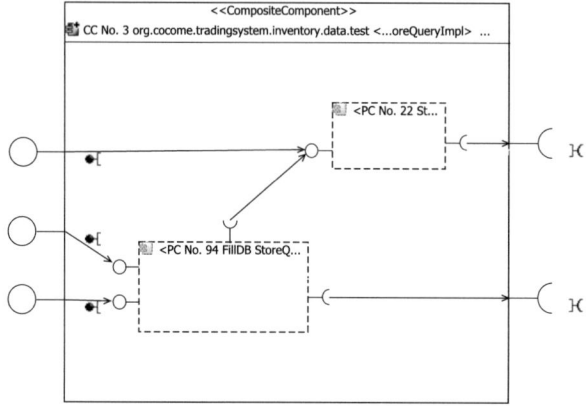

Figure 7.2.: CoCoME: Reverse engineered trading system composite component (screenshot)

- From the inventory component, which was fully recognised, most of the sub-components have been identified: The GUI of CoCoME is split into ReportingGUI and StoreGUI components in the reference decomposition but was recognised as a single component in the reverse engineered model. From the application component two out of three components have been identified (the application store component was missing). The data subcomponent of inventory was split into two composite components (enterprisequery and storequery) while the reference architecture treats both queries as a single component. The remaining three subcomponents of data had been successfully identified.

Overall, nine out of fourteen design components below the system-level have been correctly reverse engineered for CoCoME.

$$ComponentPrecision = \frac{9}{12}$$

$$ComponentRecall = \frac{9}{14}$$

When including the system-level architecture, which is the strongest abstraction level and thus hard to reverse engineer, precision slightly increases and the recall slightly drops:

$$Component Precision = \frac{10}{13}$$

$$Component Recall = \frac{10}{16}$$

The embedded part `cashdeskline` has a total of seven low level controllers in the reference architecture, one `cashdesk` and one `eventbus`. For the `cashdeskline`, eleven primitive components could be detected and five composite components. The `cashdeskline` itself was discovered. Of its subcomponents only two out of seven components were discovered (the `scannercontroller` as a single component and the remaining controllers as a single large component). The `cashdeskline` is not considered in the overall reverse engineering results (Palladio is not aiming at embedded systems) and only presented for reasons of completeness.

7.7.1.2. Interfaces

In total, the reverse engineered interfaces and also the interface ports are quite complete. The design documents of CoCoME are partially inconsistent with the implementation of CoCoME. SoMoX thus yielded interfaces which are not present in the architecture design documents but should be (interfaces missing in the design documents: `GUIRefreshable`, `FillDB`, `RMIRegistry`). Overall, the reverse engineering identified 21 component interfaces while the reference decomposition lists 15. Furthermore, dependencies which are resolved via a RMI registry led to incorrect connectors (see below) and since the creation of interfaces depends on their usage by other components (cf. Section 4.8.6), interfaces were wrongly identified.

Overall, the CoCoME reference architecture lists 15 provided component interfaces, and 20 required component interfaces (due to multiple usage, the number of provided and required interfaces does not need to be equal). The reverse engineered model identifies those interfaces correctly, except for the `StoreIf`, `ReportingIf`, `CashDeskConnectorIf`, and `ProductDispatcher`. These are assigned to the RMI registry and never provided since the connectors for these interfaces are wrong (see below). Of the provided roles, eleven out of 15 could be correctly reverse engineered and assigned.

$$InterfacePrecision = \frac{11}{21}$$

When adapting the blacklist (excluding RMI interfaces), the $InterfacePrecision$ could be further increased to $\frac{11}{11}$.

$$InterfaceRecall = \frac{11}{15}$$

$$ProvidedInterfacePortPrecision = \frac{11}{22}$$

$$ProvidedInterfacePortRecall = \frac{11}{15}$$

7.7.1.3. Connectors

The CoCoME design comprises a total of 28 connectors of which 25 could be reverse engineered. Due to the additional interfaces (discussed in the previous section) 41 connectors where created during reverse engineering.

In the reverse engineered model, some connectors were wrongly wired with the RMI registry. For example, the connection from the cashdeskconnector to applicationstore was not identified correctly. In the same way, the connectors were bound to the RMI registry for reporting, cashdeskconnector and productdispatcher. Technically, this is correctly reverse engineered but ideally the RMI communication should be transparent.

$$ConnectorPrecision = \frac{25}{41}$$

$$ConnectorRecall = \frac{25}{28}$$

The connectors successfully ensure that all required interfaces are connected. Thus, no call (inside the CoCoME system) results in an invalid callee.

7.7.2. Behaviour Analysis

The behaviour analysis focused on the classes and methods involved in the most complex Use Case 8 of the CoCoME system which deals with product exchange of trading goods among stores. This use case involves complex optimisation logic and triggers the exchange of goods which is then delivered from one store to another store of a trading enterprise.

The resulting central component service for Use Case 8 is bookSale, which covers multiple methods and classes. For it, the behaviour analysis resulted in a total 14 external calls, six internal actions, two loop actions, and one branch action. All data flow parameterisations are present in the reverse engineered models.

The control flow was entirely and correctly reverse engineered except for some missing internal actions. These internal actions where abstracted as they contained only initialisations of local variables (e.g. Integer i = null) which have only a very limited performance costs. Nevertheless, any internal calculation can, in special scenarios, potentially impact the performance of a component service (e.g. a service comprising only few calculations which is called very frequently). The abstraction is acceptable for the CoCoME example but could result in prediction errors in special cases.

The following performance prediction (next Section) judges on the deviation between measurements and prediction of the reverse engineered software system.

7.7.3. Performance Prediction

The performance prediction of CoCoME resulted in a response time of 323.0 ms, while the measurement showed a response time of 321.5 ms. Hence, the performance prediction was only 0.46% off. The performance was predicted and measured for the original Use Case 8 of CoCoME which is triggered by the test driver. The original use case is a single user use case and hence increases the chance of getting precise performance prediction results.

Until stated differently, this and all following performance predictions were performed for an Intel Core 2 Duo Processor, 4 GB of system memory and 768 MB heap space for the Sun/Oracle JVM 1.6.

7.8. SPECjbb2005

SPECjbb2005 [Sta05] is an official benchmark of the SPEC group which realises a classic three tier business application. It is intended to measure the server-side performance of Java runtime environments and is delivered with a readily available load driver. The application runs typical business logic like the creation of orders, the handling of customer data, and the delivery of goods.

259

The performance predictions for SPECjbb2005 were performed for the load generated by the load driver. The static architecture was compared to the design documents. Since the design documents of SPECjbb2005 sketch a very coarse-grained architecture, a refined architecture was made available by a developer of SPECjbb2005. This architecture served as a reference decomposition.

LOC	12,788
Classes	75
Interfaces	5
Prefixes	none
Suffix	none
Reference decomposition	
System level	1
Components	4
Reverse engineered	
Detected primitive components	4
Detected composite components	1
Performed iterations:	10
Execution time	<5 sec

Table 7.3.: SoMoX results for SPECjbb2005

7.8.1. Static Architecture

The reverse engineering of SPECjbb2005 overall resulted in high values for precision and recall of components, interfaces, roles, and connectors (cf. Figure 7.3). As SPECjbb2005 does not make use of dependency injection or other forms of late binding, reliable information on the SPECjbb2005 was available from the GAST which was extracted by SISSy. All dependencies among classes of SPECjbb2005 were fully made available via static analysis of SISSy.

7.8.1.1. Components

SPECjbb2005 comprises just a small set of five components in total, although it comprises many more classes. Thus, SoMoX is able to reverse engineer a high abstraction level for components, where each basic component covers a large set of classes. Of the reverse engineered components, two are at the system level and the remainder at the subsystem level.

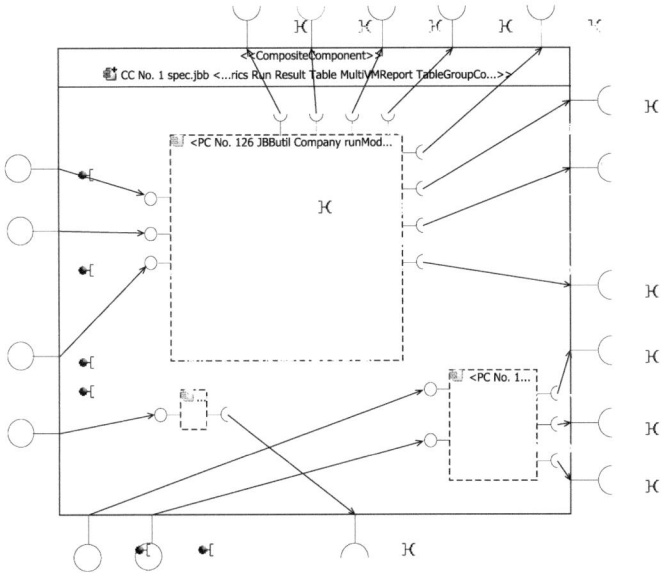

Figure 7.3.: SPECjbb2005: The reverse engineered core composite component (editor screenshot)

$$ComponentPrecision = \frac{5}{5}$$

$$ComponentRecall = \frac{5}{5}$$

With respect to the precision and recall of components, SPECjbb2005 was entirely reverse engineered. SoMoX showed to be able to deal with high component abstraction levels (*LL-high abstraction*).

7.8.1.2. Interfaces

SPECjbb2005 comprises only five Java interfaces. Thus, SoMoX reverse engineered public methods of classes as interfaces of components as a fallback strategy (see Section 4.8.6). To judge whether the reverse engineered interfaces are meaningful when using the fallback strategy, it must be investigated what precision and recall are

261

with respect to all calls passing component boundaries. For example, if component A accesses provided methods of component B, all of these calls must be captured in the interfaces (the design interfaces in this case).

The five Java interfaces and their inheritance were correctly classified as component interfaces. SoMoX detected 18 interfaces in total which were used in either provided or required roles. Of these, all correspond to design interfaces identified as explained above.

$$InterfacePrecision = \frac{18}{18}$$

$$InterfaceRecall = \frac{18}{18}$$

SoMoX reverse engineered a total of 14 provided roles and 24 required roles. Due to 14 required interfaces at the system level (i.e. dependencies to the runtime environment and library calls), only half of the required roles has a corresponding provided role. A role is expected for every interface of a component. Thus, if there is any communication via a previously identified interface, a correspondig role must be established. SoMoX successfully reverse engineered all roles.

$$ProvidedInterfacePortPrecision = \frac{14}{14}$$

$$ProvidedInterfacePortRecall = \frac{14}{14}$$

Although the component interfaces could be completely reverse engineered concerning the interfaces themselves and contained services, not all of the service signatures were complete. This was due to a special communication style in which instance variables of a class are set prior to calling the services themselves. For two component interfaces, thus further parameters had to be added, which are not present as source code parameters (see Section 7.8.2). Consider the example method doSth() which does not possess parameters and where all parameters must be passed via a setter prior to calling doSth(). In the communication style which is partially followed in SPECjbb2005, passing service parameters is realised in a comparable way.

7.8.1.3. Connectors

All connectors among the provided and required interfaces of the SPECjbb2005 component could be successfully reverse engineered. Especially, no connector was missing, delegating or assembling the wrong component. Incomplete connectors would also have impacted the performance prediction. If connectors are not present in a model, service calls end up in undefined locations. Thus, the presence of all connectors is a prerequisite to successful performance prediction.

SoMoX reverse engineered a total of 38 connectors of which 26 were delegation connectors and 12 were assembly connectors. As delegation connectors require an inner and an outer connector for a single role and since a single provided role can be connected to multiple required roles, the number of connectors does not directly relate to the number of provided and required roles but also depends on the nesting of composite components.

The 38 connectors exactly corresponded to the expected connectors from the design. Neither additional connectors nor missing connectors could be found in the reverse engineering results.

$$Connector\,Precision = \frac{38}{38}$$

$$Connector\,Recall = \frac{38}{38}$$

7.8.2. Behaviour Analysis

The high abstraction level of components implied a high abstraction level also for the behavioural model since the abstraction level of components is aligned with the abstraction level of the behavioural model in the developed approach (cf. Section 3). The behaviour analysis and subsequent performance prediction were focused on the central processTransactionLog service of SPECjbb2005. It comprises a total of 44 external calls which call 14 different services of other components and represents the most complex behaviour of a service of SPECjbb2005 (cf. Figure A.8).

Specific to processTransactionLog is the communication via instance variables. Instead of call parameters, instance variables are passed to the service before executing it. Thus, the primary *inputs* for parametric dependencies are the parameter characterisations of instance variables of the surrounding class. Formally, these parameters must hence become part of the component interface. After identifying certain parameter characterisations as performance-relevant, they had been manually

263

added to the component interface to complement it. These are parameters which are not present in the source code as call parameters.

7.8.3. Performance Prediction

In order to predict the performance (response time) of the reverse engineered system and to compare it with the response time of the actual implementation, the resource demands of all internal actions were estimated based on measurements of timing values in the corresponding code. Here, Beagle was responsible for estimating the resource demands of the internal actions. Furthermore, all other parametric dependencies (branch conditions, loop iterations, and parameter values) were reverse engineered by Beagle.

The overall predicted response time for the processTransactionLog service was $450\mu s$ (median) while the measured response time was $416\mu s$ (median). Hence, the performance prediction of the reverse engineered model is less than 8.2% larger than the measured value.

7.9. Palladio FileShare

Palladio FileShare is a client-server file sharing application. Users can upload files to the file sharing platform and share them with other users. The system is a Java-based implementation. Palladio FileShare supports different types of files. Non-compressed files are compressed prior to storing them. The storage is taken over by two separate components of which one is optimised for storing small files and one for large files. Only non-copyrighted files are being stored by the application. Therefore, file hashes are looked up in a database of copyrighted files before files are actually stored.

Palladio FileShare varies in all contexts which the reverse engineered models are parameterised over: The execution platform is being exchanged, the implementation of the compression algorithm can be exchanged by another (a LZW implementation and the compression implementation from the SPECjvm benchmark are available), and different file types and file sizes are uploaded in the investigated scenario. Thus, the case study comprises varying usage, assembly, and allocation contexts. Furthermore, the reverse engineered resource demands of Palladio FileShare are based on bytecode instructions instead of abstract CPU demands. A full architecture and control flow documentation is available for Palladio FileShare.

LOC	8,118
Classes	87
Interfaces	6
Prefixes	none
Suffix	none
Reference decomposition	
System level	1
Components	8
Reverse engineered	
Detected primitive components	6
Detected composite components	2
Performed iterations:	22
Execution time	<5 sec

Table 7.4.: SoMoX results for Palladio FileShare

7.9.1. Static Architecture

Figure A.6, page 327, visualises the reference architecture of Palladio FileShare, while Figure 7.4 depicts the reverse engineered main composite component of the system.

7.9.1.1. Components

The reverse engineered model of Palladio FileShare comprised a total of six primitive components and two composite components. Of the nine components in the reference decomposition (eight primitive components and one composite component), most components could be reverse engineered. The storage component in the reference decomposition Palladio FileShare exists in two flavours: one optimised for large and one for small files. Yet, the implementation uses the same component implementation for large and small components. The reverse engineered model cannot deal with multiple instances of a single component.

Furthermore, for the compression component, there exist two different implementations of which only one is used at a single point in time. The reverse engineered model merges the Hashing component together with the LZW compression component. Thus, in the reverse engineered model, one component represents two components of the reference decomposition.

Instead of one composite component in the reference decomposition, the reverse engineered model contains two composite components. These two composite components represent different abstraction levels of the system. The hashing component, whose implementation strongly relies on the capabilities of the Java libraries, is not

265

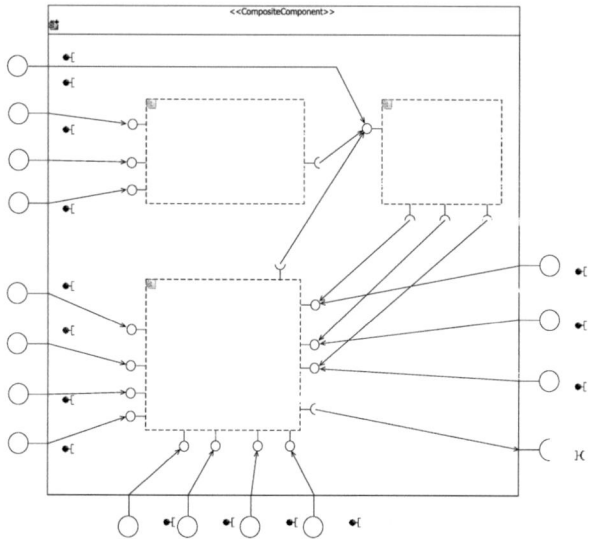

Figure 7.4.: Palladio FileShare: The reverse engineered system-level composite component (editor screenshot)

contained in the lower level composite component. The higher level composite component comprises components of the whole system.

The resulting precision and recall are:

$$ComponentPrecision = \frac{6}{8}$$

$$ComponentRecall = \frac{6}{9}$$

7.9.1.2. Interfaces

Except for one primitive component, all component roles were perfectly recognised. The combined hashing and compression component (already discussed above) has two provided roles which are not in the reference decomposition. Both roles associate interfaces created by the fallback strategy which creates interfaces from public methods. Due to the mix of compression and hashing functionality in the primitive component, these interfaces are exposed by the surrounding component. Since composite components inherit the provided roles of inner components in the applied interface strategy, the provided role of the composite components also contain these two unwanted interfaces.

Another required interface of the storage component (a util interface), is present in the reverse engineered model but not in the reference decomposition. This is actually an error in the reference decomposition which misses the dependency to the util interface which is present in the implementation.

$$InterfacePrecision = \frac{6}{9}$$

$$InterfaceRecall = \frac{6}{6}$$

The reverse engineered system contained 15 provided roles in total, compared to 8 provided roles in the reference decomposition. Additional roles arise from the additional composite component (which provides 5 roles) and the additionally recognised component interfaces. When removing the additional composite component, the precision could have been increased to $\frac{8}{11}$.

$$ProvidedInterfacePortPrecision = \frac{8}{15}$$

$$ProvidedInterfacePortRecall = \frac{8}{8}$$

7.9.1.3. Connectors

As introduced earlier, two alternative implementations of the compression component exist. Yet, only one component is bound at a single point in time. The number of connectors in the reference decomposition is nine when using only a single compression implementation.

Since there were deviations in the component structure, interface recognition, and role assignment, comparing the connectors in the reference decomposition with the connectors in the reverse engineered models would be meaningless due to subsequent errors. Instead, the connectors in the reverse engineered model should be complete and ensure model integrity to allow for simulation of the reverse engineered model. All roles should be bound to the right interfaces. Precision and recall are hence derived taking subsequent errors into account.

The reverse engineered model contains a total of 26 connectors (22 delegation and 4 assembly connectors). Given the recognised interfaces and roles, each of the connectors is required in order to form a valid model instance. No connector is missing in the model.

$$Connector\,Precision = \frac{26}{26}$$

$$Connector\,Recall = \frac{26}{26}$$

7.9.2. Behaviour Analysis

The behaviour of components of the Palladio FileShare was analysed as blackboxes (see Section 5.17). All internals of the component behaviour were reverse engineered via genetic programming. The resource demands for Palladio FileShare have been estimated based on individual bytecode instructions (see [KKR10]). Thus, the resource demands are much more fine-grained, compared to resource demands based on a single CPU demand per internal action. Resource demands were reverse engineered from dynamic bytecode instruction counts provided by the ByCounter [KKR08b] tool. To allow for precise performance predictions, the resource demands were parameterised over the input parameters of services provided by the components of Palladio FileShare.

As described in Section 5.17, the control flow in black-box scenarios is simplified to a single action and to external calls which are executed in separate loops. Due to the strong abstraction of the component behaviour, its validity is judged with respect to the predicted performance in the next section.

The parametric dependencies were learned by Beagle after processing a set of test input data. The set of test data contained files of different sizes and types (i.e. Text, JPG, ZIP) to allow for learning parameterisations of the model.

For Palladio FileShare, also the applicability of the heuristics for identifying parameter characterisations, introduced in Section 5.10.4, was validated. The parameter characterisations identified by the proposed heuristics are identical to the ones which were manually identified to be performance-relevant. The monitoring was performed based on the automatically identified parameter characterisations.

7.9.3. Performance Prediction

The performance of Palladio FileShare was predicted (cf. [KKR10]) for multiple usage scenarios where the exchanged files varied with respect to file size and type.

The files for which the performance was predicted were not identical to the set of learning data to check for the prediction capabilities of the reverse engineered model. To further demonstrate the parameterisation of the reverse engineered models, the compression component was exchanged. Thus, two further scenarios needed to be predicted: One with a LZW compression and one with a SPEC compression component. Furthermore, the execution platform was varied for prediction (Intel Pentium M 1.5 GHz single core CPU vs. Intel T2400 1.8 GHz dual core CPU). The model was reverse engineered for the first platform and then predicted for the second platform without executing Palladio FileShare or portions of it on the second platform.

For all prediction scenarios, the average prediction deviation was less than 30%. For example, the total upload process was predicted with 115 ms while the measured value was 123 ms. Figure 7.5 illustrates some of the results.

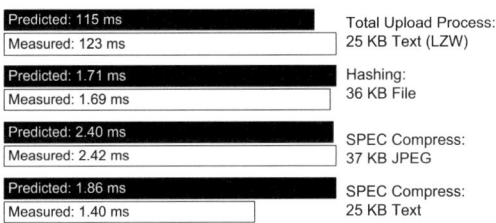

Figure 7.5.: Selected predictions and measurements for Palladio FileShare (taken from [KKR10])

The prediction for the second execution platform was off less than 10% except for one outlier where the prediction was off 30%. When using only the LZW compression, the prediction was off less than 15% even when exchanging the execution platform. For the SPEC compression component, the prediction error was less than 30% for all files and accross both platforms.

7.10. Effort Estimation

Previous work [KKKR08] showed that manual reverse engineering of parameterised performance models can consume a significant amount of time. Manually reverse engineering the CoCoME system took for example about 40 person-hours, while automated reverse engineering significantly reduces the overall time ($Effort(M)$, covering the tool execution time of SoMoX and Beagle and execution of the test cases) to about 4 hours (*LL-Effort reduction*). Externally conducted studies show that even the creation of small-sized parameterised performance models from given design documents comprising only three to five components can take about three hours of time [MBKR08b].

From the end-to-end case studies, models were reverse engineered manually and automated only for CoCoME. Hence, the comparison of manual and automated reverse engineering provides only little evidence that reverse engineering will generally save time for the creation of models. Still, the strong automation of the reverse engineering provides a base for significantly reducing the required amount of time. The tool execution duration allows the handling a large software systems (see scalability discussion in Section 7.12).

7.11. Other Case Studies

The following section briefly summarises the results of further case studies performed in the context of this thesis. These case studies have not been as extensive as the previously presented but help gaining insight whether SoMOX and Beagle are broadly applicable to different kinds of software systems.

Ohioedge CRM has a total of 78,516 lines of code and 249 classes. For the system, 13 components at the highest abstraction level could be identified in the 5th iteration (cf. [CKK08]). No reference architecture documentation was available for Ohioedge CRM. Due to the large size of the software system, the manual code analysis was based on the code artefact names and little insights into the intended architecture of the software system. The reverse engineered composite components could be evaluated as reasonable components in a manual analysis.

Rubis comprises 8,202 lines of code in total and 41 classes. Overall, 17 components in 2 iterations could be identified (cf. [CKK08]).

As for other systems, no reference architecture documentation was available for Rubis. This was compensated by a manual analysis of the code which revealed a repeated pattern which comprises a session bean that uses a home and a remote interface and which has a servlet associated with it. The presence of an intended pattern is supported by the naming of the classes and interfaces. Each instance of that pattern was identified as a single component. In total, 16 of those components could be found. Any other classes which are not included in those components are utility classes used from a larger number of components. Despite explicitly searching for higher-level components in the code, none could be found during manual reverse engineering of the system.

Of the 17 reverse engineered components, 16 were identical to the manually detected ones. A single component misses a class with a similar name as the included classes. Yet, that class is not referenced by any class of the identified component and itself only references one utility class and thus is likely to be a misplaced or outdated class. The reverse engineered software system has only little hierarchy which is also reflected in the reverse engineered model: The components are identified in the first iteration; except for a single system-level component which contains the remaining components.

openArchitectureWare was reverse engineered to check the assumption of So-MoX that the input software system must be component-based. As openArchitectureWare is actually not component-based (manual code analysis showed that), it is suitable to check the abilities of the reverse engineering approach to deal with non-component-based software systems.

openArchitectureWare yielded no component-based software architecture – neither during manual code analysis nor during the reverse engineering run. Some components were nevertheless detected, yet they do not help understanding the architecture of openArchitectureWare. Hence, SoMoX is not suitable for the reverse engineering of non-component-based software systems. Although the approach itself is able to reverse engineer components for all kinds of software systems, the results are not meaningful for systems for which the core assumptions do not hold (*LL-non-component-based systems*). The absence of a reasonable component-based architecture in the results model matches the expectations for such kinds of systems.

Behavioural Model *LZW Compression* and *SPECjvm2008 Compress* are standalone components which can be independently reused. The validation of their reverse engineered models is part of the presented case study on Palladio FileShare. For Palladio FileShare, these components serve as exchangeable compression components.

Still, the application of Beagle to parameterise the behaviour of these components provides further insights to the quality of results of Beagle (cf. [KKR10]). The main parametric dependencies for the compression components are the compression ratio and the resource demand in terms of bytecode instructions required to compress a certain file. For the compression ratio, Beagle discovered a linear dependency to the size of the input file in both cases. Such approximations are found by Beagle after about 30 seconds.

The parametric dependencies for the estimation of bytecode (cf. Section 5.16) were more complex for most bytecode instructions (some few bytecode instructions are executed with a constant number and can thus be captured by simple parametric dependencies realised by constants). The behaviour of most compression algorithms strongly depends on the inner characteristics of the data and the size of data to be compressed, but for example the type of files has less impact on the resource demand of the compression algorithm. As the inner characteristics of data are not captured in the developed approach (i.e. the values of single bytes in an array), the learned

271

parametric dependency cannot be expected to be optimal in all cases. Even if the full data to be compressed would be captured by the developed approach, it cannot be expected that parametric dependencies can be found for all bytecode instructions due to the complexity of compression algorithms.

Beagle created optimal parametric dependencies for only a few bytecode instructions. Still, the resource demand approximations are good estimators which in 98% of the cases outperform approximations by MARS [Fri91] (*LL-outperforms statistical analysis*). As mentioned in Section 7.9, the prediction error for response times based on the parametric dependencies had an error of less than 30%.

ABB Legacy Application OPC   In the context of the EU Q-ImPrESS project, a case study for the architectural reverse engineering approach was performed. The validation phase in the Q-ImPrESS project is not fully completed yet. The system is written in C and C++, having approximately 50,000 LOC and 127 files. The reverse engineering resulted in 30 primitive components and 13 composite components. Since no reference decomposition is available, the quality of the identified components cannot be judged. The processing time for SISSy were about 200 seconds and 14 seconds for SoMoX.

The OPC system is based on Microsoft COM. During the case study it was discovered that the COM interfaces were not completely present in the GAST created by SISSy. Thus, interfaces based on the recognition of COM interfaces were also incomplete when running SoMoX. When switching to public methods as a fall-back strategy, the recognised component interfaces were rather complete.

LL-C and COM support: SoMoX is applicable to reverse engineer software system written in C and C/C++ but due to the use of SISSy lacks direct support of COM interfaces.

ABB Demonstrator Subsystem   Another case study performed in the context of the EU Q-ImPrESS project is operating on an ABB application subsystem, written in C/C++, with a size of 250,000 LOC, comprising about 600 files. This case study is used to judge the scalability of the approach. The results of the scalability analysis are discussed in Section 7.12.

HSQLDB   could successfully show that SoMoX scales for real-world systems of considerable size. The following Section 7.12 discusses the scalability.

7.12. Scalability

HSQLDB   To investigate the practical scalability of SoMoX and Beagle, a large real-life software system was analysed. For the analysis, HSQLDB 2.0, a Java-based database system, was chosen. HSQLDB comprises a total of more than 158,000 lines of code, 39 Packages, 640 classes, 52 interface, and nearly 120,000 methods. Thus, it represents a typical software system of a considerable size. The scalability analysis was not used to judge the quality of the reverse engineering since no reference decomposition of HSQLDB was available and since it is not realistic to manually analyse a system of such a size to determine the quality of SoMoX and Beagle. Furthermore, only the transformation for the creation of control flow abstraction could be applied since no testbed setup was available.

The analysis on a Intel Core 2 Duo Processor, 4 GB of system memory and 768 MB heap space for a JVM 1.6 took less than 2 minutes for the SoMoX analysis and revealed 25 components (5 composite components and 20 primitive components). The precedent analysis using SISSy which creates the GAST model took 7 minutes for the system when using a DERBY database for the persistence of SISSy data. The creation of the control flow abstraction of the behaviour model took less than 10 seconds in total.

The calculation of metrics is fully multi-threaded. In a test, SoMoX was able to utilise all cores of a 24 core server machine.

The binary metric *Running* was evaluated to true since the reverse engineering could be successfully performed. The overall *ReverseEngineeringDuration* metric resulted in an overall effort of less than 2.5 minutes.

Learning a single parametric dependency in the implementation of the Beagle approach takes typically 10 seconds to 4 minutes for the selected default configuration. If optimal solutions are found, genetic programming terminates immediately; otherwise the maximum number of generation is being evolved which for the selected configuration takes about 4 minutes. When accepting a lower fitness in average, the time can also be reduced. The CoCoME model, for example, has a total of 11 parametric dependencies which could be learned in less than 10 minutes. Due to the size of HSQSLDB, the maximum number of generations needs to be reduced to limit the time per parametric dependency to a maximum of one minute. From the control flow abstraction transformation for HSQLDB, an estimation of the time demand for parametric dependencies can be derived, which, for 780 parametric dependencies results in a time demand between 2.1 (best case) and 13 (worst case) hours overall. It must be emphasised that learning parametric dependencies can run offline and does not require user interaction or multiple iterations.

A simulation of the performance of such a reverse engineered model (e.g. for the service `getSystemTable` of `DatabaseInformation` of HSQLDB) with the PCM takes less than 3 minutes (default setting of the simulation; default usage model with a single user; default allocation; default resource demand and parameterisation). Hence, even for large software systems, models are reverse reverse engineered which are suitable for performance simulations.

ABB Demonstrator Subsystem   Another scalability case study was performed for a 250,000 LOC subsystem of an ABB software subsystem. The subsystem could be analysed at ABB within about 3 hours processing time for SISSy and about 5 minutes for SoMoX. The most critical resource was the memory consumption of the SISSy step. Due to the internal usage of the Eclipse CDT parser (only for C/C++ systems), the created in-memory software model consumed about 8 GB of main memory.

LL-scalability: SoMoX and Beagle scale sufficiently well even for large-scale real world software systems. The scalability can be stated for Java and C/C++-based software systems. Software systems with more than 250,000 LOC can be successfully analysed. For the application and SoMoX, the reverse engineering is nearly interactive (the creation of the static architecture takes typically less than 5 minutes).

7.13.   Discussion and Findings

The validation of SoMoX and Beagle overall showed satisfactory reverse engineering results and high accuracy for performance predictions based on the reverse engineered models. The average precision for the static architecture across all model elements is 78%, the average recall 89% (*LL-precision recall*). Hence, nearly all model elements of the reference decompositions were also also in the reverse engineered models and little structures were identified which are not in the reference decomposition. The average precisions per architecture element were 84% for components, 73% for interfaces, 68% for provided roles, and 87% for connectors. The average recall was 76% for components, 91% for interface, 91% for provided roles, and 96% for connectors.

Overall, the recall for components themselves was slightly lower than for "surrounding" structures (interfaces, provided roles, and connectors). The reconstruction of components has to rely on more heuristics than the reconstruction for the "surrounding" structures which become visible from the results for recall. *LL-heuristic recall*: The component identified by the employed heuristics has a smaller recall than the reconstruction of the remainder of static architecture structures.

Compared to the findings of the related approach of Koschke [Kos00] (see discussion in the related work Section 8), precision and recall are comparably high. In his analysis of precision and recall for the detection of "atomic components", the recall was roughly between 75% and 34% depending on the elements which should be detected and the applied technique. About 40% of the detected atomic component candidates of Koschke were false positive and thus lowering the precision.

For SoMoX and Beagle, the performance predictions were off in average 12% and at most 30%. The accuary of the performance predictions was even high for scenarios where various elements of the reverse engineered architecture changed (e.g. in the

Palladio FileShare case study) and which by design are thus hard to predict (*LL-parameterisation*).

When viewing the reverse engineering results in detail, case study by case study, further strength and limitations of SoMoX and Beagle become visible.

CoCoME   For CoCoME, the reverse engineering revealed a mismatch between the design documentation and the implementation where the components actually communicate different than indicated by the documentation (*LL-mismatch detection*). Furthermore, CoCoME pointed to the expected shortcomings of the employed static analysis: Dependencies which were injected or introduced via service lookup cannot be handled since SISSy does not include this information in the GAST model (*LL-binding*). Dealing with dependency injection and service lookup requires an extended static analysis or dynamic analysis to find out which instances are bound at runtime (see Section 9.11). Still, for the reverse engineering results of CoCoME precision (0.74 in average) and recall (0.92 in average) remain high.

SPECjbb2005   The SPECjbb2005 reverse engineering and performance prediction results are notably good. Primarily this is due to the alignment of architecture and package structure in SPECjbb2005. Furthermore, SPECjbb2005 employs no late binding or dependency injection mechanisms and thus eases the static analysis using SISSy (*LL-binding*). The GAST model is complete and thus an optimal base for SoMoX. SPECjbb2005 makes it obvious that architecture information that is encoded into code artefacts advances the quality of reverse engineering results (*LL-architecture encoding*.

Palladio FileShare   In the Palladio FileShare case study, the strong parameterisation capabilities for models reverse engineered by SoMoX and Beagle are shown. All influence factors for component performance (cf. Section 2.6) where successfully varied in this case study. Notably, the behaviour of Palladio FileShare depends on component state which could nevertheless successfully be dealt with: Whether a file is copyrighted or not is not visible from the input data and thus disturbing the result precision (for the same input data, different results (copyrighted / non-copyrighted) could be monitored). Still, the performance prediction results in less than 30% deviation between the predicted and measured values even accross different usage profiles, assembly contexts, and allocation contexts.

Overall, typical deviations in the static architecture between the reference decomposition and the reverse engineered architecture were in the nesting of components. Instead of having a single composite component, two separate levels of components were created: The reference architecture had a composite component A holding the instances of Component B and C. The reverse engineered model had a composite component which held a sub-component B which in turn held the instance of component C (*LL-nesting*).

7.13.1. Component State

As Palladio FileShare shows, reverse engineering results and performance predictions based on them can be accurate even if component state is present. Yet, the state impact in Palladio FileShare was limited since only a small portion of files in the scenario was impacted by being copyrighted to model a realistic scenario. In other scenarios where component state has a strong impact on the behaviour (e.g. every execution is being affected), Beagle can only reverse the average or most likely behaviour induced by component state. *LL-component state*: Component state which has only small impact on the performance of components can be successfully dealt with.

Scenarios in which component state impacts component behaviour are comparable (from the perspective of Beagle) to scenarios where not all parameters are being monitored during execution: In both cases, possibly contradicting behaviour can be monitored for the same inputs. If the performance is impacted by such non-monitored parameters (state represented by internal variables or input parameters characterisation which are not identified as performance relevant and thus not monitored), Beagle creates approximations of the monitored behaviour.

7.13.2. Manual and Automated Reverse Engineering

Comparing manually reverse engineered models with automatically reverse engineered models provides useful insights. Models have been manually reverse engineered for previous publications like [KKKR08] which dealt with the CoCoME system. *LL-typical model errors automation*: Automatically reverse engineered models possess systematic errors like for example the wrong abstraction level of components, missing connectors due to the absence of information to derive them, interfaces which are considered to be component interfaces, or external calls which are present due to the wrongly identified component interfaces.

LL-typical model errors manual: Manually reverse engineered models, opposed to them, primarily suffer from inconsistent abstractions. For example small internal actions are often omitted and external actions which trigger for example logging facilities are usually neglected since they are crosscutting the architecture and increase manual modeling effort. At the same time, logging is considered to be a component service and thus explicit in the component interface. For large models, manual reverse engineering furthermore increases the risk of inconsistent abstraction levels in a single model. For example, some calls of a logging service are captured in the model but not all. The model inconsistencies imply risks for the prediction capabilities of reverse engineered models if the component context changes. If for example the connected logging component is exchanged, the performance impact of the exchanged components is only partially reflected in the reverse engineered component model.

LL-abstraction level: Getting the desired abstraction level is by definition easy for manually reverse engineered models. Human which reverse engineer a model manually, create only those components which are at the desired abstraction level. Since reference decompositions also have a fixed abstraction level, it is the challenge for automated reverse engineering to create that specific abstraction level. Nevertheless, the merge and compose thresholds are suitable to steer the abstraction levels for the automated reverse engineering (see Section 4.8.5). Since there is no direct correlation between the thresholds and the abstraction level (i.e. the resulting abstraction level of the thresholds depends on the system size and metrics; e.g. a loosely coupled system results in different abstraction levels for the same thresholds than a tightly coupled system), multiple reverse engineering iterations can be required to reach a certain desired abstraction level in automated reverse engineering. In the case studies, typically about 10 iterations where required to gain a desired abstraction level.

While automated reverse engineering is able to provide a consistent abstraction level, manually created models (which include the reference decomposition) can have inconsistent abstraction levels. In the reference decomposition of the CoCoME system, the business information system part had a much stronger abstraction than the embedded system's part where various components of the reference decomposition correspond to just a single class.

To sum up, the results of automated reverse engineering can be characterised as follows (*LL-automated characteristics*):

- The reverse engineered models posses a *consistent* abstraction level.

- The *adjustment* to the expected abstraction level requires effort.

- If model errors are present, the errors are *systematic*.

- SoMoX results in *partially incomplete* models if information is missing in the GAST.

- Beagle results in *complete* models due to strict derivation rules from given component boundaries.

Analogously, the central characteristics of manual reverse engineering can be summarised to (*LL-manual characteristics*):

- Reverse engineered models results in *intended* abstraction level.

- The reverse engineered models tend to have an *inconsistent* abstraction level.

- Models tend to be *incomplete* due to inconsistent abstractions and modeling errors (missing to model certain elements).

- If modeling errors are present, they are *sporadic* – opposed to systematic errors for automated reverse engineering.

7.13.3. Configuration

Overall, default values for the configuration of the component detection strategies of SoMoX (weights from Section 4.8.5) perform well for reverse engineering. The default values had been derived to be representative for all reverse engineered software systems in this thesis and enable all strategies. Adapting the weights per software systems is – as intended – able to prefer certain component implementation styles (e.g. ignoring the balance of abstract and concrete entities, "abstract concrete balance"). In a comparable way, for Beagle, the provided configuration defaults remained constant across the reverse engineered systems.

7.13.4. Suitable Software Architectures

LL-component based: Component-based software architectures can only be reverse engineered if a software system is created from components or at least with components in mind. The counterexample system "openArchitectureWare" (cf. Section 7.11)) showed that the base architecture of a software system must be component-based. Otherwise, no meaningful architecture which matches an expected architecture can be reconstructed. SoMoX can only identify component-based software architectures which are in some way encoded into source code artefacts. The component detection strategies fully rely on structures which are visible from the GAST model and thus must also be present in the source code of a software system.

LL-naming based strategies: The naming and hierarchy based software detection strategies performed best with respect to the component identification abilities. Although component naming can be misleading, the combination of coupling with naming proved successful for identifying components and did not lead to unexpected components, which could be the case for pure naming based component detection.

LL-SLAQ applicability: Of the remaining detection strategies, SLAQ rarely matched since it is specific to architectures which are organised in slices and layers. Due to the support of only a single architecture style which must be encoded in the implementation, SLAQ contributes only for a subset of architectures. Mostly, SLAQ matched only for some of the components of a software system (those which are organised in slices and layers). In the CoCoME example, which is partially organised in slices and layers, the strategy successfully matched.

7.13.5. Machine Learning

LL-test bed: Beagle requires a previous execution of a software system under study in a test bed to gather monitoring data. The case studies show that little variance in the input parameter space is sufficient to reconstruct models. Generally, condition coverage (C_3c, cf. [Bei90]), is sufficient to create a base for machine learning. Opposed to pure path coverage, boundaries (for branches) should be hit to improve the results. For example, a branch if(x < 1024).. depends on the value of the parameter x. If one value < 1023 and one value > 1024 are provided for x, parametric dependencies can be successfully learned. Yet, additional values do not disturb results.

LL-default heuristics: Monitoring the right parameter characterisations is supported by heuristics in the developed approach (cf. Section 5.10.4). The proposed heuristics allowed to monitor all required parameter characterisations such that the machine learning step could successfully operate on the data base. In none of the case studies, except for SPECjbb2005 (see discussion in Section 7.8), separate parameter characterisation needed to be selected. Additional studies [EKKB10, Klu10] which applied the same heuristics further show the applicability of the proposed heuristics.

7.13.6. Threats to Validity

There are two main areas for threats to validity of SoMoX and Beagle: Deviations in the reference decomposition and disturbances in the performance measurements.

If reverse engineered manually, the reference decomposition could be biased to meet the requirements on the reverse engineering approach. A biased reference decomposition has been faced by employing reference decompositions provided by third-parties which cannot be influenced. Errors in the reference decomposition where the architecture deviates from the implementation were observed for CoCoME as described above. Such errors in the reference decomposition can artificially reduce precision and recall. To at least identify deviations between the reference decomposition and the implementation, the de-facto architecture visible from the source code has been manually checked for violations. Those small deviations which were discovered are documented in beginning of Section 7.13.

To measure the performance (for the validation), the original source code has been instrumented and executed in the same test bed which was used to reconstruct the models. Still, monitoring causes runtime overhead which has to be taken into account when analysing the performance measurements. To avoid a large impact on the performance results, the developed monitoring is designed to have little overhead. For example, as much measuring data as possible is held in memory to circumvent that limited I/O performance for hard disks or networks results in wait times. Furthermore, it must be accounted for the execution environment which comprises the Windows operating system and a Java virtual machine, both of which are non real-time execution environments. For example, Windows has to handle interrupts or concurrently running processes. Therefore, the number of processes which were executed in parallel to the system under test were reduced to a minimum. The Java virtual machine employs a garbage collector which cleans up unused memory. If the garbage collector runs, outliers are being produced. All measurements were cleaned from outliers and the median instead of average values were used.

In addition to filtering the measurements, all software systems had a warm-up phase prior to starting the measurements and the software systems were executed in a Java virtual machine for which the server option was enabled. Both actions help reducing the impact of potential outliers and disturbances during measurements.

The impact of state dependencies, another factor which disturbs the monitored timing behaviour, has already been discussed above in Section 7.13.1.

7.13.7. Performance Impact Factors

A few characteristics of a software system which influence the reverse engineering performance can be derived from the case studies. The main impact factors on the performance of a reverse engineering run are (*LL-performance impact*):

- **C/C++ vs. Java** Due to the use of the Eclipse CDT for C/C++ and Recoder for Java, SISSy performs largely different for C/C++ and Java. Java systems can be analysed faster and the source code analysis consumes less memory.

- **Density of Accesses** For SoMoX, a main impact factor on performance are the number of accesses among classes. If many classes access many other classes and interfaces (a largely interconnected graph), more metrics must be calculated than for systems which are well-encapsulated on a class-level (i.e. access only a small number of classes and interfaces). Hence, the structure of a software systems impacts the overall performance of a reverse engineering run which can be expected for a software system.

- **Number of Parameter Characterisations** The key performance driver for Beagle is the number of parametric dependencies to be learned (see Section 5.18). The runtime of the Beagle approach linearly depends on the overall number. Furthermore, the larger the search space for Beagle is (number of parameter characterisations), the longer is takes to create parametric dependencies with a desired fitness. This is not an impact factor, if the number of generations to be evolved is fixed. Another performance driver for Beagle is the size of components: Large primitive components result in relatively less complex behaviour models (see discussion in Section 5.9) which in turn possess less parametric dependencies which must be calculated. Systems with only few identified primitive components typically have less parametric dependencies to be calculated. For a fixed number of generations, the calculation time for a parametric dependency is constant.

7.13.8. Further Discussion

Section 9 continues the discussion of the developed reverse engineering approach. While the discussion in this section was strongly related to the validation, Section 9 broadens the scope and discusses results and achievements of the overall context of reverse engineering.

8. Related Work

8.1. Overview

The SoMoX and Beagle approach tackle research fields for which a lot of related work exists: A vast amount of reverse engineering approaches for software is described in literature and various reconstruction approaches for performance specifications of software system exist. Machine learning is a broad research field which has been applied to numerous domains, including sub-disciplines of software engineering. Due to the broad research, many different kinds of machine learning have been developed, of which genetic algorithms and genetic programming are the most important to this thesis.

Although a lot of related research exists, no related work targets parameterised software performance models for component-based software systems, which are central in this thesis.

To structure the related work of this thesis, which is presented in the following, the related work is distinguished into four major research field. This thesis covers work from all of these research fields:

1. Reverse engineering

   - Static Architecture

   - Behaviour Models

2. Reconstruction of performance models

3. Machine learning, genetic algorithms, and statistical approximations

Of these research fields, techniques for static architecture and behaviour reverse engineering will be distinguished into static and dynamic analysis approaches, as both kinds of analysis are used in the approaches of this thesis.

The remainder of the related work section first provides an overview and summaries on related work. In the overview sections, the SoMoX and Beagle approach are classified according to standard taxonomies. Then, the related work is structured according to the above schema.

8.1.1. Summary on Related Work

The following two tables summarise the core properties of the most related reverse engineering approaches. Table 8.1 introduces reverse engineering approaches for static architectures. Table 8.2 sums up reverse engineering approaches for behaviour models. In the tables, closely related approaches are captured in a single line. The following sections detail on these and further related approaches.

Approaches	Comp.[1]	Mod.[2]	Man.[3]	Und.[4]	Sem.[5]	Comments
Koschke [Kos02, Kos00]	⊘	✓		✓	⊘	Component = Module
Keller/Sartipi [KSRP99, Sar03]	⊘	(✓)		✓	⊘	"design components": patterns, idioms, packages of structural model
Mitchell [MM06]	⊘	(✓)		✓	⊘	hill climbing and simulated annealing to modularize; cohesion and coupling
Favre [Fav04, FDE$^+$01]	⊘	(✓)		✓	⊘	do not allow composition of components
Praditwong [PHY10]	⊘	✓		✓	⊘	modules; genetic algorithm clustering
Schmerl/Yan [SAG$^+$06, YGS$^+$04]	⊘	⊘	✓	✓	⊘	deviation of intended and de-facto architecture
Anquetil [AL99a]	⊘	⊘		✓	⊘	Naming-based, SLAQ
Lundberg [LL03]	⊘	✓	✓	✓	⊘	Graph dominance analysis
Ivkovic [IG02]	⊘	✓	✓	✓	⊘	Interactive
Tools [bau, helc, helb, hela, lat]	⊘	✓	(✓)	✓	⊘	Architecture conformance, Metrics
Roeller [RLvV06]	⊘	⊘	✓	(✓)	⊘	Design decisions
						Continued on next page

Approaches	Comp.[1]	Mod.[2]	Man.[3]	Und.[4]	Sem.[5]	Comments
Müller [MOTU93]	⊘	(✓)		✓	⊘	High-level abstractions
Strein [SLLL07]	⊘	⊘		✓	✓	Source code abstractions

Table 8.1.: Related Work for Reverse Engineering of Static Architectures

Legend for Table 8.1 headings:

1. Components according to Szyperski (cf. Section 2.9)

2. Low-level component, module, class: ✓; pure clusters which are for example sets of operations without further structural details: (✓)

3. Reverse engineering is mostly a manual task

4. Main aim: Programme understanding

5. Target model possesses execution semantics

Approach	Dyn.[1]	Sta.[2]	Comp.[3]	Regr.[4]	Par.[5]	Perf.[6]	Comments
Corbett [CDH⁺00]	⊘	✓	⊘	⊘	⊘	⊘	Finite State Machines
Hrischuk [HMWR99]	(✓)	⊘	⊘	⊘	⊘	✓	Load estimations
Brand [BLL06]	✓	⊘	⊘	⊘	⊘	⊘	UML sequence diagrams
Israr [IWF07]	✓	⊘	(✓)	⊘	⊘	✓	"effective" architectures
Zheng [ZWL08]	✓	⊘	⊘	(✓)	⊘	✓	Kalman filter
Parsons [PMT⁺08, PM08]	✓	⊘	(✓)	⊘	⊘	✓	Antipatterns
Ross [Ros06, Ros90]	(✓)	(✓)	⊘	✓	(✓)	✓	Partial parameterisation
							Continued on next page

Approach	Dyn.[1]	Sta.[2]	Comp.[3]	Regr.[4]	Par.[5]	Perf.[6]	Comments
Ernst [EPG+07, ECGN01]	✓	⊘	⊘	(✓)	⊘	⊘	Invariant detection, Daikon
Nimmer [NE02]	✓	⊘	⊘	(✓)	⊘	⊘	Test cases evaluation
Woodside [WHSB01, WVCB01]	✓	⊘	✓	✓	(✓)	✓	Resource functions
Courtois [CW00]	✓	⊘	⊘	✓	⊘	✓	Regression splines
Dufour [DDHV03]	✓	(✓)	⊘	⊘	⊘	✓	Compiler optimisation
Canfora [CDPEV05]	⊘	(✓)	⊘	⊘	⊘	✓	Web service composition
Winkler [WAW04a, WAW04b]	⊘	⊘	⊘	✓	✓	⊘	Multi-dimensional dependencies, genetic programming
Support Vector Machines [CST00]	⊘	⊘	⊘	✓	✓	⊘	Polynomials
Statistical analysis [WF05]	⊘	⊘	⊘	✓	✓	⊘	domain-independent

Table 8.2.: Related Work for Reverse Engineering of Behaviour Models

Legend for Table 8.2 headings:

1. Dynamic analysis; full analysis: ✓; simplified dynamic analysis: (✓)

2. Static analysis; full analysis: ✓; simplified static analysis: (✓)

3. Any component support: ✓; architecture support: (✓)

4. Regression capabilities

5. Parameterisation; if fully parameterised over all contexts: ✓; if partially parameterised: (✓)

6. Performance properties addressed

8.1.2. Classification of this Thesis

This thesis is classified according to the work of Pollet et al. [PDP+07, DP09] and Tonella et al. [TTBS07] to ease the identification of research fields, this thesis contributes to. Furthermore, this classification shall help to understand how this thesis relates to related work, how much approaches exist in the research field, and what typical research topics are.

Pollet et al. [PDP+07, DP09] survey reconstruction approaches for software architectures and organise them in a taxonomy. Criteria of their classification include the degree of automation, input data of the analyses (e.g. source code, dynamic analysis, or human feedback), output data (i.e. visualisation support, architecture model, analysis capabilties, and architecture conformance), and the reconstruction process (e.g. top-down or bottom-up). In their survey, Pollet et al. criticise the misuse of the component term (often set equal to a paket or file) and the small number of approaches for high-level architecture abstractions.

In the taxonomy of Pollet et al., SoMox would be classified as a "bottom-up" approach while Beagle is a "hybrid" approach which employs the input of SoMoX to top-down identify relevant control flow statements at the component-level, create the instrumentation and then refined the model bottom-up. Concerning the inputs, SoMoX uses (according to the classification) "source code" and "physical organisation" input. Beagle processes "source code" and "dynamic information". Both, SoMoX and Beagle are part of the category "quasi-automatic" which subsumes quasi and fully automatic approaches. The output of SoMoX and Beagle would be classified as "architecture visualization", "architecture description", and "analysis" due to the built-in model visualisation, the architecture model (PCM), and the analyses (performance prediction) which can be executed on the result model.

Tonella et al. [TTBS07] surveys existing reverse engineering approaches from the perspective of empirical studies on them. The criteria in the survey include the type of study performed (e.g. experience reports, case studies, or experiments) and the objects of study (e.g. architecture recovery, behaviour recovery, design recovery, clone detection). The survey includes paper of four selected leading conferences from the field of reverse engineering and four selected journals. Of the 260 papers, only 26.5% have case studies (as this thesis has). A total of 31,2% of the papers tackled at least one of the research fields from this thesis.

In Table 8.1, all columns except the one for manual effort would need to be ticked for SoMoX. Beagle would receive ticks in all columns of Table 8.2. None of the presented related approaches can be classified in the same way like SoMoX and Beagle.

8.2. Related Work for Static Architecture Reverse Engineering

The overview paper by O'Brien et al. [OSV02] surveys a large number of software reconstruction approaches and evaluates them with respect to a number of criteria which are aligned with views and practice need scenarios. The survey presents selected tools from different reconstruction disciplines (e.g. manual reconstruction, query-based approaches, and data mining). O'Brien et al. extend the definition of views by Clements et al. [CBB+03] which helps in applying the definition in practical scenarios.

Canfora and Di Penta [CHDP07] provide another survey on reverse engineering approaches and identify open research directions. In their survey, they emphasize the need for combining static and dynamic analysis approaches – a research field which is addressed by this thesis.

Cornelissen et al. [CZvD+09] provide a recent overview on research in the field of program understanding by means of dynamic analysis. Besides a review on existing research fields for program understanding, the authors performed a representative literature study on 176 selected research papers presented in the top journals and conferences for software engineering and reverse engineering. The findings from the literature study identify only 13 articles which deal with design and architecture through dynamic analysis – which gives hints on the portion of approaches which address design and architecture. In should be mentioned that the survey does not explicitly list approaches for component-based software architectures.

Kosche [Kos05] (publication in German) contributes an excessive and excellent literature overview on research approaches for the reconstruction of software architectures.

8.2.1. Static Analysis

Component recovery with the aim of identifying components for programme understanding and evolution is introduced by Koschke [Kos02, Kos00]. In his approach, he distinguishes logical (expressed in explicit artefacts like files and packages) and physical components (related elements with a common purpose), and proposes means for automatically and semi-automatically recovering them. The definition of these components implies less semantics than the one used in this thesis. Futhermore, no other architecture elements like interfaces and connectors are being reverse engineering. The iterative reverse engineering approach is metric-based, uses, among others, resemblances to identify components, and integrates third-party approaches. Of the presented techniques for combining various reverse engineering inputs, the "voting approach" is most comparable to the one presented in this thesis. It also employs multiple indicators for the presence of components. The evaluation was comparable to the evaluation of the static architecture in this thesis. In both approaches, the quality of the reverse engineered components is judged by precision and recall when comparing with a reference decomposition. The approach could reach a recall for the reconstruction of about 40%. In controlled experiment, the quality of semi-automatic and manual reverse engineering approaches were compared and the approach implements an automatic metric calibration which are not present in this thesis.

Anquetil and Lethbridge [AL99a] aim at recovering software architectures from the names of source files. Based on the word analyses on common substrings in file names, deriving words from method names, and the generation of abbreviations from candidate words, a cluster analysis recovers groups of similarly named files. The approach purely relies on file names without respecting any further structure and is not capable of identifying hierarchical structures. The file name analysis of the approach is partially reflected in name resemblance, package and directory mapping of the SoMoX approach. For example, the method name identification is not part of SoMoX. Instead, SoMoX is able to respect the hierarchies expressed in names. The substring identification is partially present in the SLAQ metric.

A semi-automated iterative and interactive architecture reconstruction approach is contributed by Lundberg and Löwe [LL03]. The approach performs a dominance analysis on the base of class reachability graphs. The graph itself is created from statically analysed "create" and "uses" relations among classes. Components posses no interfaces in the approach but can be hierarchical components. The approach does not claim to exactly identify components, but help identifying "architectural entities". The authors propose the combination with further component identification methods since the dominance analysis requires "create"/"uses" relations to result in classes which dominate each other in the graph structure. SoMoX creates a richer architecture model comprising more architecture elements. Architectures which are created by SoMoX do not only rely on create and uses relation among classes but incorporates much more information sources.

Ivkovic and Godfrey [IG02] investigate the reverse engineering of software architectures from dynamically linked CORBA software. They propose a hybrid recovery approach to cope with a stated lack of support of static analysis tools to deal with dynamically linked software. The approach re-uses interactive code navigation and static analysis approaches. Ultimately, the user is guided in a proposed process to reverse engineer software architectures. SoMoX, opposed to this approach, can run fully automated but also lacks implemented support for dynamic linking.

Various industrial software (Bauhaus, Sotograph, SotoArc, SonarJ, Lattix, [bau, helc, helb, hela, lat]) is available which proposes the reverse engineering of software architectures. This software focusses on the calculation of software metric, architecture conformance checks, interactive exploration of software systems and queries on the software architecture. Furthermore, these approaches support reverse engineering capabilities for various views, the class-level, and modules. Although these approaches partially claim to reverse engineer also components and software architecture, the components are not identical with the components identified in Section 2.9. Specifically, these components do not possess all architecture elements which are required for the reverse engineering approach presented in this thesis, i.e. explicit interfaces and explicit context dependencies. The software architecture of these approaches is not component-based and does not featuring connectors and composite structures which allow for execution semantics of embedded components.

Stormer [Sto07] addresses the support of general quality attributes at the architecture level. In the approach, stakeholders identify what-if scenarios for possible architecture changes. A general software model for software quality (which can be reconstructed from existing software system) is then proposed to take over the analysis of quality attributes. The approach is not automated or tool supported. The reconstruction of architecture is only briefly addressed.

Anquetil et al. [ARA+09] reverse engineer architectural elements from Java source code. In their work, the authors concentrate on the recovery of components, the communication structure among components, and provided and required services. A compact set of five rules recovers architecture elements. They distinguish Java classes and interfaces into components and data types. All types which are not used in interfaces or inherit from types used in Java interfaces are considered as components. Composite components accumulate all classes defined in fields of the initial components. The communication structure among classes is derived from method calls among the components. Architecture elements which are identified by the approach are comparable to those of the SoMoX approach. The developed approaches targets programme understanding opposed to SoMoX which also includes performance predictions.

Roeller et al. [RLvV06] propose the recovery of architectural assumptions and design decisions from existing software systems. The approach is a manual approach which relies for example on various interviews, source code analysis, analysis of version control systems, and documentation. The approach then roughly guides the recovery of architectural assumptions. SoMoX does not deal with architectural assumptions and could be complemented by such an approach.

8.2.2. Pattern-based Architecture Recognition

Keller et al. [KSRP99] and Sartipi [Sar03] aim at identifying architecture structures using match patterns. While Keller et al. aim at "Design Components", Sartipi identifies graph patterns. Neither Keller et al. nor Sartipi identify components in the sense of Szyperski. "Design Components" are the application of, for example, a design pattern, while Sartipi supports multiple views where a query on a graph structure (which represents an attributed software model) leads to entities of a view on the software architecture. The detection strategies for components, interfaces etc. of SoMoX can also be considered as patterns. In the case of SoMoX, the patterns are fuzzy patterns which, opposed to [KSRP99, Sar03], do not immediately result in the creation of architecture elements.

8.2.3. Code analysis

Favre [Fav04] proposes an architecture reconstruction approach for software architectures described in meta-models. The paper focusses on a broad discussion of the term "software architecture" and its representation as a meta-model. In this context, foundations of model driven techniques and multiple views of a single software architecture are discussed. In earlier work, Favre et al. [FDE+01] presented an own meta-model (realised in UML and OCL) to formalise their notion of a component. This notion is influenced by the ideas of COM, Corba, and Java but does, for example, not support composite structures. Their architecture model provides constraint checking of the validity of a software architecture. Overall, the reverse engineering aspects remain vague.

Müller et al. [MOTU93] present a reverse engineering approach for the identification of subsystem structures – thus emphasizing high-level abstractions. The approach supports composite structures but no components in the sense of those utilised and required for this thesis. For Müller et al., components are aggregations of variables, procedures, modules, and subsystem. The so-called Rigi tool supports the reverse engineering process. Among others, also name-based component-identification techniques of components which well-encapsulation data and which are utilised by common clients are used.

Strein et al. [SLLL07] propose an own meta-model to language independently represent and analyse software system source code. The meta-model is comparable to the GAST model, and, in the case of Java, is based on Recoder [Rec] which is also used by SISSy [SSM06]. Due to a formalisation of their meta-model, they propose it as an exchange format and describe mappings to and from their meta-model. Finally, the paper discusses the suitability of their meta-model for program analysis. In their work, they address the handling of large meta-models – a topic which implicitly had also to be tackled for SoMoX and Beagle in order to support large-scale software systems (nevertheless the optimisations of SoMoX and Beagle have not been discussed in detail in this thesis). The approach by Strein et al. does not address the software architecture level but remains on the level of object-oriented analysis.

8.2.4. Dynamic Analysis

Schmerl et al [SAG+06, YGS+04] focus on the reconstruction of architectures from running system. They propose a process that requires a lot of manual specification to reconstruct architectures. One of their primary aims is to find deviations between reconstructed and specified / documented architectures of software systems. They do not focus on the reconstruction of components. A formal definition of their analysis model, created by defining a mapping to Petri Nets, allows exact semantics of their model.

Huang et al. [HMY06] recover low-level architectures from running software systems. Their abstraction level are EJBs. The approach is able to reverse engineer software systems at runtime to reflect forward engineering changes to the design model. The output of the approach are instances of an own architecture description language (ADL).

Systä [Sys99] reverse engineers state diagramms for Java systems based on runtime trace information. The paper contributes a case study which analyses the Fujaba [Pad, NNZ00] software system. The architecture-level is not tackled in the paper.

Aishold et al. [ABF04] discuss dynamic coupling measures for object-oriented software systems and raise awareness for the increasing popularity of dynamic binding. They validated their formally proposed metrics in an empirical case study and by showing statistical significance and contribute a meta-model for measurement data. Their results show that coupling based on dynamic analysis can significantly improve the prediction of change proneness. SoMoX uses static coupling measures to limit for example the impact of name resemblance of classes. Extending SoMoX by dynamic coupling measures could further improve the reverse engineering quality.

8.2.5. Static and Dynamic Analysis

Ernst [Ern03] discusses the advantages and disadvantages of combining static and dynamic analysis. The cited synergies which arise from combining static and dynamic analysis lay the foundation for keeping SoMoX open for static and dynamic metrics and for introducing Beagle as an approach which combines static, dynamic, and statistical analysis.

Riva and Rodriguez [RR02] combine static and dynamic analysis for the purpose of architecture reconstruction. They propose a top-down iterative approach which reverse engineers architectures described as directed graphs and message sequence charts. Dynamic and static analysis limit views in the approach. Architecture components can possess explicit interfaces and support asynchronous communication. Opposed to SoMoX and Beagle, the approach is only partially automated and integrated. Data from static and dynamic analysis has to be (manually) translated into

Prolog. The architecture reconstruction is only partially automated and requires user interaction with Prolog. The communication is limited to asynchronous communication.

Vasconcelos and Werner [AC04] combine static analysis for UML class diagrams with dynamic analysis on a per-use-case base to recognise interaction patterns from execution traces. To recover architectural elements, they are associated to the interaction patterns. Source code entities are in the approach clustered according to their use on the per-use-case base. If a single elements is predominantly used in a certain use case, a corresponding architecture elements is associated with it. The approach requires use cases to be available for the reverse engineered software. Compared to SoMoX, components in the recovered architecture are "common entities of use cases", opposed to "structurally indicated components" of SoMoX.

8.2.6. Code analysis

Plskalns et al. [PWA05] investigate the relation between code quality and cohesion and coupling and in this context critically reflect the use of pure static analysis for modern object-oriented code. They state lack of relations between cohesion, coupling and code quality and derive dynamic code metrics from that. Overall, they focus on maintainability.

8.2.7. Clustering

Anquetil and Lethbridge [AL99b] discuss the applicability of clustering as a software remodularisation approach. They present a comparative study on different clustering approaches (e.g. hill climbing and hierarchical clustering) and discuss similarity measures for software clusters. Among others, they argue for a differentiation of input data and support of informal inputs like source code comments to increase the remodularisation precision. Koschke [KE00] proposes a whole "framework" for conducting experiments on clustering and discusses a number of evaluation techniques for software clusters. Mitchell and Macoridis [MM01b] discuss the evaluation of software clustering results if reference decompositions are not available.

Maqbool and Babri [MB07] compare a total of six hierarchical software clustering approaches for the recovery of software architectures. No approach is covered which uses a precise component term. Instead, the approaches concentrate on the module viewtype [CBB+03].

Mitchell and Mancoridis [MM06] present another approach for automated iterative software modularisation via clustering. The base for modularisation is a directed graph which carries information on inheritance among classes, and the number of calls between. The kind of calls are not distinguished. Clustering is mapped to a graph partitioning problem. Detection heuristics improve the modularisation results. Components are not supported. The so-called "Bunch" tool implements the approach. A hill climbing and a genetic algorithm implementation of the clustering algorithm are implemented in it.

Another software module clustering approach related to SoMoX is presented by Praditwong et al. [PHY10]. In it, potential modules are suggested based on cohesion and coupling. The clustering appraoch is able to optimise for multiple objectives (e.g. maximise intra and inter cluster edges or additionally aiming at a certain number of clusters). The approach was validated for 17 software systems.

All of the above approaches do not deal with component-based software architectures.

The component creation of SoMoX uses component merge and composition based on the graph structure introduced in Section 4.5. It is partially comparable to a hierarchical agglomerative graph-based clustering approach (cf. [WF05, JD88, Har75]). The weights associated with every vertex here serve as distance measure.

8.2.8. Programme Comprehension

Andrews et al. [AGC02] discuss the comprehension of software systems from a cognition point of view and highlight the order in which software systems can be understood. Among others, Andrews et al. illustrate those things which need to be understood in order to re-use existing software components. According to them, component re-use starts bottom-up and relies on specifications of what a component does. Starting from that component, the impact of reusing a component to the overall system can be analysed – for performance, the impact prediction can be automated when using reverse engineered models from SoMoX and Beagle. Furthermore, according to Andrews et al., programmers start building an abstract model of a component's control flow. SoMoX and Beagle thus potentially help in understanding a component via the RDSEFF which represents a control flow abstraction.

8.3. Related Work for Reverse Engineering Behavioural Models

8.3.1. Static Analysis

Corbett et al. [CDH$^+$00] extract finite state machines from Java source code using static analysis techniques like slicing, data flow, control flow, and dependency analysis in a multi-step transformation approach. Their approach named Bandera focuses on language verification and model checking and not on component behaviour models. Nevertheless, research questions addressed in the approach are relevant for this thesis. For example, Corbett et al. automatically extract the models from source code and are able to re-translate analysis results into the original source code – the same requirements are fulfiled by Beagle in combination with the trace models. The authors emphasize the relevance of abstraction for the creation of models. Abstraction has also extensively been addressed in this thesis.

Poch and Plasil [PP09] aim at formal verification of behavioural specifications ("behaviour protocols"). These behaviour protocols are reverse engineered in the approach from object-oriented code. Comparable to Beagle, the approach requires component boundaries as input. Opposed to Beagle, the approach targets the reverse engineering of component protocols which state the functional behaviour of components. Behaviour protocols are at the level of component interfaces. Beagle targets performance models which capture the internals of single component services.

8.3.2. Dynamic Analysis

In the often-cited paper of Briand et al. [BLL06], UML sequence diagrams are reverse engineered for Java software systems. The approach traces the execution of a software system with a self-developed instrumentation and logging infrastructure based on aspect orientation. The resulting meta-modelled trace-model is specific to the approach and the base for the creation of the sequence diagrams. Comparable to Beagle, the method-call logging level provided by pure aspect orientation (AspectJ) is not sufficient for the approach. The approach does not aim at model parameterisation but also provides support for distributed software systems.

Reverse engineering of performance models using traces is performed by Hrischuk et al. [HMWR99] in the scope of "Trace-Based Load Characterisation (TLC)". TLC extracts load estimations from trace information gained by executing a prototype implementation or executable design models and it supports distributed systems with synchronous and asynchronous interaction. The approach requires to add trace IDs for tracking calls through an architecture, but Israr states [IWF07, p. 475] that "[these] traces are difficult to obtain in practice". Traces also require costly graph transformation before use, but allow TLC to deal with multi-threading and multiple instances of an object. However, the target model of TLC is not component-based, and this restriction prevents TLC from supporting changing *assembly* or *deployment* contexts or changing execution platforms and they target Layered Queuing Network (LQN) models for performance analysis, where each usage scenarios (previously identified by a performance expert) leads to a LQN submodel. TLC has a logging mechanism comparable to the one of Beagle.

Israr et al. [IWF07] use general trace data as input to determine "effective" architectures (which might also constitute of components) of a software system. No component-internal parallelism is supported by their tracing data evaluation. Supported interaction "types" include asynchronous, blocking synchronous, forwarding communication which is identified via pattern matching. In their paper, they discuss the recognition of correct traces for events/communication from logging stamps in general. Finally, they target LQNs as performance model. Intermediate models (build up by an algorithm presented in the paper) are interaction trees. Here, nodes are labeled by "component-name.ExecutionOccurrence-numer", arcs by time and message that was received. The approach supports no data flow and has no explicit notion for control flow (it assumes a 1:1 code relation), but relates calls through time stamps. The model can be build on-the-fly from an input stream of traces.

Zheng [ZWL08] focusses on runtime monitoring and online prediction of performance. The reverse engineered models are estimations produced by a Kalman filter. Thereby, they are not required to directly monitor performance values of interest but can estimate them based on known (and easily available) metrics such as response time and resource utilisation.

The models which Beagle reverse engineers also influence the component interaction. Dynamic component interaction approaches have before been surveyed by Parsons et al. [PMT$^+$08, PM08] for Java-based systems. Parsons et al. yet focus on a component-external view of interactions and do not investigate the impact on component-internal behaviour. In [PM08], they identify performance antipatterns for Java EE software systems based on "user request paths" through the architecture. These paths are not necessarily related to control flow structures in the code. These antipatterns can include multi user interaction patterns. Neither SoMoX, Beagle nor the PCM are capable of identifying such antipatterns; performance predictions based on reverse engineered models can only help software architects to manually identify antipatterns.

8.3.3. Instrumentation and Dynamic Analysis Foundations

Mueller and Whalley [MW94] discuss the minimisation of instrumentation points for dynamic analysis. The minimised set of instrumentation points in their approach is optimised to still ensure unique traces. In their approach, they use traces to perform static cache predictions at design time. The Beagle approach also minimises the number of instrumentation points in such a way that component behaviour can still be uniquely captured. According to the component boundaries, a minimal set of instrumentation points is derived for the component behaviour.

Reiss and Renieris [RR00] and De Pauw et al. [DPJM$^+$02] discuss the generation of Java trace data with a focus on programme visualisation and programme understanding. Reiss and Renieris combine static analysis with trace analysis and offline processing of data like Beagle. De Pauw et al. analyse thread interactions, deadlocks, garbage collection, and memory leaks – properties which affect the performance of software systems but which are too fine-grained to be dealt with by Beagle. The approaches emphasise the class-level and do not relate to the architecture-level.

Denker et al. [DGL06] contribute to dynamic analysis itself and address the common re-implementation of dynamic measurements frameworks with only slight variations. They introduce an intermediate level framework which allows for capturing measurement data at runtime to push the abstraction level of dynamic analysis approaches to a machine-independent level to overcome fine-grained technical details of instrumentation and data recording. The framework can be configured and adapted to a selection of measurements point and measurement criteria at runtime. Among others, the paper discusses method for dynamic instrumentation. The Beagle approach could profit from a machine-independent data gathering approach to easily support other programming languages during dynamic analysis. The instrumentation approach of Beagle does not use the proposes framework as the framework is not validated and had not been extendable at the time of development of Beagle.

Schmid et al. [STTK07] present "ARM", a standard instrumentation API for the instrumentation of application servers. Their logging approach is coarse-grained at the level of "application server to component" and "component to component" communication and aiming at capturing time stamps. Schmid et al. wrap application server calls to intercept them. Opposed to this approach, the instrumentation and monitoring of Beagle is much more fine grained at an intra component level and not specific to application servers.

8.3.4. Automated Complexity Analysis

A large number of approaches from the field of (semi-) automatic complexity analysis exists (e.g. [Weg75, HC88, NNS02, Ros90, SF96, Ros06]). Early approaches (e.g. Wegbreit [Weg75]) go back to the 1970th. Since that time, complexity analyses has been refined over and over again. While first starting with estimations in the O-notations and for example of minimal, maximal, and average execution times, later approaches (e.g. Ross [Ros06]) include control flow structures and parameters to increase the precision. Additionally, the analysis scope was broadened from single algorithms to generic programs.

Nevertheless, the focus of these approaches is different and thus the ways the complexity analysis is tackled. The approaches mostly focus on average, minimal or maximum execution times (e.g. [Weg75, HC88, NNS02] to support for example the selection of appropriate algorithms. They have no architecture relation, are not component-based approaches, and have no parameterisation over all influence factors (cf. Section 2.6).

Ross [Ros06] and Rosendahl [Ros90], for example, introduce parameterisations. In the case of Rosendahl, the parameterisation is limited to a single input dimension. Ross [Ros06] can deal with multiple dimensions but focuses on worst-case execution time. Its control flow structure is partially comparable to the RDSEFF, but has a limited data flow parameterisation and no parameterisation over the assembly and allocation context. Loop iterations need to be specified manually.

8.3.5. Invariant detection

Daikon by Ernst et al. [EPG+07, ECGN01] focusses on detection of invariants from running programs, while our approach aims at detecting parameter propagation and parametric dependencies of runtime behaviour. Analysis is in both approaches supported by machine learning. The machine learning in Daikon is an simple exhaustive random generation of all possible invariants, no combination of simple invariants to form complex ones is supported. Invariants must therefore follow a set of 75 predefined templates. Daikon can only instrument at method start and end. No automation or heuristics for identifying data properties are provided. Instead, a grammar for specifying instrumentation and monitoring exists. In Daikon load-time instrumentation is favored, but also compile-time instrumentation is featured. Invariants across multiple method executions (e.g. state effects or multi threading behaviour) are not supported.

Another approach (Nimmer and Ernst [NE02]), Ernst is involved in, discusses the suitability of available test cases to perform dynamic analyses for the identification of invariants. The author state a well applicability of test cases. Overall, Beagle, compared to Daikon, creates much more fine-grained models which are parameterised and capable of predicting performance properties. To extend Beagle, invariants could still serve as input to genetic programming to increase the convergence speed.

8.3.6. Differentiation from Static Analysis

Static source code analysis approaches are a well-researched area [Bin07], featuring sophisticated techniques. The purposes of static code analysis are varying widely and range from control flow to data flow analysis covering security aspects analysis, execution optimisations, dead code detection, problem pattern detections, etc. Still, for the field of data flow analysis, which is required in the context of this work, some limitations are preserved [Ern03]. As static code analysis approaches are used among others, the limitations must be known to explicitly deal with them: Data flow analysis through static code analysis approaches work predominantly well, if data flow is at a intra-procedural level and little knowledge about the heap is required for code understanding.

8.3.7. Static Analysis Approaches

Symbolic execution / abstract interpretation (e.g. [Kin76, CC77, Cow88]) is a static analysis technique which is perfectly applicable to reverse engineer parametric dependencies (cf. Section 5.12). It is generally capable of precisely reverse engineering parametric dependencies from code. Yet, it suffers from general limitations of static analysis such that is cannot handle arbitrarily complex code. Later symbolic execution approaches (e.g. [DLR06, Lee06]) try to push the boundaries of static analysis and overcome for example problems with the analysis of loops. Symbolic execution approaches often focus on programme verification and are thus sound – which is not the case for Beagle. Instead, Beagle is able to reverse engineer parametric dependencies for arbitrary source code.

WALA [IBM] is a generic framework for static bytecode analysis featuring for example a basic slicer. It has been used to implement symbolic execution for Beagle.

Lundqvist and Stenström [LS99] present a timing analysis method based on symbolic execution. The approach aims at real-time system and worst-case execution time, while Beagle aims at parameterised models of business information systems.

Complementary static analysis approaches like points-to-analysis (e.g. [SH97, LH99]) could help to partially overcome the limitations of symbolic executions and increase the precision loss implied by dynamic bindings. Sound approaches which account for control flow can usually handle only up to less than 100.000 LOC within acceptable time (a few minutes). Thus, relaxed approaches which accept imprecisions would be more suitable to complement Beagle which itself also is not sound.

8.4. Reconstruction of performance models

Woodside et al. [WHSB01, WVCB01] use so-called "resource functions" to characterise components for their performance. Repositories for this reason hold descriptions of components and their resource demands together with test cases. To describe resource demands, function fitting for parametric dependencies is applied. The approach is supported by tools for performing performance analysis. Bayarov [Bay99] also contributes in the context of resource functions. CPU and harddisk are considered as resources. The result of the approach is a mathematical model / equation system which is capable to predict intermediate values which have not been measured. The quality of the results is manually evaluated. Overall, resource functions primarily parameterise over the allocation context but do not create component behaviour models which allow for fully exchanging the usage and assembly context – opposed to the models created by SoMox and Beagle.

Courtois et al. [CW00] use regression splines to recognize functional dependencies. Their iterative and fully automated approach is able to refine measurements (repeat measurements) to gain certain confidence levels. The approach requires no source code analysis and can handle multiple dimensions. The output are polynomial functions which approximate the behaviour of code. In the approach, it is hard to find jump points in functions. Components are not supported and a fixed hardware is assumed (execution time is given in ms). The monolithic approach does not parameterise over external dependencies.

Dufour et al. [DDHV03] propose using a set of metrics to characterise the runtime behaviour of Java programmes. In their work, they focus on applications for compilier optimisation which could be optimised based on detailed performance characterisations or analysed for concurrency locks. Since they propose a dynamic analysis of Java programmes, they discuss representativity requirements for input data and abstract requirements to utilise metrics. Their approach operates on Java Bytecode and uses the Java Virtual Machine Profiler Interface (JVMPI) to monitor applications. Opposed to Beagle, typical performance characterisations are comparably rough, e.g. "array-intensive programme". Performance charactersisations are not parameterised as the ones of Beagle are. The PCM models created by Beagle are not suitable for detecting concurrency locks.

8.5. Machine Learning

Machine learning covers a broad field of research directions (cf. [WF05]) like support vector machines, genetic algorithms, artificial neural networks, Bayesion networks and many more. The following section present a narrow selection of approaches which are related to the domains touched by this thesis. Other approaches are cover in an overview.

Support Vector Machines (SVM) (cf. [CST00]) are typical representatives of machine learning. They are for example able to extrapolate the performance impact of a certain parameter beyond the already measured range. Typically, SVMs result in polynomial expressions. Those are hardly readable for humans. Furthermore, polynomial expressions cannot directly express non-continuous behaviour. Parametric dependencies can be polynomial but in general are not. Thus, SVMs (due to the result representation) are not optimal for the approximation of parametric dependencies.

8.5.1. Genetic Algorithms and Genetic Programming

Harman contributes a number of extensive surveys and introductions [Har07, HMZ09b, HMZ09a] for search-based software engineering – a software engineering discipline which employs meta-heuristic techniques. These surveys also address fields which are relevant for this thesis: reverse engineering, approximation, test data generation, and optimisation of software designs. The articles of Harman [Har07] and Whitley [Whi04] provide a good introduction to the field of genetic algorithms and search-based software engineering. Langley and Simon [LS95] and Goldberg [GH88] classify genetic algorithms in the field of machine learning.

Winkler et al. [WAW04a, WAW04b] propose an approach which learns non-linear and multi-dimensional dependencies from measurement data. The approach is capable to identify subsets of meaningful input variables from a number input variables. The result expressions of the genetic programming approach are mathematic expressions. The authors support the findings from this thesis: "any prior knowledge of the physical system should be included in an initial model and the function library [selection of genes]". The approach is closely related to Beagle. Opposed to Beagle, the initial generation is fully randomly generated and no capabilities to create abstractions are implemented for mutation, crossover, or fitness function. The approach of Winkler et al. is domain agnostic, aims at identifying general model structures from databases, and is thus not designed for performance properties.

Canfora et al. [CDPEV05] treat the composition of web services with attached QoS properties as an optimisation problem which is addressed with genetic algorithms. The approach solves the optimisation of the NP hard problem at runtime to be able to react to changed QoS properties and the availability of new web services. In the paper, the authors point out the applicability of genetic algorithms to non-linear optimisation problems. The approach could complement SoMoX and Beagle by optimising an architecture once it is reverse engineered.

Garousi [Gar06] addresses stress testing of distributed real-time systems. The approach relates to Beagle with respect to addressing performance attributes and adapting genetic algorithms (in this case to match the needs of optimised stress tests for a distributed system). Dolado et al. [Dol01] applied standard regression and genetic programming to predict the costs of software projects. They could not find satisfactory results, from the predictive point of view. They found no significant deviations between genetic programming and the linear model in the software cost functions.

Wegener and Grochtmann [WG98] aim at verifying timing constraints of embedded real-time systems. For the creation of tests, they use genetic algorithms which, in a comparison in multiple case studies, always performed better than random testing. As the authors point out, the inclusion of expert knowledge in the initial generation improves the genetic algorithm results. This again supports the insights gained for Beagle, which show that domain knowledge can largely improve meta-heuristic search approaches.

Section 8.2.7 discusses the application of genetic algorithms for software clustering.

8.5.2. Statistical Approaches

Large amounts of statistical approaches and theory of statistical analysis exist (e.g. [WF05, Cra07, Lin93, LC98, BL97]). Regression approaches are generally comparable to the genetic programming part of Beagle: They derive and retrieve functions on data from databases. Nevertheless, they have fully different aims compared to

Beagle. They are intended to be domain-independent. Thus they are not intended to create performance abstractions and are not supporting the inclusion and combination of static, dynamic, and statistical knowledge of other approaches.

8.6. Performance Predictions

The prediction of performance properties of software system is not a contribution of this thesis. Thus, the following paragraph just very briefly summarises the most important performance prediction approaches which relate to the Palladio Component Model [BKR09]. Woodside et at. [WFP07a] and Koziolek [Koz10] provide a recent and more detailed survey on related work from this research field.

Bondarev et al. [BCdK07] and Fredriksson et al. [FNNS06] present a performance model for component-based embedded systems, SOFA and FRACTAL [BHP06, Obj06d] are software component models with a focus on component interaction verification, Menasce et al. and Kounev [MG00, Kou06] are representatives for approaches with a strong formal foundation, Wu et al. and Eskenazi [WMW03, EFH04] emphasise component composition in the context of performance prediction, and Cortellessa et al. [CF07] highlight the feedback of performance prediction results to the software architecture.

The advantages of the selected Palladio Component Model (PCM) [BKR09] are its parameterisation capabilities, the use of general distribution function, the provision for detailed component properties, and context independent component definitions. Stable tool support, editors, and performance prediction methods make the PCM first choice for this thesis.

8.7. Conclusion

A large number of reverse engineering approaches has been proposed in literature which address static architectures as well as behaviour models. Common for all reverse engineering approaches is the use of a weak component model with a loose component definition and no execution semantics of the targeted result model. Typically, the reverse engineered components are not suitable for recomposition, possess no explicit required interfaces and often do no support composite structures.

No reverse engineering approach for components according to the definition of Szyperski (see Section 2.9) exists. No approach reverse engineers fully parameterised component models (cf. Section 2.6). Furthermore, no approach for parameterised performance models of components exists. SoMoX and Beagle represent the first approach which is fully parameterised over all influence factor at all and represents the first integrated reverse engineering approach for static architectures and behaviour.

9. Conclusion

This section briefly summarises the results and insights gained in this thesis. Lessons learned (*LL-*) are highlighted throughout this section. The discussion and lessons learned gained in the context of the validation in Section 7.13 complement this section. Section 9.12 presents a final short summary of this thesis.

9.1. Requirements Fulfilment

In the Sections 4.4 and 5.4 requirements for the reverse engineering of static software architectures and behaviour models have been stated which should be fulfiled by the developed reverse engineering approach.

- *R-Detection Mechanisms* "Detection mechanisms for components, composite components, provided and required interfaces, and connectors must be provided."

  Result: All elements of a static component-based architecture can be identified by the SoMoX approach.

  LL-Detection: Suitable heuristics and mechanisms for the detection of component-based architectures have been identified. The lessons learned include knowledge on the selection of metrics and their systematic aggregation in strategies, insights for alternative detection strategies, and means for ensuring integrity of result models. Using only metrics and a weighted sum neglects structural properties of component-based software systems. Using detection strategies which respect structural properties can significantly improve the quality of detected archtitectures.

- *R-Component Abstractions* "Component abstractions higher than classes must be reverse engineered. Besides, multiple levels of composite component structures must be supported."

  Result: The reverse engineered components comprise at least one class. The validation shows that multiple abstraction levels of components realised by multiple classes are reverse engineered.

  LL-Component Abstraction: An iterative reverse engineering approach identifies multiple abstraction levels of components. The lessons learned include knowledge on how to construct an iterative and interactive reverse engineering approach which is suitable for a fully automated execution and the systematic creation of composition and merge operators, which create composite and basic components from classes. The developed approach uses adaptive thresholds to steer the reverse engineering abstraction which showed to be well-suited to a) gain higher abstraction levels than with a single threshold, and b) guide the abstraction steepness. These means allow the creation of abstractions which match the expectations induced by a reference decomposition.

- *R-Completeness* "The completeness requirements subsume i) model integrity to have a base for model analyses, ii) the requirement of a complete static architecture which does not miss elements like connectors etc., and iii) the requirements to reverse engineer components which state explicit context dependencies through required interfaces."

  Result: The reverse engineered models are complete with respect to execution semantics. The models can be simulated using the Palladio SimuCom simulation without adaptations. Thus, they possess full model integrity (no model constraints are harmed), no calls of a required service end in undefined places (i.e. no connector for required services is missing), and all context dependencies are explicit (external calls delegate to required roles, resource demands utilise abstract resources defined in the resource environment, and the usage profile is an explicit parameter covered by the parametric dependencies).

  LL-Completeness: The lessons learned comprise means for reverse engineering *all* elements of a component-based software architecture. One important aspect is to provide fallback mechanisms (e.g. interface recognition, connector creation) which ensure the creation of all architecture elements even if information sources are incomplete (i.e. due to limitations of static analysis). Separate processing steps must ensure the creation of all architecture elements to ensure execution semantics. Genetic programming is able to identify valid parametric dependencies for few observed parameters and even if no parameters are monitored, by construction, ensures the creation of parametric dependencies. Suitable mechanisms (e.g. genetic programming adaptation, control flow construction, explicit assembly, and resource demands) are identified for every context the models are parameterised over.

- *R-Extensibility* "The developed approach must not be limited to a single object-oriented language or an implementation technology (e.g.   EJB, Spring)."

  Result: Due to the use of the language independent GAST source code presentation, the approach is generally applicable to arbitrary object-oriented languages. The approach is held extensible as discussed in Section 4.10 and 9.5.

LL-Extensibility: The application of SoMoX for Java and C/C++ software systems shows the extension capabilities. The lessons learned include that having a language-independent software source code representation (GAST) and a technology-independent core model (SAMM) largely increases the flexibility of a reverse engineering approach.

- *R-Scalability* "The approach must be scalable for up to 250,000 lines of code."

Result: The scalability analysis in Section 7.12 showed the applicability of the approach to large-scale software systems within reasonable time (overall including SISSy < 4.5 hours). No critical bottlenecks for systems of the mentioned size became visible. For smaller systems (50,000 lines of code), the reverse engineering can even be nearly interactive. For example, the software architecture (e.g. CoCoME) is typically reverse engineered within a few seconds (< 3 seconds).

LL-Scalability: The lessons learned show that designing a reverse engineering approach with scalability and performance in mind from the very beginning is crucial. While the first reverse engineering approach "ArchiRec" relied on large amounts of database requests, its successor implementation of SoMoX is running on in-memory data structures only, which is suitable to dramatically increase the performance. Parallelisation, few synchronisation points, and distinct units of processing are important to ensure a scalable reverse engineering approach. Using state-of-the-art model-driven frameworks (e.g. Eclipse EMF) nevertheless requires thoughtful performance optimisation and additional overhead to figure out how to deal with large-scale models and performance.

- *R-Automation* "The approach should be largely automated to make large system analyseable with little effort. Manual interaction should not be needed during a reverse engineering run."

Result: The reverse engineering approach is able to fully automatically reverse engineer the static software architecture and the behaviour of individual software services without user interaction, when assuming to have a test bed available and if heuristics for the identification of parameter characterisations are sufficient. The user has to provide a configuration for the SoMoX weights and strategies (or rely on defaults) and needs to manually initiate the source code instrumentation facilities and start the execution of the system under test in the test bed. The remainder is fully automatable. In the current implementation, the results of the Beagle approach (parametric dependencies) need to be manually annotated to the reverse engineered RDSEFF control flow structure. This is not a conceptual limitation but only limited in the current implementation.

Nevertheless, if needed, the user can interact in the reverse engineering approach and change settings or models. Each processing step results in valid models, which can be edited on demand.

LL-Automation: The presence of defaults and default detection heuristics for all architecture elements of a component-based software architecture proved to be beneficial for the automation. New users of the approach have little effort for creating reverse engineering results, can fully rely on the automation, and then, if needed, partially change for example the identified parameter characterisations of component interfaces to enable Beagle to capture special data properties which cannot be foreseen by the heuristics.

The presence of a valid reverse engineered model after each iteration granted the option to include fine-grained interactive feedback for the reverse engineering process. Thus, the approach by design is able to smoothly shift between full automation and interactive reverse engineering, which makes the approach flexible with respect to the desired degree of automation.

- *R-Integration* The approach should be able to combine the specific advantages of static, dynamic and statistical analysis and hence overcome the limitations of each single approach.

  Result: As presented in Section 9.5, Beagle successfully integrates static, dynamic, and statistical analysis. Beagle is able to outperform the results of each single approach. SoMoX, in the current implementation, supports only static analysis but is conceptually prepared for dynamic analysis (see Section 4.10).

  LL-Integration: Improving the quality of the initial generation and including as much domain knowledge as possible into the reverse engineering approach proved to be beneficial. The developed Beagle approach allows a seamless integration of multiple inputs which each capture domain knowledge in their results. The developed overall reverse engineering approach can then use the specific advantage of multiple approaches. The convergence speed and reachable quality of the reverse engineering results are positively impacted by the integration.

- *R-Context* The output model must be parameterised over all three contexts introduced in Section 2.8.

  Result: The reverse engineered instance of the PCM is successfully parameterised over all three contexts.

  LL-Context: Designing the reverse engineering approach to support *all* context parameterisations gave large flexibility to the reverse engineering approach since limiting the parameterisation (i.e. using constants) is no problem for the approach while the opposite would have been a lasting limitation for the reverse engineering approach.

- *R-Resource Demands* The approach must be able to integrate platform-independent resource demands.

  Result: Bytecode-based resource demands and resource demands based on abstract resource types like "CPU" and "HDD" are supported as Section 5.16 illustrates.

  LL-Resource Demands: Keeping the Beagle approach applicable to all kinds of parametric dependencies turned out to be beneficial for the reverse engineering. Having an unique representation of all parametric dependencies including those for resource demands enabled the application of the same solution to multiple search problems.

- *R-Abstraction* The reverse engineering approach must work on a component abstraction level.

  Result: The developed approach successfully reverse engineers component abstractions. Both, the static architecture and the behaviour in terms of control and data flow are – by design of the developed reverse engineering approach – abstractions, when compared to the original source code. Various means contribute in the abstraction: Merge and composition for components, the control flow abstraction which matches to the component boundaries, and all parametric dependencies which are abstractions due to the adapted genetic programming (fitness function, mutation, and crossover).

  LL-Abstraction: Reverse engineering a consistent abstraction level for the static architecture and the behaviour was crucial for the desired execution semantics of the reverse engineered models. Having an integrated reverse engineering approach for abstraction of the static architecture and behavioural models is a "must-have" requirement for all reverse engineering approaches targeting the analysis of quality of service properties of component-based software systems.

  Furthermore, the presence of strong abstractions is an important mean to make large software systems manageable. Overly detailed models are neither beneficial for understanding nor analysing real-life software systems. Due to the reverse engineering of multiple abstraction levels and the adjustability of the abstraction level (e.g. thresholds and weights), a reverse engineering approach can be much more flexibly adjusted to project needs.

9.2. Benefits of integrated Architecture and Behaviour Reverse Engineering

The developed reverse engineering approach comprising the SoMoX and Beagle approach is tightly integrated. Due to the integrated reverse engineering for static component architecture and behaviour, the abstraction level of the static architecture and the behaviour fit exactly. The component boundaries identified in the static architecture step steer the abstraction of the behaviour control flow.

The resulting parameterised models combine the power of component-based software engineering: The reconstructed component models can be re-composed like components, deployed to different execution environments, and be utilised by arbitrary other components which communicate via the same component interface. Thus, the reverse engineered models can provide answers to sizing, design optimisation, extension of legacy software systems, and reuse scenarios (cf. Section 1.2).

9.3. Reverse Engineering of Component-Based Architectures

SoMoX can only detect components which are identifyable by at least one strategy (see Section 4.8). Generally, even systems which mainly follow other architecture paradigms (e.g. service-based architectures or bus-driven architectures) could be detected by SoMoX. The openArchitectureWare example shows that ultimately, if the assumption of having a component-based architecture does not hold, no meaningful architecture can be identified any more. The quality of reverse engineering results gradually drops if less architecture assumptions hold.

The architecture reconstruction mechanism of SoMoX is intentionally designed as a kind of "fuzzy pattern detection": The input side of strategies represents detection patterns which are then translated into confidence values which indicates whether to create a component, interface, etc. from the detected structure. Due to the fuzzy translation logic and combination of various detection strategies, SoMoX becomes robust against violations of detection patterns. Typical violations, which can also contradict a component-based architecture, are architecture breakthroughs like interface bypassing.

Factors which negatively impact the reverse engineering quality of SoMoX are (*LL-negative impact*):

- inconsistent implementation style in the system (e.g. each subsystem is organised differently in packages; GUI and data persistence are partially distinct packages and partially mixed in the same package),

- inconsistent naming (i.e. no or per-subsystem naming schema which contradict each other are present), and

- the absence of interface communication.

The characteristics which negatively impact the reverse engineering results are the opposite of the expected architecture and component properties of the ones described in Section 4.8.8. Analogously, software systems which follow the assumed implementation style can be expected to lead to better results.

9.4. Reverse Engineering of Behavioural Models

The following bullet list briefly summarises aspects which positively impact the reverse engineering results of Beagle. The impact factors have already been discussed in more detail in the validation and limitations and assumptions sections (see Sections 5.20 and 7.13). *LL-positive impact*:

- Performance-relevant parameters characterisations should be identified in component interfaces.

- The algorithms of components should be oblivious. State-dependencies or dependencies to non-monitored parameter characterisations can negatively impact the fitness of reverse engineered parametric dependencies.

- The test cases which provide the base for machine learning data should cover the input parameter space. Behaviour which is not triggered during monitoring, cannot be covered in parametric dependencies.

9.5. Integration through Genetic Programming

Genetic programming, which was introduced in Sections 5.11-5.11.10 as a mean for reverse engineering parametric dependencies, will now be discussed as a more general integration approach of static, dynamic, and statistical analysis. It will be investigated, to which extend it can serve for integration of static, dynamic, and statistical analysis in the context of reverse engineering.

Results of any analysis (static, dynamic, and statistical) are mapped to valid genes. A result is not represented by a single gene (except constants) to enable optimisation not only through mutation but using crossover. Any result which is mapped to genes can then be further optimised and combined with results from other analysis approaches. The unified problem representation as measurement results from dynamic analysis and solution representation as tree structure genes enables the seamless integration of multiple reverse engineering approaches.

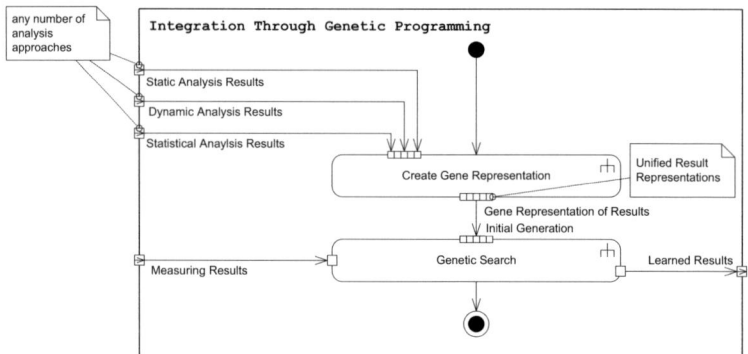

Figure 9.1.: Integration through genetic programming

Figure 9.1 provides an overview on the integration. First, results of the individual analysis approaches (dynamic, static, and statistical) must be converted to a gene representation. Then this unified representation is fed into genetic search. Genetic search interprets this input as initial generation as described in Section 5.11.10. The presented approach has neither a limitation on the upper bound of concurrently used analysis approaches nor requires complementing analysis approaches since genetic programming can always start from random initial generation and then optimise the random generation.

It could be shown for the statistical approach MARS and the application of genetic programming itself (based on dynamic analysis) that the results are better than results of a single approach. Results are by construction never worse than the results of the best input reverse engineering approach and in most cases can be improved by 5% to 25% (according to the fitness function). The improvements depend on the number of evolved generations of genetic programming and on the complexity of expression. Since other reverse engineering approaches are not designed to fulfil the requiremetns of the fitness function (for example specific abstraction needs are not supported by them) the fitness function results in worse values for their results.

LL-mars: The MARS statistical approach is well-suited to complement the search of parametric dependencies.

LL-integration improvement: The combination of multiple analysis techniques is beneficial for the reverse engineering of parametric dependencies.

9.5.1. Improving Initial Generation and Inclusion of Domain Knowledge

Improving the quality of the initial generation (derived from static and stochastic analysis instead of being randomly generated) lead to individuals with higher fitness in earlier generations. Overall, including domain knowledge on abstraction requirements, the selection of genes according to the needs of the programme code structure, the selected chromosome structure, the adapted fitness function, and the improved initial generation helped improving genetic programming when compared to unmodified genetic programming (*LL-integration*). The speed of machine learning and typical fitness values could be increased: The same fitness, when using MARS for the initial generation, could be reached after less than 1 minute compared to about 4 minutes without an optimised initial generation (*LL-convergence speed*).

Due to the random nature of evolution, the improvement can only be stated for the average case. Even "plain" genetic programming is theoretically able to result in optimal results in very few generations. It is just less likely to reach high fitness values in early generations.

9.5.2. Application to other reverse engineering problems

The presented integration method for multiple reverse engineering approaches is applicable to all reverse engineering problems which result in structured data. This data must be suitable for being split up into multiple genes forming a tree structure. The results of all reverse engineering approaches which are to be merged using genetic programming must provide results which can be transformed into genes. Furthermore, there must be an analysis method (fitness function) for the resulting genes which calculates a continuous numeric fitness value. Only continuous fitness values ensure a guided search – otherwise individuals become indistinguishable for genetic search.

To further improve genetic search, additional domain knowledge should be encoded into mutation operators, crossover operations, and fitness function. The experiences gained in this thesis show that adding domain knowledge (e.g. heuristics for more optimal solutions), increase the convergence speed of genetic search and thus result in improved results within less time *LL-domain knowledge*.

Examples for other reverse engineering domains which seem to be promising for the presented integration through genetic programming are test data generation and the creation of reliability models. Test data generation has successfully been performed using genetic search techniques (survey in [McM04]) and could profit from combining static and dynamic analysis. Reliability models are already supported by Palladio and share the same basic formalisms for control and data flow description

(RDSEFF) like the presented approach which makes them promising candidates to transfer knowledge from the performance domain to.

9.6. Genetic Programming as Approximation Approach

The Beagle approach is optimised for the reverse engineering of behaviour models with parametric dependencies. Its integrated genetic programming is nevertheless imaginable as a general multi-dimensional approximation and regression approach for the recovery of parametric dependencies in data rows. It is able to determine parametric dependencies in data while at the same time abstracting the dependencies. Characteristic curves (cf. Section 5.17) are only one application area.

The Beagle approach can handle arbitrary numbers of dimensions. It limits dimensionality by selecting the most impacting ones. Thus, it complements existing regression and approximation approaches by *abstraction* capabilities and with special support for the field of parametric dependencies in *source code* (i.e. loops and branches impacting the parametric dependencies). Hence, it covers additional kinds of dependencies which are different from, for example, citizen statistics.

9.7. Reliability and Maintainability Analysis

The target model of SoMoX and Beagle is the Palladio Component Model. Originally, the PCM has been designed to predict and analyse the performance of component-based software systems. Yet, the PCM is also the base for reliability predictions [BGKK10, BKBR10, KB09] and maintainability analyses (KAMP, [SR09]). The model instances which SoMoX and Beagle create, are complete static architectures and behaviour models with respect to performance properties. Still, the reverse engineered models are a good base for reliability and maintainability analyses as they share common model elements which are suitable for analysis of reliability and maintainability. A single PCM model instance can contain information for performance, reliability, and maintainability analysis at the same time. In order to perform reliability and performance analyses, only further model information must be added to the models reverse engineered by SoMoX and Beagle (*LL-QoS analysis base*).

Reliability   Reliability and performance prediction models share largely identical base model elements. The static architecture is the same for both, the control flow structure of the behaviour model is identical. Furthermore, the parameterisation of the behaviour model is the same (i.e. control and data flow parameterisation). The estimation of resource demands which is being reverse engineered by Beagle, is not required for reliability prediction. Instead, the model requires reliability estimations for example for internal actions. For typical scenarios, the models are identical to more than 90%.

Thus, using the models created by SoMoX and Beagle results in very little overhead (mainly reliability annotations per internal action) in order to use them for reliability predictions.

Maintainability For the maintainability analysis, the static architecture provided by SoMoX can be fully re-employed. The maintainability analysis needs a link to the original source code in order to estimate the impact of architectural changes on the source code. That link is available from the trace link model. Thus, from the perspective of the input architecture model, SoMoX provides complete results for maintainability analysis. The KAMP approach for maintainability analysis still requires further input from the user (e.g. change scenarios and effort estimations) which cannot be provided by SoMoX.

9.8. Roundtrip Engineering

Support for roundtrip engineering – the integrated cycle of forward and reverse engineering – would be desirable for the developed reverse engineering approach as a future subject. For roundtrip engineering, the stability of reverse engineering results is crucial. If the same software system is reverse engineered multiple times, the reverse engineering process should result in the same model. Without changing the software system itself, this is ensured for the static software architecture and the control flow structure by the deterministic nature of the developed reverse engineering approaches. Parametric dependencies are reverse engineered using genetic programming which by construction does not produce deterministic results. Still, if genetic programming results in the same fitness values, the parametric dependencies do not behave worse.

More challenging are scenarios where the implementation of the software system changes over time. If, for example, the reverse engineered model is used to detect architecture violations, reverse engineering results must be stable and reliable each time the software system is being reverse engineered. Desirably, small changes should not impact the reverse engineering results. Especially, the architecture should not change for small code changes (e.g. one more access to an already required component interface).

The architecture is the most-critical for stability as the lower level model elements for control and data flow should immediately reflect changes to the source code to ensure up-to-date models. For the stability of the reverse engineered software architectures, the design of SoMoX helps creating stable models. SoMoX creates components in discrete steps, according to the thresholds (for the merge and compose operation) which are set for an iteration. The thresholds are adapted according to the selected threshold stepwidth. As long as components are created within the frame between two threshold values of merge and compose, a component is stable. If the component is a "borderline" candidate, a component creation can potentially flip.

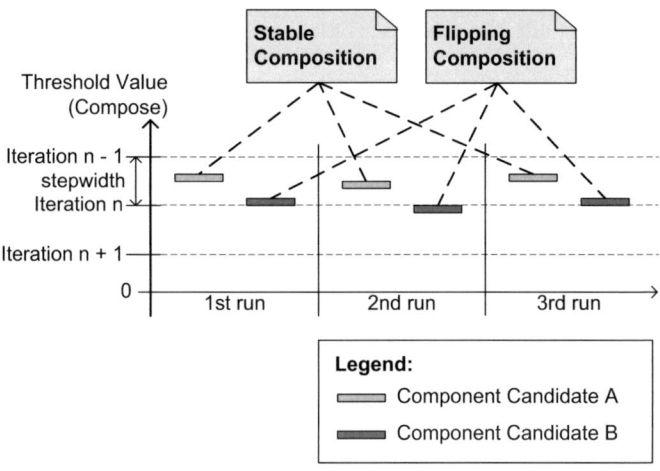

Figure 9.2.: Stability of component creation (composition case)

Figure 9.2 illustrates the composition stability of two component candidates A and B. Component candidate A has a composition value in the middle of the frame between iteration n-1 and n and thus is created in every run (x-axis). The frame is defined by the stepwidth value for composition. Component candidate B is a borderline candidate. Its composition value in the first run is sufficient to become a component in iteration n, while in the second run, the threshold is too high for component candidate B. In the third run, B again becomes a component.

The behaviour for the creation of B can depend on small changes in the source code (e.g. coupling changes). Thus, small changes in the source code can impact the creation of a component from a component candidate if the component candidate is a borderline candidate. Larger stepwidths (see y-axis) decrease the chance of borderline component candidates and hence result in more stable architecture models. In a scenario were the static component architecture result should be stable, one should chose larger values for the stepwidth.

Larger components are more stable to changes than smaller ones. If for example one class is removed from a small component, the impact to its metric is relatively larger than for small components.

If there are multiple borderline component candidates, small changes of one component can lead to "ripple effects" for other components. The missing creation of B in the example could change the metrics of another borderline component candidate which is then created or not created. Still, these "ripple effects" are rather seldom as they can only impact other borderline component candidates. Furthermore, most source metrics are calculated locally (except for package, naming metrics and the SLAQ metric) such that source code changes affect only components which immediately depend on this source code.

Generally, the stepwidth is suitable for steering the stability of a component model. Even typical values of 10 to 15 for the stepwidth provide stable architecture results. In real software systems, removing or adding an entire class of a component which comprises 20 classes for typical weights has no impact on the architecture except for candidates within a frame of 3 around the threshold borderline.

The effects of choosing the merge threshold are analog to the effects for composition. For merge, only the threshold values become larger from iteration to iteration.

One potential solution to overcome flips in the composition is to have an additional metric which indicates that a certain sets of classes of a component candidate did belong to the same component in a previous reverse engineering run. Hence, if a component candidate which existed in a previous reverse engineering run is evaluated again, the metrics can be used as an indicator to re-compose or re-merge the corresponding classes. If the architecture actually changes, the metric would be overruled by other strategies, otherwise, the old architecture can be preferred. In combination with large components which are less impacted by metric changes, such an extension could be promising for roundtrip engineering.

9.9. Extending Object-Oriented Programming Languages

The following section argues for potential extensions of object-oriented programming languages and proposes possible ways of realisation. Extending object-oriented programming languages for explicit architecture encoding would be reasonable for two reasons: i) an explicit architecture could be reverse engineered without requiring heuristics and ii) roundtrip engineering scenarios, as described in the previous section, could rely on a stable architecture definition. If an explicit architecture is changed, this could be immediately reflected in the roundtrip cycle. The core problem is the absence of full architecture information in typical object-oriented languages. When introducing explicit architecture information to object-oriented languages, additional architecture information like design decisions, intended architecture styles, and architecture constraints could also become available. Such information cannot be reverse engineered from object-oriented source code.

Explicit *components* including *composite components* would introduce high-level architecture elements that seamlessly integrate with a component's implementation. Explicit composite components are for example not present in typical component technologies like EJB [EJB07] or COM [Cor] until today. It would be desirable to have an explicit notion for *component interfaces* to distinguish them from class interfaces. Furthermore, distinguishing technical interfaces (e.g. Java API calls, JPA persistence interfaces) from business interfaces (e.g. customer management or accounting) could ease focusing on, for example, the business part of an architecture. The *provided* and *required role*, if made explicit, would support the principle of information hiding and explicit component interfaces also for composite components. In object-oriented code, the information which interfaces are being exposed, is not present. OSGi bundles [OSG09], for example, possess explicit provided and required interfaces and the package export allows further refinement of code visibility at the package level which gets into the direction of component requirements. Approaches like ArchJava [Ald03] aim at encoding the software architecture into programming languages.

From a reverse engineering perspective, these explicit elements of a programming language could be easily and uniquely identified. The ability to map architecture elements uniquely (i.e. ID-based) arises from chances of name clashes in large software architectures. Independent developers could by chance name their components identically. The proposed IDs could be for example hierarchical and comparable to package names.

Newer developments in the Java programming language picked up the need for more high-level architecture constructs like superpackages and modules [Buca, Bucb] and were in discussion for being included in the Java JDK 7. Nevertheless, these efforts focus on very lightweight programming concepts which miss for example explicit required interfaces and do not care about a high-level view on a software system.

Annotations could help distinguishing class interfaces from component interfaces and further distinguish business from technical interfaces. Components could be represented by new constructs which *obligatory* need to specify provided and required interfaces as well as its containment of other components. Having obligatory information on interfaces would for example overcome the tendency to omit optional information, which is common for Eclipse plugins (cf. studies in [DMTS10, DS10]). Eclipse plugins rarely specify extensions and extension points (their interface notion) since they are optional. Most plugins rely only on access restrictions on a package base which is inherited from the underlying OSGi bundles.

A full explicit specification of architectures would imply overhead but have advantages, for example, in reverse engineering, automated component interoperability checks, and automatic architecture conformance checking.

9.10. Limitations and Assumptions

The following section discusses limitations and assumptions which are predominantly impacting the overall reverse engineering approach. It complements the Sections 4.13 and 5.20 which presented the specific core assumptions and limitations of SoMoX and Beagle.

Component Instances The developed reverse engineering approach is not able to deal with distinct instances of the same component type. Every component type has – by assumption – exactly one assembly context. Since the reverse engineered components possess no persistent component state, the limitation does not impact the performance prediction capabilities. The component assembly can become more complex than desired since the single component instances cumulate the connectors of all component instances from the implementation of the software system. The restriction to only a single instance per component type implies that PCM component parameters (which are defined on a per assembly context; i.e. the component instance) cannot be set per instance. Instead, if there are multiple instances of the same component type which are actually configured differently, the impact is included as an average in the reverse engineered component model.

Power of the Result Model The target model of reverse engineering PCM currently has no support for event-based communication. This limitation is inherited by SoMoX and Beagle, since, even if event-based communication would be recognised, it could hardly be expressed in the PCM. Asynchronous event-based communication is currently mapped to synchronous calls.

If a framework for event-based communication is used (i.e. asynchronous calls are sent to a proxy of the communication framework), no call of the real target can be determined due to missing support of dependencies which are established at execution time (i.e. registration of listeners at runtime). This limitation is inherited from SISSy which has no support for dependency injection or other kinds of dependencies which are created at execution time.

Handling of Code Formats The primary input of the tool chain of the developed reverse engineering approach is Java source code. Java Bytecode can be easily supported as decompilers for Java are available (e.g. JAD, JDEV, or JrevPro). The decompiled source code cannot uniquely distinguish for example for and do while loops, but is complete with respect to the remaining control flow structure. The PCM does neither distinguish for and do while loops, thus no relevant information for the creation of RDSEFFs gets lost during compilation and decompilation.

Code obfuscation cannot change the control flow structure significantly since changing the order of method calls would (in general) change programme semantics. The same holds for the order of loops, branches, and external calls which, when changing the order, would result in different programme semantics. Furthermore, code obfuscation is not a problem since no human needs to understand the reverse engineered code. Only the quality of the ConsistentNaming strategy of SoMoX could drop if the names of classes would change (which cannot be the case for public APIs). Generally, compiled or obfuscated code are not a limitation to the approach.

The tooling relies on Java only for the first instrumentation step. Later steps generally could also deal with non-Java code. The GAST model is independent of a concrete object-oriented programming language.

9.11. Future Work

The future work for SoMoX includes a seamless integration with dynamic programme analysis. Dynamic metrics like the ones surveyed by Cornelissen et al. [CZvD+09] could, if integrated into SoMOX, help in program understanding. As Cornelissen et al. point out, dynamic analysis can help in program understanding. Still, only few articles deal with design and architecture by means of dynamic analysis.

Since dynamic metrics are supported by SoMoX and can be integrated with static analysis metrics, research on good combinations of static and dynamic metrics in the context of SoMoX is promising. Dynamic analysis is well-suited to complement the static analysis capabilities.

Short term extensions of SoMoX comprise the integration of a selection of module metrics and to check their applicability to component-based software architectures. Sarkar et al. [SKR08] offer a number of validated metrics for modules, which could be easily integrated into SoMoX.

The applicability of SoMoX to roundtrip engineering cycles was discussed in Section 9.8. Extending SoMoX by forward engineering capabilities to enable support for integrated roundtrip cycles is planned for future versions of SoMoX.

Furthermore, SoMoX and Beagle could be extended to create a detection mechanism for architecture violations with respect to software performance constraints. A reference architecture could be checked against a reverse engineered static architecture and behaviour model in order to identify violations of the reference architecture.

SoMoX and Beagle would need to be extended by model comparison algorithms which are able to identify mismatches between two instances of PCM models.

Beagle could be extended by the integration of further analysis information. For example, the integration of slicing information could be promising to lower the dimensionality of the search space. Slicing could identify which parameters can, at most, be involved in a certain parametric dependency. The reduced search space could then improve the convergence speed.

The application of Beagle to determine characteristic curves has been presented in this thesis (cf. Section 5.17). The field of characteristic curves for large-scale systems nevertheless sound promising as it tackles the specific requirements of industry which, for some software systems, are satisfied with rough model approximations of the real software system behaviour. An initial prototype [Rom09] already reuses Beagle. Specific abstraction requirements and corresponding support in Beagle should be researched.

9.12. Conclusion

This thesis introduced a reverse engineering approach for static architecture and behaviour models of component-based software systems. The reverse engineered models are fully parameterised performance models for component-based software systems which represent a consistent performance abstraction for static architecture and component behaviour. The execution semantics of the reverse engineered models allow performance predictions for sizing, extension of legacy software systems, component reuse, and design optimisation scenarios and helps in understanding component-based software architectures.

Through the strong integration of architectural and behavioural reverse engineering, changes in abstraction-level of the architecture are directly reflected in the behavioural model. Both models are ensured to be consistent to each other. The consistency between code and model helps avoiding misleading model prediction results, which actually do not relate to the implemented applications. By automating reverse engineering, models can stay consistent with code also for evolving applications.

The presented reverse engineering approach is based on static, dynamic, and statistical analysis. It employs genetic programming to combine static, dynamic, and statistical analysis, to create recombined results from each single approach that outperform each single reverse engineering approach. The approach is the first approach which systematically reconstructs behaviour models of components which can serve for performance predictions, and pioneers in the combination static, dynamic, and statistical analysis approaches. It is the first approach which uses genetic programming for the integration of reverse engineering approaches and contributes various unique extensions of genetic programming for the creation of performance-equivalent abstractions of component behaviour.

The approach reverse engineers component models which make no assumptions on the environment (like connected components or underlying hardware) and thus allows for composing models without changing model internals. The composition is fast and reliable as no manual effort for changing models is required. This is the first approach that provides reverse engineering for models parameterised over all influencing factors of components (assembly, deployment, and usage profile).

The contributed SoMoX and Beagle approach were successfully validated in three extensive end-to-end case studies which showed the applicability of the approach to different domain of software systems. Overall, the validation comprised 11 case studies in which the capabilities of the developed approach were analysed in detail. SoMoX and Beagle performed well in the validation: 78% precision and 89% recall were achieved in average. Performance predictions based on reverse engineered models were 12% off in average and 30% in the worst case.

The performed validation results suggest that the developed reverse engineering approach is suitable to contribute in saving a considerable amount of time for the creation of parameterised performance models when compared to the manual creation of models (4 vs. 40 hours). The automation options of the approach ease the use of the reverse engineering approach and considerably lower the time for reverse engineering. The reduced effort for the model creation and the scalability of the approach make it applicable even for large-scale real-life systems with more than 250,000 lines of code.

This thesis was complemented by foundations, and an in-depth discussion of results, assumptions, limitations, possible extensions, and future work of the developed approach.

A. Appendix

A.1. Case Study Reference Architectures

A.1.1. CoCoME

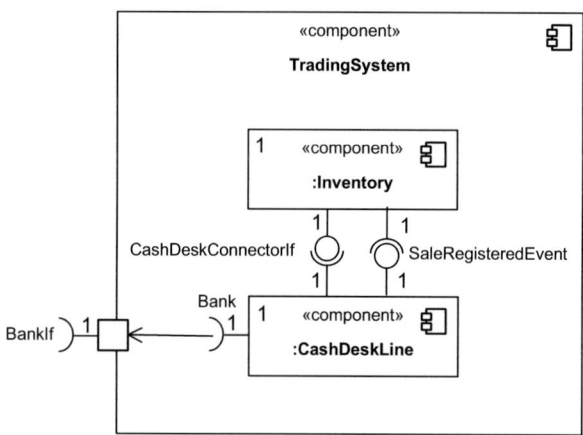

Figure A.1.: CoCoME System Level Architecture, source [HKW$^+$08]

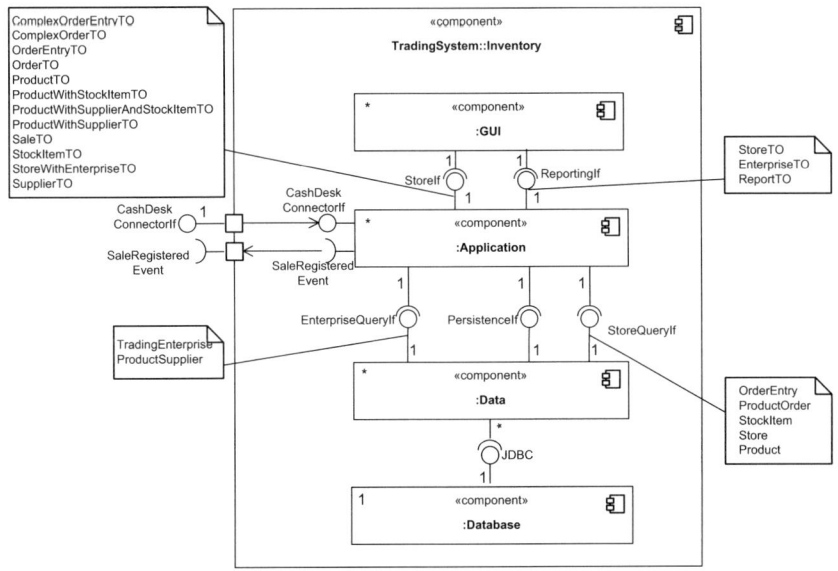

Figure A.2.: CoCoME Inventory: Subsystem Level Architecture, source [HKW$^+$08]

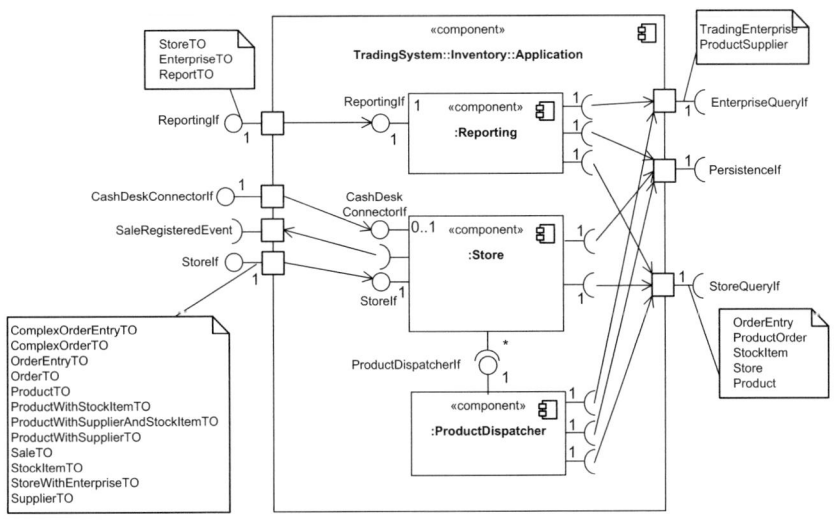

Figure A.3.: CoCoME Inventory GUI, source [HKW$^+$08]

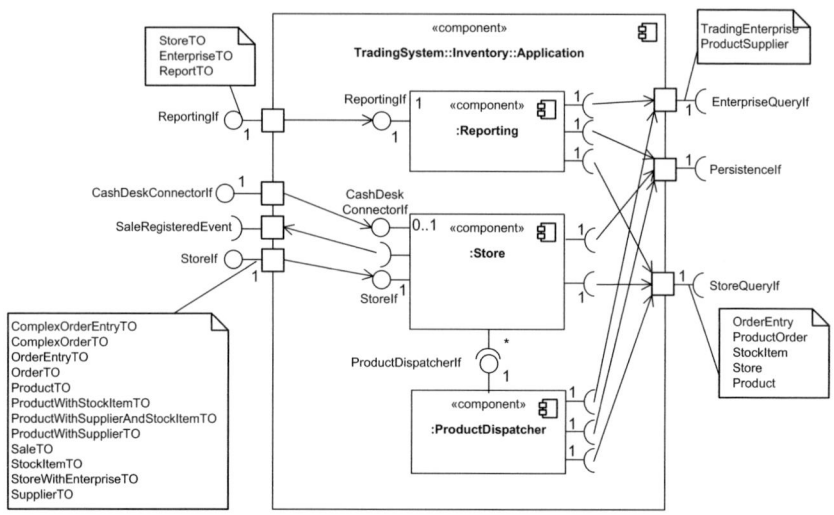

Figure A.4.: CoCoME Inventory Application, source [HKW+08]

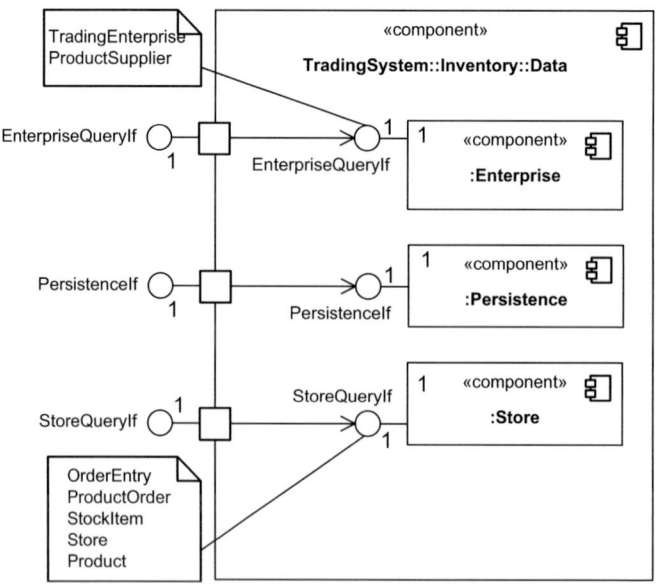

Figure A.5.: CoCoME Inventory Data, source [HKW+08]

A.1.2. Palladio FileShare

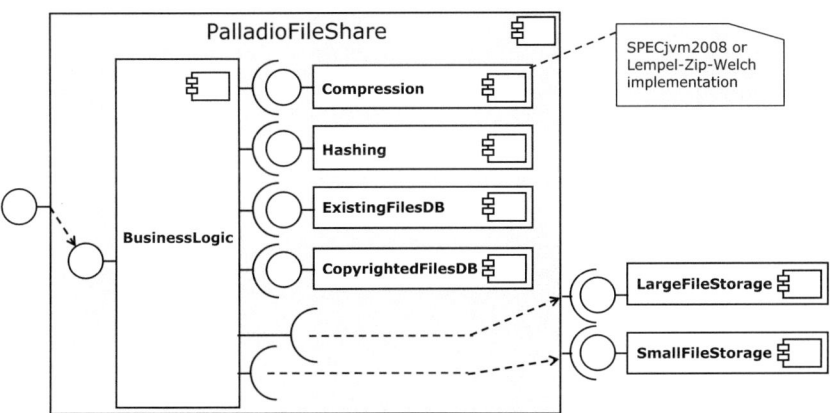

Figure A.6.: Palladio FileShare Static Architecture, source [KKR08a]

A.2. Additional Reverse Engineered Models

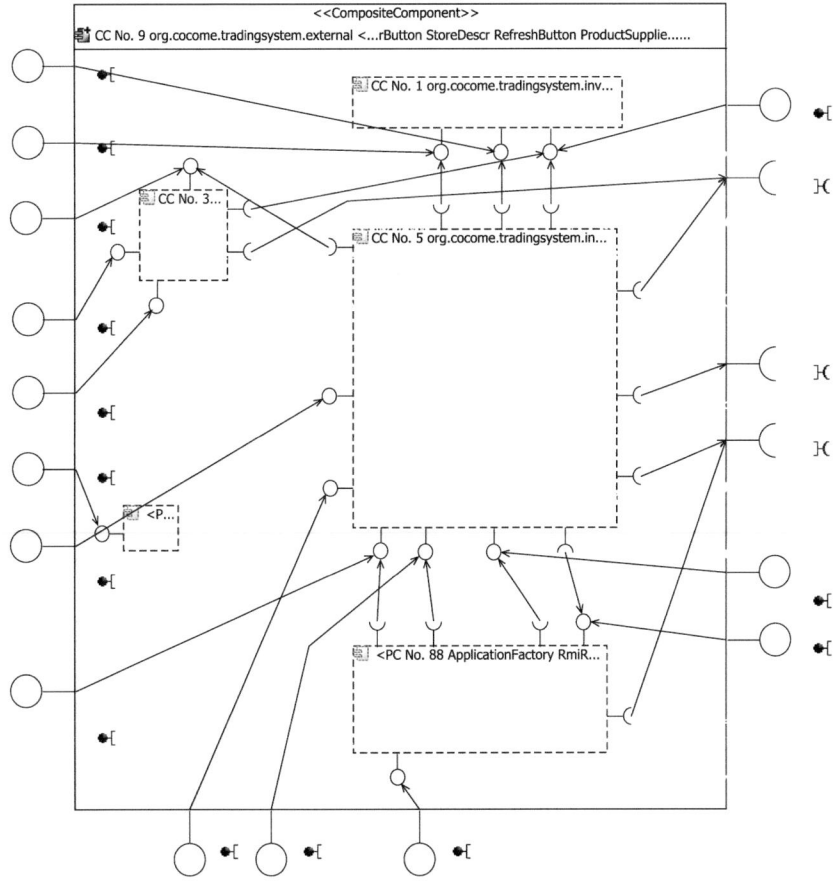

Figure A.7.: CoCoME: Reverse engineered composite component (screenshot)

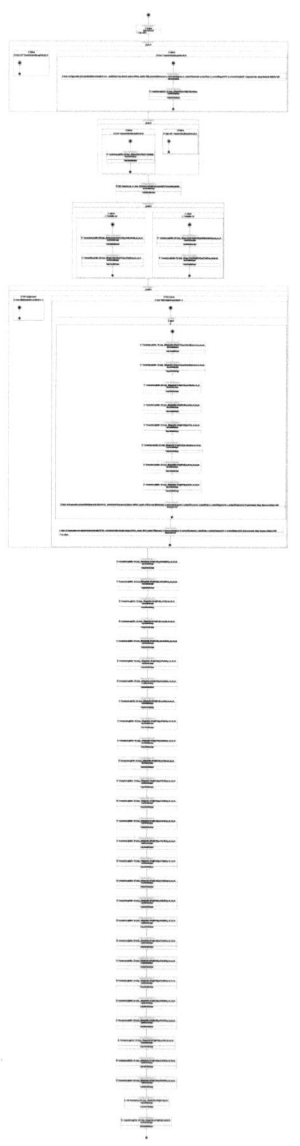

Figure A.8.: SPECjbb2005: Reverse engineered behaviour models of the process-TransactionLog service (screenshot)

List of Figures

Listings

Bibliography

[ABF04] E. Arisholm, L. C. Briand, and A. Føyen, "Dynamic coupling measurement for object-oriented software," *IEEE Transactions on Software Engineering*, vol. 30, no. 8, pp. 491–506, August 2004.

[ABM+06] J. Anderer, R. Bloch, T. Mohaupt, R. Neumann, A. Schumacher, O. Seng, F. Simon, A. Trifu, and M. Trifu, "QBENCH – Methoden und Werkzeuge zur Sicherung der inneren Qualität bei der Evolution objektorientierter Systeme," Forschungszentrum Informatik FZI, Karlsruhe, Germany, technical report FZI-Publication 1-6-6/06, July 2006. [Online]. Available: http://www.qbench.de/QBench/CMS/Members/seng/QBench-ZusammenfassenderSachbericht.pdf

[AC04] V. Aline and W. Cláudia, "Software architecture recovery based on dynamic analysis," in *XVIII Simpósio Brasileiro de Engenharia de Software, I Workshop de Manutenção de Software Moderna, 2004, Brasília*, 2004.

[AG01] F. Abreu and M. Goulão, "Coupling and Cohesion as Modularization Drivers: Are we being over-persuaded," in *Proceedings of the Fifth European Conference on Software Maintenance and Reengineering*. IEEE Computer Society Washington, DC, USA, 2001, p. 47.

[AGC02] A. Andrews, S. Ghosh, and E. Choi, "A model for understanding software components," in *Proceedings of the 18th IEEE International Conference on Software Maintenance (ICSM'02)*. Los Alamitos, CA, USA: IEEE Computer Society, 2002, pp. 359–368.

[AGP03] R. Abbott, J. Guo, and B. Parviz, "Guided genetic programming," in *Sixth International Conference on Computational Intelligence and Natural Computing, September 2003*, Department of Computer Science, California State University, Los Angeles, Los Angeles, Ca. 90032, June 2003, last retrieved 2006-09-01. [Online]. Available: http://abbott.calstatela.edu/PapersAndTalks/GuidedGeneticProgramming.pdf

[AH90]   H. Agrawal and J. R. Horgan, "Dynamic program slicing," in *PLDI '90: Proceedings of the ACM SIGPLAN 1990 conference on Programming language design and implementation.*   New York, NY, USA: ACM Press, 1990, pp. 246–256.

[AL99a]   N. Anquetil and T. Lethbridge, "Recovering software architecture from the names of source files," *Journal of Software Maintenance Research and Practice*, vol. 11, no. 3, pp. 201–221, 1999.

[AL99b]   ——, "Experiments with Clustering as a Software Remodularization Method," in *Sixth Working Conference on Reverse Engineering, WCRE.*   Los Alamitos, CA, USA: IEEE Computer Society, 1999, pp. 235–255.

[Ald03]   J. Aldrich, "Using Types to Enforce Architectural Structure," PhD Disseration, University of Washington, August 2003.

[Apa09]   Apache Foundation, "Apache Logging Service log4j," http://logging.apache.org/log4j, 2009, last retrieved 2009-12-30.

[ARA+09]   N. Anquetil, J.-C. Royer, P. Andre, G. Ardourel, P. Hnetynka, T. Poch, D. Petrascu, and V. Petrascu, "JavaCompExt: Extracting Architectural Elements from Java Source Code," in *Proceedings of the 16th Working Conference on Reverse Engineering (WCRE '09).*   IEEE, October 2009, pp. 317–318.

[AW96]   A. Avritzer and E. J. Weyuker, "Deriving Workloads for Performance Testing," *Software–Practice and Experience*, vol. 26, no. 6, pp. 613–633, 1996.

[BALS08]   A. Bertolino, G. D. Angelis, F. Lonetti, and A. Sabetta, "Let The Puppets Move! Automated Testbed Generation for Service-oriented Mobile Applications," in *Software Engineering and Advanced Applications, 2008. SEAA '08. 34th Euromicro Conference*, September 2008, pp. 321–328.

[Bar10]   Barak Naveh et al., "JGraphT," http://jgrapht.sourceforge.net/, 2010, last retrieved 2010-03-15.

[bau]   "Bauhaus homepage." [Online]. Available: http://www.iste.uni-stuttgart.de/ps/bauhaus/

[Bau93]   F. Bause, "Queueing petri nets-a formalism for the combined qualitative and quantitative analysis of systems," *Petri Nets and Performance*

338

Models, 1993. Proceedings., 5th International Workshop on, pp. 14–23, Oct 1993.

[Bay99]   S. Bayarov, "Resource Functions for Model Based Performance Analysis of Distributed Software Systems," master thesis, Ottawa-Carleton Institute for Electrical Engineering, Department of Systems and Computer Engineering, Faculty of Engineering, Carleton University, Ottawa, Ontario, Canada, June 1999.

[BBJ⁺08]   A. Baier, S. Becker, M. Jung, K. Krogmann, C. Röttgers, N. Streekmann, K. Thoms, and S. Zschaler, *Handbuch der Software-Architektur*, 2nd ed.   dPunkt.verlag Heidelberg, December 2008, ch. Modellgetriebene Software-Entwicklung, pp. 93–122.

[BBT06]   H. Byelas, E. Bondarev, and A. Telea, "Visualization of areas of interest in component-based system architectures," pp. 160–169, 29 2006-Sept. 1 2006.

[BC88]   V. R. Basili and G. Caldiera, "Reusing existing software," Institute for Advanced Computer Studies, Department of Computer Science, University of Maryland, College Park, MD, USA, Tech. Rep. IMIACS-TR-88-72, CS-TR-2116, Oct. 1988.

[BCdK07]   E. Bondarev, M. R. V. Chaudron, and E. A. de Kock, "Exploring performance trade-offs of a JPEG decoder using the DeepCompass framework," in *WOSP '07: Proceedings of the 6th international workshop on Software and performance*.   New York, NY, USA: ACM Press, 2007, pp. 153–163.

[BCR94]   V. R. Basili, G. Caldiera, and H. D. Rombach, "The Goal Question Metric Approach," in *Encyclopedia of Software Engineering - 2 Volume Set*, J. J. Marciniak, Ed.   John Wiley & Sons, 1994, pp. 528–532.

[BDD⁺06]   S. Becker, A. Dikanski, N. Drechsel, A. A. E. Ghazi, J. Happe, I. El-Oudghiri, H. Koziolek, A. Kuperberg, R. Rentschler, R. H. Reussner, R. Sinawski, M. Thoma, and M. Willsch, "Modellgetriebene Software-Entwicklung - Architekturen, Muster und Eclipse-basierte MDA," Universität Karlsruhe (TH), Tech. Rep., 2006. [Online]. Available: http://digbib.ubka.uni-karlsruhe.de/volltexte/documents/2918

[BDH08a]   S. Becker, T. Dencker, and J. Happe, "Model-Driven Generation of Performance Prototypes," in *Performance Evaluation: Metrics, Models and Benchmarks (SIPEW 2008)*, ser. Lecture Notes in Computer Science, vol. 5119.   Springer-Verlag Berlin Heidelberg,

2008, pp. 79–98. [Online]. Available: http://www.springerlink.com/content/62t1277642tt8676/fulltext.pdf

[BDH+08b] T. Bures, M. Decky, P. Hnetynka, J. Kofron, P. Parizek, F. Plasil, T. Poch, O. Sery, and P. Tuma, "CoCoME in SOFA," in *The Common Component Modelling Example: Comparing Software Component Models*, ser. Lecture Notes in Computer Science, vol. 5153. Springer-Verlag, Berlin, Germany, 2008.

[BDIS04a] S. Balsamo, A. Di Marco, P. Inverardi, and M. Simeoni, "Model-Based Performance Prediction in Software Development: A Survey," *IEEE Transactions on Software Engineering*, vol. 30, no. 5, pp. 295–310, May 2004.

[BDIS04b] ——, "Model-Based Performance Prediction in Software Development: A Survey," *IEEE Transactions on Software Engineering*, vol. 30, no. 5, pp. 295–310, May 2004.

[Bec08a] S. Becker, "Coupled Model Transformations for QoS Enabled Component-Based Software Design," Ph.D. dissertation, University of Oldenburg, Germany, Mar. 2008.

[Bec08b] ——, *Coupled Model Transformations for QoS Enabled Component-Based Software Design*, ser. Karlsruhe Series on Software Quality. Universitätsverlag Karlsruhe, 2008, vol. 1.

[Bei90] B. Beizer, *Software Testing Techniques*, 2nd ed. International Thomson Computer Press, 1990.

[Ber06] P. Berkhin, *Grouping Multidimensional Data*. Springer, 2006, ch. A Survey of Clustering Data Mining Techniques, pp. 25–71.

[BGdMT98] G. Bolch, S. Greiner, H. de Meer, and K. S. Trivedi, *Queueing Networks and Markov Chains*. John Wiley & Sons Inc., 1998.

[BGKK10] F. Brosch, R. Gitzel, H. Koziolek, and S. Krug, "Combining architecture-based software reliability predictions with financial impact calculations," in *International Workshop on Formal Engineering approaches to Software Components and Architectures (FESCA)*, ser. ENTCS, vol. 264, no. 1. Elsevier, 2010, pp. 3 – 17.

[BHK06] S. Becker, J. Happe, and H. Koziolek, "Putting Components into Context: Supporting QoS-Predictions with an explicit Context Model," in *Proc. 11th International Workshop on Component Oriented*

Programming (WCOP'06), R. Reussner, C. Szyperski, and W. Weck, Eds., July 2006, pp. 1–6. [Online]. Available: http://research. microsoft.com/~cszypers/events/WCOP2006/WCOP06-Becer.pdf

[BHP06]   T. Bures, P. Hnetynka, and F. Plasil, "Sofa 2.0: Balancing advanced features in a hierarchical component model," in *SERA '06: Proceedings of the Fourth International Conference on Software Engineering Research, Management and Applications.*   Washington, DC, USA: IEEE Computer Society, 2006, pp. 40–48.

[BHS07]   B. Beckert, R. Hähnle, and P. H. Schmitt, Eds., *Verification of Object-Oriented Software: The KeY Approach*, ser. LNCS 4334.   Springer-Verlag, 2007.

[BHT⁺10]   S. Becker, M. Hauck, M. Trifu, K. Krogmann, and J. Kofron, "Reverse Engineering Component Models for Quality Predictions," in *Proceedings of the 14th European Conference on Software Maintenance and Reengineering, European Projects Track.*   IEEE, 2010, pp. 199–202. [Online]. Available: http://sdqweb.ipd.kit.edu/ publications/pdfs/becker2010a.pdf

[Bin07]   D. Binkley, "Source Code Analysis: A Road Map," in *FOSE '07: 2007 Future of Software Engineering.*   Washington, DC, USA: IEEE Computer Society, 2007, pp. 104–119.

[BJH⁺05]   D. A. Bacigalupo, S. A. Jarvis, L. He, D. P. Spooner, D. N. Dillenberger, and G. R. Nudd, "An investigation into the application of different performance prediction methods to distributed enterprise applications," *J. Supercomput.*, vol. 34, no. 2, pp. 93–111, 2005.

[BK96]   F. Bause and P. S. Kritzinger, *Stochastic Petri Nets: An Introduction to the Theory.*   Vieweg-Verlag, 1996.

[BK02]   ——, *Stochastic Petri Nets*, 2nd ed.   Vieweg, 2002.

[BKBR10]   F. Brosch, H. Koziolek, B. Buhnova, and R. Reussner, "Parameterized Reliability Prediction for Component-based Software Architectures," in *International Conference on the Quality of Software Architectures (QoSA)*, ser. LNCS, vol. 6093.   Springer, 2010, pp. 36–51.

[BKK09]   F. Brosig, S. Kounev, and K. Krogmann, "Automated Extraction of Palladio Component Models from Running Enterprise Java Applications," in *Proceedings of the 1st International Workshop on Run-time mOdels for Self-managing Systems and Applications (ROSSA 2009).*

In conjunction with Fourth International Conference on Performance Evaluation Methodologies and Tools (VALUETOOLS 2009), Pisa, Italy, October 19, 2009. ACM, New York, NY, USA, Oct. 2009.

[BKR07]   S. Becker, H. Koziolek, and R. H. Reussner, "Model-based Performance Prediction with the Palladio Component Model," in *WOSP '07: Proceedings of the 6th International Workshop on Software and performance.* New York, NY, USA: ACM, February 5–8 2007, pp. 54–65. [Online]. Available: http://sdqweb.ipd.uka.de/publications/pdfs/becker2007b.pdf

[BKR09]   S. Becker, H. Koziolek, and R. Reussner, "The Palladio component model for model-driven performance prediction," *Journal of Systems and Software,* vol. 82, pp. 3–22, 2009. [Online]. Available: http://dx.doi.org/10.1016/j.jss.2008.03.066

[BL97]   A. L. Blum and P. Langley, "Selection of relevant features and examples in machine learning," *Artificial Intelligence,* vol. 97, no. Issues 1-2, pp. 245–271, December 1997. [Online]. Available: http://www.sciencedirect.com/science/article/B6TYF-3SNYS10-8/2/a3721939d19c9fa9909fcf950003499d

[BLL05]   L. Briand, Y. Labiche, and J. Leduc, "Tracing distributed systems executions using aspectj," in *Proceedings of the 21st IEEE International Conference on Software Maintenance (ICSM'05),* Sept. 2005, pp. 81–90.

[BLL06]   L. C. Briand, Y. Labiche, and J. Leduc, "Toward the Reverse Engineering of UML Sequence Diagrams for Distributed Java Software," *IEEE Transactions on Software Engineering,* vol. 32, no. 9, pp. 642–663, September 2006.

[BM03]   A. Bertolino and R. Mirandola, "Towards component based software performance engineering," in *Proc. 6th Workshop on Component-Based Software Engineering: Automated Reasoning and Prediction, ACM/IEEE 25th International Conference on Software Engineering ICSE 2003,* I. Crnkovic, H. Schmidt, J. Stafford, and K. Wallnau, Eds., 2003, pp. 1–6.

[BMR⁺96]   F. Buschmann, R. Meunier, H. Rohnert, P. Sommerlad, and M. Stal, *Pattern-Oriented Software Architecture – A System of Patterns.* Wiley & Sons, New York, NY, USA, 1996.

[BNKF98]   W. Banzhaf, P. Nordin, R. E. Keller, and F. D. Francone, *Genetic Programming – An Introduction*. Heidelberg: dpunkt Verlag, Heidelberg, 1998, ralfs Book.

[BOR04]   S. Becker, S. Overhage, and R. H. Reussner, "Classifying Software Component Interoperability Errors to Support Component Adaption," in *Proceedings of the 7th International Symposium on Component-Based Software Engineering (CBSE 2004), Edinburgh, UK*, ser. Lecture Notes in Computer Science, I. Crnkovic, J. A. Stafford, H. W. Schmidt, and K. C. Wallnau, Eds., vol. 3054. Springer-Verlag Berlin Heidelberg, May 2004, pp. 68–83. [Online]. Available: http://springerlink.metapress.com/content/yk87fnn309wf2fgh/

[BP89]   T. J. Biggerstaff and A. J. Perlis, *Software Reusability*. ACM Press, Addison-Wesley, Reading, MA, USA, 1989, vol. I & II.

[BR88]   V. R. Basili and H. D. Rombach, "Towards a comprehensive framework for reuse: A reuse-enabling software evolution environment," Institute for Advanced Computer Studies, Department of Computer Science, University of Maryland, College Park, MD, USA, Tech. Rep. UMIACS-TR-88-92, CS-TR-2158, Dec. 1988.

[BR08]   R. Böhme and R. Reussner, "Validation of Predictions with Measurements," in *Dependability Metrics*, ser. Lecture Notes in Computer Science. Springer-Verlag Berlin Heidelberg, 2008, vol. 4909, ch. 3, pp. 14–18. [Online]. Available: http://www.springerlink.com/content/662rn13014r46269/fulltext.pdf

[Buca]   A. Buckley, *Improved Modularity Support in the Java Programming Language*, Java Community Process Java Specification Requests JSR 294.

[Bucb]   ——, *Java Module System*, Java Community Process Java Specification Requests JSR 277.

[BW99]   M. Büchi and W. Weck, "The greybox approach: When blackbox specifications hide too much," Turku Center for Computer Science, Tech. Rep. 297, Aug. 1999. [Online]. Available: http://www.abo.fi/~mbuechi/publications/TR297.html

[CBB+03]   P. C. Clements, F. Bachmann, L. Bass, D. Garlan, J. Ivers, R. Little, R. Nord, and J. Stafford, *Documenting Software Architectures*, ser. SEI Series in Software Engineering. Addison-Wesley, 2003.

343

[CC77]   P. Cousot and R. Cousot, "Abstract interpretation: a unified lattice mo-
           del for static analysis of programs by construction or approximation
           of fixpoints," in *POPL '77: Proceedings of the 4th ACM SIGACT-
           SIGPLAN symposium on Principles of programming languages.* New
           York, NY, USA: ACM, 1977, pp. 238–252.

[CC90]   E. J. Chikofsky and J. H. Cross, "Reverse engineering and design
           recovery: a taxonomy," *IEEE Software*, vol. 7, pp. 13–17, January
           1990. [Online]. Available: http://ieeexplore.ieee.org/iel1/52/1647/
           00043044.pdf?tp=&arnumber=43044&isnumber=1647

[CCMW01]   E. Christensen, F. Curbera, G. Meredith, and S. Weerawarana, *Web
           Services Description Language (WSDL)*, http://www.w3.org/TR/wsdl,
           World Wide Web Consortium (W3C) W3C Note, Rev. 1.1, March
           2001.

[CDE08]   C. Cadar, D. Dunbar, and D. Engler, "KLEE: Unassisted and
           Automatic Generation of High-Coverage Tests for Complex Systems
           Programs," in *8th USENIX Symposium on Operating Systems
           Design and Implementation*, San Diego, CA, December 2008, last
           retrieved 2009-03-31. [Online]. Available: http://www.usenix.org/
           events/osdi08/tech/full_papers/cadar/cadar.pdf

[CDH+00]   J. Corbett, M. Dwyer, J. Hatcliff, S. Laubach, C. Pasareanu, Robby,
           and H. Zheng, "Bandera: extracting finite-state models from java
           source code," in *Proceedings of the 2000 International Conference
           on Software Engineering.* Limerick, Ireland: IEEE, 2000, pp.
           439–448. [Online]. Available: http://ieeexplore.ieee.org/xpls/abs_all.
           jsp?arnumber=870434

[CDPEV05] G. Canfora, M. Di Penta, R. Esposito, and M. Villani, "An approach
           for QoS-aware service composition based on genetic algorithms," in
           *Proceedings of the 2005 conference on Genetic and evolutionary com-
           putation.* ACM Press New York, NY, USA, 2005, pp. 1069–1075.

[CE00]   K. Czarnecki and U. W. Eisenecker, *Generative Programming.* Ad-
           dison-Wesley, Reading, MA, USA, 2000.

[CF07]   V. Cortellessa and L. Frittella, "A Framework for Automated Genera-
           tion of Architectural Feedback from Software Performance Analysis?"
           EPEW 2007, no. LNCS 4748, pp. 171–185, 2007.

[CH89]   P. P. Chang and W.-W. Hwu, "Inline function expansion for compi-
           ling C programs," in *PLDI '89: Proceedings of the ACM SIGPLAN*

344

1989 Conference on Programming language design and implementation. New York, NY, USA: ACM, 1989, pp. 246–257.

[CHDP07]   G. Canfora Harman and M. Di Penta, "New Frontiers of Reverse Engineering ," in *Future of Software Engineering (FOSE '07)*. Los Alamitos, CA, USA: IEEE Computer Society, 2007, pp. 326–341.

[Chi]   S. Chiba, "Javassist (Java Programming Assistant)," http://www.csg.is.titech.ac.jp/projects/index.html, last visit: October 9th, 2009. [Online]. Available: http://www.csg.is.titech.ac.jp/ projects/index.html

[Chi08]   I. I. Chirila, "Parameter Analysis in Software Components using Symbolic Execution," Bachelor Thesis, Faculty of Informatics, University of Karlsruhe (TH), Karlsruhe, Germany, 2008.

[Cho07]   L. Chouambe, "Rekonstruktion von Software-Architekturen," master thesis, Institute for Program Structures and Data Organisation, Chair Software Design and Qualitiy (SDQ), Faculty of Informatics, Universität Karlsruhe (TH), Karlsruhe, Germany, May 2007.

[Cia10]   A. Ciancone, "Mapping the Service Architecture Meta-Model to the Palladio Component Model," Master's thesis, Politecnico di Milano, Dipartimento di Elettronica e Informazione, Piazza L. Da Vinci 32, 20133 Milan, Italy, 2010.

[CKK01]   E. S. Cho, M. S. Kim, and S. D. Kim, "Component metrics to measure component quality," in *APSEC '01: Proceedings of the Eighth Asia-Pacific on Software Engineering Conference*. Los Alamitos, CA, USA: IEEE Computer Society, December 2001, pp. 419–426.

[CKK08]   L. Chouambe, B. Klatt, and K. Krogmann, "Reverse Engineering Software-Models of Component-Based Systems," in *12th European Conference on Software Maintenance and Reengineering*, K. Kontogiannis, C. Tjortjis, and A. Winter, Eds.   Athens, Greece: IEEE Computer Society, April 1–4 2008, pp. 93–102. [Online]. Available: http://sdqweb.ipd.uka.de/publications/pdfs/chouambe2008a.pdf

[CL02]   Y. Cheon and G. T. Leavens, "A simple and practical approach to unit testing: The JML and JUnit way," in *ECOOP 2002 – Object-Oriented Programming*, ser. Lecture Notes in Computer Science, vol. 2374.   Springer, 2002, pp. 1789–1901.

[CLGL05] S. Chen, Y. Liu, I. Gorton, and A. Liu, "Performance Prediction of Component-based Applications," *Journal of Systems and Software*, vol. 74, no. 1, pp. 35–43, 2005.

[CM98] V. Cherkassky and F. Mulier, *Learning from Data: Concepts, Theory, and Methods*. John Wiley & Sons, Inc. New York, NY, USA, 1998.

[CMRT10] V. Cortellessa, A. Martens, R. Reussner, and C. Trubiani, "A process to effectively identify guilty performance antipatterns," in *Fundamental Approaches to Software Engineering, 13th International Conference, FASE 2010*, D. Rosenblum and G. Taentzer, Eds. Springer-Verlag Berlin Heidelberg, 2010, pp. 368–382. [Online]. Available: http://www.springerlink.com/content/wl11718486334174

[CMST90] G. Ciardo, R. Marie, B. Sericola, and K. S. Trivedi, "Performability analysis using semi-markov reward processes," *IEEE Transactions on Computers*, vol. 39, no. 10, Oct. 1990.

[Cor] M. Corp., "The COM homepage," http://www.microsoft.com/com/, last retrieved 2006-10-30. [Online]. Available: http://www.microsoft.com/com/

[Cow88] P. Coward, "Symbolic execution systems-a review," *Software Engineering Journal*, vol. 3, no. 6, pp. 229–239, November 1988. [Online]. Available: http://ieeexplore.ieee.org/xpls/abs_all.jsp?arnumber=28077

[Cra07] M. J. Crawley, *The R Book*. Chichester: Wiley & Sons, 2007.

[CST00] N. Cristianini and J. Shawe-Taylor, *An introduction to support Vector Machines and other kernel-based learning methods*. Cambridge University Press, New York, NY, USA, 2000.

[CW00] M. Courtois and C. M. Woodside, "Using regression splines for software performance analysis," in *Proc 2nd Int. Workshop on Software and Performance (WOSP2000)*. Ottawa, Canada: ACM, September 2000, pp. 105–114.

[CZvD+09] B. Cornelissen, A. Zaidman, A. van Deursen, L. Moonen, and R. Koschke, "A Systematic Survey of Program Comprehension through Dynamic Analysis," *IEEE Transactions on Software Engineering*, vol. 99, no. 2, pp. 684–702, 2009.

[Dah01]   M. Dahm, "Byte Code Engineering with the BCEL API," Freie
            Universität Berlin, Tech. Rep. B-17-98, 2001. [Online]. Available:
            http://bcel.sourceforge.net/downloads/report.pdf

[DDHV03]   B. Dufour, K. Driesen, L. Hendren, and C. Verbrugge, "Dynamic me-
            trics for java," in *Proceedings of the ACM SIGPLAN 2003 Conference
            on Object-Oriented Programming, Systems, Languages, and Applica-
            tions (OOPSLA '03)*. ACM Press, 2003, pp. 149–168.

[DGL06]   M. Denker, O. Greevy, and M. Lanza, "Higher abstractions
            for dynamic analysis," *2nd International Workshop on Program
            Comprehension through Dynamic Analysis (PCODA 2006)*, pp.
            32–38, 2006. [Online]. Available: http://ieeexplore.ieee.org/xpls/abs_
            all.jsp?arnumber=792487

[Die05]   R. Diestel, *Graph Theory*, 3rd ed. Berlin: Springer, 2005.

[DLR06]   X. Deng, J. Lee, and Robby, "Bogor/Kiasan: A k-bounded Symbolic
            Execution for Checking Strong Heap Properties of Open Systems,"
            in *21st IEEE/ACM International Conference on Automated Software
            Engineering, 2006 (ASE '06)*. IEEE, September 2006, pp. 157–
            166. [Online]. Available: http://ieeexplore.ieee.org/xpls/abs_all.jsp?
            isnumber=4019544&arnumber=4019571&count=72&index=24

[DMM99]   D. Doval, S. Mancoridis, and B. Mitchell, "Automatic clustering of
            software systems using a genetic algorithm," in *Software Technology
            and Engineering Practice, 1999. STEP '99. Proceedings*, 1999, pp.
            73–81.

[DMM03]   N. Dumitrascu, S. Murphy, and L. Murphy, "A Methodology for
            Predicting the Performance of Component-Based Applications," in
            *Proceedings of the Eighth International Workshop on Component-
            Oriented Programming (WCOP'03)*, W. Weck, J. Bosch, and C. Szy-
            perski, Eds., Jun. 2003.

[DMTS10]   J. Dietrich, C. McCartin, E. Tempero, and S. M. A. Shah, "Barriers to
            Modularity – An Empirical Study to Assess the Potential for Modula-
            risation of Java Programs," in *QoSA 2010*, ser. LNCS, G. Heinemann,
            J. Kofron, and F. Plasil, Eds., vol. 6093. Springer, 2010, pp. 135–150.

[Dol01]   J. J. Dolado, "On the problem of the software cost function," *Infor-
            mation and Software Technology*, vol. 43, no. 1, pp. 61–72, January
            2001.

[DP09]   S. Ducasse and D. Pollet, "Software Architecture Reconstruction: a Process-Oriented Taxonomy," *IEEE Transactions on Software Engineering*, vol. 35, no. 4, pp. 573–591, 2009.

[DPJM⁺02]   W. De Pauw, E. Jensen, N. Mitchell, G. Sevitsky, J. Vlissides, and J. Yang, "Visualizing the Execution of Java Programs," in *Software Visualization: International Seminar, Dagstuhl Castle, Germany, May 20-25, 2001: Revised Papers.* Springer, 2002.

[DS10]   J. Dietrich and L. Stewart, "Component Contracts in Eclipse – A Case Study," in *CBSE 2010*, ser. LNCS, L. Grunske, R. Reussner, and F. Plasil, Eds., vol. 6092. Springer, 2010.

[ECGN01]   M. D. Ernst, J. Cockrell, W. G. Griswold, and D. Notkin, "Dynamically discovering likely program invariants to support program evolution," *IEEE Transactions on Software Engineering*, vol. 27, no. 2, pp. 99–123, February 2001.

[Ecl09]   Eclipse Foundation, "AspectJ Homepage," http://www.eclipse.org/aspectj/, 2009, last accessed 2009-12-29. [Online]. Available: http://www.eclipse.org/aspectj/

[Edm08]   J. Edmonds, *How to think about Algorithms*, 1st ed. Cambridge University Press, New York, NY, USA, 2008.

[Edv99]   J. Edvardsson, "A survey on automatic test data generation," in *Proceedings of the Second Conference on Computer Science and Engineering in Linköping.* ECSEL, October 1999, pp. 21–28.

[EFH04]   E. Eskenazi, A. Fioukov, and D. Hammer, "Performance Prediction for Component Compositions," in *Component-Based Software Engineering (CBSE 2004)*, ser. Lecture Notes in Computer Science, I. C. et al., Ed., vol. 3054/2004. Springer Berlin / Heidelberg, 2004, pp. 280–293. [Online]. Available: http://springerlink.metapress.com/content/n8951bh11162y4hc/?p=f75f502238d84e0ea6db958a449d05ac&pi=17

[EJB07]   "Sun Microsystems Corp., The Enterprise Java Beans homepage," 2007, last retrieved 2008-01-06. [Online]. Available: http://java.sun.com/products/ejb/

[EKKB10]   F. Eichinger, K. Krogmann, R. Klug, and K. Böhm, "Software-Defect Localisation by Mining Dataflow-Enabled Call Graphs," in *Proceedings of the 10th European Conference on Machine Learning and Principles and Practice of Knowledge Discovery in Databases*

(ECML PKDD), Barcelona, Spain, 2010. [Online]. Available: http://digbib.ubka.uni-karlsruhe.de/volltexte/1000019636

[EPG⁺07] M. D. Ernst, J. H. Perkins, P. J. Guo, S. McCamant, C. Pacheco, M. S. Tschantz, and C. Xiao, "The Daikon system for dynamic detection of likely invariants," *Science of Computer Programming*, vol. 69, no. 1–3, pp. 35–45, Dec. 2007.

[Ern03] M. D. Ernst, "Static and dynamic analysis: Synergy and duality," in *WODA 2003: ICSE Workshop on Dynamic Analysis*, Portland, OR, May 9, 2003, pp. 24–27. [Online]. Available: http://pag.csail.mit.edu/ ~mernst/pubs/staticdynamic-woda2003.pdf

[Est95] J. C. Esteva, "Automatic identification of reusable components," in *Proceedings: Seventh International Workshop on Computer-Aided Software Engineering*, H. A. Müller and R. J. Norman, Eds. IEEE Computer Society Press, 1995, pp. 80–89.

[Fav04] J. M. Favre, "CacOphoNy: Metamodel-Driven Software Architecture Reconstruction," in *Working Conference on Reverse Engineering, WCRE2004*, Delft, The Netherlands, November 2004. [Online]. Available: http://citeseer.ist.psu.edu/favre04cacophony.html

[FDE⁺01] J.-M. Favre, F. Duclos, J. Estublier, R. Sanlaville, and J.-J. Auffret, "Reverse engineering a large component-based software product," in *Fifth European Conference on Software Maintenance and Reengineering*. Lisbon, Portugal: IEEE, March 2001, pp. 95–104. [Online]. Available: http://ieeexplore.ieee.org/iel5/7309/19763/ 00914973.pdf?tp=&isnumber=&arnumber=914973

[FK96] R. Ferguson and B. Korel, "The Chaining Approach for Software Test Data Generation," *ACM Trans. Softw. Eng. Methodol.*, vol. 5, no. 1, pp. 63–86, 1996.

[FNNS06] J. Fredriksson, T. Nolte, M. Nolin, and H. Schmidt, "Predicting execution time for variable behaviour embedded real-time components," *to appear / RTSS Workshop The 27th IEEE Real-Time Systems Symposium December 5-8, 2006 Rio de Janeiro, Brazil*, 2006.

[Fri91] J. H. Friedman, "Multivariate Adaptive Regression Splines," *The Annals of Statistics*, vol. 19, no. 1, pp. 1–141, 1991.

[Gar06] V. Garousi, "Traffic-aware Stress Testing of Distributed Real-Time Systems based on UML Models using Genetic Algorithms," phd, Ottawa-Carleton Institute of Electrical and Computer Engineering, Department of Systems and Computer Engineering, Carleton University, Ottawa, Ontario, Canada, August 2006. [Online]. Available: http://shannon2.uwaterloo.ca/~garousi/downloads/vahid-garousi-phd-thesis.pdf

[GCL01]   J. Grundy, Y. Cai, and A. Liu, "Generation of Distributed System Test-beds from High-level Software Architecture Descriptions," *Proceedings of the 2001 IEEE International Conference on Automated Software Engineering, San Diego, CA.*, Nov. 2001.

[GG75]   J. B. Goodenough and S. L. Gerhart, "Toward a theory of test data selection," *ACM SIGPLAN Notices*, vol. 10, no. 6, pp. 493–510, 1975.

[GG07]   I. Galvao and A. Goknil, "Survey of traceability approaches in Model-Driven Engineering," in *Proceedings of the 11th IEEE International Enterprise Distributed Object Computing Conference (EDOC 2007)*. IEEE, October 2007, pp. 313–326.

[GH88]   D. E. Goldberg and J. H. Holland, "Genetic Algorithms and Machine Learning," *Machine Learning*, vol. 3, no. 2-3, pp. 95–99, October 1988.

[GHJV95]   E. Gamma, R. Helm, R. Johnson, and J. Vlissides, *Design Patterns: Elements of Reusable Object-Oriented Software.* Addison-Wesley, Reading, MA, USA, 1995.

[GL03]   J. Gelissen and R. M. Laverty, "Robocop: Revised specification of framework and models (deliverable 1.5)," Information Technology for European Advancement, Tech. Rep., 2003.

[GMS05]   V. Grassi, R. Mirandola, and A. Sabetta, "From Design to Analysis Models: a Kernel Language for Performance and Reliability Analysis of Component-based Systems," in *WOSP '05: Proceedings of the 5th international workshop on Software and performance.* New York, NY, USA: ACM Press, 2005, pp. 25–36.

[GSTH08]   D. Gross, J. F. Shortle, J. M. Thompson, and C. M. Harris, *Fundamentals of Queueing Theory*, 4th ed., ser. Series in Probability and Statistics. Wiley, 2008.

[GWTH98]   S. Gokhale, W. Wong, K. Trivedi, and J. Horgan, "An analytical approach to architecture based software reliability prediction," 1998. [Online]. Available: citeseer.nj.nec.com/article/gokhale98analytical.html

350

[Ham50]   R. W. Hamming, "Error detecting and error correcting codes,"
           Bell System Technical Journal, vol. 26, no. 2, pp. 147–160,
           1950, mR0035935. [Online]. Available: http://www.caip.rutgers.edu/
           ~bushnell/dsdwebsite/hamming.pdf

[Hap08]   J. Happe, "Predicting Software Performance in Symmetric Multi-
           core and Multiprocessor Environments," Dissertation, University
           of Oldenburg, Germany, August 2008. [Online]. Available: http:
           //oops.uni-oldenburg.de/volltexte/2009/882/pdf/happre08.pdf

[Har75]   J. Hartigan, *Clustering Algorithms*. New York: Wiley, 1975.

[Har07]   M. Harman, "The current state and future of search based software
           engineering," *Future of Software Engineering, 2007. FOSE '07*, pp.
           342–357, May 23-25 2007.

[HBR$^+$10] N. Huber, S. Becker, C. Rathfelder, J. Schweflinghaus, and
           R. Reussner, "Performance Modeling in Industry: A Case Study on
           Storage Virtualization," in *ACM/IEEE 32nd International Conference
           on Software Engineering, Software Engineering in Practice Track,
           Capetown, South Africa*. New York, NY, USA: ACM, 2010,
           pp. 1–10, acceptance Rate: 23% (16/71). [Online]. Available:
           http://sdqweb.ipd.uka.de/publications/pdfs/hubern2010.pdf

[HC88]   T. Hickey and J. Cohen, "Automating program analysis," *Journal of
           the ACM (JACM)*, vol. 35, no. 1, pp. 185–220, 1988.

[HC91]   J. W. Hooper and R. O. Chester, *Software Reuse – Guidelines and Me-
           thods*. New York, NY, USA: Plenum Press, 1991.

[HC01]   G. T. Heineman and W. T. Councill, Eds., *Component-Based Software
           Engineering*. Addison Wesley, 2001.

[hela]   hello2morrow, "SonarJ homepage." [Online]. Available: http:
           //www.hello2morrow.com/products/sonarj

[helb]   ——, "Sotoarc homepage." [Online]. Available: http://www.
           hello2morrow.com/products/sotoarc

[helc]   ——, "Sotograph homepage." [Online]. Available: http://www.
           hello2morrow.com/products/sotograph

[HH01]   M. Harman and R. Hierons, "An Overview of Program Slicing," *Soft-
           ware Focus*, vol. 2, no. 3, pp. 85–92, 2001.

[HHK02]   H. Hermanns, U. Herzog, and J.-P. Katoen, "Process algebra for performance evaluation," *Theoretical Computer Science*, vol. 274, no. 1-2, pp. 43–87, 2002. [Online]. Available: http://www.sciencedirect.com/science/article/ B6V1G-4561J4H-3/2/21516ce76bb2e6adab1ffed4dbe0d24c

[HKW⁺08]   S. Herold, H. Klus, Y. Welsch, C. Deiters, A. Rausch, R. Reussner, K. Krogmann, H. Koziolek, R. Mirandola, B. Hummel, M. Meisinger, and C. Pfaller, *The Common Component Modeling Example*, ser. Lecture Notes in Computer Science. Springer-Verlag Berlin Heidelberg, 2008, vol. 5153, ch. CoCoME – The Common Component Modeling Example, pp. 16–53. [Online]. Available: http://springerlink.com/content/a04pr72354648281/ ?p=34d1b831d92a42359a30ecad99939785&pi=2

[HL00]   D. Hosmer and S. Lemeshow, *Applied Logistic Regression*. Wiley-Interscience, 2000.

[HMRT01]   B. R. Haverkort, R. Marie, G. Rubino, and K. S. Trivedi, *Performability Modelling : Techniques and Tools*. Wiley & Sons, New York, NY, USA, 2001.

[HMWR99]   C. Hrischuk, C. Murray Woodside, and J. Rolia, "Trace-based load characterization for generating performance software models," *Software Engineering, IEEE Transactions on*, vol. 25, no. 1, pp. 122–135, Jan/Feb 1999.

[HMY06]   G. Huang, H. Mei, and F. Yang, "Runtime recovery and manipulation of software architecture of component-based systems," *Automated Software Engineering*, vol. 13, no. 2, pp. 257–281, 2006.

[HMZ09a]   M. Harman, S. A. Mansouri, and Y. Zhang, "Search Based Software Engineering: A Comprehensive Analysis and Review of Trends Techniques and Applications," Department of Computer Science, King's College London, Technical Report TR-09-03, April 2009. [Online]. Available: http://www.dcs.kcl.ac.uk/technical-reports/ papers/TR-09-03.pdf

[HMZ09b]   ——, "Search based software engineering: A comprehensive review," 2009, unpublished.

[Hua08]   J. C. Huang, *Path-Oriented Program Analysis*. Cambridge University Press, New York, NY, USA, 2008.

[IBM]   IBM T.J. Watson Research Center, "T.J. Watson Libraries for Analysis (WALA)," http://wala.sourceforge.net/, last retrieved 2010-01-07. [Online]. Available: http://wala.sourceforge.net/

[IG02]   I. Ivkovic and M. W. Godfrey, "Architecture recovery of dynamically linked applications: A case study." in *IWPC*, 2002, pp. 178–186. [Online]. Available: http://plg.uwaterloo.ca/~migod/papers/ iwpc02-nautilus.pdf

[IWF07]   T. Israr, M. Woodside, and G. Franks, "Interaction tree algorithms to extract effective architecture and layered performance models from traces," *Journal of Systems and Software, 5th International Workshop on Software and Performance*, vol. 80, no. 4, pp. 474–492, April 2007. [Online]. Available: http://www.sciencedirect.com/science/article/ B6V0N-4KSSW5C-1/2/be38c84d6892a796dc2833b6622f66d3

[Jai91]   R. Jain, *The Art of Computer Systems Performance Analysis*. John Wiley & Sons, New York, 1991.

[JD88]   A. K. Jain and R. C. Dubes, *Algorithms for clustering data*. Upper Saddle River, NJ, USA: Prentice-Hall, Inc., 1988.

[KB09]   H. Koziolek and F. Brosch, "Parameter dependencies for component reliability specifications," in *Proceedings of the 6th International Workshop on Formal Engineering approaches to Software Components and Architectures (FESCA)*, ser. ENTCS, vol. 253, no. 1. Elsevier, 2009, pp. 23 – 38. [Online]. Available: http://www.koziolek.de/docs/ Koziolek2009.pdf

[KBH07]   H. Koziolek, S. Becker, and J. Happe, "Predicting the Performance of Component-based Software Architectures with different Usage Profiles," in *Proc. 3rd International Conference on the Quality of Software Architectures (QoSA'07)*, ser. Lecture Notes in Computer Science, vol. 4880. Springer-Verlag Berlin Heidelberg, July 2007, pp. 145–163. [Online]. Available: http://sdqweb.ipd.uka.de/publications/ pdfs/koziolek2007b.pdf

[KBHR08]   H. Koziolek, S. Becker, J. Happe, and R. Reussner, "Life-Cycle Aware Modelling of Software Components," in *Proceedings of the 11th International Symposium on Component-Based Software Engineering (CBSE)*, ser. Lecture Notes in Computer Science. Universität Karlsruhe (TH), Karlsruhe, Germany: Springer-Verlag Berlin Heidelberg, October 2008, pp. 278–285.

[KE00]   R. Koschke and T. Eisenbarth, "A framework for experimental evalua-
              tion of clustering techniques," in *IWPC 2000. 8th International Work-
              shop on Program Comprehension*.   Limerick, Ireland: IEEE, June
              2000, pp. 201–210.

[Kin76]   J. C. King, "Symbolic execution and program testing," *Communica-
              tions of the ACM*, vol. 19, no. Issue 7, pp. 385–394, July 1976.

[KKKR08]   T. Kappler, H. Koziolek, K. Krogmann, and R. H. Reuss-
              ner, "Towards Automatic Construction of Reusable Predic-
              tion Models for Component-Based Performance Engineering,"
              in *Software Engineering 2008*, ser. Lecture Notes in Infor-
              matics, vol. 121.   Munich, Germany: Bonner Köllen Ver-
              lag, February 18–22 2008, pp. 140–154. [Online]. Available:
              http://sdqweb.ipd.uka.de/publications/pdfs/kappler2008a.pdf

[KKR08a]   M. Kuperberg, K. Krogmann, and R. Reussner, "Performance
              Prediction for Black-Box Components using Reengineered Parametric
              Behaviour Models," in *Proceedings of the 11th International
              Symposium on Component Based Software Engineering (CBSE
              2008), Karlsruhe, Germany, 14th-17th October 2008*, ser. Lecture
              Notes in Computer Science, vol. 5282.   Springer-Verlag Berlin
              Heidelberg, October 2008, pp. 48–63. [Online]. Available: http:
              //sdqweb.ipd.uka.de/publications/pdfs/kuperberg2008c.pdf

[KKR08b]   M. Kuperberg, M. Krogmann, and R. Reussner, "ByCounter: Portable
              Runtime Counting of Bytecode Instructions and Method Invocations,"
              in *Proceedings of the 3rd International Workshop on Bytecode Seman-
              tics, Verification, Analysis and Transformation, Budapest, Hungary,
              5th April 2008 (ETAPS 2008, 11th European Joint Conferences
              on Theory and Practice of Software)*, 2008. [Online]. Available:
              http://sdqweb.ipd.uka.de/publications/pdfs/kuperberg2008a.pdf

[KKR10]   K. Krogmann, M. Kuperberg, and R. Reussner, "Using Genetic
              Search for Reverse Engineering of Parametric Behaviour Models
              for Performance Prediction," *IEEE Transactions on Software
              Engineering*, vol. 36, no. 6, pp. 865–877, 2010. [Online]. Available:
              http://sdqweb.ipd.kit.edu/publications/pdfs/krogmann2009c.pdf

[Kla08]   B. Klatt, "SoMoX: SOftware MOdel eXtractor," study thesis, Univer-
              sität Karlsruhe (TH), 2008, to appear.

[KLM+06]   T. Kalibera, J. Lehotsky, D. Majda, B. Repcek, M. Tomcanyi, A. To-
           mecek, P. Tuma, and J. Urban, "Automated Benchmarking and Ana-
           lysis Tool," in *Proceedings of First International Conference on Per-
           formance Evaluation Methodologies and Tools (VALUETOOLS 2006)*.
           Pisa, Italy: ACM, October 2006.

[Klu10]   R. Klug, "Fehlerlokalisierung in Software durch Analyse des Daten-
           flusses in Call-Graphen," Diploma Thesis, Fakultät für Informatik,
           Karlsruhe Institute of Technology (KIT), 2010, thesis in german.

[Kna10]   T. Knapp, "Reverse Engineering of Software Components using Sym-
           bolic Execution," Bachelor Thesis, Faculty of Informatics, Karlsruhe
           Institute of Technology (KIT), Karlsruhe, Germany, March 2010.

[Kos00]   R. Koschke, "Atomic Architectural Component Recovery for Program
           Understanding and Evolution," phd thesis, Institut für Software-
           technologie, Abteilung Programmiersprachen, Fakultät Informatik,
           Elektrotechnik und Informationstechnik, Universität Stuttgart, Ger-
           many, Stuttgart, Germany, August 2000. [Online]. Available: http://
           elib.uni-stuttgart.de/opus/volltexte/2000/669/pdf/Koschke.Thesis.PDF

[Kos02]   ——, "Atomic architectural component recovery for program unders-
           tanding and evolution," in *Proceedings of the 18th IEEE International
           Conference on Software Maintenance (ICSM'02)*. Los Alamitos, CA,
           USA: IEEE Computer Society, 2002, pp. 478–481.

[Kos05]   ——, "Rekonstruktion von Software-Architekturen – Ein Literatur-
           und Methoden-Überblick zum Stand der Wissenschaft," *Informatik
           – Forschung und Entwicklung*, vol. 19, no. 3, pp. 127–140,
           April 2005, springer Berlin / Heidelberg. [Online]. Available:
           http://www.springerlink.com/content/n2634176w28m2034

[Kou06]   S. Kounev, "Performance modeling and evaluation of distributed
           component-based systems using qucucing petri nets," *IEEE Transac-
           tions of Software Engineering*, vol. 32, no. 7, pp. 486–502, July 2006.

[Koz93]   J. R. Koza, *Genetic Programming – On the Programming of Computers
           by Means of Natural Selection*, 3rd ed. The MIT Press, Cambridge,
           Massachusetts, 1993.

[Koz08a]   H. Koziolek, *Parameter Dependencies for Reusable Performance Spe-
           cifications of Software Components*, ser. The Karlsruhe Series on Soft-
           ware Design and Quality. Universitätsverlag Karlsruhe, 2008, vol. 2.

[Koz08b] ——, "Parameter Dependencies for Reusable Performance Specifications of Software Components," Ph.D. dissertation, University of Oldenburg, 2008. [Online]. Available: http://sdqweb.ipd.uka.de/publications/pdfs/koziolek2008g.pdf

[Koz10] ——, "Performance evaluation of component-based software systems: A survey," *Performance Evaluation*, vol. 67, no. 8, pp. 634–658, 2010, special Issue on Software and Performance. [Online]. Available: http://www.sciencedirect.com/science/article/B6V13-4WXC21F-1/2/602bed8a6bd384b5516b8f84ac82c672

[KP05] B. Ko and J. Park, *Component Architecture Redesigning Approach Using Component Metrics*, ser. Lecture Notes in Computer Science. Berlin / Heidelberg: Springer Berlin / Heidelberg, 2005, vol. 3397/2005, ch. Artificial Intelligence and Simulation, pp. 449–459.

[KR08a] H. Koziolek and R. Reussner, "A Model Transformation from the Palladio Component Model to Layered Queueing Networks," in *Performance Evaluation: Metrics, Models and Benchmarks, SIPEW 2008*, ser. Lecture Notes in Computer Science, vol. 5119. Springer-Verlag Berlin Heidelberg, 2008, pp. 58–78. [Online]. Available: http://www.springerlink.com/content/w14m0g520u675x10/fulltext.pdf

[KR08b] K. Krogmann and R. H. Reussner, *The Common Component Modeling Example*, ser. Lecture Notes in Computer Science. Springer-Verlag Berlin Heidelberg, 2008, vol. 5153, ch. Palladio: Prediction of Performance Properties, pp. 297–326. [Online]. Available: http://springerlink.com/content/63617n4j5688879h/?p=9666cb29a31b453aba8a1ae6ee7831b6&pi=11

[Kru92] C. W. Krueger, "Software Reuse," *ACM Computing Surveys*, vol. 24, no. 2, pp. 131–183, 1992.

[KSRP99] R. K. Keller, R. Schauer, S. Robitaille, and P. Pagé, "Pattern-based reverse-engineering of design components," in *ICSE '99: Proceedings of the 21st international conference on Software engineering*. Los Alamitos, CA, USA: IEEE Computer Society Press, 1999, pp. 226–235.

[Kup10] M. Kuperberg, "Platform-Independent Performance Predictions," Ph.D. dissertation, Karlsruhe Institute of Technology (KIT), Faculty of Informatics, Karlsruhe, Germany, 2010, to appear. working title.

[KZM+10]   L. Kapova, B. Zimmerova, A. Martens, J. Happe, and R. H. Reussner, "State dependence in performance evaluation of component-based software systems," in *Proceedings of the 1st Joint WOSP/SIPEW International Conference on Performance Engineering (WOSP/SIPEW '10)*. New York, NY, USA: ACM, 2010, pp. 37–48. [Online]. Available: http://sdqweb.ipd.uka.de/publications/pdfs/kapova2009b.pdf

[lat]   "Lattix homepage." [Online]. Available: http://www.lattix.com/

[Lau06]   K.-K. Lau, "Software Component Models," in *Proceedings of the 6th International Conference on Software Engineering (ICSE06)*.   ACM Press, 2006, pp. 1081–1082.

[LC98]   E. L. Lehmann and G. Casella, *Theory of Point Estimation*, 2nd ed., ser. Springer Texts in Statistics.   Springer Verlag, New York, 1998.

[Lee06]   J. Lee, "Program Validation by Symbolic and Reverse Execution," PhD thesis, BRICS Ph.D. School, Department of Computer Science, University of Aarhus, Aarhus, Denmark, November 2006. [Online]. Available: http://www.brics.dk/~jlee/papers/thesis-jooyong.pdf

[LFG05]   Y. Liu, A. Fekete, and I. Gorton, "Design-Level Performance Prediction of Component-Based Applications," *IEEE Transactions on Software Engineering*, vol. 31, no. 11, pp. 928–941, 2005.

[LH99]   D. Liang and M. Harrold, "Efficient points-to analysis for whole-program analysis," in *Software Engineering – ESEC/FSE'99*, ser. LNCS, vol. 1687.   Springer, 1999, pp. 199–215.

[Lin93]   B. W. Lindgren, *Statistical Theory*.   New York: Macmillan, 1993.

[LL03]   J. Lundberg and W. Löwe, "Architecture Recovery by Semi-Automatic Component Identification," *Electronic Notes in Theoretical Computer Science*, vol. 82, no. 5, pp. 98–114, 2003.

[LMS+99]   S. Lapierre, E. Merlo, G. Savard, G. Antoniol, R. Fiutem, and P. To-nella, "Automatic Unit Test Data Generation Using Mixed-Integer Linear Programming and Execution Trees," in *15th IEEE International Conference on Software Maintenance (ICSM'99)*, vol. 00.   Los Alamitos, CA, USA: IEEE Computer Society, 1999, p. 189.

[LS95]   P. Langley and H. A. Simon, "Applications of machine learning and rule induction," *Communications of the ACM*, vol. 38, no. 11, pp. 54–64, 1995.

357

[LS99]   T. Lundqvist and P. Stenström, "An Integrated Path and Timing Analysis Method based on Cycle-Level Symbolic Execution," *Real-Time Systems, Springer Netherlands*, vol. 17, no. 2-3, pp. 183–207, November 1999. [Online]. Available: http://www.springerlink.com/content/n85l7k240p716837/

[Luc01]   A. D. Lucia, "Program Slicing: Methods and Applications," in *Proceedings of the First IEEE International Workshop on Source Code Analysis and Manipulation*, Florence, Italy, 2001, pp. 142–149.

[LW05]   K.-K. Lau and Z. Wang, "A Taxonomy of Software Component Models," in *Proceedings of the 31st EUROMICRO Conference*.   IEEE Computer Society Press, 2005, pp. 88–95.

[LW07]   ——, "Software component models," *IEEE Transactions on Software Engineering*, vol. 33, no. 10, pp. 709–724, October 2007.

[Map]   Maplesoft, "Maple," http://www.maplesoft.com/products/Maple/, last accessed 2010-04-23.

[Mar94]   R. Martin, "OO Design Quality Metrics – An Analysis of Dependencies."   Object-Oriented Programming Systems, Languages, and Applications (OOPSLA), October 1994.

[Mar05]   A. Martens, "Empirical Validation and Comparison of the Model-Driven Performance Prediction Techniques of CB-SPE and Palladio," Carl-von-Ossietzky Universität Oldenburg, Aug. 2005, study thesis.

[Mar07]   ——, "Empirical Validation of the Model-driven Performance Prediction Approach Palladio," Master's thesis, Carl-von-Ossietzky Universität Oldenburg, Nov. 2007.

[MB07]   O. Maqbool and H. Babri, "Hierarchical Clustering for Software Architecture Recovery," *IEEE Transactions on Software Engineering*, vol. 33, no. 11, pp. 759–780, 2007.

[MBKR08a] A. Martens, S. Becker, H. Koziolek, and R. Reussner, "An Empirical Investigation of the Applicability of a Component-Based Performance Prediction Method," in *Proceedings of the 5th European Performance Engineering Workshop (EPEW'08), Palma de Mallorca, Spain*, ser. Lecture Notes in Computer Science, vol. 5261.   Springer-Verlag Berlin Heidelberg, 2008, pp. 17–31.

358

[MBKR08b] ——, "An Empirical Investigation of the Effort of Creating Reusable Models for Performance Prediction," in *Proceedings of the 11th International Symposium on Component-Based Software Engineering (CBSE'08), Karlsruhe, Germany*, ser. Lecture Notes in Computer Science, vol. 5282. Springer-Verlag Berlin Heidelberg, 2008, pp. 16–31.

[MBTS04] G. Myers, T. Badgett, T. Thomas, and C. Sandler, *The Art of Software Testing*, 2nd ed. Wiley, 2004.

[McI69] M. D. McIlroy, ""Mass Produced" Software Components," in *Software Engineering*, P. Naur and B. Randell, Eds. Brussels: Scientific Affairs Division, NATO, 1969, pp. 138–155, report of a conference sponsored by the NATO Science Committee, Garmisch, Germany, 7th to 11th October 1968.

[McM04] P. McMinn, "Search-based software test data generation: a survey," *Software Testing, Verification and Reliability*, vol. 14, no. 2, pp. 105–156, June 2004.

[Mef] K. Meffert, "JGAP – Java Genetic Algorithms Package," http://jgap.sourceforge.net/, last retrieved: 2010-01-04. [Online]. Available: http://jgap.sourceforge.net/

[MG00] D. A. Menasce and H. Gomaa, "A method for design and performance modeling of client/server systems," *IEEE Transactions on Software Engineering*, vol. 26, no. 11, pp. 1066–1085, November 2000. [Online]. Available: http://ieeexplore.ieee.org/xpls/abs_all.jsp?arnumber=881718

[Mil56] G. A. Miller, "The magical number seven, plus or minus two: Some limits on our capacity for processing information," *Psychological Review*, vol. 63, no. 2, pp. 81–97, 1956.

[MIO87] J. D. Musa, A. Iannino, and K. Okumoto, *Software Reliability – Measurement, prediction, application*. New York: McGraw-Hill, 1987.

[MJS+00] H. A. Müller, J. H. Jahnke, D. B. Smith, M.-A. Storey, S. R. Tilley, and K. Wong, "Reverse engineering: a roadmap," in *ICSE '00: Proceedings of the Conference on The Future of Software Engineering*. New York, NY, USA: ACM, 2000, pp. 47–60.

359

[MM01a]   B. S. Mitchell and S. Mancoridis, "Comparing the decompositions produced by software clusteringalgorithms using similarity measurements," in *Proceedings of the IEEE International Conference on Software Maintenance, CSMR 2001*, 2001, pp. 744–753.

[MM01b]   ——, "CRAFT: A Framework for Evaluating Software Clustering Results in the Absence of Benchmark Decompositions," in *Proceedings of the 2001 Working Conference in Reverse Engineering (WCRE'01)*. Stuttgart, Germany: IEEE, October 2001, pp. 93–102, best Paper Award. [Online]. Available: http://www.cs.drexel.edu/~spiros/papers/WCRE01a.pdf

[MM06]   B. Mitchell and S. Mancoridis, "On the automatic modularization of software systems using the Bunch tool," *IEEE Transactions on Software Engineering*, vol. 32, no. 3, pp. 193–208, March 2006. [Online]. Available: http://ieeexplore.ieee.org/iel5/32/33822/01610610.pdf

[MOTU93]   H. Muller, M. Orgun, S. Tilley, and J. Uhl, "A reverse engineering approach to subsystem structure identification," *Journal of Software Maintenance: Research and Practice*, vol. 5, no. 4, pp. 181–204, December 1993.

[MPP07]   L. Mariani, S. Papagiannakis, and M. Pezzè, "Compatibility and regression testing of cots-component-based software," in *ICSE'07, Proceedings of the 29th International Conference on Software Engineering*, Minneapolis, MN, USA, May 23–25, 2007, pp. 85–95.

[MW94]   F. Mueller and D. B. Whalley, "Efficient on-the-fly analysis of program behavior and static cache simulation," *Lecture Notes in Computer Science*, vol. 864/1994, pp. 101–115, 1994.

[Mye75]   G. J. Myers, *Reliable software through composite design*. New York: Petrocelli/Charter, 1975.

[NE02]   J. W. Nimmer and M. D. Ernst, "Automatic generation of program specifications," *ACM SIGSOFT Softw. Eng. Notes*, vol. 27, no. 4, pp. 229–239, 2002.

[NK05]   P. Niemeyer and J. Knudsen, *Learning Java*, 3rd ed., M. Loukides and D. Cameron, Eds.   O'Reilly, Sebastopol, 2005.

[NNH99]   F. Nielson, H. R. Nielson, and C. Hankin, *Principles of Program Analysis*.   Berlin: Springer, 1999.

[NNS02]   F. Nielson, H. R. Nielson, and H. Seidl, *Proceedings of the 11th European Symposium on Programming, Programming Languages and Systems: , ESOP 2002*, ser. Lecture Notes in Computer Science. Springer Berlin / Heidelberg, April 2002, vol. 2305/2002, ch. Automatic Complexity Analysis, pp. 237–261.

[NNZ00]   U. A. Nickel, J. Niere, and A. Zündorf, "Tool demonstration: The FUJABA environment," in *Proc. of the 22nd International Conference on Software Engineering (ICSE), Limerick, Ireland*, 2000.

[Obj05a]   Object Management Group (OMG), "UML Profile for Schedulability, Performance and Time," January 2005. [Online]. Available: http://www.omg.org/cgi-bin/doc?formal/2005-01-02

[Obj05b]   ——, "Unified Modeling Language Specification: Version 2, Revised Final Adopted Specification (ptc/05-07-04)," 2005. [Online]. Available: http://www.omg.org/spec/UML/2.0/

[Obj06a]   ——, "CORBA Component Model, v4.0 (formal/2006-04-01)," 2006. [Online]. Available: http://www.omg.org/technology/documents/formal/components.htm

[Obj06b]   ——, "MOF 2.0 Core Specification (formal/2006-01-01)," 2006. [Online]. Available: http://www.omg.org/cgi-bin/doc?formal/2006-01-01

[Obj06c]   ——, "UML Profile for Modeling and Analysis of Real-Time and Embedded systems (MARTE) RFP (realtime/05-02-06)," 2006. [Online]. Available: http://www.omg.org/cgi-bin/doc?realtime/2005-2-6

[Obj06d]   Object Web, "The Fractal Project Homepage," 2006, last retrieved 2008-01-06. [Online]. Available: http://fractal.objectweb.org/

[Obj07]   Object Management Group (OMG), "CORBA 3.0 - OMG IDL Syntax and Semantics chapter," 2007. [Online]. Available: http://www.omg.org/docs/formal/02-06-39.pdf

[OD08]   D. L. Olson and D. Delen, *Advanced Data Mining Techniques*. Springer Verlag, February 2008.

[Ora10]   Oracle, Sun Developer Network, "The Java Tutorials, Lesson: Exceptions," http://java.sun.com/docs/books/tutorial/essential/-exceptions/index.html, January 2010.

[Ori05]   C. Oriat, *Jartege: A Tool for Random Generation of Unit Tests for Java Classes*, ser. Lecture Notes in Computer Science. Heidelberg: Springer Berlin, September 2005, vol. 3712/2005, pp. 242–256. [Online]. Available: http://dx.doi.org/10.1007/11558569_18

[OSG09]   *OSGi Service Platform*, OSGi Alliance Std., Rev. 4.2, June 2009. [Online]. Available: http://www.osgi.org/

[OSV02]   L. O'Brien, C. Stoermer, and C. Verhoef, "Software architecture reconstruction: Practice needs and current approaches," Software Engineering Institute, Carnegie Mellon University, Pittsburgh, Tech. Rep. CMU/SEI-2002-TR-024, August 2002. [Online]. Available: http://www.sei.cmu.edu/pub/documents/02.reports/pdf/02tr024.pdf

[OSV08]   M. Odersky, L. Spoon, and B. Venners, *Programming in Scala*, 1st ed. artima, November 2008.

[Pad]   U. Paderborn, "Fujaba Tool Suite RE," last retrieved: 2010-07-24. [Online]. Available: http://www.fujaba.de/

[Par93]   C. Y. Park, "Predicting program execution times by analyzing static and dynamic program paths," *Real-Time Systems, Springer Netherlands*, vol. 5, no. 1, pp. 31–62, March 1993.

[PDP+07]   D. Pollet, S. Ducasse, L. Poyet, I. Alloui, S. Cimpan, and H. Verjus, "Towards A Process-Oriented Software Architecture Reconstruction Taxonomy," in *11th European Conference on Software Maintenance and Reengineering, 2007 (CSMR '07)*.   Los Alamitos, CA, USA: IEEE Computer Society, March 2007, pp. 137–148.

[PE88]   F. Pfenning and C. Elliot, "Higher-order abstract syntax," *ACM SIGPLAN Notices*, vol. 23, no. 7, pp. 199–208, 1988.

[Pet80]   C. A. Petri, "Introduction to general net theory," in *Net theory and applications : Proceedings of the advanced course on general net theory,processes and systems (Hamburg, 1979)*, ser. Lecture Notes in Computer Science, W. Brauer, Ed., vol. 84.   Springer-Verlag, Berlin, 1980, pp. 1–20.

[PHY10]   K. Praditwong, M. Harman, and X. Yao, "Software Module Clustering as a Multi-Objective Search Problem," *IEEE Transactions on Software Engineering*, vol. 99, no. PrePrints, 2010.

[PM08]   T. Parsons and J. Murphy, "Detecting Performance Antipatterns in Component Based Enterprise Systems," *Journal of Object Technology*, vol. 7, no. 3, pp. 55–90, March-April 2008. [Online]. Available: http://www.jot.fm/issues/issue_2008_03/article1/

[PMT$^+$08]   T. Parsons, A. Mos, M. Trofin, T. Gschwind, and J. Murphy, "Extracting Interactions in Component-Based Systems," *IEEE Transactions on Software Engineering*, vol. 34, no. 6, pp. 783–799, 2008.

[PP09]   T. Poch and F. Plasil, "Extracting Behavior Specification of Components in Legacy Applications," in *Proceedings of the 12th International Symposium on Component Based Software Engineering (CBSE 2009)*, ser. LNCS, no. 5582.   Springer, June 2009, pp. 87–103.

[PV09]   C. Păsăreanu and W. Visser, "A survey of new trends in symbolic execution for software testing and analysis," *International Journal on Software Tools for Technology Transfer (STTT)*, vol. 11, no. 4, pp. 339–353, October 2009.

[PWA05]   O. Pilskalns, D. Williams, and A. Andrews, "Defining Maintainable Components in the Design Phase," in *Proceedings of the 21st IEEE International Conference on Software Maintenance (ICSM'05)*.   Los Alamitos, CA, USA: IEEE Computer Society, 2005, pp. 49–58.

[qim09]   "EU project Q-ImPrESS, Quality Impact Prediction for Evolving Service-oriented Software," 2009, http://www.q-impress.eu/, last retrieved 2009-10-20. [Online]. Available: http://www.q-impress.eu/

[Rec]   Recoder Team, "Recoder homepage," http://recoder.sourceforge. net/, last retrieved 2007-10-25. [Online]. Available: http://recoder. sourceforge.net/

[Rei85]   W. Reisig, *Petri Nets: An Introduction*, ser. EATCS Monographs on Theoretical Computer Science.   Springer-Verlag, Berlin, Germany, 1985.

[Rei08]   S. P. Reiss, "Controlled dynamic performance analysis," in *WOSP '08: Proceedings of the 7th international workshop on Software and performance*.   New York, NY, USA: ACM, 2008, pp. 43–54.

[Rin01]   M. Rinard, *Static Analysis*.   Springer, 2001, vol. 2126/2001, ch. Analysis of Multithreaded Programs, pp. 1–19.

[RJ01]   B. Ramesh and M. Jarke, "Toward reference models for requirements traceability," *IEEE Trans. Softw. Eng.*, vol. 27, no. 1, pp. 58–93, 2001.

[RK09]   C. Rathfelder and S. Kounev, "Model-based performance prediction for event-driven systems," in *Proceedings of the Third ACM International Conference on Distributed Event-Based Systems*, ser. DEBS '09. New York, NY, USA: ACM, 2009, pp. 33:1–33:2. [Online]. Available: http://doi.acm.org/10.1145/1619258.1619300

[RLvV06]   R. Roeller, P. Lago, and H. van Vliet, "Recovering architectural assumptions," *The Journal of Systems and Software*, vol. 79, pp. 552–573, April 2006.

[Rom09]   A. Romito, "Performance-Kennlinien nachrichtenbasierter Systeme," Diploma Thesis, Karlsruhe Institute of Technology (KIT), Karlsruhe, Germany, October 2009, thesis in German.

[Ros90]   M. Rosendahl, "Automatic complexity analysis," in *FPCA '89: Proceedings of the fourth international conference on Functional programming languages and computer architecture*. New York, NY, USA: ACM Press, 1990, pp. 144–156.

[Ros06]   K. D. Ross, "Towards an automatic complexity analysis for generic programs," in *WGP '06: Proceedings of the 2006 ACM SIGPLAN workshop on Generic programming*. New York, NY, USA: ACM, 2006, pp. 87–95.

[RR00]   S. P. Reiss and M. Renieris, "Generating Java trace data," in *JAVA '00: Proceedings of the ACM 2000 conference on Java Grande*. New York, NY, USA: ACM, 2000, pp. 71–77.

[RR02]   C. Riva and J. V. Rodriguez, "Combining Static and Dynamic Views for Architecture Reconstruction," in *Proceedings of the Sixth European Conference on Software Maintenance and Reengineering (CSMR 2002)*. Los Alamitos, CA, USA: IEEE Computer Society Press, 2002, pp. 11–13.

[RRMF08]   A. Rausch, R. Reussner, R. Mirandola, and FrantisekPlasil, Eds., *The Common Component Modeling Example: Comparing Software Component Models*, ser. Lecture Notes in Computer Science. Springer-Verlag Berlin Heidelberg, 2008, vol. 5153. [Online]. Available: http://springerlink.com/content/l8t37r416121/

[RSP03]   R. H. Reussner, H. W. Schmidt, and I. Poernomo, "Reliability Prediction for Component-Based Software Architectures," *Journal of Systems and Software – Special Issue of Software Architecture – Engineering Quality Attributes*, vol. 66, no. 3, pp. 241–252, 2003.

[RvHG+08] M. Rohr, A. van Hoorn, S. Giesecke, J. Matevska, W. Hasselbring, and
S. Alekseev, "Trace-context sensitive performance profiling for enterprise software applications," in *Performance Evaluation: Metrics, Models and Benchmarks*, ser. LNCS, S. Kounev, I. Gorton, and K. Sachs,
Eds., vol. 5119.   Springer, 2008, pp. 283–302.

[SAG+06] B. Schmerl, J. Aldrich, D. Garlan, R. Kazman, and H. Yan, "Discovering architectures from running systems," *IEEE Transactions on Software Engineering*, vol. 32, no. 7, pp. 454–466, July 2006.

[Sam97] J. Sametinger, *Software engineering with reusable components*.
Springer Verlag, Heidelberg, 1997.

[Sar03] K. Sartipi, "Software architecture recovery based on pattern matching,"
in *International Conference on Software Maintenance, 2003. ICSM
2003. Proceedings.*   Los Alamitos, CA, USA: IEEE Computer Society, September 2003, pp. 293–296.

[Sch07] S. E. Schaeffer, "Graph clustering," *Computer Science
Review*, vol. 1, no. 1, pp. 27–64, 2007. [On-
line]. Available: http://www.sciencedirect.com/science/article/
B8JDG-4PBG1S7-1/2/6537f3d1ffbf391086c60dbeba874b13

[SF96] R. Sedgewick and P. Flajolet, *An introduction to the analysis of algorithms*.   Addison-Wesley Longman Publishing Co., Inc. Boston, MA,
USA, 1996.

[SGM02] C. Szyperski, D. Gruntz, and S. Murer, *Component Software: Beyond
Object-Oriented Programming*, 2nd ed.   New York, NY: ACM Press
and Addison-Wesley, 2002.

[SH97] M. Shapiro and S. Horwitz, "Fast and accurate flow-insensitive points-
to analysis," in *POPL '97: Proceedings of the 24th ACM SIGPLAN-
SIGACT symposium on Principles of programming languages*.   New
York, NY, USA: ACM, 1997, pp. 1–14.

[SKK+01] M. Sitaraman, G. Kuczycki, J. Krone, W. F. Ogden, and A. Reddy,
"Performance Specification of Software Components," in *Proceedings
of the 2001 symposium on Software reusability: putting software reuse
in context*.   ACM Press, 2001, pp. 3–10.

[SKR08] S. Sarkar, A. C. Kak, and G. M. Rama, "Metrics for Measuring the
Quality of Modularization of Large-Scale Object-Oriented Software,"
IEEE Transactions on Software Engineering, vol. 34, no. 5, pp. 700–
720, 2008.

[SLLL07]   D. Strein, R. Lincke, J. Lundberg, and W. Löwe, "An Extensible Meta-Model for Program Analysis," *IEEE Transactions on Software Engineering*, vol. 33, no. 9, pp. 592–607, 2007.

[SLS77]   G. Seber, A. Lee, and G. Seber, *Linear Regression Analysis*.   Wiley New York, 1977.

[Smi90]   C. U. Smith, *Performance Engineering of Software Systems*.   Addison-Wesley, Reading, MA, USA, 1990.

[Som10]   "SoMoX – The SOftware MOdel eXtractor," http://www.somox.org, 2010, last retrieved 2010-03-15.

[SP94]   M. Srinivas and L. Patnaik, "Adaptive probabilities of crossover and mutation in genetic algorithms," *IEEE Transactions on Systems, Man and Cybernetics*, vol. 24, no. 4, pp. 656–667, Apr 1994.

[Spr06]   "The Spring Framework Homepage," 2006. [Online]. Available: http://www.springframework.org/

[SR09]   J. Stammel and R. Reussner, "Kamp: Karlsruhe architectural maintainability prediction," in *Proceedings of the 1. Workshop des GI-Arbeitskreises Langlebige Softwaresysteme (L2S2): "Design for Future - Langlebige Softwaresysteme"*, G. Engels, R. Reussner, C. Momm, and S. Sauer, Eds., 2009, pp. 87–98. [Online]. Available: http://ftp.informatik.rwth-aachen.de/Publications/CEUR-WS/Vol-537/

[SRK06]   G. Snelting, T. Robschink, and J. Krinke, "Efficient path conditions in dependence graphs for software safetyanalysis," *ACM Transactions on Software Engineering and Methodology*, vol. 15, no. 4, pp. 410–457, October 2006. [Online]. Available: http://pp.info.uni-karlsruhe.de/uploads/publikationen/snelting06tosem.pdf

[SSM06]   O. Seng, F. Simon, and T. Mohaupt, *Code Quality Management*. dpunkt Verlag, Heidelberg, 2006.

[Sta73]   H. Stachowiak, *Allgemeine Modelltheorie*.   Springer Verlag, Wien, 1973.

[Sta05]   Standard Performance Evaluation Corporation (SPEC), "SPEC-jbb2005 Java Server Benchmark," http://www.spec.org/jbb2005/, 2005, last accessed 2010-07-25.

[Sta08]   Standard Performance Evaluation Corp., "SPECjvm2008 Bench-marks," 2008, URL: http://www.spec.org/jvm2008/, last visit: October 9th, 2009. [Online]. Available: http://www.spec.org/jvm2008/

[Sta09]   StatSoft, "Multivariate Adaptive Regression Splines (MARSplines)," Website, 2009, last retrieved 2009-04-09. [Online]. Available: http://www.statsoft.nl/ik/textbook&stmars.html

[Sto07]   C. Stormer, "Software quality attribute analysis by architecture recons-truction (squa3re)," in *11th European Conference on Software Main-tenance and Reengineering, 2007 (CSMR '07)*.   Los Alamitos, CA, USA: IEEE Computer Society, March 2007, pp. 361–364.

[STTK07]   M. Schmid, M. Thoss, T. Termin, and R. Kroeger, "A Generic Application-Oriented Performance Instrumentation for Multi-Tier En-vironments," in *10th IFIP/IEEE International Symposium on Integra-ted Network Management (IM2007)*.   IEEE, May 2007, pp. 304–313.

[Su09]   T. Sag and M. Çunkas, "A tool for multiobjective evolutionary algo-rithms," *Advances in Engineering Software*, vol. 40, no. 9, pp. 902–912, 2009. [Online]. Available: http://www.sciencedirect.com/science/article/B6V1P-4VP12DC-4/2/d3574c82b60ff338ba2e154c3f2b0e37

[SW02]   C. U. Smith and L. G. Williams, *Performance Solutions: A Practical Guide to Creating Responsive, Scalable Software*.   Addison-Wesley, 2002.

[Sys99]   T. Systä, "Dynamic Reverse Engineering of Java Software," in *ECOOP '99 Workshop Reader*, ser. Lectural Notes in Computer Science, S. Ducasse and O. Ciupke, Eds., no. 1743.   Springer-Verlag London, UK, 1999, pp. 174–175, last retrieved: 2006-10-23. [Online]. Available: http://www.cs.tut.fi/%7Etsysta/papers/ecoopnew.pdf

[Sys00]   ——, "Static and Dynamic Reverse Engineering Tech-niques for Java Software Systems," Ph.D. dissertation, Uni-versity of Tampere, Finland, 2000. [Online]. Available: http://acta.uta.fi/pdf/951-44-4811-1.pdf

[TH99]   V. Tzerpos and R. Holt, "MoJo: A Distance Metric for Software Clus-terings," in *IEEE, Sixth Working Conference on Reverse Engineering (WCRE)*.   Los Alamitos, CA, USA: IEEE Computer Society, 1999, p. 187.

[The09]   The Q-ImPrESS consortium, "Service Architecture Meta-Model (SAMM)," http://www.q-impress.eu/wordpress/wp-content/uploads/2009/05/d21-service_architecture_meta-model.pdf, May 2009, project Deliverable D2.1, last accessed 2010-04-03.

[Tho68]   K. Thompson, "Programming Techniques: Regular expression search algorithm," *Communications of the ACM*, vol. 11, no. 6, pp. 419–422, 1968.

[Tri01]   K. S. Trivedi, *Probability and Statistics with Reliability, Queuing and Computer Science Applications*, 2nd ed.   Wiley & Sons, New York, NY, USA, 2001.

[TS05]   M. Trifu and P. Szulman, "Language independent abstract metamodel for quality analysis and improvement of oo systems," in *Proceedings of the 7th German Workshop on Software-Reengineering (WSR 2005), Bad Honnef, Germany*, ser. Softwaretechnik-Trends, vol. 25, no. 2, 2005.

[TS06]   N. Tillmann and W. Schulte, "Unit tests reloaded: parameterized unit testing with symbolic execution," *IEEE Software*, vol. 23, no. 4, pp. 38–47, July-Aug. 2006.

[TTBS07]   P. Tonella, M. Torchiano, B. D. Bois, and T. Systä, "Empirical studies in reverse engineering: state of the art and future trends," *Empirical Software Engineering, Springer*, March 2007, published online first. [Online]. Available: http://www.hitech-projects.com/euprojects/serious/public_papers/EmpiricalStudies.pdf

[VGM+09]   L. Vanneschi, S. Gustafson, A. Moraglio, I. D. Falco, and M. Ebner, *Genetic Programming – Proceedings of the 12th European Conference, EuroGP 2009 Tübingen, Germany, April 15-17, 2009*, ser. LNCS.   Springer Berlin/Heidelberg, April 2009, vol. 5481.

[WAW04a]   S. Winkler, M. Affenzeller, and S. Wagner, "Identifying Nonlinear Model Structures Using Genetic Programming Techniques," in *Cybernetics and Systems 2004*, 2004, pp. 689–694. [Online]. Available: http://www.heuristiclab.com/publications/papers/winkler04a.pdf

[WAW04b]   ——, "New methods for the identification of nonlinear model structures based upon genetic programming techniques," *Proceedings of the 15th International Conference on Systems Science*, vol. 1, pp. 386–393, 2004, last retrieved 2006-09-01. [Online]. Available: http://www.heuristiclab.com/publications/papers/winkler04b.pdf

[Weg75]   B. Wegbreit, "Mechanical program analysis," *Communications of the ACM*, vol. 18, no. 9, pp. 528–539, 1975.

[Wei81]   M. Weiser, "Program slicing," in *ICSE '81: Proceedings of the 5th international conference on Software engineering.* Piscataway, NJ, USA: IEEE Press, 1981, pp. 439–449.

[WF05]   I. H. Witten and E. Frank, *Data Mining: Practical Machine Learning Tools and Techniques*, second edition ed., ser. Morgan Kaufmann Series in Data Management Systems. San Francisco, CA: Morgan Kaufman, 2005.

[WFP07a]   M. Woodside, G. Franks, and D. Petriu, "The future of software performance engineering," in *Future of Software Engineering (FOSE '07).* Los Alamitos, CA, USA: IEEE Computer Society, May 2007, pp. 171–187.

[WFP07b]   M. Woodside, G. Franks, and D. C. Petriu, "The Future of Software Performance Engineering," in *Proceedings of ICSE 2007, Future of SE.* IEEE Computer Society, Washington, DC, USA, 2007, pp. 171–187.

[WG98]   J. Wegener and M. Grochtmann, "Verifying Timing Constraints of Real-Time Systems by Means of Evolutionary Testing," *Real-Time Systems*, vol. 15, no. 3, pp. 275–298, 1998.

[Whi04]   D. Whitley, "A genetic algorithm tutorial," *Statistics and Computing*, vol. 4, no. 2, pp. 65–85, June 2004. [Online]. Available: http://www.springerlink.com/content/wh2681221ml68873/

[WHSB01]   M. Woodside, C. Hrischuka, B. Selic, and S. Bayarov, "Automated performance modeling of software generated by a design environment," *Performance Evaluation*, vol. 45, no. 2-3, pp. 107–123, July 2001.

[Win06]   W. E. Winkler, "Overview of Record Linkage and Current Research Directions," Statistical Research Division, U.S. Census Bureau, Washington, Research Report Series, RRS 2006-2, 2006. [Online]. Available: http://www.census.gov/srd/papers/pdf/rrs2006-02.pdf

[WMW03]   X. Wu, D. McMullan, and M. Woodside, "Component Based Performance Prediction," in *Component-Based Software Engineering (CBSE 2003)*, I. Crnkovic, H. Schmidt, J. Stafford, and K. Wallnau, Eds. Carnegie Mellon University, USA, and Monash University, Australia, May 2003.

369

[Wol] Wolfram Research, "Mathematica," http://www.wolfram.com/products/mathematica/, last accessed 2010-04-23.

[WSH08] Z. Wang, A. Sanchez, and A. Herkersdorf, "Scisim: a software performance estimation framework using source code instrumentation," in *WOSP '08: Proceedings of the 7th international workshop on Software and performance.* New York, NY, USA: ACM, 2008, pp. 33–42.

[WVCB01] M. Woodside, V. Vetland, M. Courtois, and S. Bayarov, *Performance Engineering: State of the Art and Current Trends*, ser. Lecture Notes in Computer Science. Heidelberg: Springer, Heidelberg, 2001, vol. LNCS 2047/2001, ch. Resource Function Capture for Performance Aspects of Software Components and Sub-Systems, pp. 239–256. [Online]. Available: http://www.springerlink.com/content/71k0ka2c1l7fn99q/

[WW04a] X. Wu and M. Woodside, "Performance modeling from software components," *SIGSOFT Softw. Eng. Notes*, vol. 29, no. 1, pp. 290–301, 2004.

[WW04b] ——, "Performance Modeling from Software Components," *SIGSOFT Softw. Eng. Notes*, vol. 29, no. 1, pp. 290–301, 2004.

[WYF03] H. Washizaki, H. Yamamoto, and Y. Fukazawa, "A metrics suite for measuring reusability of software components," in *Proceedings of the Ninth International Software Metrics Symposium (METRICS'03)*, ser. IEEE. IEEE Computer Society, 2003, pp. 211–223. [Online]. Available: http://ieeexplore.ieee.org/xpls/abs_all.jsp?arnumber=1232469

[Yac02] S. M. Yacoub, "Performance Analysis of Component-Based Applications," in *SPLC 2: Proceedings of the Second International Conference on Software Product Lines.* London, UK: Springer-Verlag, 2002, pp. 299–315.

[YGS+04] H. Yan, D. Garlan, B. Schmerl, J. Aldrich, and R. Kazman, "Discotect: A system for discovering architectures from running systems," in *ICSE '04: Proceedings of the 26th International Conference on Software Engineering.* Washington, DC, USA: IEEE Computer Society, 2004, pp. 470–479.

[ZHM97] H. Zhu, P. A. V. Hall, and J. H. R. May, "Software unit test coverage and adequacy," *ACM Comput. Surv.*, vol. 29, no. 4, pp. 366–427, 1997.

[ZWL08]   T. Zheng, C. Woodside, and M. Litoiu, "Performance model estimation and tracking using optimal filters," *IEEE Transactions on Software Engineering*, vol. 34, no. 3, pp. 391–406, May-June 2008.